PRESSTITUTES

*reprise of *Journalists for Hire /
Bought Journalists*
by
UDO ULFKOTTE

About the Title

"In the Pay of the CIA" is a figure of speech, a bit of poetic license. This book is not so much about the spies employed as journalists by the CIA. It's more a first-person account of the ways ordinary journalists are bribed through their regular paychecks and perks, being used as intelligence assets indirectly. They also get favors and speaking fees from those they please, as Ulfkotte himself did from heads of state, oil companies, as well as the BND, or German CIA. And they must toe the party line. If journalists don't stay on message about events, they aren't invited again, they can lose their job.

Ulfkotte's target is the corruption of Elite Organizations and Mainstream Media, which set the tone and rules of the game for the puppets of the press. The *entire* political and media network is not only bought, it was installed by the Allies after WW2. It ensures permanent control over Germany through organizations like the Atlantic-Brücke, the CFR, or NATO. The media serve the interests of NATO, the war party, and big business, not their readership.

Ulfkotte's original title translates to *Bought Journalists: How Politicians, Intelligence Agencies and High Finance Control Germany's Mass Media,* which is a good description of his revelations. So he blames *Politicians* first and foremost. The greatest corruption is at the highest levels.

About the Translator

Andrew Schlademan, the translator, has taught English for over 15 years in public and private schools in Germany and the Czech Republic and also lectures at the Augsburg University of Applied Sciences. As a German-to-English non-fiction translator, he specializes in memoirs, alternative medicine, physics, spirituality and, increasingly, political corruption.

Schlademan's most recent non-fiction translations include: *European Politics on Drugs* by Christoph Klein, an inside view of the "atmed Affair," a multi-billion-euro corruption scandal that has kept a drug-saving metered-dose inhaler actuator off the European and world markets for over 25 years. *NO LOVE* by Marion Kohn, a revolutionary insight into the causes and resolution of narcissism and altruism. Björn Eybl's *The Psychic Roots of Disease*, the definitive New Medicine desk reference, and *Thinking Tools for Creativity and Innovation* by Florian Rustler. Schlademan is currently translating *The Source within You* by Fabian Wollschläger.

When he's not teaching or translating, Schlademan spends most of his free time watching lectures and documentaries, ever amazed by the incredible universe around us.

PRESSTITUTES

Embedded In the Pay of the CIA

By

Udo Ulfkotte
1960-2017

ProgRESSive

2019

Presstitutes Embedded in the Pay of the CIA
A Confession from the Profession

Authored by Udo Ulfkotte,
translated by Andrew Schlademan.
First Paperback Edition, Published October, 2019
All Rights Reserved © Progressivepress.com
Length: 99,000 words plus notes, index, and glossary, on 256 pages
ISBN 1-61577-017-8, EAN 978-1-61577-017-5
Version 1.7, 1/2020

English translation from the original German,
*Gekaufte Journalisten: Wie Politiker, Geheimdienste und Hochfinanz
Deutschlands Massenmedien lenken,*
Kopp Verlag, Rottenburg, 2014.

Preface, "What is Freedom of the Press?" by John-Paul Leonard, Publisher. Biography of the Author, Dr. Udo Ulfkotte, by Andrew Schlademan.

Library of Congress Subject Heading
Z657 659 Freedom of the press. Censorship

BISAC Subject Area Codes
POL039000 Political Science / Censorship
POL064000 Political Science / Corruption & Misconduct
BUS070060 Business & Economics / Industries / Media &
    Communications Industries
POL047000 Political Science / Imperialism
HIS014000 History / Europe / Germany

NOTICES

If you were to jail all the journalists, such as they are, you'd surely put fewer innocents behind bars, than are locked up already.
— Christian Friedrich Hebbel (1813-1863), German dramatist and poet

Who has his own pen, is not a pen.
— *Saying*

I no longer think journalists should be treated with a special kind of immunity when they get a story this wrong, repeatedly, and people die in the process. I prefer to call them "media combatants," and I think that is a fair and accurate description of the part they play in wars today.
— Sharmine Narwani, interview with Salon.com on the war on Syria

On August 16, 2014 my friend Peter Scholl-Latour passed away. He was like a father to me. Some years before, in 2010, he was the one who encouraged me to write this book. I thank him for his friendship and for his advice, and I bow in respect for his life's work. Without him, this book could never have been written as it was.

This book is also dedicated with great gratitude to my wife Doris, and the physician Dr. Thomas Urbach, who saved my life when I was in an almost hopeless condition. Without their prompt, self-sacrificing and selfless help, I could never have completed this work.

Everyone named in this book denies having close, intimate contacts to elite organizations. Moreover, they deny being lobbyists. They also deny being "corrupted" by their proximity to the elite. And, they deny having lost their journalistic edge, working as they do in such close proximity to the aforementioned groups. They deny that this proximity has any influence on their reporting.

All the organizations named in this book deny being lobbies, they deny any desire to influence journalists or public opinion, and they also deny having any contacts to intelligence services.

— Udo Ulfkotte

Contents

What Is Freedom of the Press?   8

  How this Book Came to Be   10

Foreword   14

Chapter 1. Fake Freedom of the Press: My Life as a Reporter   27

  The Truth – A Journalist Exclusive?   27

  "Truths" on Sale from Our Sponsors:
    Elite Networks and Intelligence Agencies   30

  How an Oil Company Greased my Palms   38

  FAZ Façade: A Corrupt Mind Lurks Behind   41

  How do Journalists Pay for their Villas in Tuscany?   49

  Well-Greased: The Sleazy System of Journalism Prizes   52

  Courtesy Interviews, PR Trips and Tax Fraud   59

  Depraved Drinking Buddies: Glimpses of Journalistic Dirty Work   64

  Low-Down Dirty Tricks: How They Cheat Advertisers   66

  The Spiral of Silence: The News is Not in the Newspaper   68

  Here Today, Gone Tomorrow: Off With Their Headlines   74

Chapter 2. Our Lockstep Media:
Synchronized, Obedient and No Questions Asked   77

  Thilo Sarrazin: The Character Assassination of a Folk Hero   77

  Propaganda: The Prussians of the Balkans Are Coming   78

  Tricks of the Tongue in Politics and Media   80

  The Loss of Credibility   81

Chapter 3. The Undercover Truth:
Alpha Journalists Toe the Line for the Elites   83

  Bild Your Own Opinion   86

  Groomsman Journalism: *Bild* Up Your Power   90

  What Makes Kai Diekmann Tick?   92

  Bridge over the Atlantic   97

  In the Stranglehold of the Intelligence Agencies   104

  The Names: Controversial Contacts   110

  Embarrassing Adulation   116

  Undercover Power: Classic Propaganda Techniques   119

  Kallmorgen and Bohnen –
    Dubious PR Experts and Prestigious Newspapers   124

Obama's Trolls: America's Fifth Column   127

Rockefeller's Ghost – The Trilateral Commission   129

In Memory of FAZ Chief Schirrmacher:
    Tank Driver in the Civil Service   138

Buying Contacts with Big Names? Nobility Eradicated   141

The Power of the Bilderbergers: Conspiracy Theory or Reality?   145

Chapter 4. Buy a Journalist – See How Money Talks   150

Two in Three Journalists are for Sale   150

Favoring Favors: How to Bend the Media's Knees   154

Exposed: The Side Hustle   161

Brainwashing: Power Scissors in Your Head   162

Voting with Our Wallets: Turning Journalists into Welfare Recipients   167

Nonpartisan? The SPD's Media Empire   170

Chapter 5. Case Histories from the Propaganda Front   175

The Higher Goal: Amputating Germany's Identity   180

Merkel's Fairy-Tale Hour:
    How the German Government Lies to Its Citizens   182

Battle of Lies: The Propaganda Spiel
    of Sabine Christiansen and Ulrich Wickert   185

Soap Commercials for the Euro: The Mannstein Advertising Agency   194

Democracy Failed   197

Crime Scene Editorial Suite: the Shady Side of the Media   200

What Should We Do?   204

Afterword   211

After the Afterword: the Editor's Last Word   216

Notes   217

Index of Names   242

Author Biography   246

Glossary   250

What Is Freedom of the Press?

Can censorship be freedom of the press?

Legal minds favoring the interests of capital may be quick to claim that newspaper owners and editors have a freedom-of-speech right to print what *they* think is fit to print. They affirm a right of censorship or advocacy, above the duty to hew the line of objective reporting. Business, but not government, they say, may restrict press freedom.

However, this attitude confuses two very distinct classes of law, the Bill of Rights and civil contract law. The First Amendment merely forbids the government from infringing on freedom of expression. Thus if communist and nationalist parties each wish to publish their own books or newspapers, congenial to their respective viewpoints, the state should not intervene.

Most newspapers, however, claim to be independent, objective or non-partisan. Thus there is an implied contract to provide an *information service* to readers. Advertising in the paper should be clearly labeled as such.

Truly independent media are a public service entrusted with a fiduciary duty, similar to civil servants. The power and influence of their office is under their care, it is not theirs personally. Thus arises the temptation of corruption, of selling favors. For a large corporation, the financial value of a decision by an official or a newspaperman may easily dwarf the salary of the poor fellow, who may sell himself for pennies on the dollar.

A paper that claims to be independent when it actually serves hidden interests is guilty of fraud. That of course comes under another branch of law, the criminal code.

We hear much more about political corruption, but media corruption may actually be worse. Media reporters are our eyes and ears. What if our senses didn't reflect what is happening around us, but instead some kind of fantasy, or even remote programming? (Which sounds a lot like TV;-) If our eyes fooled us like that, we would be asleep and dreaming with eyes open, or disabled, hospitalized for hallucinations. We could never be masters of our own affairs, without a reliable sensorium. So the media must serve the nation just as our senses must faithfully serve each one of us. But they serve themselves. With the media we have, we are a zombie nation.

Of course, it's hard to be objective on topics like politics which are matters of opinion. That's what the op-ed page is for. The problem is systematic bias, when money talks in the news pages.

As a freshman in college, I once volunteered to be a stringer on the college paper, and was sent out to interview some subjects on a campus controversy. I didn't seem to be cut out for a hard hitting journalist either! The episode always reminds me of a Mulla Nasrudin story.

Mulla was serving as judge in the village, holding court in his garden. The plaintiff came and pleaded his case so convincingly, that the Mulla blurted out, By Allah, I think you are right! His assistant demurred, But Mulla, you haven't heard the other side yet! So now the defendant entered his plea, with even greater vigor and eloquence. Once again, the Mulla was so impressed, he cried out, By Jove, I believe you are right! And once again his clerk protested: But Mulla, they can't both be right! Oh my God, exclaimed the Mullah, I guess you are right, too!

My junior high school journalism teacher never tired of telling us, Journalism is a business. In theory it's a public trust, but money makes the world go round. We all have to please the boss to keep our job. We are all bought one way or another. As Ulfkotte points out, there are thousands of journalists looking for a job, not the other way about. So his original title *Bought Journalists* (*Gekaufte Journalisten*) was kinder and more modest than my more sensational *Presstitutes* — but as he had a pithy sense of humor, I think he would have liked it anyway. The "privished" edition title *Journalists for Hire* seems to downplay the matter a shade though. It's perfectly normal to be hired as a journalist, isn't it?

Perhaps we have to escalate the term to investigative journalist, because a journo is just somebody who writes things down.

In an interview (https://www.paulcraigroberts.org/2019/10/14/journalists-are-prostitutes/), Ulfkotte tells about his first assignment, during the Iran-Iraq war. The international press corps set out from Baghdad into the desert with extra jerry cans of gasoline — to set alight some long-destroyed tanks for a film shoot. Innocent sensationalism perhaps? But a million people have died in Iraq, Libya and Syria because the press didn't just report the news, didn't just lie about the news,

but they invented and sold the events that served as pretexts for wars.

That is way out of line.

There is no free speech protection for setting fire to a crowded theater!

In my book *ISIS IS U.S.*, in fury at the fakery of these warmongers, I castigate the mainstream media, the MSM, as the MMM: the Mass Murdering Media, as well as the Military-Monetary- Media complex. Notice how the media only point the finger at the military and industry, but mum's the word about the money masters and the media manipulators, they who control the nerve system of the zombie nation, military-industrial complex and all? Political candidates who tackle the media do so at their peril.

Sharmine Narwani is right. These are media combatants, these are war criminals, the lowest circle of hell in the ranks of crimes. We have million-dollar penalties for accidental product liability, but the salesmen of genocide get off scot-free!? 3,000 died on the spot on 9/11, followed by two decades of wars. The key suspect: Netanyahu crony Larry Silverstein. His reward: a $3 *billion* insurance payout – pure profit, as he was only leasing the Towers. The MSM cover it up, and revile you as a "conspiracy theorist" if you protest. "Presstitutes" is too light-hearted a word for them. The tragedy is that many social media agitators for the destruction of Syria were fools, who *thought* they were being oh so cool. Remember the Milgram experiment?

I like my book covers to be a depiction of the title, an allegory, which led to the most salacious cover art on "Presstitutes" I've ever dealt with. "Bought Journalists" could have been a covey of journos in a shopping cart, picking up their perks. Light satire blending to comedy, but this isn't really a funny story. Too many people, including the author, have given their lives.

One nice thing about this book is you get to know a real nice guy. I like Udo. Decent, intelligent, good sense of humor, conscientious, level-headed. He tells how he fell into this because he was just out of college and needing a job. We all have our compromises and our confessions to make. Ulfkotte relates the moment when it became too corrupt for him, when politicians offered him €5000 to use his cover as a journalist to spy and dig up dirt on the private life of their rival. That was too low down and dirty, too criminal for him, although it seemed to be expected and natural to them. Ulfkotte was the rarest of courageous whistleblowers.

How this Book Came to Be

I'm lucky to publish this book. Titles that are too hot for anyone else to handle are all that keep my tiny press going. A major bestseller in Germany, *Bought Journalists* was slated to be published in English in 2016, by Tayen Lane, an even more obscure imprint. After Ulfkotte passed away in January 2017, and the book kept getting postponed, suspicions of foul play and "privishing" ran rife on the Internet.

A number of activists were brainstorming how to get their hands on an English translation. A special thanks is due to Paul Barbara, who contacted Kopp about the English rights, and then found me through a mutual friend, Ian Fantom. The chief problem was that translation is expensive from German to English, which is why the book is not cheap.

To this day, Tayen Lane's non-existent edition has remained "on sale" for over $900 on Amazon. That sounded like a pretty good deal, about ten times cheaper than the going rate for a new translation. But each time I placed an order for the book, it was canceled. Supposedly this priceless tome had been misplaced in the warehouse, yet the sellers still kept offering it again. This odd detail inclines me to the theory that there was indeed a conscious effort to suppress the translation. Making it look as if the first publisher still had the rights to the book would discourage others from trying. An ex-employee of Tayen Lane did confirm to me that their "German to

English translation never moved forward." Another curiosity: during the nearly three years *Journalists for Hire* was "on sale" but unavailable on Amazon, it garnered only five-star reviews, 24 of them, from customers who wanted to read the book. Then the day this edition became available, that edition got a 1-star troll review, virulently attacking the author as a "yellow journalist" – which happens to mean "warmonger." Weird.

Of course, there could be some mundane explanations for the failure of the first, or rather zero edition. Business failure. Language barrier. Death of the author — for a small publisher, a proactive author promoting the book is a necessity. It was spooky, too, that the only book Tayen Lane seemed to have published before was a non-starter about suicide...

And what if the author's death was a key part of the pattern of suppression? There we go full conspiracy. It's not that incredible, though. Ulfkotte's last page here is a declaration of war: "This book is the first volume of an explosive three-part series." It's been alleged that the CIA has a weapon that works by triggering a heart attack. And like the Mafia, their code of silence calls for punishing ex-colleagues who took the oath of secrecy and then turned against them, more than mere bystanders like Joe Blogger or Johnny Publisher.

So I hope I'm lucky to publish this book. Hopefully it will get reviews in the alternative media, or interviews with our translator or myself. This is the second time I've published a German bestseller. The first was Mathias Broeckers' *Conspiracy Theories and Secrets of 9/11*. It didn't turn a profit, but was a very interesting treatment. In the first part of the book he shows that conspiracy – in the broadest sense, grouping together against outsiders – is one of three basic principles of life and evolution. Darwinians normally only talk about competition, but the second one is cooperation, and the hybrid of the two is conspiracy. Our body consists of a collective of cells cooperating and conspiring together against competing organisms! Conspiracy is as common as the air we breathe. Even the official story of 9/11 is a theory about a conspiracy of 19 hijackers, who weren't even on the passenger lists... Then there is the conspiracy theory about conspiracy theories, that the CIA purposely turned the term into an epithet to cover up the JFK assassination.

Of course not everything is a conspiracy. You have to remain skeptical, keep your balance and common sense. We need the flexibility to add new perspectives, and not try to reduce everything to one perspective. Our brains are perfectly capable of this, we just have to use them. Don't believe what they tell you, if it doesn't stand to reason. On 9/11, three towers fell at free-fall speed, but only two were hit by airplanes – which were 5,000 times lighter than the steel buildings anyway. Anyone can do the math. The perps didn't even bother to make it plausible, having the media to cover it up.

When a huge revelation like 9/11 hits, like it did some of us back in 2002, when I published the first "truther" book in English, it's a big shock. This can make people either deny the new information, or go overboard with it. Sometimes the shock of losing the mainstream world view is so great that people switch to the reverse explanation for everything. Yet most of life is still banal or benign. Major criminal political conspiracies like 9/11 require a lot of effort, and are used strategically.

Although 9/11 showed that these people are capable of almost anything, that doesn't mean they can or will do everything. For instance, I don't believe in chemtrails, because it doesn't make sense, and the contrails persist mostly on days when there are natural cirrus clouds in the upper atmosphere.

Manipulation is even more common than conspiracy. We all do it to get other people to do things. Ulfkotte shows that mass media manipulation is business as usual. It is so prevalent that it starts to get into the realm of a matrix, a wall-to-wall pseudo-reality. The spider army spins its web 24/7. Their thread is a mix of outrages and banalities, bread and circuses.

The formula is clear to see in the major German tabloid *Bild.* Its readers go for simplified and emotional narratives, like a cheap novel with themes of love and hate: "The reader's attention is steered away from what's objectively important and diverted to what's trivial." Yes, there IS a sucker born every minute. We are still just creatures that go too much on impressions and emotions rather than logic, and the media play on that with sensationalism and simplified images. Sure, our brain has amazing powers, but it can only focus on one thing at a time. (Luckily, that's at least one more than machines, that have no awareness of anything.)

Simplification, love and hate, enemy images. Our bane as a nation is our bent for political correctness and demonization. We are the heirs of the Puritans, who had a nasty habit of picking on little old ladies, demonizing them and then burning them at the stake. Who were the real demons there? Or in the tragedies of Libya and Syria??

We never learn. Hitler with us is as immortal as Satan, constantly recycled as the evil icon dictator of the day, sometimes complete with moustache. This is how they demonize populism. Ulfkotte asks, why should populism be unpopular? Lincoln expounded populism when he spoke of a government by and for and of the people. Each time you spend a $5 greenback with his icon on it, you distribute a piece of populist propaganda!

Trump is right to use the term "witch hunt" against the puritanical attack dogs of impeachment. He wouldn't have needed to ask favors of foreign potentates if the MSM, the mainstream media, were doing their job and investigating the Bidens. The pot calling the kettle black, because it sees itself on the politically correct moral high ground. More important, without the color revolution launched by the MSM and the Obama regime, Ukraine wouldn't have sunk into this cesspool of corruption. Even Trump won't say what the Bidens were really up to: stirring up war in East Ukraine so they could get their hands on the oil shale fields of the Donbass, or that they are investors in the illegal occupation of oil fields in the Golan Heights. Can't remember anyone ever fishing in more troubled waters. What about the suspicions that the Clintons have murdered people, such as Seth Rich, those are just conspiracy theories and not to be investigated either. Did the DNC kill this whistleblower and blame Putin instead for losing the election? The Mueller report won't say. But people do get killed. Like JFK, RFK, MLK. These are not minor matters they are getting away with behind the protective mask of the media which "covers" the news. Surveys do reflect declining public faith in the mainstream media – except among Democrats. Tell people what they want to hear: a basic marketing principle.

You may have heard of Operation Mockingbird and how the CIA plays our domestic media like a Wurlitzer. Ulfkotte explains how in Germany, CIA media operations started with the postwar occupation. It's part of the declared intention (most infamously but not only by Winston Churchill) to destroy the German people, the German identity. Control of the global media is the firm foundation of the Anglo-American-Zionist empire.

In his parting shot, "What should we do," Ulfkotte sees one simple ray of hope. "Everyone reading this book has the ultimate power over the journalism I have described here. All we have to do is stop giving our money and our attention to these 'leading media.' When enough of us stop buying the products offered by these media houses, when we no longer click on their Internet articles and we switch off their television or radio programs – at some point, these journalists will have to start producing something of value for their fellow citizens, or they're going to be out of a job. It's that simple." Instead, we can patronize sources like https://eluxemagazine.com/magazine/honest-news-sites/ . They note that, according to *Business Insider*, 90% of US media are owned by just six corporations, a similar problem of lockstep media as in Germany. They recommend these "Honest News Sites Way Better Than Mainstream Media."

The Corbett Report	Consortium News
Moon of Alabama	StormCloudsGathering
The Anti-Media	Truth In Media
Global Research	Media Roots
We Are Change	21st Century Wire

And The OffGuardian, which incidentally was one of the strongest voices for publishing this suppressed book.

– John-Paul Leonard,
ProgressivePress.com,
October 2019

Foreword

LSD? Crack? Datura tea? Cocaine? Crystal meth? In light of the reporting being done by our mainstream media in Germany, the question we find ourselves asking more and more often these days is: What drugs are they on in the editorial offices? It seems like they've definitely lost their minds. What in the world are they mixing in their muesli every morning? Many journalists have evidently lost their grip on reality. While millions of Germans are worrying about how they can manage the rising prices of rent and food and electricity, some journalists are trying to cozy up to the elites, the very elites who are responsible for more and more of our suffering. And, while the EU can only delay its inevitable bankruptcy by printing money around the clock, our leading media are encouraging us to bring even more bankrupt countries and their crises into the EU – of course, to benefit the financial elite. Too much crack? Too much LSD? Or is it all that cocaine in the editorial offices? While German citizens are already fed up with the casualties being brought home from foreign wars, select media pundits are strapping on steel helmets and enthusiastically cheering on plans for even more American wars. Is this what happens when you take crystal meth?

At the same time here in Germany, our alpha journalists seem to be experiencing a total blackout. Somehow, they cannot or do not want to remember the inspiring words they used to glorify the Iraq War or our military deployment in Afghanistan. Or, how they first realized the financial crash was upon us and the euro was tanking until only after every German citizen was already suffering the consequences. When a commercial airliner exploded over Ukraine in 2014, they would have loved nothing more than to send German soldiers to fight Russia, even before anyone knew who was actually responsible for the crash. Preventing bloodshed by demanding more bloodshed – a killer idea. Alone in Iraq, the more than 100,000 civilians who died are a testament to this, because the German media – with very few exceptions – cheered on the war in a delusional frenzy. Who or what controls these psychopaths in Germany's leading media? Are they really on drugs? Or does this systematic insanity have completely different causes? Are there propaganda specialists operating behind the scenes? In the past, we would have likely dismissed this as a simple conspiracy theory, but we now know that journalists from prestigious media outlets are the main target of the "spin doctors" who want the power to determine our news. This is primarily how the US government and the Israelis operate. There are even handbooks on how to influence the mainstream media.[1] One thing is clear: If you work in the mainstream media, you should exercise extreme caution towards lobbying groups, also around American and Israeli ones. As we will see, some journalists are doing just the opposite. They obviously feel right at home in the web of influential American and Israeli organizations. They even boast about being caught up in these networks too, proudly listing their "memberships" in the most controversial of circles.

When you keep uncovering more and more credible information about what's going on behind the scenes, you'll definitely begin to see our "news" in a completely different light. However, you better not talk about it. Our media representatives can't take a joke, even in satire. Author Josef Joffe, a "big-time journalist,"[2] and convicted tax evader Theo Sommer,[3] a managing director at the weekly newspaper *Die Zeit*, showed that they're big party poopers when they split legal hairs in order to sue a satirical program on Zweites Deutsches Fernsehen (ZDF), one of the two main public broadcasting channels in Germany. Joffe and Sommer's legal antics came after the show reported on their controversial contacts to questionable networks.[4] Still, wouldn't it be better if the folks out there could get a peek at the powers behind the curtain? Media specialist Thomas Stadler wrote: "For a flagship like *Die Zeit,* Joffe's legal proceedings (...) against ZDF are equivalent to a journalistic declaration of bankruptcy."[5] Nevertheless, it isn't only the likes of Josef Joffe that we need to be keeping a very close eye on.[6]

Do you ever get the feeling that you are being constantly lied to and manipulated by the media? Then you have something in common with the majority of the German population and with one of richest men in Germany, Karl Albrecht. Albrecht recently passed away, in July òf 2014 at the ripe old age of 94. Even though his estate was estimated at more than 18 billion euros at the time of his death, the German media simply didn't know what to say about his life. They just printed a photo and didn't include any of the details from his successful career. Albrecht, the founder of the Aldi supermarket chain, believed that politics was a dirty business. His whole life, he never wanted to meet any of the German Chancellors, he relied on his own family instead of elite networks, and he despised banks and credit institutions. He turned down all the honors and awards he was ever offered, even the Federal Cross of Merit. And, he never gave an interview. Why? One thing is clear: this ambitious family man didn't want to be used by anyone. He didn't want to be manipulated either. He was convinced that it would be best to steer clear of all these temptations. So, why are more and more people out there starting to think like Karl Albrecht?

In 1991, Professor Hans-Jürgen Bücher, a media scientist from Tübingen, published a research paper entitled "Media Language." In it, he said we can't overlook "that the interaction between the press and politics today follows a complicated set of rules: through staged reporting events like press conferences, so-called off-the-record conversations, or also through subtle forms of press control." Subtle forms of press control? Excuse me? We have a "controlled press?" To the average citizen, this sounds outrageous, but as we will see, it is our reality.[7]

Up until very recently, it was considered the stuff of "conspiracy theory" whenever anyone questioned why our media often seemed to be synchronized across the board. We're supposed to be living in a democracy with a diversity of opinion. Yet this alleged "conspiracy theory" is now becoming our bitter reality. This book will expose an elite network of lobbyists, one that is operating within our media. Did the billionaire Karl Albrecht know this and was this the reason he kept his distance from the media?

It should go without saying that journalists shouldn't be active in lobbying organizations or shadowy, elite networks, but many are – and they hate being unmasked.[8] You can expose them, one step at a time. After all, there are many publicly available studies that clearly show the power of their opinions, based on their presence in the most influential newspapers and magazines. All you have to do is comb through the electronic databases to see how frequently they are referenced.[9] Taking a further step, you can compare the names you find like this with the official lists of lobbyists registered with your national government. Since I am concentrating on the German media in this book, I compared them with the register kept by the German Bundestag[10] and with the lists maintained by Lobbypedia,[11] a project of *LobbyControl*. (The Bundestag or German Parliament / House of Representatives will generally be referred to as the Bundestag throughout this English translation).

When you then take look at the lobbying groups that these media personalities represent with their powerful opinions, you end up with a small circle of secretive, elite organizations. Suddenly, some of these journalists don't look like journalists anymore, but more like actors posing as journalists. It appears as though they're only simulating their independence and impartiality in front of their audience. In other words: As a journalist, if you are getting exclusive access to powerful elite circles, doesn't this also mean that you have gotten much too close to the ones making this access possible? As a journalist, aren't you already long since "corrupted" at this point? Haven't you been pulling punches for so long, you don't even notice you're doing it anymore? All of the journalists named in this book deny that they pull any punches or that they've been "corrupted" by getting too close to elite networks, but how are the readers going to see this? Especially if the names of the organizations or journalists listed here can also be found in the *WikiLeaks* documents from the secret US embassy reports?[12] Why do the names of certain mainstream, German media organizations show up there over and over again?

What this book will make clear is: There is an entire army of agents who appear respectable at first glance, but they are making money by influencing the German media on behalf of foreign interests. They do this, for example, through supposedly charitable "transatlantic friendship organizations." Their job is to keep German political and media elites from building any intellectual alliances with Russia and holding them on a pro-American course. After all, Washington is pursuing clear objectives in Europe and a new Cold War is one of them.[13] To achieve their ends, they need the mainstream media in Germany as an ally. Our first example: the US Department of Defense alone has spent billions of dollars on targeted propaganda over the years to influence media coverage around the world.[14] It is also easy to document the effects that this public opinion manipulation has had on the German-speaking world as well.[15] In recent months, you could even apply for grant money from the US embassy in Berlin to subversively direct public opinion in Germany toward America's interests – I will document this.

In his book The Warmongers: A History of US Propaganda, 1917-2005 *(Die Kriegsverkäufer: Geschichte der US-Propaganda (not available in English))*, the historian and media scientist Andreas Elter proved how the Americans exert their influence on our journalists. Amazingly, and unfortunately, his work went largely unnoticed. Since then, however, the WikiLeaks documents have been published. With the help of a WikiLeaks search engine, anybody can easily look up[16] how often certain, leading German media outlets have been mentioned by name in these secret diplomatic cables for their pro-American reporting. It is also conspicuous that the media outlets that are clearly very sympathetic to Germany's former occupying power, the USA, neglect to publish any reporting critical of the US. Are they doing this in Washington's interests? What is actually going on here?

The operators of the WikiLeaks internet platform are dedicated to making all types of classified documents accessible to the public. Among other documents, a memorandum classified as "CONFIDENTIAL/NOFORN (US)," which means confidential and only accessible to US citizens, was available for download in 2010. The author turned out to be the "CIA Red Cell," a team of intelligence officers who were appointed by the CIA Director, in his own words, "to think outside the box," "encourage thinking" and "offer alternative views." This is where I found a document from the spin doctors in the CIA with the title: "Afghanistan: Sustaining West European Support for the NATO-led Mission – Why Counting on Apathy Might Not Be Enough."[17] This secret document dealt with ensuring support among NATO's Western European allies for the war in the Afghan Hindu Kush. The Western European public was to be persuaded to tolerate the increase in casualties, both among their own soldiers and the Afghani civilian population, expected for the spring and summer of 2010. For this, a customized "strategic communication program" would be required for the NATO states providing troops. Germany was one of the countries included in the list. This secret document is nothing more than an instruction manual, prepared by the CIA, on how to influence public opinion in the German-speaking world. Surprisingly, the CIA justified the need to influence German public opinion based on the findings of a transatlantic organization: the *German Marshall Fund of the United States.* They had determined that only about one percent of the Germans they polled felt that stabilizing Afghanistan was Germany's most important national goal.[18] Therefore, this is exactly what needed to change. The German public was then inundated with US propaganda through the mainstream media – with war propaganda.

Aren't secret documents like the ones WikiLeaks published reason enough for leading German media groups to try and avoid any suspicion of influence by US organizations and their propaganda? If the CIA is creating "strategic communication programs" for the German-speaking media, then our "quality media" should have to steer clear of any organizations showing up in the sphere of US intelligence services. Yet the opposite is the case. The German mainstream media are drooling at the mere prospect of being tolerated by elite transatlantic organizations, if not joining them directly. The result is shocking in my opinion: one-sided and freely interchangeable propaganda. Today, this can be found increasingly often in the German media.

It used to be that intelligent, well-informed people would read several newspapers a day. It gave them differing points of view and a more accurate picture of current events. This is no longer worth the effort these days, because editorial content is freely interchangeable and basically identical. One example: On one day in July 2014, photos of Angela Merkel cooking were published on the front page of all leading media in Germany.[19] Why would they do that? If Angela Merkel is cooking, that's about as important to the average German citizen as a sack of rice falling over in China. If you place the newspapers next to each other, the mainstream monotony is unmistakable. What was once reserved for the tabloids in the supermarket checkout lane – that is, the German Chancellor in her kitchen – can now be found on the front pages of the so-called "quality media." At the same time, Germany's national newspapers now stand out for constantly delivering reporting and commentary that contradicts the perceptions and opinions of a clear majority of the population.

The newspaper analyst Professor Andreas Vogel from Cologne says, "Consumers today can generally choose between different features when they're purchasing products and services, only the daily newspaper publishers believe that they can serve every single reader with one standard product."[20] In his view, the publishers themselves are responsible for the rapid decline in German daily newspaper sales, not the internet.[21] One example: Among the Madsack publishing group (including the *Leipziger Volkszeitung* and *Ostsee-Zeitung),* the various papers' content is often identical. This means that one article can appear in up to 18 newspapers.[22]

This loss in the diversity of opinion, the standardization of the product and the increasingly extreme one-sidedness can only be understood by those who know how the "flows of information" are being channeled behind the scenes. The shady network of media, lobbyists and politics has been well-disguised up to this point. In the following chapters, we will identify this network and ask the following questions: Who is being influenced by whom? And even more importantly: Who is bribing whom and why? And how are we as (German) citizens being manipulated by the media? Now, let's set out on an exciting search for clues.

The first thing we notice: University students learn very early on that our "leading media" does not inform them truthfully. When it comes to the daily manipulation by the media, the university magazine *uni.de* writes:

Through language alone, the media manipulates our perception. This even occurs in surveys that should actually be serving the purpose of finding out what the majority thinks. The political barometer (Politbarometer) used by ZDF is a sad example of this. However, wherever opinion is increasingly being manufactured by the media and simply accepted by its users, democracy is in danger. (...) The manipulation of how opinion is formed begins with biased language. We can also see how this is used in articles of objective genres in the so-called quality media like the SZ (Süddeutsche Zeitung) *or FAZ* (Frankfurter Allgemeine Zeitung).[23]

Excuse me? Students at universities today are being warned that public broadcasting stations such as ZDF or that supposedly prestigious newspapers are manipulating the people? This provides us with some deep insight. According to a study done by the University of Mainz, which was reported by the political magazine *Cicero* in 2014, ZDF is even responsible for publishing polls that led to the Free Democratic Party (FDP) losing their seats in the Bundestag.[24] Only four (!) percent of viewers believe that they are better informed thanks to ZDF. And only five percent of Germans under 30 watch ARD (Germany's first public television station) – but this state-funded broadcaster collects more than 7.7 billion euros a year in mandatory television licensing fees.[25] As we will see in the chapter "Case Histories from the Propaganda Front," they also engage in the direct manipulation of German public opinion on behalf of the ruling political parties.

I, myself, used to work for the renowned "quality media," at the *Frankfurter Allgemeine Zeitung* (FAZ). Honestly: Today, I am ashamed of this. As we shall see, my reporting wasn't independent. It wasn't unbiased. It wasn't and still isn't neutral. The truth from my point of view: Sometimes I was even bribed for my reporting. In other cases, it coincided with the interests of a particular network.[26] As we shall see, I was even officially declared an honorary citizen of the State of Oklahoma by its Governor while I worked for the FAZ – just so that my reporting would be pro-American.

Later, I will describe that in more detail. The FAZ was pleased with my honorary citizenship. At the time, a lot of things were considered natural at the FAZ that I find to be more than problematic today. Looking back, it all seems like a fraud in my opinion – the readers were actually paying money for the "information" in the FAZ. I can't change what I have done, but I can tell the reader about what's really going on out there in the media: The bigger the BS the "quality media" dishes out, the thicker they lay on the buzzwords and catch phrases to cover the stench. Today, what we find in the media boardrooms is a kind of megalomaniacal way of thinking. The way I see things, nothing is really being questioned anymore, instead, all that counts are money and perks.

Many years ago I published a bestseller on the media business: *How Journalists Lie (So lügen Journalisten (not available in English))*. However, once you read the following chapter, you will never look at the "leading media" in the same light again. After all, this is a media establishment that has led the German-speaking world into unimaginable suffering over the last few years. One example would be our financial woes. As we will see, they tricked us into believing that the euro would be a strong currency with a glorious future. They even did this against the will of a people who wanted to keep the D-Mark and the Schilling. The people on the streets are still footing the bill for this today, their savings are vanishing right before their eyes. Today, we are paying for the devastating financial consequences of this manipulation. The same thing goes for the financial crash that our mainstream media didn't want to see coming as they kept the Champagne corks popping on the business pages. Only one editor-in-chief of a business newspaper, Lionel Barber, formerly of the *Financial Times Deutschland,* ever publicly apologized to his readers. He admitted that his paper neither saw nor understood the financial crisis on the horizon and that he gave his readers incorrect information – up until every average person on the street was already experiencing the financial crisis up close and personal.[27] The *Financial Times Deutschland,* however, which publicly excused itself for its ineptitude, has gone out of business in the meantime.

We, the people, aren't just paying a high financial price for this manipulation by the leading media either. The body count is devastating as well. This is because our popular media is painting a very clear image of the enemy: Russia. The evil Russians and the good Americans, that is the predominant view. This is a psyop, a psychological warfare tactic. Where wars were once fought by soldiers, they are now waged by the media. Many people recognize that the media is planting this bogeyman in our minds. Once respectable newspapers like the FAZ are now regularly referred to as the "yellow press" and "disgusting warmongers."[28] Based on his extensive studies, the Austrian conflict expert, Dr. Kurt Gritsch, also accuses our traditional, "quality newspapers" of being "warmongers." He writes:

Do you like to read the newspaper? And if so, are you also one of the many who enjoys reading the traditional broadsheets like the "FAZ," the "Neue Züricher Zeitung (NZZ)," the "Süddeutsche Zeitung" or "Die Zeit"? I admit: I do not. Not since I figured out, over the course of many years, that this is where the journalistic preparations for war take place (...) It is warmongering, and should be characterized as such.[29]

This rabble-rousing and warmongering recently reared its head in a display of historic proportions after the Malaysia Airlines passenger flight (MH-17) crashed in eastern Ukraine in mid-July of 2014. The wreckage had barely hit the ground before an opinion cartel was spreading the "news" everywhere that Russia was behind the crash. The *Bild* newspaper was way out at the front of this psychological manipulation of the German populace. "Does EU only stand for 'Egregiously Useless?" asked the paper within days of the crash, claiming a rocket from Moscow had killed the 298 people on board. At the time, it was definitely not yet clear who had owned or who had fired the rocket.[30] On the same day the *Bild* (and other German media) complained about the "uselessness" of the EU in standing up to Russia, American intelligence services were even stating that they didn't have any evidence of "Russian complicity" in the crash.[31] It soon became clear that the Americans, unlike the German media, had good reason to exercise caution.[32]

In this book we will tackle the question, all plane crashes aside, of why the leading media in Germany are purveying alarmingly one-sided propaganda and disinformation (psyops), which sometimes leads directly into outright warmongering. We will also take a closer look at the media scientist Uwe Krüger's work and see why his studies of the German media led him to the alarming realization of how the "quality media" in the German-speaking world is being intellectually controlled by the EU, the arms industry, NATO and the USA.[33] When you look back at the articles today, you can understand the statements made by the scientists Krüger and Gritsch. Many years ago, under the headline, "Cowardice in the Face of the Public," the *FAZ* published lines like: "Germany can no longer afford to be a geopolitical bystander."[34] The message in the article, at least as I understood it: We need to send even more German soldiers to Afghanistan. Much to the delight of the arms industry, NATO, and the political and financial elite, our mainstream media doesn't just report on the combat missions taking place in Afghanistan. These opinion-makers are echoing Germany's pro-American political elite, just as they did when the Americans invaded Iraq. Ready and willing, they sugarcoated the "revolutions" in North Africa and the Middle East that the USA wanted. They promised us peace and democracy there if we all just joined in the choir controlled from Washington loudly enough. Since then, however, all we have gotten is more and more terror and hate… and dead and horribly wounded soldiers coming back from foreign deployments. After our warmongers in the press fanned the fires consuming the Middle East, they continued by unabashedly crying out for "war" in

Ukraine and on the Crimean Peninsula. They also wanted to "make a military statement" on NATO's eastern border with Russia. As we will see, American propaganda organizations were pulling the strings behind the scenes. Thanks to their interdependence with US lobbies, our mainstream media functions as the extended arm of the NATO press office, the arms industry and a small clique of leading politicians.[35] We will illustrate this in detail.

Today it is perfectly clear to the average citizen that these "revolutions" in the Middle East, for example, have achieved absolutely nothing. Also shocking is what the pro-American, German-speaking mainstream media is keeping secret from us: The situation, for example, under the Egyptian President Al-Sisi is even ghastlier than it was under President Mubarak. Now, the Egyptians are so anti-American that during his visit in July 2014, the US Secretary of State John Kerry had to undergo an embarrassing security check, being frisked and having to go through a metal detector, before he was received by the Egyptian President.[36] Our pro-American media prefers to hide things like that from the German-speaking world. They keep it secret, like so many other things, because they simply can't explain this to the public. Especially after having written all those articles celebrating the wave of Western peace and democracy that was supposedly washing over the Middle East.

If you want to know why European news is so one-sided, get familiar with the networks operating behind the scenes, the ones where the alpha journalists are embedded. Evidently, they can hardly wait to send our soldiers into the next American war. So far, more than 100 German soldiers have been killed in foreign deployments that were prepared journalistically in our leading media. What do these German journalists, who so loudly demanded the end of the political "cowardice in the face of the public," say to the parents of the German soldier Georg Kurat? He died in Afghanistan at the age of 21. Or to the parents of Konstantin Alexander Menz (22) and the relatives of more than fifty other German soldiers who lost their lives in Afghanistan alone? And the worst part of it is: They lost their lives for absolutely nothing. The billions of dollars in development aid and the blood we've shed there hasn't changed a thing. Have our mainstream media ever publicly apologized for their share in the responsibility for all the bloodshed and suffering, and not just in Afghanistan, that has resulted from their biased reporting?

Here, our alpha journalists prefer to remain silent. As Markus Wiegand, editor-in-chief of the *Wirtschaftsjournalist (Business Journalist)*, aptly described these colleagues: "The elite in this industry live in a bubble where you don't harm one another, instead, you just pat each other on the back."[37]

From Alexander the Great (356 to 323 BC) to the Roman Empire and the British Empire and up to World War II, history has taught us one thing: The world cannot be controlled, governed or pacified by one person or one group.

Just as Alexander the Great, who once dreamed of bringing peace to the whole world, was unable to keep the peace among his own European troops on their way from Macedonia to what is present-day Afghanistan, now, nearly 2,500 years later, American and German soldiers haven't been able to change anything there either. As we know, the entire German military tried in vain to succeed where Alexander the Great had failed.[38] No German soldiers would have ever been sent to war by our politicians if our leading media hadn't submissively prepared the ground for them with their clever, psychologically potent rhetoric. I personally experienced this, up close and personal, for almost two decades. In the meantime, many people are now sick and tired of the biased reporting coming from our "quality media." I also wouldn't be surprised if the friends and relatives of fallen German soldiers start to blame the mainstream media and their network of friends after reading this book. The following chapters are definitely going to bring the structures operating behind the scenes into much better focus.

"Friendly fire" is what it's called when you fall victim to your own side's weapons. In this book, I will show how opinion makers in the German-speaking world cheer on the "transatlantic friendship," while shooting at their own helpless population. The weapons at the media's disposal are far more dangerous than the soldiers' noisy ammunition. Their lies creep quietly, deep into our brains. We alluded to this out a few paragraphs ago in connection with the articles glorifying the revolutions in North Africa and the combat operations in Afghanistan and Iraq.

Something that never ceases to amaze the careful observer in this battle for public opinion is what our mainstream media always leaves out when they provide important background information. One example: In the summer of 2014, *Human Rights Watch* published a long report about the restrictions on the freedom of the press in Western democracies due to the increasingly intensive monitoring and surveillance measures carried out by US intelligence services. The report documents how journalists have had to change the way they work in order to even get their hands on any independent information at all.[39] The German-speaking mainstream media didn't waste a word on this report, but then again, they boast an extremely close relationship to American propaganda organizations. If the same report would have discussed the restrictions on Russian journalists because of state-sponsored surveillance and monitoring in Moscow, this story would probably have been on the front page of every paper. In plain language: Instead of neutral news, more and more often we are being served increasingly selective information. Our thinking is being channeled in the process – and this certainly isn't happening by accident.

I don't know what is going to happen after this book is published. After all, I am exposing networks that prefer working in the dark. I'm also naming the names of hundreds of journalists.[40] The purpose of providing these names or identifying people, organizations or companies is not for defamation or slander. Rather, this is necessary in the public interest, because the horrific damage resulting from what I describe in this book affects us all. The only way this damage can be prevented is by making it public. This is because, as opposed to corrupt politicians, corrupt journalists cannot be prosecuted if they manipulate or suppress the truth – even when they take bribes to do so. I wrote a few of the people listed here by name and asked them for a statement. In response, I received letters from lawyers, threats of lawsuits and hints of possible steps being taken in the direction of criminal prosecution. For these reasons, I didn't bother any of the large media companies with any more questions. I'm anxious to see what will happen. Markus Wiegand, editor-in-chief of the *Wirtschaftsjournalist*, said that on closer inspection, the German media elite is made of up of a "club of wimps."[41] If you criticize them, they start screaming like a nest full of hungry chicks.

One thing is very important: before I unmask other journalists, I must admit to my own wrongdoing. I have written about how corrupt I was in my reporting and which networks had an influence over my reporting – always with my employer's blessing. After that, it'll get really exciting. My goal? I want to use the truth concentrated in the following chapters, which is proven with sources, paragraph for paragraph,[42] not only to inform, but also to affect a change – together with the readers of this book and their friends. Will we be able to do it together? Usually, you never end up with exactly what you intended. In the late 80's, the East German opposition would have never believed you if you told them that the Berlin wall was going to fall and Germany would be reunited. They only wanted to relieve some of the problems within the system. Instead, they brought it down. In 1906, the American author Upton Sinclair wrote a muck-raking novel because he wanted to improve the working conditions in the Chicago slaughterhouses of the time. What resulted instead were sweeping laws for better food hygiene. Looking back, he said, "I aimed for the public's heart, and by accident I hit it in the stomach." With this in mind, I hope the following chapters will reach people's hearts. And, I hope that one day, this will help bring an end to the growing frustration so many people have with fake journalists and the media they work for.

"If you don't buy, you won't get lies." This was the slogan of Malaysian activists calling for a nationwide boycott of the newspapers. More and more Malaysians were unhappy with their reporting and wanted to teach the ruling elite a lesson. This widespread dissatisfaction is also present in Germany. Do we really have independent media? Or has it all just become pure fiction in the meantime? Who decides on what news we get to hear? Why is every minor facet of an American presidential election now more important than any local German news? If you're reading this, you can probably guess the answer: In democracy's shadows, information is molded by the invisible hand of an opinion cartel. In the background: There are elite organizations with close ties to intelligence agencies. They are active among the think tanks and "charitable" foundations. You can only be accepted into this exclusive society, a fifth column of the powerful, through personal recommendations. You can't purchase a ticket to get inside. They have amassed so much wealth, they don't need to charge entrance fees.

When do we really feel well-informed? When we know that Angela Merkel chews on her fingernails?[43] That may be true,[44] but is this information really important? Do we have to know that the former Minister-president of Saxony, Kurt Biedenkopf, likes to play with a toy train? And that the former head of Deutsche Bank, Hilmar Kopper, "collects the wispy pieces of paper that they used to wrap around oranges for transport to identify their place of origin?" He irons them out and then glues them in an album?[45] In our modern information society, there are endless streams of news. It is important to sort your information… and to know what you can believe. Before, the "quality media," public broadcasting stations, newspapers of record and the radio used to do this for us. Everything is different today.

The actress Hildegard Knef once said to me, "It is unbelievable how much the media can lie. I don't even know what I should believe any more." We met in August 1997, at the Bremen-based talk show *III nach Neun (Three after Nine)*.[46] We drank a glass of wine after the show in a local hotel. Indignantly, Hildegard Knef related the liberties journalists had taken in reporting about her life. She said, "Only one thing is true about journalists: they are in the business of lying." A few months before that and nearly 5600 kilometers away from Bremen, I heard something similar while I was on a trip in Ethiopia. This time I was talking with Karlheinz Böhm, the actor who played Emperor Franz Joseph at Romy Schneider's side in the "Sissi" film trilogy about Empress Elisabeth of Austria. I visited him in the highlands of Ethiopia. Hildegard Knef and Karlheinz Böhm – two legends of the German cinema – no longer trust the German media. This gave me a lot to think about. After all, "Thou shalt not bear false witness," was one of the highest moral commandments at one time. Alas, now we consider journalists to be the greatest liars out there. Udo Lindenberg, a German rock music legend, didn't have the best opinion of the media either. We had a chance to discuss this in a television studio's greenroom. Likewise the journalist Peter Scholl-Latour, whom I met many times in war zones around the world since the late 80s. He liked to paraphrase Hiram Johnson's old adage saying, "The first thing that falls by the wayside in war is the truth." When I was younger, these comments by Hildegard Knef, Karlheinz Böhm, Udo Lindenberg and Peter Scholl-Latour seemed like conspiracy theories to me. Are they really? Later on, I started to hear things like this more frequently, for example, from my friend, Professor Wilhelm Hankel, a man who always seemed like a father to me. He was the man who developed the German treasury bills.

What bothered him the most was that our media were becoming increasingly uncritical, frequently distributing biased propaganda, and the information they offered was completely generic and unoriginal.

So, how can you as the reader be certain that the following information I provide isn't just fiction too? First of all, I specify names, companies, times and places. I have also included hundreds of footnotes with additional sources. If even just a tiny piece of this information is wrong, I will be sued. Secondly, I can boast of a journalistic accolade that you only get if you most definitely *have* been telling the truth: My house has been searched more than once for suspicion of having betrayed state secrets. They don't barge into your house if you're a liar. You only get them when you reveal something that the public isn't supposed to find out about. I am probably, unfortunately, the German author whose house has been searched the most times for just doing his job. However, you can think of it this way: Each time, the state was simply adding another feather to my cap of honest reporting.

One more important note before we get started: In the following chapters, I often speak of "these" journalists. Please keep in mind that this definitely does not include the many respectable and serious, poorly paid and hard-working, freelance or salaried editors who want to promote the ideals and values of a free press and do so with great commitment. The ones who incessantly reveal abuses through impeccable research and want to provide truthful reporting. Despite their great dedication, they will eventually lose their jobs too.[47] This book is about those journalists who float on a level above us, removed from the common folk, and make common cause with the elites, sometimes corrupt and allowing themselves to be bribed for their courtesy reporting. But that's enough of an introduction. Let's find out how this manipulation works in the real world.

Chapter 1. Fake Freedom of the Press: My Life as a Reporter

Everyone named in this book denies having close, intimate contacts to elite organizations. Moreover, they deny being lobbyists. They also deny being "corrupted" by their proximity to the elite. And, they deny having lost their journalistic edge, working as they do in such close proximity to the aforementioned groups. They deny that this proximity has any influence on their reporting.

The Truth – A Journalist Exclusive?

How can it be that our mainstream media celebrate the European Union and the euro currency as a project for the future, even though millions of people throughout Europe are critical of the EU and the euro? Jean-Claude Juncker, longtime head of Luxembourg's government and the current President of the European Commission, tells us how this works:

"We decide on something, put it out there and wait and see what happens. If no one kicks up a fuss, no rioting in the streets, since most people haven't a clue what's been decided, we continue, step by step, until there is no turning back."[1]

Why does our mainstream media cheer on these politicians instead of denouncing them? The answer: They're working together. They stick to these elites. How can it be that our mainstream media is always demanding that German soldiers should be sent on new military adventures in foreign countries, even though the majority of the population is clearly against this? The answer: Our alpha journalists are nothing more than the long arm of the NATO press office. We will also go into great detail to prove this in this book. How can it be that our mainstream media continues to celebrate mass immigration from all over the world as "enrichment," even though the majority of Germans would rather close the borders to certain migrants today rather than tomorrow? The answer: Industry and the financial elite want it this way, because a massive influx of cheap labor serves their interests.

This list of piercing questions could go on forever. However, the most important question behind all of it is: Who is really governing Europe? It surely isn't the citizens of the EU, because what's going on in Europe has little to do with democracy. It is more of an illusion of democracy, a well-crafted illusion. Still, if the citizens aren't in charge, then who is? Could it be a group of opinion makers, a group of the most important and influential heavyweights from industry, finance and politics who are pulling the strings behind the scenes and controlling our thinking through the mainstream media?

That sounds like a conspiracy theory, but you can find astonishing statements to this effect, even in the big newspapers, and they will make you think twice. The *Frankfurter Rundschau* (FR), for example, reported that the euro can be traced back to the secretive, elite network of the Bilderberg Group.[2] This statement, which according to the FR was confirmed by one of the Bilderberg Group's own honorary chairmen, is just one of many examples that hint at how elite networks are obviously orchestrating our lives from the shadows. Later, in its own chapter, we will use the euro as an example of how this network uses propaganda to impose the interests of the political and the financial elite – against the will of the people. Nevertheless, this wouldn't be possible without control over the flow of information – and this flow is influenced by a small number of opinion makers.

An interesting undergraduate thesis from Munich put together a list of the adjectives and adverbs used in select articles about Obama (USA) and Putin (Russia) in the *Frankfurter Allgemeine Zeitung* between 2000 and 2012. The words selected were ones that implied a value judgement in their description of Obama or Putin. The adjectives used in the FAZ to describe Putin had overwhelmingly negative connotations, including: threatening, rough, aggressive, confrontational, anti-western, power-political, untruthful, cool, calculated, cynical, harsh, abrasive, non-substantive (arguments) and implausible (arguments). The words used to describe Obama had a completely different tone: committed, fanatically welcomed, enthusiastic, conciliatory, praised, hopeful and resolute.[3] In plain language: The reporting in the once renowned FAZ newspaper is definitely not neutral, independent, unbiased nor objective these days. So where is this bias coming from? Does this style of reporting possibly have anything to do with the closeness that the FAZ's writers have to certain elites and powerful circles? In the following chapters, we won't only be considering the FAZ when it comes to this question. We will also look into why the mainstream media doesn't even want you to imply that they're close to the elite.

Chapter one, scene two: A few years ago, the reporter Thomas Leif painted a rather conspiratorial picture in the ARD television documentary *Strippenzieher und Hinterzimmer (Puppet Masters and Back Rooms)*. In it, journalists, ministers and party officials appeared to all be sitting in the same boat, isolated from the common folk and getting along like gangbusters. Viewers got to see how politics is made in secret meetings behind the scenes.

The film was about a corrupt world of cozy connections.[4] What was being shown, however, wasn't a conspiracy theory. The film was controversial, because the people being shown in it were the perpetrators. They thought that this form of corruption was completely normal. The journalists portrayed in the documentary took it as an affront when they were simply asked about these secret networks operating in the background. When the NDR news magazine *Zapp* questioned a member of one of these shadowy groups, they got the response, "We're dealing with secret things, and this means: We want to be the ones to understand politics. A viewer or listener, or reader doesn't need to know that. They only have to understand what we say."

The viewers and readers only have to understand what the journalists report? They shouldn't even get to know who wants which news and what messages distributed at all? Regarding secret meetings, NDR cited a journalist as follows: "What we do there is an industry secret. The same thing goes for lobbying. A lobbyist never talks openly about who they talk to, which documents they receive, where they pass them on and what happens as a result. This is comparable." A former editor at ZDF said: "The advantage is simply that we get to learn the truth and then – as bitter as it may be for some – we aren't allowed to publish or broadcast it."[5] Really? The truth is reserved exclusively for journalists? And then they're not allowed to publish it? What is really going on out there? If anyone still believes that the news is balanced, honest and reliable, this book is going to shatter those illusions for you.

Personally, the illusions I had about journalism and truthful reporting were shattered many decades ago. I can remember the exact day it happened: It was August 2, 1990, the day the Iraqi army marched into Kuwait. At the time, Saddam Hussein had always been shown in the best light by the German media. Suddenly, they needed a story to make the Iraqis look like the very definition of evil. This was done by the PR agency *Hill & Knowlton*. They specialize in lies. They made up a story about Iraqi soldiers going into Kuwaiti hospitals, tearing helpless babies out of their incubators and leaving them on the concrete floors to die, and then taking the incubators from Kuwait to Baghdad as war booty. This horror story was cooked up to justify the USA's entry into the war to "free" Kuwait. *Amnesty International* helped spread the incubator lie.[6] In December of 1990, AI published a report about the human rights violations in Kuwait where the incubator lie was depicted as the alleged reality.[2] On January 12, 1991, the US Congress voted in favor of the war against Iraq.

At a US Congressional hearing on October 10, 1990, a young girl by the name of "Nayirah" testified that she had seen with her own eyes how Saddam Hussein's soldiers threw the babies on the cold cement floors of the hospital in Kuwait and steal the incubators. This heartbreaking testimony, about how evil Saddam Hussein and his henchmen supposedly were, was broadcast into every living room in America – and of course in Germany as well – and it produced the desired mobilization of public opinion in favor of the war. Later, it came out that the whole story was made up. The girl turned out to be the daughter of Saud bin Nasir Al-Sabah, the Kuwaiti ambassador in Washington. We also learned that she had received acting lessons from the *Hill & Knowlton* PR agency before delivering her tear-jerking testimony. The Kuwaiti government had paid the media and PR agencies a total of 12 million USD for this propaganda campaign. At the time, I was already an editor at a newspaper. I witnessed first-hand how these made up lies were printed in many German newspapers with the purpose of bringing German public opinion to the boiling point: Before that, Saddam Hussein had been portrayed as a "good leader" in Germany, but overnight, along with the people of Iraq, he was to be downgraded into some kind of insect. The German media's efforts were a success.

Not too long before that, I just happened to be on the front lines of another war, shortly after the Iraqis had launched a chemical weapons attack. Saddam Hussein's soldiers had just massacred Iranians with poison gas made in Germany. That was at Zubai in July of 1988. I will describe that in more detail later.[7] I took horrifying photos of the Iranian victims of this gas attack, whose brains had flowed out of their eyes, noses and mouths. You would suppose there would have been a wave of outrage in Germany after this. Instead, there was basically silence among German journalists. In contrast to the incubator lie described above, the gassing of the people I saw in Iran was a brutal reality. None the less, once the wave of incubator propaganda hit, it was like the masses' brains had been hacked. All at once, everyone began to scream: War! War! War! This wouldn't have been remotely possible if Germany's alpha journalists hadn't marched in the vanguard with their disinformation campaign – and I was enlisted in the opinion cartel's disinformation troops.

This book is the first part of three explosive publications about the media industry. In the following chapters of this book, you will learn how secretive networks actually control the flow of information in Germany. This book deals with the sticky proximity of the German media to elite circles, with its shocking consequences. In a subsequent book, we will learn about the tricks the large German publishing houses use to systematically deceive their advertisers. You'll get a little taste of this here in this book first. In the third book, I will reveal which journalists are on which internal PR industry lists. This will also be devastating, because German reporting has already been bought for the most part. Still, I will also reveal some of the names in this book as well. So, let's get this book started by concentrating on the simulated freedom of press, especially the lobbying work, the secret networks of our opinion-makers and the consequences these have on reporting in Germany.

"Truths" on Sale from Our Sponsors: Elite Networks and Intelligence Agencies

The first thing I have to say again is that I, myself, the author of this book, was guilty of this. Looking back, I was corrupt, I was manipulative, and I dealt in disinformation. It was exactly this same inability to keep a distance, what I accuse other journalists of doing in the following chapters, that led me to believe it was perfectly normal for such a long time. With my boss' approval, I took advantage of the press discounts, accepted the all-inclusive invitations to 5-star hotels and went on buddy-buddy trips with top politicians. I held positions in various foundations, and I gave lectures at organizations affiliated with intelligence agencies. When I look back, I can see that as an employee of the *Frankfurter Allgemeine Zeitung* (FAZ), I was often bought for positive reporting – and I let them buy me. What's more, my employer had my back, because they expected it from me like it was a given. Today, I can talk about it – but that doesn't make it any better.

Some things have changed since then. Today, however, bought reporting is still taken for granted. For example, the EU presently pays "independent" journalists to polish the EU's image in the supposedly "independent" media. Thus, both private and public media companies court the EU to get their hands on the PR money they make available. This is known as bought journalism.[8] It also works in the opposite direction as well: Two British reporters offered EU delegates money to change some laws – and they were successful.[9] In Switzerland, journalists often receive envelopes with 500 Swiss francs (around USD 500) for participating in "press conferences."[10] A publisher in Switzerland also offered politicians very flattering biographies if they would also purchase an advertisement along with it as well.[11] If it is called journalism, then it should also have something to do with journalism. Günther Jauch, for example, the former host of the critical news magazine *Stern TV* and one of the most well-recognized journalists in Germany, "in a 20-minute infomercial for Amway," pitched "a US company that sells detergent and personal hygiene products by means of a pyramid scheme."[12] As a critical journalist, can you do something like this? Where are the boundary lines? As a journalist in Germany, should you be hawking products? Well, it's something that happens every day in the real world. At any rate, nothing stuck to the Teflon-man Jauch. However, looking back, it is extremely embarrassing for him. Moreover, how embarrassing is it if a university thesis on biased reporting in the German media ("Biased Attribution in German Print Media"[13]) includes the following about an article written by Horst Bacia, a journalist at the FAZ:

The analysis of this article with regard to its development of the topic, thus, at best, results in an argumentation that, in its presentation, can be compared to that of an advertising text.[14]

Excuse me? After a detailed analysis, a university thesis certifies that one of the most celebrated FAZ columnists writes at the level of advertising copy? Boundaries that should remain clear are obviously getting blurred here. So, how does the communications scientist Wolfgang Donsbach describe the general relationship between truth and journalism in Germany?

In Germany, this tendency to evaluate and select information corresponding to one's own opinion is much more profound than it is in other countries.[15]

The manipulation of the readers has been noticeable at the FAZ for many years. Dr. Heinz Loquai gave a famous speech in 2003 where he said the following about the FAZ:

*We learn from the FAZ's Washington correspondents that, among other things, Bush studies the bible every day, prays regularly and bases his actions on the question, "What would Jesus do?" The president is a "paragon of modesty and close to his people." There may be "an arrogant bone or two in Bush's body," but he is "a man of love." His "portion of missionary fervor" is "softened by statesmanlike prudence," through "patient waiting," the "natural political talent's decision" has been "expressed." Although Bush may know that he is not an intellectual, he can rely on "his political instinct, his wisdom and his natural wit." So (...) lectured, we can continue to count on the judgement and objectivity of leading German daily and weekly newspapers' America correspondents! Embedded with the allied troops, embedded in the political-media network in Washington – what's the difference?*16

The former FAZ Washington correspondent Matthias Rüb wrote the adulation to US President Bush cited above shortly before the Iraq War began in 2003, in violation of international law. One year later he received the Arthur F. Burns Award for a different article. The Arthur F. Burns Award is presented by Germany's Foreign Minister. So, who selects the winners today? The jury includes, for example, the journalists Sabine Christiansen and Stefan Kornelius (Süddeutsche Zeitung).[17] Keep these names in the mind. We will come across them and their interesting connections quite often.

In Germany, economic correspondents from respected daily newspapers also write for corporate magazines under pseudonyms, so they can report on the newspapers where they're employed. Editors at state-owned, public broadcasting companies also take money from political parties to instruct politicians on how they can keep their distance from rabid journalists. All of that is taken for granted these days. Business reporters give us the financial reports about banks on TV, finish recording and then go play the host at bank-sponsored events, receiving princely sums for their services. Germany is at the same time both the Bought and the Sold Republic. At any rate, we're being drenched in bought truths around the clock – especially when it comes to politics and the economy.

As a journalist, in certain networks you can learn how to create or strengthen the public's opinions. It's all about courtesy reporting in the best interest of politicians, parties, associations or institutions. I witnessed it over decades and actively participated in it – as a vain employee at the FAZ. I will describe it to the best of my ability. It gets really scary when politicians, the lords of privileged information, dictate the use or non-use of news to journalists. A nice way of saying this is calling it "authorizing." A politician is allowed to give their blessing to what they said and even to what they were asked. Anything undesirable is redacted. As the SpiegelBlog wrote about it in 2012:

> *As a German journalist, when you are interviewing an American and you give them the option of reviewing their own statements at the end, they will sometimes look at you like an extra-terrestrial in jihadist's clothing. Isn't that incredibly stupid? Giving the interviewee so much power? In Germany, authorization has been nurtured for decades. Although DER SPIEGEL didn't invent it in the 1950s, (...) they have cultivated it so ardently, it has become the industry standard in this country, at least for interviews.*[18]

When you think about it, all authorizing means is that the interviewer is bowing down to an authority. Journalists are therefore simply submitting to the powerful. Politicians can make any unpleasant news disappear by claiming that it was an "unauthorized" interview.[19] In this way, the lords of privileged information dictate journalists' use or non-use of information in Germany – and we think it is completely "normal" – just like people in the Middle Ages thought the reports coming out of the nobility's courts were "normal." Today, just like in the Middle Ages, a few court minions get to sit very close to the powerful and feast on their words. The staging, the costumes of this drama may have changed over the centuries, but it's still being directed by the same entity: the network of the powerful.

Leading journalists are surrounded by the networks of the elites, from which, normal citizens are simply excluded. Journalists like to claim that they fulfill an important function of criticism and control. Allegedly, they want to track down and reveal persistent abuses. Above all, they want to "keep tabs on the powerful." That is why journalists like to refer to themselves as "the Fourth Estate." The function of providing information is the media's and journalists' central function. This means providing their audience with information on things they didn't know about before – and doing so in a comprehensive, objective and understandable way. They should also be doing this in a way that doesn't remind us of the way journalism is practiced in a dictatorship.

What should we think when the ZDF anchorman Claus Kleber compares his own program, Germany's state-sponsored public news program, the *Tagesschau*, with North Korean government television?[20] Furthermore, how can it be tolerated that somebody like Kai Diekmann, the editor-in-chief of the "independent" *Bild* newspaper, is a member of the controversial Atlantik-Brücke organization?

Are you still really neutral if you, as the publisher of the weekly newspaper DIE ZEIT, like Josef Joffe, are also sitting on the board of the pro-American and "CIA-related think tank"[21] the *Aspen Institute*? Josef Joffe even said the following about his lobbying work for the USA in Germany, "Since the majority of the people in our country do not think very highly of the USA, I like to write against this majority."[22] Doesn't Josef Joffe, a litigious party pooper,[23] know that the Aspen Institute's office in Berlin is suspected of having also been the office that US intelligence agency officers were working out of?[24] This is the conclusion of a study on the transatlantic relations of Shepard Stone, the first director of the Aspen Institute in Berlin:

One is only extremely reluctant to disturb this "picturesque still life" with the suspicion that Stone was a case officer for one or even several American intelligence agencies. His "office": the Berlin Aspen Institute.[25]

Can you – like the very likeable and liberal-minded journalist Stefan Kornelius from the *Süddeutsche Zeitung* – be connected to a bunch of political lobbying organizations and then still report independently on political processes? I would say: No, you certainly can't. The *Süddeutsche Zeitung* even wrote that themselves. When the ZDF correspondent Udo van Kämpen, who went to music school to study the drums,[26] played a song at a press conference in the summer of 2014 for Angela Merkel's birthday, the Munich-based paper (SZ) was outraged: "Journalists don't do that. They are observers, not participants. (…) If you get too close to a politician, you should not report on them or their policies, otherwise your trustworthiness and independence go overboard. (…). Journalists don't have the best reputation as it is."[27] So, if the SZ also agrees that journalists aren't allowed to get this close to politicians or their organizations, then how do these words fit in with the longstanding connections of the SZ journalist Stefan Kornelius? In the meantime, the SZ columnist Stefan Kornelius has hit rock bottom. That same USA that he energetically defended against all attacks in his articles throughout the years still went and stabbed the Germans in the back by spying on our citizens here. That apparently also led Kornelius to adopt a new posture towards the USA. Here is what one newspaper wrote about Kornelius' new, apparently reformed attitude:

Kornelius' last commentaries awaken the impression of an insulted writer-for-hire who realized he might have been backing the wrong horse. With growing foreign policy tensions between Germany and the USA, it may not only mean fewer cocktail receptions and award ceremonies on the other side of the Atlantic. They will also be appreciated less among the German elite.[28]

Everybody bets on the wrong horse once in a while. That doesn't interfere with their independence, does it? But how can the editor-in-chief of the popular weekly business magazine *Wirtschaftswoche,* Roland Tichy, simultaneously be the chairman of the board of the CDU-connected Ludwig

Erhard Foundation,[29] member on the advisory board of the Johanna Quandt Foundation[30] (founded by the billionaire Johanna Quandt) and also on the advisory board of the radical Friedrich August von Hayek Foundation?[31] Holger Steltzner, the publisher responsible for the prestigious business section of the once so renowned FAZ, is also a member of the radical Friedrich August von Hayek Foundation's advisory board.[32] He does not mention this in his official FAZ biography.[33] Friedrich August von Hayek (1899-1992), despised democracy as "a system produced through the blackmail and corruption system of politics," as a "word fetish."[34] *Cicero* writes about Hayek: "Hayek's dogmas also include that democratic decisions may only be made by those who are affected by them. This means: Only the rich should be able to decide how much in taxes the rich pay to the state, i.e. the general public. This is also one way to eliminate democracy."[35] Is this something that a leading German journalist can support? Whose lobbying work are they doing? Is that what independent journalism looks like? Are you able to report freely if you support that?

Even more shocking: Transatlantic organizations based in Germany were able to apply for US grants if they used this money for influencing Germans to support pro-American interests, such as the free trade agreements promoted by the USA. You think that's just a crazy conspiracy theory? Then you can't believe what the renowned *Washington Post* and the US embassy say anymore, because they both reported on it in 2014.[36] Every well-prepared manipulation of leading German opinion makers in Germany would earn you between $5000 and $20,000 from the US embassy – depending on the importance of the elites influenced. While I was writing this manuscript, the American embassy in Berlin had forms available online where US-related organizations in Germany could apply for money to carry out Washington's propaganda objectives in Germany. The US embassy in Berlin even expressly thanked the numerous participants in this manipulation project.[37] Do the German alpha journalists, the ones that still boast or have boasted of their close, intimate contacts to such pro-American organizations in Germany, really want to claim that they didn't know anything about all this?

And what's with the sponsorship of journalists by political parties? Do the citizens out there really believe that the graduates from the CDU-sponsored journalist academy at the Konrad Adenauer Foundation[38] or the SPD-sponsored journalist academy at the Friedrich Ebert Foundation[39] will just flip a switch in their heads after getting this party-affiliated education and then simply provide neutral reporting for the rest of their careers?

My long years of experience only tell me one thing: No, that is impossible. I was also sponsored and trained by that elite network, one that subtly wraps itself around influential journalists and guides their pen like a kraken. It all seemed so natural to me: At the same time that I was supposedly an independent journalist at the *Frankfurter Allgemeine Zeitung*,

I was also a member of the planning committee at the Konrad Adenauer Foundation – with its close connections to the CDU.

Looking back, I was a lobbyist. A lobbyist tries to, for example, influence public opinion through mainstream media in favor of special interest groups. I did that. Like for the German Foreign Intelligence Service. The FAZ expressly encouraged me to strengthen my contact with the Western intelligence services and was delighted when I signed my name to the pre-formulated reports, at least in outline, that I sometimes received from them. Like many of the reports I was fed by intelligence services, one of many examples I can remember well was the exposé, "European Companies Help Libya Build a Second Poison Gas Factory" from March 16, 1993. Needless to say, the report caused a stir around the world. However, I watched as two employees of the German Federal Intelligence Service (the German CIA, the *Bundesnachrichtendienst* or BND), drafted it in a meeting room of the FAZ offices at Hellerhofstrasse 2 in Frankfurt. In other words: They basically told me what to write, paragraph for paragraph, right there in the FAZ editorial offices and then the article was published. One of the duties of these two BND employees was writing reports for large-circulation German newspapers. According to employee accounts, the BND fed reports to many German newspapers at the time – with the knowledge of their publishing houses. The Federal Intelligence Service even had a little front company with an office directly above a shop on the Mainzer Landstrasse in Frankfurt, only two blocks away from the FAZ's main office. In any case, they had classified materials there that came from the BND.

Once you became a "player" on the team that drafted such articles, this was followed by the next level of "cooperation": You would be given stacks of secret documents that you could evaluate at your leisure. I remember we brought in a steel filing cabinet just for all the secret reports at the FAZ. (When I was visiting colleagues at a magazine in Hamburg, I saw that they'd done the same thing in their editorial offices).

Back then, I didn't know how contemptuously intelligence agencies spoke about journalists. "You can get a journalist for less than a good whore, for a few hundred dollars a month." These are the words of a CIA agent, as quoted by the *Washington Post* editor Philip Graham. The agent was referring to the willingness and the price journalists would accept to spread CIA propaganda reports in their articles. Of course, this was also with the approval of their employers, who knew about and encouraged all of this. In Germany, the Federal Intelligence Service was the extended arm of the CIA, basically a subsidiary. I was never offered money by the Federal Intelligence Service, but they never even had to. I, like many of my German colleagues, found it thrilling to be a freelance writer for an intelligence agency or to be allowed to work for them in any capacity at all.[40]

Some of the things I found out, I wasn't allowed to report on. These were actually tests of my reliability as a water boy and lackey for the intelligence agencies. Foreign intelligence agencies also financed my travels. Like the British Service for my trip to the intelligence agency conferences at Wilton Park.[41] After the Second World War, this English country estate was initially used by the British as a re-education camp[42] for select Germans and was later also used to provide guidance to Germans, including journalists such as myself. The British Services financed it. However, there doesn't appear to be anything at all on this among the classified documents released by the NSA whistle-blower Edward Snowden.

During the summer of 2005 when I was the "chief correspondent" of the glossy magazine *Park Avenue*, I had a phone call with the Director of the CIA James Woolsey, which lasted more than an hour. His wife is active in the transatlantic propaganda organization *German Marshall Fund* (but we'll touch on this later). Sitting in my Hamburg office at Grüner + Jahr publishing, I was amazed that I didn't lose the connection, because at the beginning of our conversation Woolsey was sitting in his office in Virginia, then he was in a limousine and after that in a helicopter. The connection was so good, it was as if he was sitting right next to me. We spoke about industrial espionage. Woolsey wanted me to publish a report through Grüner + Jahr that would give the impression that the USA doesn't carry out any industrial espionage in Germany through their intelligence services. For me, the absurd thing about this conversation wasn't its content, which was fortunately never printed. What I really found absurd was that after the conversation, Grüner + Jahr sent the CIA henchman Woolsey's secretary in Virginia a bouquet of flowers after the call, because someone at Grüner + Jahr wanted to keep the line to the CIA open.

Yes, looking back, I was one of the perpetrators who was fed materials from the outside and exploited. I was a lobbyist who was supposed to influence public opinion through the mass media. I just didn't want to believe it back then. That's why I can understand when my former colleagues who still do the same things today and, for example, are members of pro-American lobbies or are close to these lobbies, don't want to believe it either. Regardless, looking the other way doesn't make it right. A lobbyist reports with bias. This biased reporting in the German mainstream media (based on multiple examples from sources such as the FAZ) is also confirmed in a 2012 undergraduate thesis out of Munich titled, "Biased Attribution in German Print Media."[43] A while ago, I came across the following headline: "Study: For lobbyists, FAZ is way up at the top of the reading list."[44] The article states: "The publication read most frequently by German lobbyists is the *Frankfurter Allgemeine Zeitung*. It is at the top of the reading list for 88 percent of them." Why is that? Let's take a closer look.

How an Oil Company Greased my Palms

The former President of Germany Johannes Rau (SPD) once said, "It becomes dangerous when journalists influence political processes or even the outcome of elections through active meddling, which is guided by outside interests. It becomes dangerous when sentiments are deliberately intensified or even fostered in the first place by aggravation or half-truths."

Looking back, I was one of those people who was supposed to influence political processes by my reporting. When I was supplied with "information" for my articles during my countless foreign assignments, by Federal Intelligence Service field agents among others, I thought this was "normal." However, it was almost always impossible to confirm if the information was accurate. Still, I published it with the full support of my former editor-in-chief. The phrasing I was expected to use was "according to information from within intelligence circles." At the FAZ, we were really proud of having good contacts within "intelligence circles." Nevertheless, nobody was able to verify any of the "information" they were leaking to us. We just printed it. In retrospect, it's embarrassing to me. Even though I was participating in it voluntarily, I was also told that I could be fired if I didn't play along. Yes, that actually does happen. Yes, I had studied law at university and, just to be sure, I even asked some colleagues who were lawyers. They confirmed the fact that an employer can fire an employee if they refuse to work with the Federal Intelligence Service. Later, verdicts confirming this have become a matter of the public record.

For example: A pilot working for Aero-Flugdienst, an affiliate of ADAC (Germany's largest automobile club with their own fleet of air ambulances), who didn't want to work undercover for the Federal Intelligence Service, was fired for "endangering national security." The labor court also approved of this dismissal.[45] Many readers might think that something like this isn't possible in a democracy, associating acts like these with countries such as the former East Germany, but that's exactly what happened. The large network of German foreign correspondents was also very tempting to the Federal Intelligence Service. It was the perfect cover, letting innocent "journalists" do their sensitive research for them. Colleagues who did that told me about it while we were abroad together, because I was a part of this network as well. We promised each other we would never tell anyone else.

Moreover, don't forget that in addition to 6,000 salaried employees, the Federal Intelligence Service has around 17,000 more "informal" employees. They have completely ordinary day jobs, and would never openly admit that they also work for the Federal Intelligence Service. It is the same all over the world. As I inevitably found out during my decades abroad, almost every foreign reporter with an American or British newspaper was also active for their national intelligence services. That's just something to keep in mind whenever you think you've got "neutral" reporting by the media in front of you.

I remember when I got involved with the Federal Academy for Security Politics, with their close ties to intelligence agencies. This was encouraged by my employer. I also remember that in the late summer of 1993 I was given time off to accept a six-week invitation from the transatlantic lobbying organization, the *German Marshall Fund of the United States*. All of this surely affected my reporting. The German Marshall Fund sent me to New York, and I did a night shift with police officers in the Bronx. I wrote an article for the FAZ about this titled: "The toughest policemen in the world go through these doors." It was one of many positive articles I wrote about the USA – discreetly organized by the German Marshall Fund. It may be hard to believe, but I was actually given a loaded firearm in New York. There's even a photo of the New York City Police Department handing it to me. The reader didn't learn anything about what was going on behind the scenes, behind this favorable reporting in the FAZ. They also didn't find out about the discreet contacts I made during my stay in the US. These included a meeting with Reza Cyrus Pahlavi, the son of the Shah of Persia, who still hoped to regain the throne in Tehran with the help of the CIA. Reza Cyrus Pahlavi needed one thing above all else: attention in the media. Thus, as one of the world's many prestigious newspapers, the FAZ should support these plans through the media when the time was ripe, or so I found out when we met.

This German Marshall Fund is a propaganda organization of the USA, one of the great powers that occupied Germany after the war. It was founded by Guido Goldman, son of Nahum Goldman, the founder and president of the World Jewish Congress. According to their own information, the *Marshall Fund* exists to "develop leaders who are committed to transatlantic relationships." That may sound positive, but it really means the following: They want to recruit and train pro-American lobbyists.

You're having trouble picturing what that means? One example: On July 22, 1993, the then Governor of Oklahoma officially proclaimed me an honorary citizen of the State of Oklahoma. Governor David Walters signed the certificate of honorary citizenship, which was then framed and given to me at an official ceremony (Honorary Citizen of the State of Oklahoma). The German Marshall Fund surprised me with the ceremony, organizing it without my knowledge. The certificate, with the state's seal and Governor's signature on official parchment, is still hanging in my office today. It hangs as a reminder of the perfidious tricks that are used to entice mainstream media journalists. Needless to say, I wasn't awarded honorary citizenship in the US because my name is Udo Ulfkotte and I had a hobby of collecting inkwells at the time. I was given the honor because the transatlantic German Marshall Fund wanted to bring me so deep into the fold, that as an honorary citizen, I had no other choice but to produce pro-American reporting. For six weeks in the USA, I got to experience this perfidious lobbying work up close and personal. In the meantime, I have broken off all contact. However, I can't say this about Klaus-Dieter Frankenberger, my former FAZ colleague and the current head of the foreign policy desk at the FAZ. His name continues to show up again and again in connection with the German Marshall Fund.[46]

Naturally, I also went on business trips with politicians who handed me portfolios with their "background information." Naturally, I was to incorporate this "information" in the newspaper without any changes. That was all lobbying in its purest form. The only ones left in the dark were the readers. My long-standing employer, the FAZ, reassured my belief that journalists aren't "prostitutes." Their journalists also weren't selling themselves, even if they accepted invitations on expensive foreign trips from companies like *Shell* on behalf of the FAZ – and then wrote flattering articles about it in the FAZ. After one of these trips, when another journalist accused me of corruption, ("Bribed by *Shell*"), the FAZ sued my accuser in the District Court of Cologne (case no.: 28 0 19/97) – and lost. That was in 1997. Since then, anyone can rightfully claim that I was "bribed" by *Shell*. This is because, in one of the articles I wrote about *Shell* in Nigeria, what the reader didn't learn was that my entire, luxurious research trip to the oil-producing region, including the use of a helicopter on location, was financed for the FAZ by *Shell*. Even though I did note that Shell paid for the trip in my original text, this was later cut out by a colleague in the editorial office so the article would fit on the page – hence, the FAZ and I had to own up to it.[47]

The judges ruled that: "The required consideration between the protection of the plaintiff's honor," that was mine, "and the defendant's freedom of opinion leads to the presumption that the contested statements are permissible. According to the opinion of the Chamber, this is not a case of prohibited, abusive criticism."

Now, anyone thinking my *Shell*-sponsored trip for the FAZ, which left me officially designated as being "bribed," was a nice 5-star experience, only needs to take a look at an article by one of my colleagues who accompanied me on the trip. Klaus Podak from the *Süddeutsche Zeitung* wrote about our experiences together during that *Shell* trip in Nigeria. In his article, he wrote: "A young man, jumping around in perfectly ironed fatigues, is apparently about to lose it. He's waving his machine gun around, finger on the trigger. Just a few seconds before this, he was holding the gun to my colleague's head through the window of our small bus, his finger on the trigger." Podak's colleague whose life was threatened like that during his field research was Udo Ulfkotte. Can you imagine how it feels, after experiencing something that approaches a mock execution, to have to swallow being called "bribed?"

Yet, in retrospect, I can only agree with everyone who called me that at the time.

A few of my first trips abroad on behalf of the FAZ took me to southern Africa in the 1980s – of course, these were completely paid for by what was still the South African apartheid regime at the time, the South African airline, South African mining companies and/or the local tourism industry. These trips were signed off and approved by my superiors at the FAZ. None of this was mentioned in any of my articles. And, because it was so "beautiful" there in the Country on the Cape, I got to tape a few videos with the team from the FAZ's own private TV station at the time ("Tele FAZ"). Of course, these videos painted my trip's financiers in a very positive light. Of course, they were also paid for by the backers of the apartheid regime. In southern Africa, they flew us around in a private plane. My FAZ colleagues and I were courted and ultimately bought. The viewers, (if I remember correctly, a few of the reports were broadcast on RTL), were also oblivious to this. RTL probably didn't even know that South Africa had financed this propaganda garbage the FAZ was passing off on them.

FAZ Façade: A Corrupt Mind Lurks Behind

Bribed reporting at such an ostensibly serious newspaper like the FAZ? You can't believe it? FAZ journalist Werner Sturbeck, one of the FAZ correspondents in Düsseldorf, let himself be bribed by Thyssen-Krupp in 2012. At least that is my interpretation of the ruling handed down by the District Court in Cologne (case no.: 28 0 19/97). Not a word about this verdict can be found in his official resume at the FAZ.[48] On August 3, 2012, Sturbeck wrote the courtesy article "The Other Side of Thyssen-Krupp" in the business section of the FAZ. With it, the FAZ was prostituting itself for the Thyssen-Krupp corporation. In July, 2012, before the courtesy article appeared, Werner Sturbeck took the Thyssen-Krupp corporate jet to Munich and then flew first class with Lufthansa for a five-day trip to Beijing. He spent his nights in the five-star hotels, "China World" in Beijing, "Ritz-Carlton Pudong" in Shanghai and "Sofitel" in Nanjing – without having to pay a cent. Thyssen-Krupp financed everything. In return for this, they expected favorable reporting. The FAZ saved around 15,000 euros on travel costs alone. Nothing about this was included in the article that Werner Sturbeck wrote after his trip, even though the German Press Council's code requires it for invitation trips like this.[49] Boundaries were clearly crossed at the FAZ, just as so often has been the case. All's well as long as the paying readers don't notice. I list other unpleasant facts in the section "Favoring Favors: How to Make the Media Compliant." Looking back at Sturbeck's luxury trip, the FAZ admits to their guilt by saying, "The first class trips with Thyssen-Krupp are not normal and not okay."

Not normal? I was laughing pretty hard when I heard that. Now, let's take a closer look at one of the sponsors of typical luxury trips like these. One that the FAZ, of course, always reported on favorably throughout the past.

In retrospect, I'm no longer quite sure how many luxury trips were financed for FAZ journalists by one of the richest men in the world, the fairytale Sultan, Qabus of Oman.[50] The man is a billionaire – and a classic dictator. *CBS News* in America is not the only outlet that refers to the ruler of Oman as a dictator.[51] The London *Guardian* calls him an "autocrat."[52] The daily newspaper *Die Welt* calls him the "most likeable dictator" in the world. He is one of the few dictators the USA officially supports.[53] Nevertheless, he is a dictator and remains a dictator. Is it best practice for a respectable newspaper to be accepting invitations from dictators? Regardless, the senior executives at the FAZ had no qualms about repeatedly accepting luxurious invitations from this dictator, sending their employees to visit Oman on several occasions. I will describe this in detail. When an all-expenses paid invitation arrived from this dictator's little empire, the FAZ was always eager to accept – and not just from this dictator, but they never shared this part of the story with their readers.

Firstly, if they did, the average reader would get a completely wrong impression. A reader would think: Okay, someone is paying for a reporter's trip. However, in light of the aforementioned country of Oman, which we will use as a representative example, this would be an extreme understatement. The reality: With these invitations from Oman, we travelled like FAZ VIPs, flying first class or business, at the head of state's expense. The Sultan's personnel were waiting at the airport to quickly and very discretely whisk their guest – a simple journalist – past the "ordinary mortals" and through security. At this point, at the very latest, you don't feel like a simple journalist anymore, but more like a true VIP and somehow extremely important. Here, I should also mention that this special treatment isn't particular to the exotic Sultanate of Oman, it is something that journalists experience quite often – especially journalists from the "mainstream media."

Back to Oman: In front of the airport, an air-conditioned, luxury limousine with chauffeur and interpreter were waiting for me and would accompany me for the rest of the trip. The interpreter was also a kind of talking wallet and would practically ensure that I never paid for anything myself, anywhere on my trip. They were skilled at anticipating a guest's every wish, simply from the look in your eyes. At the end of the day, all of this was financed by the billionaire and dictator Sultan Qabus, who was undergoing cancer treatment in Germany as I was writing this manuscript.[54]

Once, during one of my trips for the FAZ, I was staying at the Omani 5-star luxury hotel, the Al Bustan Palace, in an expansive suite overlooking the

Gulf of Oman. Of course, this was completely paid for by the government of Oman. There at the bar, I ran into the actor Diether Krebs (who passed away in 2000) and we started talking. Krebs was amazed that a German journalist could afford such an expensive, luxury hotel. He complained to me about how incredibly expensive the internationally-recognized PADI diving courses taught by the Greek, Jason Erodottu, were at this hotel. His sons Moritz and Till were taking these courses. I didn't tell him that all I had to do was book my dives to the room and the Sultan would pay for them. Yes, the Sultan even paid for my training to become a PADI-certified rescue diver with Jason Erodottu as my private diving instructor. The Sultan paid for everything that was booked to the room. The dirty laundry that I had washed and pressed before I left for the airport, the post cards from the souvenir shop, the expensive phone calls to the office in Frankfurt, the evenings at fine dining establishments. According to my state escorts, this was the custom among the Sultan's guests in his country. I was naive and stupid to accept that, but then again, I was also corrupt. That's how we were baited, only to be caught in the trap. Admitting to all of this now doesn't right any of my wrongs – but it could serve as a warning to others.

All of this only had one purpose: As long as you get into that air-conditioned limousine with its chauffeur and interpreter and indulge in that super-rich lifestyle, letting them drive you around and cover all your expenses, you are constantly under their control. The security services in the country (and the Omani dictatorship has a very extensive security network) and the Minister of Information, who was also the acting intelligence director, were constantly informed of every step their guest journalists took. They also controlled the people you talked to and the impressions you got from the country. They knew who you talked to on the phone. Naturally, you never had a conversation with any unhappy citizens, let alone any "dissidents" on trips like these. How could you? You were constantly surrounded by the intelligence director's "guides," who any normal citizen in that country would immediately recognize as secret service agents. If you opened a local newspaper, it would only be full of praise for the Sultan. The media, of course, were also owned by the Sultan. Noble court reporting. At the German embassy, it wasn't any different either. After all, the diplomats didn't want to risk a word of criticism appearing in the FAZ. Who wants to get thrown out of a country where you live like you're in paradise, when all you have to do is keep your eyes shut tightly enough? Of course, you couldn't fail to notice how Omanis got preferential treatment, getting served first in stores. Foreigners, and not just foreign workers from the Indian subcontinent, were obviously seen as second-class human beings in Oman. Of course, there were also human rights violations happening under this dictatorship that I and many other journalists "sugarcoated" in our articles.

5-star, air-conditioned, luxury limousine, 5-star suite, blue skies, sandy beaches and an atmosphere of being on vacation: That was the sugarcoated reality as I perceived it. It was better to just ignore everything else. That's what everyone else from the German-speaking world was doing in those days, when they received their invitation to visit the Sultan and do PR for him. Still, that doesn't make it any better.

Imagine a young man from a poor family who had to work hard for everything he had, because his father had died early. Delivering newspapers, working on construction sites, standing in assembly lines – just to be able to go to college and improve his career prospects – and then he hits the jackpot. For free. Without any effort. Wait, without any effort? All he had to do was just ignore everything he didn't want to see. All he had to do to win the big jackpot was write what the nobility wanted to hear. Naturally, after my first trip to Oman, I shared my experiences with my colleagues and not just at the FAZ. Needless to say, I had a lot of fellow journalists who also wanted to finally hit the jackpot too.

I will never forget my friend Klaus Bering, a diplomatic correspondent for the dpa news agency at the time. Receiving an invitation through the dpa, he also enjoyed the seductive, 5-star treatment in Oman. On our flight back to Germany from Muscat, the capital of Oman, this respected journalist drank so much in the business class that he unabashedly threw up in front of the other passengers several times. Even after the fact, Bering thought it was perfectly natural that the stewardesses would clean the vomit off him like he was a little sheik – after all, the Sultan was paying for everything. I can also say that one of Germany's former foreign ministers, Klaus Kinkel, probably has a memory of this dpa correspondent that he would rather forget. One time, when I was flying with Kinkel and Bering in a tiny air force jet for a short visit to the Near East, Bering, a chain-smoker, constantly kept lighting up one cigarette after another, even though Kinkel kept asking him politely, yet firmly, to show some consideration for the non-smokers in the airplane. Kinkel probably still remembers this to this day, because the air in that little plane was simply unbearable. Some journalists really don't know where to draw the line when they're travelling at somebody else's expense.

As I recall, one of these beneficiaries, who reported compliantly and, from my personal point of view, not neutrally after being invited on trips to Oman was Klaus-Dieter Frankenberger. Don't get me wrong, there were many others as well, particularly outside of the FAZ, who suddenly wanted to travel to Oman in those days. To clarify: I don't know if and I'm also not claiming that my former FAZ colleague Frankenberger accepted gifts in Oman. However, we often talked about these kinds of things and he also received the same 5-star luxury treatment as a guest of the Sultan, which I experienced many times in Oman. Similarly to how I felt about it at the time, Frankenberger didn't think it was inappropriate and didn't feel like he had been "corrupted" when we spoke about this in the office. During these luxurious trips, we were like kids in a candy store who didn't know which glass we should reach into first. Of course, we took advantage of it. After all, it was a job and we didn't ask questions. In sports, you never hear a top scorer say: I want less, because I don't think it's fair that I'm earning more than a defender. At the FAZ in those days, we were living in a microcosm which, in my view, had lost its bearings and taken on a corrupt set of values. What was right? What was wrong? Yet in retrospect, we were defining a set of values for other people through our articles that was crazy. Today, after the revelations about him, Frankenberger has become rather controversial,[55] but he is still in charge of the foreign affairs desk at the FAZ. We both started at the FAZ at around the same time in 1986.

Frankenberger reports with a bias. This was shown in another context in a 2012 bachelor thesis out of Munich, which used one of his articles as an example.[56] I used to do that too. The truth is this: Since the 1990s, Frankenberger and I accepted invitations for luxury travel in and paid for by Oman. We did this without our readers ever finding out who picked up the bill for these all-inclusive, full-service packages for the FAZ: the billionaire Qabus from the Sultanate of Oman. So, what can the critics of today say about people like me and the current head of the foreign affairs desk at the FAZ? Based on the aforementioned ruling from the District Court of Cologne (case no.: 28 0 19/97; see the long footnote[57] for details), can they say that we were "bribed" for our Oman reporting in the past? Looking back at what I did, I would definitely have to say: I was bought. This proximity to power corrupts. The Sultan had his own symphony orchestra.[58] He had everything a human being could ever wish for. All of the world's finest automobiles were parked on exquisite carpets in his huge underground garage. Then, all of a sudden, you were sitting next to him on the couch in his palace. In reality, you were nothing other than one of his many paid lackeys. Still, you didn't feel like just a cog. Instead, you somehow felt like you were a part of a powerful network. This was also because a Sultan, worth billions of dollars, took the time to sit down with you.

However, things like this sometimes develop completely differently than expected. During my first meeting with Sultan Qabus for the FAZ, I didn't even know that Sultan Qabus was allegedly a homosexual and had only been married for a short time in order to keep up appearances in his Islamic country.[59] Before my first interview with the Sultan, I was briefed in the Sultan's antechamber by Anthony Ashworth,[60] a British consultant and MI6 secret service agent. He prepared me for the meeting, expecting that I would be alone with the Sultan for a few hours. At the time, Ashworth told me something strange that I still remember to this day: "If he offers you a Ferrari and you don't want it, then simply decline it with gratitude. You just have to say it to him very politely, but also very clearly." I thought his words were absurd, assuming it was his very dry, British humor, but I didn't understand the background behind what he was telling me yet. Why would the Sultan want to give me a Ferrari? Plus, I'm not really into Ferraris anyway. I prefer old Deutz tractors from the 60s with a top speed of 18 km/h. As I mentioned, it hadn't dawned on me that this billionaire, with his own symphony orchestra and a palace where I never saw any women, but only a lot of boyish-looking young men, could allegedly get very comfortable with you when you were sitting all alone with him on his couch. Here, so as not to create the wrong impression, I have to say: The Sultan's behavior toward me was impeccable. He never offered me a Ferrari either. Still, the secret service agent Anthony Ashworth and, above all, the German embassy were extremely nervous, because they were afraid that the Sultan would hit on me over the course of a private meeting lasting a few hours (which was not the case). On the contrary, the Sultan told me how lonely he was in his palaces and how comfortable he felt in the bar he bought near Garmisch-Partenkirchen. In the rare hours he got to spend there, he could be a completely normal person and enjoy a German beer in the company of his male friends. Here, I feel it's important to emphasize again that this proximity to power corrupts. If Sultan Qabus is financing these trips for the FAZ and the dictator is sitting on his couch, telling droll stories about his life, then everything that happens is ice cold and calculated. My colleagues at the FAZ and I all fell for it. Of course, all of this influenced our reporting in the FAZ – without a doubt.

This is because, despite all his affected friendliness, Sultan Qabus is nothing other than a despot. Almost all of the human rights reports from the US State Department confirm this. The reports are critical of the fact that any form of criticism directed at the Sultan is prohibited by law and the Omani people have no right to replace the government. The Sultan alone has the power of disposition in all national and international matters. In plain language: He is a dictator. According to reports from the State Department, government officials do not have to disclose their finances and police officers do not need a search warrant to enter homes. Furthermore, it also states that the laws of the country are abused to silence government critics or anyone who advocates undesirable opinions. Publications and the importing of books and other media products are also restricted as well.[61] Now, try and find any of this in the reports that we wrote in the *Frankfurter Allgemeine Zeitung* after accepting those luxurious invitations from Oman. Clearly, up to the present day, hardly anything has changed in this respect. In newspapers like the FAZ, you'll almost always see the smiling, benevolent, super Sultan who almost everyone supposedly likes. Looking back, I have to say: This is lobbying, propaganda and disinformation in its purest form. How embarrassing.

We were literally supporting a brutal dictator. If we had been honest, we would have reported in the FAZ about the many human rights abuses happening in Oman. However, since the Sultan bought off so many foreign journalists like us with luxurious trips, he has been able to continue his reign for many years. One example: In July, 2014, two young Omani bloggers were arrested because they dared to mention human rights violations in Oman online. These adolescents were not allowed to contact a lawyer. They were simply locked up. One of them was even sent to a psychiatric ward, because he dared to criticize the Sultan.[62] It has gone on like this for years: Whoever opens their mouth gets arrested.[63]

Knowing this now as a reader, if you look back and consider who financed some of our 5-star Oman trips in the 90s with their accompanying courtesy reports, then you would see those articles on Oman in an entirely new light. Using the analogy of the ruling handed down by the District Court of Cologne I mentioned above, is it safe to say that the FAZ not only "prostituted" itself with the *Shell* stories, but also with its Oman-friendly reporting?

Just to be clear: My colleague Klaus-Dieter Frankenberger is a thoroughly agreeable person, a jovial cigar aficionado who appreciates fine wines. We just want to stick to the truth, yet I was also "bribed" by Oman back in the 90s. What would be interesting to know, from the point of view of today's readers, would be the question of who has been arranging the trips to the Sultanate of Oman in recent years? Is everything still being arranged through Renate Kornes and the German press office for Oman like it was back in my day?[64]

In hindsight, I was witnessing Frankenberger, my colleague at the time, cross one invisible line after another with every luxury trip to the billionaire dictator's country – just like I did. And I saw this from inside the editorial offices of the *Frankfurter Allgemeine Zeitung*. It started with his first trips to Oman in the 90s ("Oman is on its way to become an Arab jewel"[65]) covering the "improbable success story of Oman"[66] and it continued with his "voice of compromise and reason"[67] and "festive ceremony to open the second session" of the "Council of Oman."[68] I would like to emphasize here that I am only using Oman as a synonym for a multitude of similar examples to be found in the German media. However, I can say that I never experienced anything like this at *Der Spiegel*. *Der Spiegel* journalists, as far as I know, never accepted any dictators' invitations to go on luxury trips like these. For them, it was a question of honor, and everyone stuck to it. The same cannot be said for the FAZ. When I look back, we were completely corrupt.

Are people like Frankenberger, the ones who have climbed up through the media hierarchy, aware of all this today? They probably are. I say this because after a scandal over the FAZ accepting paid luxury trips in another context and the corruptibility of FAZ journalists, there was talk about the FAZ wanting to provide "transparency" from now on.[69] Carsten Knop, in charge of corporate reporting at the FAZ told *medium magazin* in 2012, "In the future, we will provide transparency with regard to trips that we are invited to go on." After revelations that certain corporations had paid for first class trips on Lufthansa and five-star hotels, Knop said of the FAZ's new transparency, "This is not a temporary measure, but a new standard. This is how it will be from now on."[70] If you're a reader, you should try and keep tabs on whether this transparency only goes for the business section or if they're also going to practice this when it comes to paid trips and invitations from political interests.

Michael Spreng, a political consultant who was once the editor-in-chief of the *Kölner Express* and the *Bild am Sonntag*, is also very familiar with these generous invitations for journalists and the special treatment they get. He wrote the following:

> *The last stop on my South America trip with Helmut Schmidt was the Dominican Republic, governed by a self-proclaimed social democratic party at the time. (...) On the last evening of our official visit, Schmidt invited me to a reception on a German Navy training ship, the "Deutschland," where I met the Secretary General of the governing party. He invited me to stay for a few more days and get to know the country better. I stayed and the next morning I was picked up in an army vehicle and taken to the airport. I was joined by a very amiable person from the Foreign Ministry who was also along for these three extra days. He told me that the President's helicopter would be at my disposal the whole time. For three days, we flew all over the country and, wherever I felt like landing, the helicopter with the presidential seal would land – and hundreds of people came running, because they all thought "El Presidente" had arrived.*[71]

The reason I mention this is because the luxury treatment that journalists from mainstream media get is definitely not limited to the FAZ. Anyone who still thinks that my portrayal of events, using Oman as an example, is totally atypical for mainstream media journalists, well you are sorely mistaken. Moreover, journalists' bosses are fully aware of this as well. I will explain this in even more detail in the chapter "Buy Yourself a Journalist." This is because either the boss receives an invitation personally and passes it on to an editor, knowing what it entails, or an editor receives an invitation and they need to get it approved by the boss. Trips like these always need to be approved by superiors in advance – if nothing else, for insurance reasons. Then, when you're filling out a travel request, you have to make an estimate of how much the trip is going cost the publisher. If your application for a business trip only includes the costs for travel to and from the airport, your boss knows exactly what they're authorizing. Back then, my superiors at the FAZ were authorizing a lot of trips like this – and not just for me.

Let's forget about Oman in this context. You can just as easily replace the Sultan with an industrial company or another country. In this book, Oman is simply a synonym for corruption, for bought reporting. However, from my point of view at the time, it was a win-win situation for everyone involved. On the one hand, for their investment, the host would get advertising copy that wasn't clearly labeled "paid advertisement" or "sponsored by." Far from it, they were getting an ostensibly authentic text in the editorial part of the newspaper. From my point of view today, I know this wasn't anything other than bought reporting, but it wasn't labeled as PR. Also, the buyer wasn't just getting just one advertising text, they were usually getting a whole series of advertisements in this form. From a business point of view, this made an invitation a good investment. At any rate, it was definitely less expensive than buying a whole page of advertising in any of the German-speaking "quality media." On the other hand, for a journalist, it was like hitting the jackpot. Finally, the publisher got to fill up a few pages with exotic stories for next to nothing.

So, why did I describe all of this in such detail and also mention Frankenberger's name several times? Because, as the head of the foreign affairs desk, this former colleague of mine is now the one approving the business trip applications for a younger generation of journalists. Also, because it is well known how extremely badly the FAZ is doing these days. This once flourishing company is hemorrhaging (according to the management's statement at the June 2014 general meeting, official losses for 2013 were 8.3 million) and that employees have not received a pay increase since 2014 (personnel costs in 2013 were 86.7 million euros).[72] Nevertheless, I am warning him and my other former colleagues against signing off on any business trip applications for invitations that appear irresistibly inexpensive at first glance. We all know from experience that nothing good can come of it. We also know what it means for those readers who are paying good money for their information and think that they're getting the unvarnished truth for it.

By the way, there is even one more discreet way that this can be taken up a notch, and I have often seen it practiced by journalists in the German-speaking media. They take their wife or lover and sometimes even their kids along like they were invited too when they go on one of these all-expenses paid, luxurious invitation trips. All they have to do is make sure that the host will cover all the costs beforehand. With all of the trips that the Sultan alone has financed over the years, if he started naming names, you would have endless material for a new tabloid television show.

How do Journalists Pay for their Villas in Tuscany?

By employing a few tricks of the trade, journalists – and I'm not referring to any of the aforementioned journalists or publishing houses here – can amass a considerable fortune. This doesn't have anything to do with any particular media group, but rather the German income tax code. That is to say, the German taxpayers are subsidizing all of this out of pocket. And no, I'm not just referring to the frequent flyer miles that journalists can exchange for any number of goods, which can then be sold via platforms like eBay. Ultimately, petty tricks like these usually come at their employer's expense or whoever paid for the flights, and no number of frequent flyer miles is going to buy you a vacation home.

So, why do so many alpha journalists in Germany's mainstream media have houses in Tuscany and in other popular regions of Italy, southern France or Spain? By now, you probably have a basic idea of how you, as a journalist, can sell your soul to the devil in return for luxurious trips to exotic countries – all at somebody else's expense – but this isn't the half of it. Once you find a rich sponsor like the Sultan (and behind the walls of the PR agencies there are quite a few of them out there), all-inclusive, 5-star service is the standard for journalistic PR trips. And this doesn't just mean three trips to the buffet every day. On the contrary: This means you can order from exquisite, gourmet menus to your heart's content. Keeping this in mind, the German tax code provides a daily allowance for foreign business trips. However, as a journalist, it isn't very fair to your fellow taxpayers if you claim this allowance on your income tax return for every day you got pampered and didn't even have to spend a penny for it. I can't tell you how many journalists I've met abroad who couldn't resist this generous offer from the German welfare state. For every day you spent in Oman in 2014, for example, you could claim 48 euros, for one day in an American city like Houston or Miami: 57 euros, for one day in Norway: 64 euros, for a day in Sweden: 70 euros, and for a day in Africa, for example, in Angola, you could claim 77 euros. Thus, the German taxpayers sponsor journalists' trips on a country by country basis. In reality though, the journalist gets a free, all-inclusive travel package, pockets a taxpayer subsidized per diem and also gets their fee or their regular paycheck for the story. At some point, it dawned on me that this is how shrewd and unscrupulous alpha journalists in Germany's mainstream media were financing their vacation homes in Tuscany on the side.

I've seen a lot of unethical tricks like this. I'll never forget how a reporter/photographer charged his employer in Hamburg thousands for supposed "exclusive photos." He told them that he bought the rights to the photos for a lot of money during a trip to Baghdad. Then, he billed the publisher with a "personal invoice" for expenses that he had never even actually incurred. Unfortunately for him, he was trying to pass off photos that had been distributed by the Iraqi dictator Saddam Hussein's press office in the Baghdad Press Center for free. At some point, his boss in Hamburg got wind of this – and the reporter had to go. Since then, this man has been saying that he got fired because his reporting was "too critical" of the USA. Now, he is one of the most celebrated undercover journalists in Germany, giving lectures on good journalism and checking the accuracy of PR claims for the media. In short: This man is now the epitome of "serious journalism" in the German-speaking world – another ironic paradox in the annals of history. However, it is a good thing that his publishing house showed him the red card at the time and is now being discreet, remaining silent about his past. I visited the man a few years ago in Hamburg – he didn't show any regrets. He really didn't seem to understand why he had been fired. He told me over dinner at a rustic, old seafood restaurant near Hamburg's fish market that he hadn't behaved any differently than his colleagues. He was probably even right about that. The only difference was that he got caught. In many other cases, the editorial office simply didn't notice, for example, when personal invoices were submitted for bribes made to alleged paid informants. After all, the bribes that journalists paid out were tax deductible – so this form of corruption was also being subsidized by German taxpayers. That was the everyday reality. Corrupt journalists submitting personal invoices to milk their employers and the system for as much as they could get away with.

Looking back at all of this, however, the paid, all-inclusive trips that were also subsidized by our taxpayers were just the tip of the iceberg. What was truly corrupt and absolutely unforgivable were the gifts. A good example is the annual meeting of the Gulf Cooperation Council (Saudi Arabia, United Arab Emirates, Qatar, Oman, Bahrain and Kuwait). It is held in a strictly Islamic country, right before Christmas when the news cycle is always slow. Here, Western journalists weren't attending in droves because they wanted to escape their fattening Christmas roast and all that alcohol. Every participant who stuck around until the end of that terribly boring, multi-day meeting and filed their reports from the conference's press center (which was always more of a propaganda center) like a good little boy, was rewarded with valuable gifts at the end: one year a golden Rolex, the next year a golden fountain pen, another year a set of valuable coins – always something that would please everyone. The gifts (each year was different, but all journalists attending an annual meeting received the same thing) were either placed discreetly in the hotel room or you could pick them up in the "press center" on the final day of the conference. Everybody knew it. Nobody turned it down. In any case, I never saw any fellow journalists leaving their gifts behind. We were all infinitely corrupt. So, the next time you see, hear or read a report about the annual meeting of the Gulf Cooperation Council, you can rest assured that it's basically a bought PR report. Moreover, our mainstream media are even thankful and report on it eagerly, because it usually takes place during a lull in the annual news cycle and they get to fill up a few pages free of charge. Something else to keep in mind: The propaganda…, excuse me, press centers in Arabian countries always have a 24-hour buffet. Therefore, the journalists don't spend anything on food. What's more, for every day they're in Saudi Arabia, a journalist can deduct an additional 48 euros from their income tax. Every day in the Emirates and Kuwait it's 42 euros, in Oman it's 48 euros, and it's 56 euros a day in Qatar. And what do the German-speaking viewers, readers or listeners get as a thank you for their generosity? A fat load of paid reporting. This is pure contempt. They're making a mockery of the public.

Well-Greased: The Sleazy System of Journalism Prizes

As if everything I just mentioned wasn't already enough, journalists also receive additional rewards for their reporting – and these come in the form of "journalism prizes." Explaining this raffish system is best done by comparing it with certain distinctions that are awarded to various foods. Every country in the world probably has similar organizations, but in Germany you will see gold, silver and bronze DLG Quality Seals on thousands of foods. Make of it what you will, you should at least know what's going on behind the scenes: Every year, around 27,000 products are "tested" by the Association of German Agriculture, a food industry organization, for their appearance, smell and taste. Chemical or microbiological tests are only carried out in exceptional cases. Afterward, every product that doesn't show a "deviation from the expected quality" receives the best classification – that is, a gold quality seal.[73] The testing procedure also doesn't say much about a product's ingredients and its actual quality.[74] Consumers can see what a DLG quality seal is worth every time the media publicizes another scandal involving a DLG endorsed food. Like the recent hygiene scandal at the industrial Müller-Brot bakery, where mouse droppings and insects were found in Müller-Brot ingredients and baking machinery[75] – DLG award-winning products.[76] The DLG seal is definitely one of the more dubious distinctions found in the German-speaking world. This is because they also award their quality seal to foods that use additives and artificial flavors to enhance their taste. These include, for example, the strawberry cream yogurt from Zott. This yogurt's rosy color doesn't come from its strawberries alone, but through the addition of red beet food coloring. Consumer protection advocate Silke Schwartau finds this unbelievable, "How can it be that an artificially flavored product is still awarded a distinction for great taste?"[77] Yet additives and artificial flavors have never seemed to concern the DLG's taste testers. Even the Haribo gummy bears that contain additives (such as carnauba wax, aka E903) sport the DLG's official seal. Another example: the "Meister Krüstchen" bake-at-home rolls from "Harry" are distinguished with the DLG's golden seal. In the Stiftung Warentest, (Germany's most reputable organization providing consumer product comparisons), the same rolls received an "unsatisfactory" (lowest) rating. Stiftung Warentest's explanation: The rolls tasted "old, bland, only slightly aromatic..." The DLG couldn't explain the serious differences between these test results.

Still, all of this is easy to understand if you know how the system works: The DLG is an organization made up of lobbyists from the agriculture and food industries. It is definitely not a consumer protection organization. The association has more than 20,000 members and it finances itself through the revenues it generates with its services. Needless to say, this includes awarding their DLG quality seal on a massive scale. Nearly all of the products they "test" – up to over 90 percent – receive one of these "quality seals." Although, to feature it on your product, you need to pay a licensing fee. So, when it comes to "journalism prizes," we'll be talking about a rather undignified system that basically functions in the same way.

Do you think that newspaper readers, radio listeners or television viewers – that is, neutral consumers – are the ones who decide which journalists will get which prizes? Nope, the system simply hands out awards to itself, just like in our example of the DLG quality seal. The committees that decide who's going to get a journalism prize are almost exclusively made up of journalists from media companies who then "reward" other journalists. They don't care about being nonpartisan, independent or truthful – just like with the DLG seal, they only care about mediocre quality and anything that promotes sales. Just like foods full of artificial additives get a golden seal slapped on their packaging, journalists who deliver mediocre quality, toe the politically correct line and kowtow to the elite get these (supposedly) prestigious media prizes as a "thank you." In many cases, this system practices the same style of consumer deception, it just uses journalists as its product. If you dig deeper, you'll find that media companies – like newspapers – love to feature their award-winning journalists to sell more copies, but they are often the ones who financed and presented the awards in the first place. Of course, the journalists who rack up these honors keep their mouths shut. After all, they're not going to turn down the "prize money." These accolades are often accompanied by thousands of euros. I've been to a lot of these award ceremonies. Whenever organizations close to a political party presented awards to media journalists, and I mean organizations so close that any rookie investigative journalist could find out in minutes that they were owned by that same party through a network of other companies, then the consumer deception was pretty obvious – but we played along with the system. We were corrupt. Just look at how many companies finance journalism awards these days. Do you think that any of these companies want to give their support to any reporting that is critical of themselves and their products?

It is a well-greased system – and yet some consumers out there still believe in a system of "independent" journalism. The truth: When German-American think tanks and foundations present awards for allegedly excellent journalism, they are merely distinguishing the journalists who propagated their organization's point of view in a particularly positive manner to the people out there who don't know any better. So, we're back where we started, the proximity of our alpha journalists to the elites. These alpha journalists, and we'll get to know many of them in this book, are eager to accept these awards and their self-satisfaction is unmistakable. I know it all too well. After all, I used to be involved in the decision-making process for award ceremonies like these and I'm speaking here about something that was never meant to be revealed to the general public.

A typical example for the debasement of journalism prizes is the Hanns Joachim Friedrich Award, once a highly prestigious distinction for journalists. Now it is an award given to propagandists.[78]

Did you know that many large electricity companies also give journalist awards? Many of the leading media outlets are happy to report on how "progress" is making its way into German households: The old, analog electricity meters with the rotating discs are being replaced by supposedly modern, digital devices. In Germany alone, five million of these new digital electricity meters will be installed by the summer of 2015. Many of the journalists who praised this "progress" were subsequently awarded media prizes by electricity companies. Funny enough, not one of these high-quality journalists ever mentioned the business model behind this "progress." The manufacturers love this digital "progress," and this is because the new calibration guidelines call for the digital meters to be replaced every eight years. (Somehow, the old analog meters didn't need to be calibrated and lasted for decades). In other words: We are installing electronic garbage in our homes. What's more, this first wave of newly installed meters won't even put in eight years' worth of service before they are tossed on the electronic scrap heap. They will have to be replaced faster than planned, because the EU just decided to regulate the electricity consumption of the new digital meters themselves, something that went unregulated up to this point. All we know is that these new digital devices, with their interactive communication modules and measuring systems that make consumers transparent to the electricity companies, use up a lot of electricity themselves and they won't come close to fulfilling the latest EU guidelines. Put simply: They will first have to be replaced to meet newly updated regulations. The basis for this is the EU eco-study for intelligent electricity networks with the lot number 33 ENER. Needless to say, all of this will be paid for by the consumer, that is, the rate payers who use electricity. Meanwhile, the power companies push these new devices with big advertisements in the media, thus financing the jobs of those journalists who are happily reporting on this counterproductive "progress." Whoever works hard and cooperates with this well-greased system, there's a good chance they'll secure additional rewards – and these come in the form of "journalism prizes."

Among these prizes, you'll find the "Liberty Award", which has been presented by the cigarette manufacturer Reemtsma every year since 2007. This award is given to honor journalists "who give voice to the daily fight for freedom." The "Liberty Award" for journalists from the Reemtsma tobacco company is accompanied by 15,000 euros. This journalism prize is extremely controversial, receiving widespread, vociferous criticism, and not just because it is completely financed by the tobacco lobby. Hans Leyendecker from the Süddeutsche Zeitung refused his nomination for the following reason: "When I received the offer, I knew immediately: I won't let them nominate me. A journalist has to know where he's going, who he is allowing to invite him, who he is allowing to pay him. It doesn't matter if it's an award, a speech or he's taking on the role of the host. A journalist doesn't allow himself to be bought, a journalist doesn't go to such events."[78a] Others didn't seem to have any problem accepting this award from the tobacco industry, such as the ARD journalist Thomas Roth (2009) and the FAZ reporter Konrad Schüller (2012).

Their jury also includes people such as the *Die Zeit* journalist Theo Sommer,[79] who is a legally convicted tax evader and for this reason alone, surely not a role model for honest citizens (an immoral moralist[80]). We will come to him later in connection with controversial organizations such as the Atlantik-Brücke, the Bilderbergers, the Trilateral Commission and the German Council on Foreign Relations. Theo Sommer is an expert for positive reporting on military operations. The media journalist Uwe Krüger depicts this in his book, "Meinungsmacht" *(Power of Opinion (not available in English))*. From his point of view, Krüger shows how journalistic research is bent into shape when it produces unwanted findings that contradict political aims. One example is the harmful effects of the depleted uranium munitions used by NATO in the Yugoslav Wars. When the first reports on this surfaced in the beginning of 2001 and put the then Minister of Defense Rudolf Scharping (SPD) on the defensive, he reacted as politicians are wont to do in tricky situations: He appointed an expert committee to examine the accusations. He entrusted the leadership of the committee to Theo Sommer, the former editor-in-chief at *Die Zeit*. Sommer enjoyed the Minister's trust because, in his first life, he had led the planning staff at Hardthöhe (the headquarters of the Federal Ministry of Defense) and had also been a member of the Federal Government's Defense Structure Commission. Six months later, the commission under Theo Sommer gave the all-clear signal: Depleted uranium munitions were classified as harmless and a leading story appeared in Theo Sommer's *Die Zeit* with the headline, "The Alarmists' Embarrassment."[81] With that, the case was closed and, according to Uwe Krüger, Scharping presented Sommer with the German Bundeswehr's Gold Cross of Honor.[82] Theo Sommer shortened this story on his homepage and in his "Awards" section, it merely lists: "2002: Bundeswehr's Gold Cross of Honor."[83]

Embarrassing: In 2014, The Bundestag members Ulla Jelpke, Christine Buchholz and Jan van Aken submitted an inquiry to the Federal Government with printed document 18/2307 in which it stated that in a letter dated July 21, 1999, in connection with the Kosovo deployment, the Ministry of Defense had warned the Bundeswehr about physical contact with uranium contaminated dust. In the 1999 letter to the Bundeswehr, they pointed out that "the absorption of DU particles by the body is to be avoided by wearing a dust mask and washing hands before eating because of its radiological and toxic effects." Furthermore, upon entering a military vehicle, "dust is to be shaken off clothing and footwear, footwear is to be washed off." This means that Scharping's friend, Theo Sommer, was whitewashing something that they had been warning the Bundeswehr about internally since 1999.

Incidentally, sitting alongside Theo Sommer and 13 military journalists, there was also an additional alpha journalist in the "Dr. Sommer Working Committee": Nikolas Busse from the *Frankfurter Allgemeine Zeitung*. At first, he had been the FAZ's NATO correspondent, then the foreign policy desk's deputy editor in-chief at the FAZ. We'll get to him later, in connection with some controversial Transatlantic networks where Busse even swore an oath of allegiance to the USA before the illegal Iraq War in 2003 (for this, see the section: "The Names: Controversial Contacts" in chapter 3).

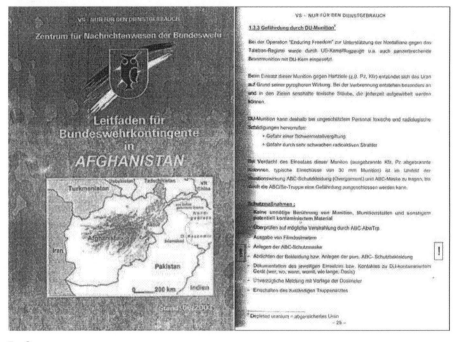

Left:
Cover of an internal, classified Bundeswehr document on the dangers of depleted uranium. The classification as "CLASSIFIED MATERIAL (VS) – FOR OFFICIAL USE ONLY" means that knowledge of the content by unauthorized individuals (therefore you as a reader) may be detrimental to the interests of the Federal Republic of Germany.

Right:
Page 25 of the "Guidelines for Bundeswehr Contingents in Afghanistan"
CLASSIFIED MATERIAL – FOR OFFICIAL USE ONLY

1.3.3 Dangers of DU munitions (Depleted Uranium)
During the operation "Enduring Freedom" to support the Northern Alliance
against the Taliban regime, US combat aircraft employed, among other
munitions, armor piercing uranium, incendiary munitions with a DU core.
When using this munition against hard targets (e.g. tanks, motor vehicles),
the uranium ignites due to its pyrophoric effect. While it burns, persistent
toxic dusts are created, particularly on and in the targets, that can be stirred
up at any time.
DU munitions can therefore cause toxic and radiological damage to
unprotected personnel.
• Risk of heavy metal poisoning
• Risk through very weak radioactive emitters
If the use of this munition is suspected (burned out motor vehicles, tanks,
burned out columns, typical entry holes from 30 mm ammunition), ABC
protective clothing (overgarment) and ABC masks are to be worn in the area
surrounding the munition's effects until a ABC/Self-Defence unit can rule out
any hazard
Safety Measures:
- No unnecessary contact with munitions, munition pieces and other
potentially contaminated material
- Check for possible radioactivity by ABC defence unit
- Issuance of film dosimeters
- Donning of the ABC protective mask
- Sealing of the clothing or donning the personal ABC protective clothing
- Documentation of the respective mission or contact with the DU-
contaminated device (who, where, when, how, how long, dose)
- Immediate notification with submission of the dosimeter
- Contact the responsible unit doctor

The bombshell: Even though depleted uranium munitions were officially
considered as allegedly safe after the "Dr. Sommer Working Committee"
sounded the all-clear signal, the Bundeswehr issued another directive in
2003, after the Committee's report was published, in which they warned of
the munition's danger and pointed out protective measures. In a classified
document issued by the Bundeswehr, "Danger from DU Munitions" mention
is made of radiological damage that could be caused by the armor-piercing,
incendiary munitions with a DU core employed (by US combat aircraft)
during the Operation "Enduring Freedom." It advised that soldiers wear ABC
protective clothing, do not touch the munitions, are issued film dosimeters,
report any contact immediately and immediately call in the troop's doctor.[84]
In plain language, all this means is: Since "Dr. Sommer's Working
Committee," soldiers who were harmed by the aforementioned munitions
cannot hope to receive any financial compensation for its adverse health
effects. At the same time, however, the armed forces were issuing internal

warnings on the danger of the munitions. An absurd situation. In Great Britain, the situation is completely different: In 2004, a court officially confirmed for the first time that a British war veteran's illnesses and deformities were due to depleted uranium munitions.

Today, Theo Sommer, whose background includes whitewashing depleted uranium munitions in the media for the Ministry of Defense[85] as described above, now selects suitable journalists to receive awards from the tobacco industry.[86] But we don't want to get bogged down here talking about controversial journalism prizes, where a certain elite are in a class among themselves.

Just one more note: The appropriation of the term "freedom" in tobacco lobbying is not a new invention by the Reemtsma corporation. LobbyControl, an initiative for transparency and democracy, explains: "In Anglo-Saxon countries, the tobacco industry has even supported or helped establish organizations who are active in the name of freedom and are against smoking bans and all prohibitions in general. E.g., the *Center for Consumer Freedom* (USA, see: *SourceWatch*) or the *Freedom Organisation for the Right to Enjoy Smoking Tobacco* (FOREST) in England. According to *Action on Smoking and Health*, they receive over 90 percent of their financial means from the tobacco industry."

Don't forget: In Germany, tobacco advertising was banned in print media at the beginning of 2007. The advertising ban passed in EU directive 2003/33/EC also covers image advertising by the tobacco industry, and this was confirmed in August of 2009 through two rulings by the Higher Regional Court in Hamburg. According to the European Commission, any form of image advertising by tobacco companies falls under the tobacco advertising ban. In its May 2008 report, the Commission indicated any public relations work that portrays tobacco manufacturers as "responsible," as "a means of marketing the company's image and products." However, reporting on the tobacco industry's awards ceremonies does not fall under the EU's 2007 advertising ban. Now, this begs the question: How long have they been handing out the "Reemtsma Liberty Award" to "brave journalists?" That's right: Since 2007. Enough said.

So, you now know how tobacco companies use journalism awards to advance their PR interests. And, since I'm already in the process of shattering the illusions you have about the lily-white tobacco industry, I would also like to mention how they bribe the political parties in Germany. Of course, there are ways to make political donations that German citizens won't recognize as donations. This is done by bribing the media arms of the various political parties. All of the political parties in Germany publish magazines for their members. The CDU's youth organization, Young Union, has the magazine *Entscheidung (Decision)*, the CDU itself has the *Union Magazin* – and the SPD has enough newspapers to fill a whole bookstore (see the chapter on that later in this book). Tobacco companies pay fantastic prices for advertisements in these party magazines and thereby sponsor the parties. They rent booths at every state and national party conference. Through the booth rentals alone, covert donations flow into the parties' coffers at a tune of one million euros a year.[87] The average German citizen has no idea that the parties are being bribed in this way. Apparently, there isn't a big difference between bribing politicians and buying favorable reporting.

Courtesy Interviews, PR Trips and Tax Fraud

Looking back, I find it particularly macabre that my trips to war zones were financed by various war parties or their supporters. Many of these trips would never have been possible without this "support," because I wouldn't have been issued a visa or gotten any protection. Plain and simple, these were nothing but PR trips for war parties. The invitations for such trips were normally sent to my superiors, who then distributed the invitations to the editors and approved the travel applications. On trips like these, the intimacy with power, that is, to those who decide over life and death, was somehow fascinating.

At this point, I can't remember how many courtesy interviews I did with Near Eastern or African heads of state or their ministers during my travels. All I know is that two-thirds of the statements from these allegedly very important people were a pack of lies. However, these lies were just what the local German embassy or the representatives of corporate enterprises doing business in these countries wanted to hear – and the FAZ was eager to print all of it. In Khartoum, the capital of Sudan, it was bad. North of the capital, where the Blue and White Nile converge at Omdurman, the Israeli Mossad had rented a property disguised as an "agricultural business." Living on a neighboring property was Bin Laden's group, which would later become world famous. At the request of the German embassy, I was to write a descriptive article for the FAZ about Ronny S. (an Israeli). He was in Sudan selling milk from German cows, milked in air-conditioned stables, to a small ruling elite. What I wasn't to write about: Thanks to the milk, the Mossad-man Ronny S. got closer to this closed circle of elites in Sudan than he ever would have been able to otherwise. Moreover, sitting right next to Bin Laden, he could watch everything happening on his neighbor's property from up in a small lookout tower on the "dairy farm." So, in the FAZ, at the German embassy's request, I wrote about the milk produced by the happy German cows on the Nile and ignored a good part of what was really going on there – as I often did. My superiors at the FAZ always liked it when I worked closely with the local German embassy during trips like these.

It was even worse in Iran. The German embassy in Tehran was constantly trying to promote German-Iranian trade. Since the largest companies in Iran belong to the Mullahs, every time I was there, the embassy was pressuring me into doing courtesy interviews with the foreign minister, any available Ayatollah or other Iranian dignitary I could find, or at least mentioning one or more of them in an article. When the Iranians were more interested in one of these interviews, then they would also pay for the trips (as I depicted them in Oman). Simply put: The FAZ accepted invitations and published courtesy interviews. The FAZ archives are full of these courtesy interviews that they lined up for me. That's how it went from Afghanistan to Algeria and from South Africa to the Horn of Africa. Needless to say, as a reporter for a famous German daily newspaper, the German embassy was always at the forefront of everything else going on behind the scenes.

Of course, the embassy had an influence on our writing. Especially on the stories that were never meant to be written truthfully. I'm reminded of a dinner I had with German diplomats in Baghdad. I can't remember if it was at the ambassador's house or at another top diplomat's. From the neighboring property, I could hear horrifying voices, a heart-wrenching wail. I wanted to know what was going on and I found out that an Asian diplomat lived behind the wall of the neighboring property. He liked to eat dog and behind the wall, which was between the properties, he had the dogs slaughtered slowly, while they were still alive. First, they would cut off their legs, then their tail and their head. Supposedly, an agonizing death makes the meat taste better, at least that's what this Asian believed. The German diplomats begged me not to mention this in my reports from Baghdad. It could harm our relationship with that country. Looking the other way when animals are being tortured? It was horrible.

Accompanying German politicians on international trips was just as bad. There were folders with language rules for every conceivable situation. If you were lazy, all you had to do was copy a few of the pre-formulated clichés and pep it up with a few of your own impressions from the surroundings. That made everybody happy. It had nothing to do with honest journalism. It was more about feeding the people a line of BS – and if you did it, you would always make the short list for the next round of journalism awards.

It didn't matter whether I was working for 17 years of my previous life at the FAZ or afterwards as a correspondent for Grüner + Jahr, for the ddp news agency, the Axel Springer publishing house, or for television stations and many other well-known media companies – I usually experienced the same thinking at the management level: Only the others are corrupt and indecent. Once again: Confessing my own mistakes doesn't make it any better, but hopefully the younger generation will be able to learn from my mistakes.

Without thinking, I would jump at the chance to fly with the former head of the German Federal Intelligence Service, Klaus Kinkel, at the time when he was the acting Minister of Foreign Affairs. Together with a colleague from the German Press Agency (DPA) in a small luxury jet owned by the German government, I was brimming with pride at being this close to him and I reported positively about it afterwards. I also did this noble court reporting for Helmut Kohl and many other politicians. In retrospect, I am ashamed, and I apologize for this. I can't undo it, but I can own up to it.

As I briefly mentioned, while travelling along with a group of top German politician in Africa, I once got to visit Karlheinz Böhm (the actor who played Emperor Franz Josef in the "Sissi" movies). At the time, if I would have told the truth, I would have written that this visit to see Böhm and his aid projects was just a "PR gag" in the eyes of the politicians. They were only there to get a group photo that would look good in the eyes of the German voters, standing next to a respected actor, surrounded by black children. As soon as these politicians had their photos, Karlheinz Böhm and the African children were completely meaningless. Böhm was just a political prop – just like so many others. For my part, just like in so many other situations, I didn't describe the encounter truthfully. I was, as often is the case, also corrupted by my proximity to power. Seriously: How sincere can someone be when they can fly into the hot highlands of Ethiopia from their 5-star hotel in the capital, Addis Ababa, in the comfort of an air-conditioned helicopter? When they only have enough time for a quick interview on poverty with an actor turned philanthropist before they have to fly back to their 5-star, air-conditioned hotel? When they can write that article about Ethiopian poverty sitting at a luxury buffet – while people all around them are starving?

When I traveled with presidents, chancellors or ministers, I didn't get checked at the borders. When we landed on the military airfield of the Cologne/Bonn airport, customs looked the other way. Everybody knew it, we even expected it. Many took advantage of it. Even the politicians, even the ministers. People found out about this double standard through the "Carpet Affair," (where *Spiegel* reported on how Dirk Niebel, the Minister for Economic Cooperation and Development, bought a $1,400/30kg Persian carpet in Kabul when he was flying on a commercial airline, so he left it at the German embassy for another diplomat to bring back on a government aircraft).[88] Many, too many, simply thought it was normal to either skip paying customs duties on the luxury goods they brought back from trips or they would have them delivered discretely as I just mentioned. I can remember a colleague from a high-circulation newspaper who even brought back a completely disassembled, used Harley Davidson when he flew back from a business trip to the USA with the German Air Force. He sold the parts in Germany and made a few thousand in profit. This is called tax evasion and the German taxpayers also financed his transport costs through the German

Air Force. Many of us were criminals. The worst part: This mutual knowledge created an invisible bond between politicians and journalists.

After the fact, a journalist described in his blog everything you needed to do when you were travelling with a top German politician, say the German Chancellor, and you knew you weren't going to get checked:

The Peruvians also gave us a tip where we could buy burial objects from the Inca culture. The archaeologist told us that they came from grave robbers and were very valuable. A colleague and I drove to a house on the edge of town and bought (illegally) a headdress (250 dollars) and a piece of a burial shroud. Exporting it was the easy part, because the luggage of anyone accompanying the Chancellor wouldn't be inspected.[89]

All of that took place well over a decade ago, but I can provide the names of many colleagues who still do this. I don't blame them. After all, I used to take part in this depraved system myself. With any luck, I might get them to think about what they're doing and encourage them to change their ways. Perhaps they'll never admit to it openly, so I will make it very clear: The direction of the bias found in articles and editorials is definitely influenced by a close contact to elites as I describe it in this book. Therefore, what I'm talking about doesn't have anything to do with independent and non-partisan journalism.

Another example: After the former Chancellor Helmut Kohl stopped by the FAZ's Frankfurt offices to have confidential discussions with the chief political editors at the time, Johann Georg Reißmüller and Fritz Ullrich Fack, all of us on the editorial staff were proud to have had such a "distinguished guest" in our offices. The idea that this proximity could also corrupt us never crossed our minds. On the contrary, we wanted to be able to command the same respect from these elites. Some, like the FAZ man Frankenberger, managed to achieve this, but at what price? We are going to examine this question in more detail.

The former editor-in-chief and media consultant Michael Spreng writes about Kohl and his relationship with journalists:

It is well known that Helmut Kohl only knew two types of people: those who were with him and those who were against him. That is how he also classified journalists. His relationship to press freedom was purely instrumental: A good journalist was the one who allowed himself to be instrumentalized. Those of us – like me – who had a certain underlying sympathy toward him were quickly appropriated as "Kohlians" and had to follow him unconditionally.[90]

I would've never believed a word of that back when Kohl came to visit Reißmüller and Fack in the editorial offices, but that's really how it was. Kohl was instrumentalizing Fack and Reißmüller at the FAZ for his own objectives. Today, other journalists are being instrumentalized by other politicians – and maybe they don't even notice it or don't want to.

By the way, people like the FAZ directors I named dictated newspaper editors' thinking to a certain extent, for example, through the language we were supposed to use. I will never forget when the political editor-in-chief, Johan Georg Reißmüller, stormed into the office with a text in his hand and yelled out, "Who edited this?" The text included "Sinti and Roma" somewhere and Reißmüller said loudly, clearly and undeniably, "Those are Gypsies! Remember that: Gypsies!" So, the FAZ's political editors weren't supposed to write "Sinti and Roma." That was way back at the beginning of my training to become a journalist. My colleague, Reinhard Olt, a Professor of German studies and I just looked at each other for a long time after that in the FAZ's newsroom. "Gypsies" – something like that sticks in your mind. Your thinking is guided in certain ways. This is how we are influenced through language, and it starts during our education when we're young.

Up to this point, I have written much too much about the *Frankfurter Allgemeine Zeitung*. I hope I haven't awoken any crazy suspicions that all of this was only typical at the FAZ, specifically among the political editorial staff, at least during the time when I was working there. However, that's not entirely true. That's why this book isn't an attack on the FAZ per se, but incitement for all media companies to set their own houses in order. That said, I'd also like to mention that when I was at the FAZ, this "bribed" reporting was most prominent in the features section. At least the travel and tourism desk of the features section always had a stack of invitations so high, you could hardly see over it. The invitations were for all-expenses paid (luxury) trips to faraway countries. These were free trips where those paying for them surely expected to see certain content published on certain topics. Thus, they were expecting PR in return. The editorial staff wasn't forbidden from financing a trip directly through the subject of our reporting, for example, an airline or a tour company. So, we readily divvied up these trips among ourselves. In the ensuing articles, we usually never indicated who financed these trips. As far as I can remember, that was also completely "normal" in other media companies too. In July of 1987, I hadn't even been at the FAZ for a year and I published a long report under the title: "In the Shade of the Khat Tree." The invitation and financing came from the Yemeni airline Yemenia. It was pure PR. I got the invitation from the travel desk of the features section. The folks at Yemenia were so excited that the PR I wrote appeared in the features section, they asked me if there was anything I desired, aside from going on an all-expenses paid vacation to Yemen in the future. More as a joke, I blurted out that I'd never eaten grilled king prawns as delicious as the ones I had in the little Yemeni city of Mocha (where mocha coffee gets its name). A few days later, we received an express delivery at the FAZ's editorial offices. It was a box full of shrimp that had been grilled in Yemen only a few hours earlier. Of course, my colleagues helped themselves to this "Molle" (that's what we called a free round in the office) and thought it was completely "normal." No one ever paused to make any moral or ethical considerations.

In the offices of the FAZ's features section, there was also a bookcase full of unsolicited books that publishing companies sent to be reviewed. The more positive reviews these publishing house promotional copies got in newspaper, the more new releases the publishing house would send to the features section. Sometimes I would go to the features department and get a box full of brand-new books for my colleagues in the political office to pick and choose from. Nobody there thought there was anything wrong with this. New books written by FAZ editors were also mentioned in the FAZ. I can still remember my first bestseller that was published by a FAZ publishing company. Naturally, the FAZ publisher advertised *Verschlusssache BND (Classified Information: Federal Intelligence Service (not available in English))* by organizing a press conference for its release at the FAZ's main office.

I can also still remember that I was classified by the German Federal Criminal Police Office as "at risk of attack" for many years, due to my public criticism of Islamic ideology. I was probably the only journalist in Germany who was legally allowed to conceal and carry a loaded firearm in the FAZ's editorial conferences. For several months, BMW provided me with a bullet-proof sedan, equipped with a television and every other luxury extra, free of charge. The FAZ wasn't only aware of that, but I was able to bill the FAZ for all of the car's running costs. They were actually saving money because my FAZ company car wasn't putting on any mileage while I drove the BMW. All of these things were somehow taken for granted.

To sum up, everything always revolved around one thing: no, not around truthful reporting. It all revolved around money and personal perks. We were chasing our dreams.

Depraved Drinking Buddies: Glimpses of Journalistic Dirty Work

I can tell you the exact second that I personally stopped what I was doing, because I was so disgusted with myself. It was the day I called Hans Wolfgang Euler, a criminal lawyer in Frankfurt, and asked him for advice. I called him because one of the most popular CDU politicians in Germany, in the presence of witnesses, asked to assign me the task of spying on the former SPD Prime Minister of the Rhineland-Palatinate, Kurt Beck, at his office. One of the witnesses was a former managing director for the CDU in the Rhineland. This man has gone through a lot for the CDU and has been keeping quiet about a lot of things for a long time. If he decides he ever wants to publicly name the people behind this, he still has my promise to stand by him in public or to testify in court. This well-known managing director of the CDU was – as I said – not the initiator of the proposal. He was merely sitting there with me as a well-known CDU politician offered me 5,000 euros to approach Kurt Beck's wife "as a journalist," so I could spy on her married life. In the interest of the Beck family's privacy, I do not want to and will not furnish any details here, but I can say this: At the time, the CDU already had access to the Beck family's bank statements. Allegedly, a bank employee with close ties to the CDU was already on board. Apparently, this State Prime Minister could hardly do anything without the CDU knowing about it. The one thing they lacked was obviously the little details of the Beck family's private life, and the CDU wanted me to document this too.

The politician sitting across from me was a true Machiavellian prince and he belonged to a well-known CDU commission. After listening to what he wanted for nearly two hours, I was too agitated to say anything. It was at this point that I wondered just how low I must have sunk, that a politician assumed I would do the dirty work for him and his party in exchange for a secret payment (disguised as a lecture fee). I pretended to accept the offer at the State Parliament building in Mainz and then, even though it was a hot day, I immediately called the criminal lawyer Hans Wolfgang Euler from inside my sweltering car. He arranged a meeting with the director of Kurt Beck's office. There, we learned that Beck's office staff already knew about the assignments, because I wasn't the only journalist the CDU had unleashed on Kurt Beck. None of this would have ever happened to me if I hadn't had this sticky proximity to so many politicians. They just took it for granted that I was ready, willing and able to do their dirty work.

In those days, I was enjoying a lot of perks: I could come and go as I pleased at Konrad Adenauer's holiday residence, a villa with a pool and park in Cadenabbia on Lake Como, in Italy. The Villa La Collina belonged (and still does) to the Konrad Adenauer Foundation, which is associated with the CDU, and I was associated with them.[91] I always met all the big names in German politics there, because, for one thing, I was a member of the Adenauer Foundation's planning staff during those years. The CDU also organized a number of well-paid lectures for me, especially at the Villa La Collina. It was still private in those days, and without any unapproved guests, it was dangerously intimate. There, we enjoyed delicious food and far too much alcohol. My wife and I will never forget the night that one of the leading CDU politicians from the Rhineland-Palatinate stumbled into our room on the top floor of the villa. In the stately house that had once been Konrad Adenauer's residence, the first Chancellor of post-war West Germany, he thought our room was a bathroom and he proceeded to empty the contents of his stomach out on our bed. So this proximity to politicians could sometimes be disgusting, in the truest sense of the word.

Once you were through the gates to the old Villa La Collina, you felt like you were among family and nobody locked their doors – and then this drunk CDU bigwig barged in. At the time, I was still able to grin and bear it. But when I was asked to spy on the private life of the Prime Minister of the Rhineland-Palatinate, right there in the state parliament building in Mainz, it was too much. I had to draw the line. I knew they were going to be angry and try to pressure me if I didn't play along, but I didn't care. I wanted to finally be able to look at myself in the mirror again.

By the way, Konrad Adenauer's Villa La Collina hides another secret. It sits on a hill above Lake Como with a view of the little village of Bellagio, just a few minutes away by ferry on the opposite shore.[92] In Bellagio, the Rockefeller Foundation, which draws the power elite to it through a network of secretive organizations, just happens to have a secluded training center.[93] When Germany's elite politicians really need to have a confidential meeting with American elites to discuss political strategy, they stay at the Villa La Collina. From there, they take the ferry to Bellagio and then they go to the Grand Hotel Villa Serbelloni where they are discreetly picked up by a Rockefeller Foundation chauffeur. This covert procedure reminded me of what went on at the German embassy in Iran, at 324 Ferdowsi Street in Tehran. The Turkish embassy is also located on Ferdowsi Street, right next door. The two embassies are connected by a top-secret underground tunnel, so that the ambassadors and their closest employees can escape to the neighboring embassy in the event of an emergency. When Federal Intelligence Service agents wanted to get me into the German embassy without any of the embassy staff even noticing, I had to go through the Turkish embassy. I would be met there and then taken through the underground tunnel. Many German embassies are connected to underground tunnel systems, (particularly in Arab and African countries; American services also used these to get people in, but that's beside the point). Needless to say, this was all very mysterious and exciting for me, but pretty crazy when you think about it. Just like the top German politicians taking the ferry from the Villa La Collina to Belaggio, so they could pick up their political marching orders in secret meetings at the Rockefeller Foundation. It was only later that I found out the Rockefeller Foundation uses affiliate organizations like the Trilateral Commission to win over top German journalists. Like a spider's prey, they get wrapped up in silky favors until there's no more escaping, but we'll get to more on that in a later chapter.

Low-Down Dirty Tricks: How They Cheat Advertisers

Through the type of journalism I have been describing here, media consumers are being lied to. The reader is surely aware of this by now. However, we have forgotten about the ones who buy the advertising in the hopes that their investment will generate a resonating effect. Unfortunately, the advertising customers paying those horrendous prices for ads in newspapers are being deceived. The big publishing houses have long been competing with each other over circulation numbers, and advertising prices are based on actual sales figures. At the beginning of my journalism career, I was stunned when I stumbled across the methods that different publishing companies use in the fight for these sales figures. At the time, these methods were (and apparently still are!) completely "normal" for the industry. Being in the business, I quickly learned: While the newspapers were still hot off the publishers' presses in the evening, a portion of the print run, which had been bought up by their own marketing department through a multitude of tricks, was loaded onto a truck and driven around Germany on the autobahn for 24 hours — so this is what they mean by "circulation"! The next day, when the "returns" (those that were not sold in stores and were picked up again) came back, they would be combined with the portion of the "run" that had been joyriding on the autobahn for a whole day, and taken for paper recycling.

Back in the good old days, a publishing company could pay their employees' salaries for four weeks with the profits they made on all the advertisements placed in a single Saturday edition, (this is no longer the case today). Those were the boom times of the publishing industry, but nobody on the outside had a clue of what was going on behind the scenes. I still have a faint recollection of how proud the managing directors at newspaper publishers were when their "stupid" advertising customers fell for the trick of buying ads in "paid circulation" that never even actually existed. In the 1990s, a certain leading employee at a southern German publisher quit his job and joined a publisher based in Hessen. He showed the managing director proof that his former employer in Bavaria had been increasing the alleged sales figures of a large German daily newspaper in the aforementioned way – on a daily basis. This defector thought that his new employer would praise his courage and make the fraud public. What the man didn't realize: The publishing company in Hessen was doing the exact same thing. With that, his compromising evidence disappeared into a safe where it has remained to this day.

Since, as I mentioned, that story was only a faint recollection, I wanted to refresh my memory. On June 9, 2014, I asked a former head of marketing who had worked at one of the publishers at the time. I assumed he had to have gotten wind of the situation. His written response: "Dear Udo, since I have always trusted you: Yes! 3 years before [X's (name of the publisher's managing director)] death, he was even visited by a defector from the [newspaper XY], who wanted to fire back at his old employer with this pertinent evidence. [Managing director X] didn't go along with it. The proverbial glass house, you know, where they were sitting themselves… Aside from that, I know from a good source that the publisher XY still turns about 20,000 copies to account in the way you described on a daily basis."

If you're asking yourself: Why didn't I name the names and companies in this section, something that is completely unusual for this book so far? The answer is simple: I'm working on a book about the dirty tricks of the publishing industry with the help of a retired insider. Therefore, it doesn't make any sense to give them a heads up before the book is published in its entirety. We would also have to waste valuable time on lawyers and court dates. Regardless, prestigious publishing companies have been systematically defrauding their big advertising customers for years. After the next book is published, advertisers will be able to demand a refund for the large sums of money they have been paying all these years for nothing.

When it comes to fraud in the media, we're not only talking about publishing companies. The fraud has been and still is lurking everywhere in the media business – as I came to realize over and over again. It can literally be found around every corner, and in places you'd never expect. The first time I was in Namibia, I checked into a well-known hotel in the capital of Windhoek. Upon entering my room, I found a strange woman lying in my bed, smiling at me with a cheeky grin. Tired and irritable after the long flight, I went straight back down to the front desk, assuming the room had been double-booked by accident. Without any difficulty, they gave me another room. I only realized what had transpired the next morning when the other journalists on the excursion asked, "And? How was yours?" The woman in "my bed" hadn't been a coincidence at all. I was young. I was naive. I still had a lot to learn about how journalists are bribed and bought and the kinds of tricks they used in the industry. It was an all-expenses paid invitation that the FAZ had sent me on. As I recall, it had been financed by some South African tourism agency. Looking back, the pattern always seemed to play out in exactly the same way more or less.

The Spiral of Silence: The News is Not in the Newspaper

It took a quarter of a century before the truth came out and was officially confirmed. In June, 2014, after more than 25 years, the employers' liability insurance association finally recognized that as a former war correspondent for the FAZ, I am a victim of chemical weapons used on the battlefield. I am probably the last living Western witness of a mass poison gas attack that took place in July of 1988. In the attack, several hundred people were killed over the course of just a few hours with German-manufactured poison gas. In all likelihood, many more lives were lost. Gas masks were certainly no help against the "sulfur mustard." Now that 25 years have passed, the CIA has also released internal documents about this use of poison gas I mention here.[94] So, in a book about the German media and truth in reporting, why am I starting off this section with information like this? Because it is a typical example of how politics and the media operate in Germany. If you go very deep into the archives of the *Frankfurter Allgemeine Zeitung*, the paper I was reporting for at the time, you'll find an article I wrote with the title "Near Zubeidat, evidence of the battle is being buried."[95] Another reference to what happened on an Iraqi battlefield with German involvement can be found in the released archives of the CIA.[96] Otherwise, there's only a small photo with a caption. That's it. You'd think that if people were suffering agonizing deaths somewhere in the world thanks to German-manufactured poison gas, then as a well-informed citizen, you would have heard something about it. The reality is completely different. I still have a lot of color photos of this mass gassing, but they have never been published to this day. Better said: With the exception of one very small image, they were censored. My superior at the time, the former editor-in-chief of FAZ's foreign policy desk, Fritz Ullrich Rack, didn't want them published. When I returned from the battlefield with the photos, he merely sent me off to the Association of Chemical Industries (VCI) . All the FAZ published was a short, rather anecdotal report on the battlefield use of poison gas and one small photo. That was it. My editor-in-chief at the FAZ instructed me not to share the photos with any other media houses, even though I held the rights to them. The *Stern* wanted the photos back then, but it would have cost me my job. My subjective impression at the time was that the public was to learn as little as possible about it.

I already suspected this while I was still in Iraq, struggling with the physical effects of the poison gas. With difficulty, I wrote down all the incomprehensible details of what had happened there. It was an unbearably hot day and after the poison gas attack, people were lying on the battlefield with their brains flowing out of their mouths, eyes and noses. The Iraqis were using bulldozers, which of course were also Made in Germany, to push great heaps of corpses together before covering them with the desert sands. Back then, we didn't have cell phones or the internet and I also didn't have a satellite connection. I was already starting to suffer severe symptoms and the trip back to Baghdad from the battlefield was pure hell. Nevertheless, I managed to submit all the details of my report there in Baghdad over the phone. Today, when I read what little they published of it back at the FAZ in Frankfurt, I can only shake my head.

After my return to the newsroom, my then colleague Klaus-Dieter Frankenberger told me that he had edited the piece and took out all the horrific details. Brains leaking out of gassed human beings wasn't something they printed in the FAZ. The FAZ readership obviously shouldn't be exposed to any of the unappetizing details. It was only in fall of 1990, around two years after my report appeared in the FAZ, that the Germans who helped the Iraqis produce the poison gas behind the scenes were arrested.[97]

On December 19, 2013, around 25 years after the gassing, I wrote the former FAZ editor-in-chief Fack, long since retired, and asked him to explain his behavior at the time. Among other things in my letter, I wrote:

Upon arrival in Frankfurt, you had me provide the Association of Chemical Industries with the countless photos I took of the gassing – as far as I can remember. Before this, member companies had delivered the necessary components for the mustard gas to the Iraqis so they could gas the Iranians. At the time, only a single, harmless photo from the horrible photo series of the gassed Iranians on the battlefield was allowed to be published in the FAZ, because the FAZ believed the images were unacceptable for the readers.

To this day, this former FAZ editor-in-chief couldn't, or hasn't wanted to explain any of this to me. A half-century after the Jews were gassed, people were being gassed again with German involvement, to the best of my knowledge – and the entire story was suppressed by the media.

German Chancellors have asked Israel for forgiveness, because Nazis gassed Jews generations ago. German Chancellors have knelt down in Paris and in Warsaw and asked our neighbors to forgive us for wars that took place generations ago. How can it be that the German politicians and media of today are nowhere to be found when Iranians are being gassed with German chemical weapons? Did I miss something? Did you ever hear of Kohl, Schröder or Merkel asking the Iranian people for forgiveness? The flow forming machines used to make the gas grenades' shells in Iraq, as well as the chemical components used to produce the poisonous gases: sulfur mustard, tabun and sarin, were from German production facilities. We delivered all of this, right to the middle of the war zone, disguised as "agricultural pesticide." We pretended like the Iraqis wanted to spray the desert with thousands of tons of pesticide. We are liars.

That being said, I am still under the impression that certain things shouldn't be made public. Long after Iraq, I also got this impression while working at Grüner + Jahr. In November 2005, I wrote an exposé for them titled: "The Underworld Nobility of Berlin." In it, Steffen Jacob, the king of Berlin's underworld, reported how his "career" began when Willy Brandt, the mayor of Berlin at the time, was one of his first customers for the "liberal ladies" of a certain industry. Steffen Jacob, who died many years later in August of 2014,[98] used the opportunity to try and get me to ghostwrite his memoirs. He was a fan of my non-fiction books and hoped that, in addition to my exposé for Grüner + Jahr, he could also immortalize his "ascent" in the underworld, in all its glory, in the form of a book. This man, who made hard cash with easy girls, had a suitcase full of thank you letters. A treasure trove of embarrassment. One of the letters was from a defense minister. This well-known minister thanked him for the "beautiful evening." Steffen Jacob told me what wasn't in the letter: He claimed that the minister was into torturing women sexually with bottles. I didn't know if I should believe that or not. The details sounded incredible to me. These were excesses that I was reminded of again, years later, when the head of the International Monetary

Fund, Dominique Strauss-Kahn's red light escapades and rape accusations were made public. What was clear was that Steffen Jacob had many people in the palm of his hand. I'm not saying this here because the minister financed these escapades himself or with taxpayer money. They were paid for through the Berlin office of lobbyists working for a German arms manufacturer. Steffen Jacob showed me the corresponding bank statements. He also insisted that such "services" were often officially taxed, (thereby the state also got their cut in the process). Steffen Jacob told me about the general secretary of a political party, the head of the CIA's Berlin office and a German defense minister, all amusing themselves at his establishment with ladies like these. He also showed me the corresponding "thank you letters." Apparently, nothing is too embarrassing for some people. As I was writing my report, Steffen Jacob claimed that he also entertained the Foreign Office as well as the Federal Criminal Police Office and their guests. Another informer showed me a playground on the Fuggerstrasse in Berlin where the men back then could allegedly drive by slowly to pick out children for "free delivery" to their place for sex. Ali Kepenek, a photographer from Berlin, was also party to some of these details, because he was assigned to photo illustrate the statements of Steffen Jacob and the other big names from the Berlin underworld.[99] I don't know which photos Ali Kepenek still has from this. A Polish lumber importer explained how the illegal weapons business works in Berlin and who the customers are. Frank Warneck, also known as "Wanne" (Tub) and a member of the Hells Angels, came clean in the report. His last words during our meeting then were, "Conscience can only exist where there is knowledge. But do your readers really want to know all this? I'm excited to see if it will actually get printed."

Well, none of it has ever been printed to this day. The research cost a lot of money, but contemporary witnesses, giving their accounts of Willy Brandt with prostitutes or well-known politicians out cruising for children – that would have caused a political earthquake. Therefore, the story disappeared into the archives. My subjective impression, though I may be wrong: Grüner + Jahr didn't actually want to cover these issues. [Such photos are also valuable for blackmail… Ed.] The few personal experiences I've had have at least shown me that publishing houses don't like to "tackle" certain issues. There may be different reasons for this, but one thing is sure: Nothing that we see, hear or read is ever a complete reflection of reality.

The founder of the Allensbach polling institute, Elisabeth Noelle-Neumann, once told me while she was visiting the offices of the *Frankfurter Allgemeine Zeitung*, "What you find in people's heads today, it's often not even the reality at all, but rather a reality created and manufactured by the media." In the 1990s, she was a regular visitor to the FAZ's editorial offices. She was a professor of communication sciences and a public opinion researcher who enjoyed international respect. However, when she died in 2010 at the age of 94, she didn't have many friends in the German media.

Many journalists despised her, because she dared to address something that is considered taboo in Germany: the systematic influencing and control of the masses through a small minority of journalists. Noelle-Neumann called it the "Spiral of Silence," when mass media, e.g. television, publicly depicts minority opinions as majority opinions and then people refrain from speaking their mind, simply remaining silent instead, because they're afraid of socially isolating themselves. Noelle-Neumann originally formulated the Spiral of Silence as a scientific theory during her research into mass communication in the 1970s. In the intervening decades, it has become an even more powerful and vicious demon, never loosening the firm grip it has on the populace. It is manipulating us.

This demon also lies. Especially during wartime. During the early phases of the Lebanese Civil War (1975 to 1990), television viewers couldn't get enough of the house-to-house fighting in Beirut every evening. Alas, as a television journalist, this kind of reporting can get you killed. So war correspondents of all nations came up with a style of reporting that didn't only add to their life expectancy, it also made their jobs a lot easier: They would make friends with one of the parties involved in a civil war, give them a camera and then pay them to deliver the latest video. Afterwards, the correspondent could tape their report standing in front of some burned out ruins, which a little fuel would quickly bring back to smoky life for the viewers. The addition of a few mean-looking militants shooting their machine guns behind them would ensure that a war correspondent's reports were coming from "right in the middle of the action." Everyone was happy: The German broadcasters received first-class video material, the viewers shivered at the sight of the bravado, the correspondents proved they were worth their war correspondent's bonus and a few extras from one of the militias got enough money to smoke and drink for another day.

The author of this book has been to many battlefields around the world – from Afghanistan to Angola and the Congo countries, back to Iraq and Iran. Time and again, he met television teams carrying gasoline canisters along with them in their hunt for video material. Far from any fighting, they would set long-since burned out military vehicles on fire again and a stage a surreal play in front of this scenery: Experienced correspondents would begin ducking regularly, acting harried and twitching, which, needless to say, looked pretty funny when you're only standing a few meters away. You can only understand it once you get a glimpse of the finished segment. A few machine gun bursts or, in more extreme cases, even mortar impacts would be added to the audio track after the fact. We also have "heroes" like these working for German broadcasters. Today, because of their extraordinary accomplishments, they have long since been promoted to program management, so it wouldn't be appropriate to mention their names here. Others have had to endure setbacks, because they were outed as plagiarists.

Personally, I preferred not to write about a lot of situations I experienced back then – even when I was directly involved. It probably wouldn't have come across very well with the readers if I would have told them in all honesty how I reported from Afghanistan. I was heavily armed with a fully-automatic Kalashnikov and wearing an ammo belt stuffed full of magazines. I still have the photos. A German reader, sitting in their peaceful world and sipping their morning coffee, wouldn't have understood that as a foreign "infidel" in a Afghani war zone in those days (long before the arrival of the first Western troops), we were fair game and the Mujahedin shot at us whenever they pleased. However, you could keep them at a safe distance with a few targeted bursts of rifle fire. At any rate, you definitely wouldn't have survived a day with the cotton balls in your luggage alone. When I was there, I even converted to Islam for the sake of appearances in the western Afghan city of Herat. This was officiated by a Mujahideen leader named Ismail Khan, and word of my conversion quickly spread among the other Mujahideen in the war zone. For those who hadn't gotten word of it and still shot at me for fun, I could keep them at a distance with the rifle.

There were other journalists who were totally against defending themselves with weapons, even though they were in an unstable area of an Islamic country, completely alone and without protection. The US journalist Daniel Pearl, for example, never understood why I never trusted any of the warring parties in ongoing civil wars. He always put his full trust in these people. Later, Muslims wound up cutting off his head while he was fully conscious, filming the act and posting it online.[100] The Swedish journalist Nils Horner never protected himself either. He was always unarmed and never even wanted an armed escort. He was shot to death in Kabul by followers of the Islamic ideology.[101] The same thing happened to two French reporters in Mali.[102] And the German photographer, Anja Niedringhaus, who hailed from the eastern part of Westphalia just like me, was simply shot dead like so many others in Afghanistan.[103] This is the daily reality in such countries, but our media preferred to show a different picture.

I personally learned to not trust anyone in a war zone back in 1987. During the Angolan civil war, I found myself in a camp that belonged to the pro-Western bush fighter Jonas Savimbi. A German journalist from the magazine *Quick* thought it would be fun to throw me one of the grenades that were lying around all over the camp. He was convinced that a camp full of bush fighters wouldn't just leave real, live grenades lying around, so he pulled out the pin before he tossed me the grenade. He was wrong. The grenade was live and it detonated within seconds. I had managed to catch it and throw it further away before I dove behind some sandbags. The *Quick* journalist happened to take a black-and-white photo at exactly that second, and I still have a copy of it today. It's a reminder to never to trust a stranger in a war zone.

Here Today, Gone Tomorrow: Off With Their Headlines

As we'll see, journalists and the media are manipulating us around the clock, everywhere. In the meantime, our brains have somehow been able to come to terms with this. Of course, we know that the media often lies to us, but it really starts getting scary when the manipulation is also designed to influence and move us emotionally – when journalists themselves are manipulated by the state to spread rumors in the background.

I personally experienced this myself. From one moment to the next, I was "shut down" by the same intelligence agencies that had been feeding me information while I worked at the FAZ. I left the FAZ at the end of 2003. At the beginning of 2004, I was giving a lecture in Dresden when I was informed that the police and public prosecutor's office were searching my home, several hundred kilometers away. Their grounds: "suspicion of disclosing classified information." The news of this "raid" appeared everywhere, from the *Tagesschau* to *Der Spiegel*.[104] The FAZ also reported: "A terrorism expert's premises searched" and published my name in connection with the event. In one fell swoop, I wasn't just a criminal in the eyes of my neighbors who had witnessed it. What I found surprising was that what the state had been encouraging me to do for years, (receiving and analyzing confidential documents), was somehow a criminal offence all of a sudden. It took me a while before I began to understand that this was all for show and I was only being discredited and "shut down" in public. The signal going out to everyone who had ever provided me with material was: Effective immediately, Ulfkotte is finished. In retrospect, I can understand everything they did, but there's one thing I can't understand: To this day, neither the *Tagesschau*, *Der Spiegel* nor the FAZ have followed up by reporting that no charges were ever filed and the criminal investigation was closed. No classified information had been disclosed nor had any other crime been committed. They can publicly execute a person – at least that's the way I felt about the news at the time – and later, they don't even have to set the record straight. Regardless of my insignificant case, the reader should understand that this is simply a media tactic. Now, I always have to smile when I hear "revelations" about politicians in the news or every media outlet simultaneously reports that somebody's house was searched on the "suspicion" of something. Sometimes this is being done for very different reasons than what we're being told, as I found out myself. Nevertheless, journalists are not obligated to report the truth after the fact and rehabilitate anyone they've executed like this. I think it's a shame that the FAZ, which reported on my place being searched in 2004 (correct), never restored my good name once the criminal investigation was dropped and they never apologized for their behavior. For my part, I have endeavored to remain objective in the writing of this book, also with regard to the FAZ. Still, it didn't surprise me when the media journalist Stefan Niggemeier wrote, in reference to another case, "the FAZ conceals relevant criticism from its readers."[105] He also reported that a local chairman of the Young Union (CDU) canceled his FAZ subscription because of its biased reporting.[106] I can entirely understand why someone would want to do that these days.

One more thing: In those years, when the elites of the time were literally burying me in classified materials, I maintained a very close relationship with Bernd Schmidbauer (CDU). Up until 1998, he was the Intelligence Coordinator at the Chancellery. I had already written in a few articles about how he had me locked in a room in the Chancellery so I could analyze some classified documents in peace and write down the most important points. Later, I was simply handed documents like these or they even had them delivered to me.

Many of the documents that were seized when my home was searched came from Schmidbauer's office, bore his signature and could be traced directly back to him. The public prosecutor's office that had been investigating based on this suspicion of "disclosing classified information" wasn't interested in this. From a legal point of view, Schmidbauer could have been considered a traitor.

I can still remember once, when I was on a talk show, how I pulled a handful of documents out of my pilot case in front of the rolling cameras. The other participants in the discussion had doubted me when I told them the statements I had made were coming from intelligence circles. So, I reached into my pilot case and pulled out some files at random, holding them up in front of the camera. Later, after a picture of the television screen had been enlarged, you could see a folder from Schmidbauer's office with his personal shorthand on top. This caused a flurry of excitement at the Chancellery. They were afraid that the opposition would demand proceedings against Schmidbauer, a recipient of the Federal Cross of Merit 1st Class, and this would lead to his immunity in the Bundestag being removed. Amazingly, this didn't happen. One of my top informers at the time, Bernd Schmidbauer, was obviously immune. Today, he collects his tidy pension and is the honorary president of the Federal Association for Professional Nature and Species Conservation (BNA), the nation-wide, umbrella organization for animal and plant owners. The fact remains: Certain people can commit crimes and still get the Federal Cross of Merit 1st Class. Their accomplices are like figures on a chess board and our "quality media" plays along willingly. This is just one of the many pieces of evidence that show that democracy and the rule of law are only being simulated in Germany, they are simply illusions.

In the section, "In the Stranglehold of the Intelligence Agencies," I will also describe how I was recruited for the Federal Intelligence Services (BND) by a university professor when I was a student (initially without my knowledge) in the 1980s. Starting in 1999, I also lectured at the university in

Lüneburg. In the business administration department, I taught a class on security management for several years. Together with other lecturers (including Rolf-Wilhelm Dau, the former head of security at Philips), I secretly selected university students who were of interest to the BND based on their personality structure, their political views and their abilities. You could recognize this very easily in the seminars I organized. We talked a lot about politics. We did role playing exercises. During the seminars, I also asked the students about their hobbies and personal views through innocent small talk on the side. Many of my students will certainly remember how we occasionally watched James Bond movies. Afterward, I would ask them if they could imagine working for an intelligence service later themselves. They always laughed. My students thought I was really funny. None of them suspected the truth. That's how the BND wanted it and the university supported it. After many years, an unmistakable signal also brought my teaching days to an abrupt end: The searches I just mentioned were also carried out at the University of Lüneburg. The federal goons who arrived to "shut down" Ulfkotte marched into the university president's office and notified everyone there that they were investigating me for "disclosing classified information." From that moment on, I was met with contempt on campus. Shortly thereafter, my lecturing position was taken away. Other lecturers there will have long since taken over my task of screening the suitability of unwitting students for the BND. That's the way it works in Germany. You just aren't supposed to talk about it.

Chapter 2. Our Lockstep Media: Synchronized, Obedient and No Questions Asked

Everyone named in this book denies having a clingy, sleazy closeness to elite organizations. Moreover, they deny being lobbyists. They also deny being "corrupted" by their proximity to the elite. And, they deny having lost their journalistic edge, working as they do in such close proximity to the aforementioned groups. They deny that this proximity has any influence on their reporting.

Thilo Sarrazin: The Character Assassination of a Folk Hero

The evil demon that possesses German journalists can be found quite easily if you take a look into our leading editorial offices. Let's take the case of Thilo Sarrazin as an example. A long-time member of the SPD and former board member of the Deutsche Bundesbank, Sarrazin published *Deutschland schafft sich ab* (*Germany Abolishes Itself*) in 2010, which took a critical look at Germany's post-war immigration policy. The book shot to #1 on the bestseller list and remained there for 21 weeks, selling over 1.5 million copies. According to serious polls, more than two-thirds (70 percent) of Germans essentially agree with Sarrazin.[1] Polling data also revealed that Thilo Sarrazin could be regarded as a kind of folk hero. In the German media, however, he is largely portrayed as exactly the opposite – the archetypical "villain." And that, simply because he dared to write what the majority of Germans are already thinking. The *taz* called Sarrazin a "demagogue,"[2] and so did the *Kölner Stadt-Anzeiger*.[3] Deutschlandradio branded him as a "right-wing populist."[4] Journalist Mely Kiyak went so far as to characterize Sarrazin, whose face is partially paralyzed on right side, as a "lisping, stuttering, twitching caricature of a human being."[5] So, a person who openly expresses what the majority thinks gets bullied in our oh-so-politically-correct media as a "lisping, stuttering, twitching caricature of a human being." Seriously? A man with the polling numbers of a folk hero gets ridiculed across the board by our mass media. As I mentioned, you can find the evil demon responsible for this demonization in nearly every editorial office these days. When asked in all seriousness whether Thilo Sarrazin should even be discussed in the media at all, the weekly newspaper *Die Zeit* responded, "By doing so, aren't we only spreading the thoughts that almost all journalists and politicians condemn these days? Yes, we're doing Thilo Sarrazin (...) a favor in the process. (...) Thilo Sarrazin is on his way to becoming a folk hero..."[6] Obviously, this can't be allowed to happen – the opinions held by a majority of Germans also being articulated or represented in the media, God forbid!

The German-speaking world is reputed to have an extensive selection of newspapers, television channels and other such media with a broad spectrum of opinions. From the far left to the far right. German journalists today are also reputed to be completely independent of the people and things they report on. Reputedly, their only allegiance is to objectivity and the truth. However, as we will soon see, this is all just an illusion.

An illusion is a deception of the senses, a representation of something, different than it is actually present in reality. Our "quality media" are perfect masters in the art of creating illusions. They only simulate this diversity of opinions, independence and true reporting they present to us. The truth of the matter is that we are all being manipulated, disinformed and controlled by the media – to suit the wishes of the political establishment.

Propaganda: The Prussians of the Balkans Are Coming

On the 1st of January, 2014, the gates to the German labor market were once again opened up to a new wave of migrants, this time from Bulgaria and Romania. It was a very controversial issue at the time. Among the voices in the debate, there were some who warned of "poverty immigration" into the German social systems. The Federal Chancellor, however, was not amused by this discussion. The media took the hint. There was an immediate flurry of reports that Romanians and Bulgarians were extremely hard-working people who would surely fill our social coffers and not empty them by any means. The evening news on the *heute-journal* outdid all of the other courtiers of politically correct reporting and referred to the Romanians and Bulgarians as the hard-working "Prussians of the Balkans." The astonished public was reassured, "You will see the confirmation of this if you look into the labor market statistics. The unemployment rate of migrant Bulgarians and Romanians is even lower than that of the population as a whole."[7] Apparently, unfounded fears were being stirred up over the citizens of Bulgaria and Romania coming to raid the German social welfare system. The *heute-journal* even assured their viewers: "Most of them fill the gaps in the German labor market where there is a shortage of skilled workers."[8] The state-run propaganda channel, ZDF, took the lead in generating a wave of disinformation and propaganda aimed at assuaging the German people's fears of their new, fellow-citizens. There were reports in which the Romanians and Bulgarians were portrayed as an extremely hard-working, new population group who, compared to the German population as a whole, were hardly ever unemployed.[9] All – literally all – of the leading German media outlets ran with this and repeated it without any verification. After all, the figures published to back up the statements made by the *heute-journal* came directly from the Federal Government. All this was going on only a few months before both local and European elections were due to take place in 2014. The voters needed to be kept in a good mood. In those days, even renowned business papers like the *Handelsblatt* used their headlines to reassure us that, "Bulgarians and Romanians: The Mass Exodus Is a Bust."[10] Additionally, since Germans weren't supposed to be discussing this topic in the first place, new language barriers were also quickly erected: "poverty immigration"[11] and "welfare tourism"[12] were to become "Un-words of the Year." On the *Tagesschau*, the state-run evening news on ARD, the language police used their prime time slot to explain why we're not allowed to use these words anymore:

They discriminate against people who are looking for a better future in Germany out of sheer necessity and it obscures their fundamental right to do so. According to the Un-Word of the Year's jury, the term "welfare tourism" takes its place in a tangle of other un-words that together, serve to promote this sentiment: "poverty immigration." This was originally used in the defamatory sense of "immigration into welfare systems," and is now increasingly used in an undifferentiated way, as an objectively neutral term. The term "welfare tourism," however, takes this allegation of malicious intent to the extreme.[13]

The European and local elections held in May of 2014 were barely six days behind us when the German voters were finally presented with the truth: "Welfare Recipients: Increasing Numbers of Immigrants from Bulgaria & Romania" ran as the *Bild* tabloid's main headline. The first two lines of the article already said it all: "The number of poor immigrants from East-EU countries and euro-debt states who receive Hartz IV (welfare) in Germany continues to rise significantly. At the end of February, according to the latest figures from the Federal Employment Agency (BA), 290,760 people from the 10 Eastern and 4 debt countries were receiving support. This was 21 percent (50,226) more than in February 2013. Accordingly, the number of Bulgarians and Romanians receiving welfare exceeded 50,000 for the first time in February. At the end of February, the BA counted 28,705 welfare recipients from Bulgaria and 24,098 from Romania."[14]

Then, in June of 2014, the German media reported: The number of Hartz IV recipients from Bulgaria and Romania had risen significantly by about 60 percent compared to the previous year.[15] This was according to current data from the Institute for Labor Market and Occupational Research (IAB). In the words of their study, many of the new citizens depending on welfare live in a few large cities, primarily in Dortmund, Duisburg, Stuttgart and Hamburg. Once again: *sixty* percent more Hartz IV recipients from Bulgaria and Romania. Shortly before this, they had claimed exactly the opposite. There you have it for the allegedly hard-working "Prussians of the Balkans."

In plain language: The ones who had warned us of these developments before the elections were right. There were, and still are, masses of poverty immigrants. Still, politicians and the media sold them to us before the election as the "Prussians of the Balkans" and backed up this bold statement with statistics that were likely fabricated, specifically for this disinformation campaign. It was a typical simulation of credible and independent reporting. A pure illusion.

So why did they do all this? Marco Arndt of the Konrad Adenauer Foundation in Sofia hinted at this years ago in a conversation he had with Deutschlandradio. When it came to the question of whether Bulgaria had been admitted to the EU prematurely, Arndt answered, "If you take the formal criteria at face value, then it is certainly correct that Bulgaria and Romania did not fully meet these criteria, that the European Union made a political decision to admit both states." Furthermore, he stated, "Bulgaria lies on the border of Europe. When I think of Russian influence – it would be much stronger than it already is in that country if Bulgaria wasn't in the EU. Let me just say, 'energy policy.'"[16] So, what we're dealing with here is purely power politics and geostrategic considerations, both of which led to Bulgaria's 2007 admission to the EU. The Eastern Bloc states, once under the influence of the former Soviet Union, Estonia, Latvia, Lithuania, Poland, the Czech Republic, Slovenia, Slovakia and Hungary all joined the EU in 2004. With the admission of Bulgaria and Romania in 2007, Russia is now completely isolated from Western Europe. Behind the scenes, it was all about power politics.

Tricks of the Tongue in Politics and Media

It's not only our evening news programs that have become a permanent source of deception. Every day, the streets of Germany are getting sketchier as crime takes over more and more neighborhoods. Plaster is falling from the walls of public schools while the gap between the rich and the poor continues to widen. The people's rage is reaching unprecedented proportions, yet the "quality media" in Germany continues to lull us along with meaningless drivel from an endless line of interchangeable politicians. While everything out there is slowly but surely falling apart and rotting away, our "quality media" continues to serve up fresh illusions of stability, prosperity and financial security.

We owe a debt of gratitude to the constitutional lawyer, Hans Herbert von Arnim, for showing us just how the established political parties regard the state as their rightful spoils and eagerly plunder us, the common citizenry. In this endeavor, the "quality media" are their willing accomplices. They second them and assist them by keeping the victims calm and even in good spirits while they're being looted. These days, what most of the media in the German-speaking world consistently churns out has absolutely nothing to do with their touted virtues of truth, objectivity and independence. It is much more a kind of enforced conformity.

However, upon closer inspection, this forced conformity allows us to easily see through the verbal duplicity used in politics and the media: When they tell us what to think, they call it, "Education for becoming a responsible citizen." If immigrants lack any and all respect for the natives of their new country, then we should respect that as a "cultural idiosyncrasy." If all the major media groups essentially report exactly the same thing in all newspapers and on all TV stations around the clock, like in a dictatorship, then we should understand this as the "diversity" of our media landscape. It's no different when it comes to the euro: When politicians from every party increasingly threaten our savings with "euro rescue packages," then they speak of "stability" (like in the case of the Stability and Growth Pact). As soon as you start to think about the names they use for all these new political concepts, you can quickly get an idea of the lies behind them. Everybody knows we're being fed a daily ration of convoluted notions and outright lies, served up with a smile by our politicians and the media – in unison. When all of the major political parties and media outlets all hold essentially the same position on all important issues, be it climate change, gender quotas or rescuing the euro, then our media simply calls this, "Democracy in action." In actuality, the "quality media" is leading us around by the nose. When the energy supply in Germany is constantly on the verge of collapse due to the "green energy revolution," then the media simply calls this precarious state of affairs "sustainable." No one protests against this idiotic distortion of terms being implemented across the board. And at some point, we even wind up believing it – even though we know the opposite is true. It's gone so far that we even think that the fraud these journalists are perpetrating against us on a daily basis is completely normal. Many have simply resigned themselves to being lied to and deceived by politicians and their willing accomplices in the "quality media." The result? We no longer trust journalists at all, and rightly so.

The Loss of Credibility

For a myriad of reasons, journalists in German-speaking countries now have one of the worst reputations of all occupational groups – and this is no fluke. For decades, they have been working hard to earn this miserable reputation. In the fight for circulation and ratings, they have bent the truth and lied so often that it's hard to believe them at all anymore.

Doctors, nurses and policemen are popular – but journalists from the "quality media?"[17] Let's not kid ourselves: The reputation of mainstream journalists is at rock bottom.[18] Asked to rank various professions according to prestige, the average German citizen places journalists somewhere between politicians and prostitutes. Nobody is surprised anymore that once respected media companies are now regularly referred to as "presstitutes" on the Internet. Even *Der Spiegel* (*The Mirror*), for example, a magazine many people used to rely on for quality news, has taken on the inglorious nickname, "Der Speichel" (The Spittle).

In a study conducted by the Allensbach Institute for Public Opinion Research in 2013, television presenters, together with bankers, took last place in the popularity rankings. The television presenters themselves, however, consider themselves to be the greatest. Among them is a certain Johannes B. Kerner. In a March 2014 edition of *Bild der Frau*, a weekly women's magazine you can find in supermarket checkout lanes, he couldn't contain his brilliance, declaring, "My IQ is somewhere around and near 130" (irgendwo um und bei). Another classic example comes from the narcissistic TV host Michel Friedman who, after being caught in an affair involving Ukrainian girls who were forced into prostitution, confessed in all seriousness, "I didn't love myself enough."[19]

Foreign journalists don't hold their German-speaking colleagues in very high regard either. As Roger Boyles, the Germany correspondent for the *London Times*, said two decades ago, "German newspaper journalists seem to be very dependent on the press agencies. Many articles that appear under their name are identical to dpa or German AP reports from the previous day. If there is a difference, it is that the journalist has added his opinion – without doing any research."[20] Brandon Mitchener, from the renowned *International Herald Tribune*, also criticized German journalists with the words: "Very many newspaper articles do not contain any individual research, rather they're largely uncritical. With a few exceptions, I think the journalists are too passive and perhaps also a little lazy. They are always well informed, but also obedient to authority."[21] Lazy, obedient and reluctant to do research – this is how our foreign colleagues see German journalists. And what about our citizens? The communications sciences Professor, Wolfgang Donsbach from Dresden, has investigated this in a study entitled "Disenchantment of a Profession." In it he says:

The majority of citizens attest to journalists' enormous influence in many areas of their lives: what is discussed in daily conversation, attitudes toward politicians, which party they will vote for and in questions of buying commercial products. That said, journalists are thus more powerful than politicians for more than half of those involved in the study, and almost all of them think that this isn't good. Additionally, political reporting is criticized by almost two-thirds of the public as not being objective enough, although objectivity is something that two-thirds of the public expect. For them, journalists just aren't honest brokers. Almost two-thirds believe that journalists often suppress the comments of experts who disagree with their own personal opinions.[22]

Chapter 3. The Undercover Truth:
Alpha Journalists Toe the Line for the Elites

Everyone named in this book denies having intimate, cozy relationships with elite power structures. Moreover, they deny being lobbyists. They also deny being "corrupted" by their proximity to the elite. And, they deny having lost their journalistic edge, working as they do in such close proximity to the aforementioned groups. They deny that this proximity has any influence on their reporting.

If you're working around a lot of the pro-American propaganda organizations that this former occupation force left behind on German soil, as a politician or a journalist, you can quickly find yourself in bizarre conflicts of interest. An example: *Die Zeit* author Jochen Bittner and a colleague of his wrote an article on German foreign policy in 2014.[1] The article is about the Munich Security Conference and a speech by German President Gauck, who supports the deployment of German soldiers abroad. The article in *Die Zeit* praised Gauck's speech. What the readers didn't learn: Gauck's speech is partially the result of a project by a transatlantic organization, the German Marshall Fund (GMF), who developed it together with the German Institute for International and Security Affairs (Stiftung Wissenschaft und Politik (SWP), funded by the Federal Foreign Office). Furthermore, *Die Zeit* journalist Bittner worked on this project and was directly involved in the project's paper.[2] Bittner himself calls it an "open concept paper" – a kind of position paper.[3] An article on it states:

According to Bittner, however, it is true that during the course of 2013 he "participated in a discussion group organized by the Institute for International and Security Affairs (SWP) and the GMF." The aim of the group was to draw up a position paper with regard to a new German security strategy. According to Bittner, though, this was merely an "open concept paper."[4]

A lawyer additionally noted:

Bittner did not only participate in a conference or discussion round of the GMF and the SWP (...). Rather, what we're dealing with here was a project that stretched out over the course of a year and resulted in a paper on the subject of German foreign and security policy. This project therefore had the character of a think tank, one which also made concrete recommendations on diverse issues.[5]

Thus, Bittner was writing in *Die Zeit* about a speech that had been developed in part by the lobbying organization *German Marshall Fund* and SWP, together with Bittner. Furthermore, this speech was given on the occasion of a pro-American lobbying event, the Munich Security

Conference. Readers of *Die Zeit* had no idea that what Bittner was apparently praising as an "open concept paper," was something that he himself had worked on, at least in part. All this was so absurd that the satirical TV program *Die Anstalt* (The Institution) decided to give their take on the issue. It was only after this piece that *Die Zeit* decided to publish the following notice under their online version of the article:

Editor's note: In this article from ZEIT no. 7/14, the authors mention a study project by the Institute for International and Security Affairs and the German Marshall Fund on the building blocks of a German security strategy. One of the authors of the article, Jochen Bittner, was a member of this project.[6]

The above-mentioned *Anstalt* show, airing on April 29, 2014, also took a closer look into the propaganda the German media uses to praise Washington and denounce Moscow. One scene showed a chart with the names of five leading German journalists – Stefan Kornelius from the *Süddeutsche Zeitung*, Josef Joffe and Jochen Bittner from *Die Zeit*, as well as Günther Nonnenmacher and Klaus-Dieter Frankenberger from the *Frankfurter Allgemeine*. They also included the names of twelve transatlantic think tanks – among them the *Aspen Institute*, the Trilateral Commission, the German Council on Foreign Relations and the Federal Academy for Security Policy – in which, as they explained, "military men, economic bosses and politicians discuss foreign policy strategies *in a discreet atmosphere*."

Then they revealed all the lines showing the ties between these five journalists and the government-related think tanks. The resulting chart formed a dense network.[7] "Thus, all these newspapers are basically something like the local editions of the NATO press office," they said on the air. This triggered fierce protests from the media outlets mentioned. Media scientist Uwe Krüger later stated, "I take it that the pressure they felt after a television show like this with millions of viewers was pretty high. At any rate, a storm of controversy erupted under online articles, and apparently subscriptions were also cancelled."

In the *New York Times*, conflicts of interest like the one that appeared in *Die Zeit* are prohibited. In Germany it's different. In Germany, this is called "quality journalism." So, looking at the other German newspapers behaving in the same way toward the many US lobbying organizations, you could get the impression that they are in fact only something like the local editions of NATO's central press office.

But, how did *Die Zeit* react to the *Die Anstalt*'s satire?

Josef Joffe, publisher-editor of DIE ZEIT, complained to the editor-in-chief at ZDF, Peter Frey, about the alleged misrepresentations in the satirical show. The "Anstalt's" editorial staff had the pleasure of dealing with cease-and-desist letters sent by the liberal newspaper's publisher and an editor. And, Stefan Kornelius, a lead columnist for the Süd–deutsche Zeitung mentioned in the program, rejected criticism of his proximity to the elite when this was brought up by NDR's (Northern German Broadcasting) media magazine Zapp.[8]

Josef Joffe has become extremely controversial in publishing circles and I believe his chutzpa is ruining the reputation of the once well-respected weekly newspaper *Die Zeit*. Still, he, along with the other journalists named in the ZDF program, like to emphasize the claim that the organizations they belong to or have belonged to are not lobbying organizations. According to his own admissions, Joffe is no longer a member of the *Aspen-Institute*, American Council on Germany (ACG) and The Atlantik-Brücke. Joffe claims that the ZDF team "fell for" the doctoral thesis of the scientist Uwe Krüger, (already mentioned several times in this book), who investigated these past network connections.[9] If I was in Josef Joffe's position, I would be careful about using the phrase "fell for." I say this because shortly before this 2014 incident, the media journalist Stefan Niggemeier verified that Joffe, who considers himself to be a serious individual, was circulating nonsense that originated in a newspaper hoax himself. In one of his articles, as Niggemeier explains, he "fell for a fictitious hype agency."[10]

According to media reports, the journalists at *Die Zeit* even filed a temporary restraining order against the satirical television show, which prohibited ZDF from rebroadcasting the aforementioned episode of *Die Anstalt*. According to a report on this, "For a flagship newspaper like *Die Zeit*, the legal action taken by Joffe and Bittner against ZDF amounts to a journalistic declaration of bankruptcy. Unfortunately, the big newspapers such as the *SZ*, *FAZ* or *Spiegel* didn't report on Joffe and Bittner's dispute with ZDF. Shame be to him that thinks evil of it."[11]

You read that right: An allegedly "independent" and allegedly "democratic," journalistic newspaper is taking legal action against satire. The "free" press v. satire! For anyone who doesn't yet have a clue as to what's going on in the German mainstream media, now you have your answer.

Interestingly enough: Even after Josef Joffe wrote in a May 2, 2014 letter that he was not a "member of the *Aspen Institute*, ACG and the Atlantik-Brücke," his own homepage at Stanford University, where he teaches, still listed him as being associated with these organizations for months afterward. Among his many functions listed there (I saved a screenshot of it) are:

Boards: American Academy in Berlin, International University Bremen, Ben Gurion University, Israel; Goldman Sachs Foundation, New York; Aspen Institute Berlin, Leo Baeck Institute, New York; German Children and Youth Foundation, Berlin; European Advisory Board, Hypo–vereinsbank, Munich (2001-2005). Editorial Boards: The American Interest, (Washington); International Security (Harvard), and Prospect

(London), The National Interest, Washington (1995-2000). Trustee: Atlantik-Brücke (Berlin), Deutsches Museum (Munich), Abraham Geiger College (Berlin). Member: American Council on Germany, Intl. Institute for Strategic Studies.[12]

Apparently, he can't even keep track of this confusing tangle of networks himself. Or, the person who updates his homepage I cited is also bewildered. It was only after reading through Josef Joffe's self-portrait for a second time that I noticed something between the lines of the other statements this list was making: He sat on the advisory board of the Hypovereinsbank. What's more, he sat on the editorial board of the *Goldman Sachs Foundation.*

What on Earth is a German journalist doing in the obscure *Goldman Sachs Foundation?* The *Handelsblatt* warns its readers about this institution with the following words:

Reuters have their doubts about the activities of the Goldman Sachs Foundation, a global charitable foundation created by the Goldman Sachs Group. The fact that the foundation's tax return consists of over 200 pages of single-spaced descriptions shows just how much Goldman itself invests and deals in its own charitable activities. The strange thing about it is that although Goldman has invested 501 million dollars in the foundation since 1999, only a fraction of around five percent has been distributed and invested in projects – the minimum requirement for non-profit status. Goldman itself profits from most of the foundation's activities. As an example, Reuters calls the Asia Society on Park Avenue in New York: a 'talking shop' where the Goldman bankers can 'butter up' foreign clients.[13]

Goldman Sachs is the epitome of the greedy, US financial elite that made billions in profits while ordinary people lost their homes and savings at the height of the financial and commercial crisis. The greedy Goldman bankers' mysterious charity just serves to add a little shine to these money-grubbers' tarnished reputation. What on Earth is a German journalist doing in the *Goldman Sachs Foundation?* It doesn't get any worse than that! Or does it?

Bild Your Own Opinion

Who still remembers Mao Tse-Tung, the communist leader of the People's Republic of China? If nothing else, that man loved his cult of personality. The Chinese media had to pay him constant homage. Had Chairman Mao been able to see Angela Merkel's sixtieth birthday, he would have been green with envy. Mao forced the media in his country to praise him under the threat of draconian punishment. Today in the German media, this kind of praise seems to be fully automated. Everybody loves "Mutti." Leading the vanguard in this modern cult of personality: the *Bild* newspaper.[14]

The professor Brigitte Witzer asserts that we live in a "dictatorship of the dumb," in an "idiocracy."[15] Our society is getting dumber. Always way out front in this dumbing down: the *Bild* newspaper. Professor Witzer has observed how our leading media also "inform" themselves with the *Bild*, she writes:

Of course, there are differences between the Bild and other newspapers, let's take our erstwhile quality media, the FAZ or Süddeutsche Zeitung for example. They put together highbrow information for a nation-wide readership, but they also follow the Bild's lead when it comes to the agenda for public discourse. At least this is what my personal experience tells me from the time I've spent in a café in Berlin's Prenzlauer Berg. I was able to personally follow the newspaper reading habits of a well-known FAZ editor there for three years. He, with a copy of the Bild, I, at a loss for words. This may be an exception, but I am surrounded by people who earn a living in the media and honestly, I hear nothing else. This is why I would like to insist: The Bild sets the agenda. It is merely given a makeover by FAZ and the Süddeutsche, intellectualized and fortified with science (...). This has taken reporting to a different level. But does it have a different objective?

So, what is the "objective" of the *Bild* newspaper? And what's going on there behind the scenes?

Our former Chancellor Gerhard Schröder once said that he only needed "*Bild*, BamS (*Bild* on Sunday) and boob tube" to govern. Get power over a few mass media outlets – and you can easily steer the masses. The main thing is having a small handful of opinion makers who play along in manipulating the masses. When you are finished reading the following sections, you will probably see media outlets like the *Bild*, *Süddeutsche Zeitung*, *Frankfurter Allgemeine*, *Die Zeit*, ZDF and ARD through completely different eyes.

Heinz Oskar Vetter, the former chairman of the German Trade Union Confederation (DGB), coined the phrase, "Whoever *resorts* to the *Bild* will perish in it," but today, the *Bild* has taken its place in the center of German society. Being associated with the paper no longer brings anyone into disrepute. Even serious journalists accept it as a source of information. Artists like the German rock legend Marius Müller-Westernhagen and award-winning actress Veronika Ferres have been in advertisements for the *Bild*. Germans can all remember the billboards featuring celebrities such as Til Schweiger, Armin Rohde, Thomas Gottschalk, David Garrett, Udo Lindenberg, Michelle Hunziker, Peter Scholl-Latour, Katharina Witt or Bill Kaulitz expressing their opinions on the *Bild*. The aim of the ad campaign was to offer "top-notch celebrities a stage" to "share their open, candid and honest opinions about the *BILD*."

The former German President Richard von Weizsäcker advertised for the *Bild* with the words, "'*Bild*': exciting politics, (multi-) color style." On the poster with Alice Schwarzer, a women's rights activist and tax evader, it went, "Every truth needs a courageous person to speak it." Peter Scholl-Latour was quoted as saying, "My main interest in the '*Bild*' is that it reflects the big trends in opinion – and sometimes even sets them in motion." Handball all-star Stefan Kretzschmar boldly claimed, "The '*Bild*' can come up with headlines, but the '*Bild*' never has an opinion." Former Foreign Minister Hans-Dietrich Genscher, "When I'm done reading the '*Bild*' – every day –, I don't yet know what Germany thinks, what it feels, but I do – in the opinion of '*Bild*'"[16]

The *Bild* newspaper is Germany's highest-circulation print newspaper. It has a paid daily circulation of about 2.4 million. The target audience of the *Bild* is neither the university professor nor the unskilled worker, but the average consumer. 63 percent of its readers are men, 43 percent of all readers have a lower secondary school leaving certificate (10th grade) with an apprenticeship, 35 percent have a secondary school diploma (12th grade) and four percent are college graduates. Seven percent of its readers are self-employed, 34 percent are employees or civil servants and 37 percent are skilled workers. Overall, the *Bild* reaches about 18 percent of Germans – almost one in five. 4.3 million women and 7.3 million men read the *Bild* every day for an average of 45 minutes.

For the rebellious students of 1968, the *Bild* was still an inflammatory tabloid inciting reactionaries. It called out for someone to stop the Marxist political activist Rudi Dutschke, shortly before an anti-communist shot him in the head. Afterward, Springer publishing's delivery trucks were burning in the streets. Heinrich Böll's novel "The Lost Honor of Katharina Blum" is a literary tribute to this conflict. Today, all of that is long forgotten. Today, the *Bild* is hip. The paper largely owes this turn-around to one person: Kai Diekmann. At the latest, Diekmann was catapulted up amongst the Olympians of language creation when he went with the headline "We Are Pope" (Wir sind Papst), upon Pope Benedict XVI's election.

In their own advertising, the *Bild* still refers to itself as "independent" and "non-partisan." But is it really? And was it ever? Whenever a *Bild* editor asked me for a column, an interview or some sort of collaboration, the answers or "research results" they wanted from me already had at least a certain direction I needed to follow. My experiences tend to corroborate the findings of a 2011 study released by the Otto Brenner Foundation. When describing *Bild* editors they state:

The editors develop their stories less according to an objective reality than according to objective efficacy. Anything that doesn't fit the pattern will be made to fit. Editors don't hesitate to ask potential collaborators if they are willing to express the desired opinion – and many play the game.[17]

You get the same manipulative impression if you analyze the "Winners & Losers" column, a regular feature the *Bild* has been printing for decades. Seen over the years, right-wing politicians are statistically more likely to be winners than left-wing politicians by a wide margin.[18]

Still, Michael H. Spreng, a former editor-in-chief of the *Bild am Sonntag* (*Bild* on Sunday), has had a very different experience with this column:

The Bild and I have had a clearly defined relationship since January 1, 2001: The Bild newspaper doesn't like me and I don't like it. It expresses its occasional vulgar opinion of me, printed in the millions. In 2002, when I was working for Edmund Stoiber, I appeared in Oskar Lafontaine's column "IM Cohiba" because I occasionally smoked a good cigar with Gerhard Schröder. Eventually, I was named as one of the "30 most annoying" talk show guests and in 2004, when I was an advisor to Jürgen Rüttgers, I was named "Loser of the Day." Here's the story: Rüttgers was campaigning through North Rhine-Westphalia before the election in his town hall-style format "Rüttgers – up close and personal." In Bielefeld, the applause was less than enthusiastic, and this led me to make the – certainly careless – remark in front of two or three people, well, you know the Westphalians aren't known for their excitement. When a Bielefelder nods his head, that's ecstatic applause. What I didn't know: The Bild boss Kai Diekmann grew up in Bielefeld and so the next day I was the "Loser of the Day" on the front page.[19]

Even the study published in 2007 entitled, "*Bild* – Independent, Non-partisan? The election reporting of Germany's most successful tabloid newspaper," also paints an unpleasant picture of the *Bild*. It includes:

On the evening of the 2005 Bundestag elections, Gerhard Schröder took the media to task in the ZDF program "Berliner Runde," in a discussion panel involving top politicians from the parties represented in the Bundestag. The chancellor, who is said to have once claimed that he only needed "Bild, BamS and boob tube" to govern (...), complained in an aggressive tone about the machinations of the media. He claimed that he had to campaign against "what was written and broadcast there" (Schröder in the program "Berliner Runde," ZDF). What did he mean by these accusations? Did the media want to bring on a change in government through their writing? This question is particularly interesting regarding the Springer publishing house's various media, since these newspapers, and the Bild newspaper in particular, were increasingly accused of favoring the Union parties (CDU/CSU) during Schröder's time in office (...). After the election, the publisher's ties to the Union were evident when Friede Springer, widow of the publisher's founder Axel Springer and majority shareholder of the company, was sitting in the visitors' gallery of the Bundestag during Angela Merkel's election as Chancellor. So, did Schröder have to govern or lead an election campaign against the Bild, instead of being helped by this paper? Furthermore, was Merkel able to count on this tabloid's support during the election campaign?[20]

Many studies by communication scientists draw the same conclusion. For the Bundestag elections, there was direct campaign advertising for the Union parties, although the *Bild* newspaper described itself as "non-partisan" and had previously condemned an explicit election recommendation by the *Financial Times Deutschland*. Not only in 2002, but also in the Bundestag elections of 2005[21] and 2009, the newspaper campaigned for the Union parties and Angela Merkel, who was once a propaganda functionary with the Free German Youth (FDJ) in the communist German Democratic Republic (DDR).[22]

According to my subjective experience, the *Bild*'s primary intention has nothing to do with independent journalism. Its intention is to generate as much profit as possible for Springer publishing. To this end, the *Bild* uses every means of publishing at their disposal, regardless of the rules, whether this is journalism, PR or advertising. Whether the information they publish is accurate information about important news isn't something that's decided based on any democratic need or journalistic rule; it's all based on how it affects the company's bottom line. At the *Bild* newspaper, journalism isn't a time-honored trade whose rules set any limits on their business. Here, journalism is cannon fodder for their return on investment. *Bild* journalism is manipulation of the masses – in partnership with the political elite.[23]

Groomsman Journalism: *Bild* Up Your Power

The most poignant example of the intimate proximity between journalists and the elites is when journalists are invited to be in a politician's wedding party or vice versa. When Helmut Kohl married his partner Maike Richter in 2008, the *Bild* was in on the action. Daniel Biskup, Kohl's favorite photographer, was snapping the photos and *Bild* editor-in-chief Kai Diekmann reported on the wedding. Diekmann, along with Leo Kirch, were groomsmen at Kohl's wedding.[24] Just as Kohl was likewise a groomsman at Diekmann's wedding in 2002.[25] In this example, the separation of politics and journalism is not quite so clear.[26] So, does *Bild* stand for "*Bild* up your power?" In retrospect, the *Bild*'s overwhelmingly positive reporting on Helmut Kohl throughout the past appears in a completely different light.

Among our French neighbors, groomsman journalism isn't an unknown phenomenon either. The French journalist Augustin Scalbert, writing when

Nicolas Sarkozy was still the President of France, reported on a groomsman belonging to the French media:

The billionaire Bernard Arnault, for example, owner of the most important daily business newspaper in France (Les Echos) and the world's largest luxury goods group (LVMH), is simply friends with Sarkozy. This friendship goes deep – he was also a groomsman at Sarkozy's wedding. Moreover, when Arnault was "only" the owner of La Tribüne (a competitor of Les Echos), his newspaper supported Sarkozy wholeheartedly and, from time to time, this came at the expense of Sègoléne Royal, Sarkozy's opponent for the French presidency.[27]

Just how this groomsman journalism works in France was described in an impressive 2010 report by the *Süddeutsche Zeitung*:

When the photo of Sarkozy's wife with another man appeared on the front page of Paris Match, in the middle of a heated election campaign last summer, the conservative politician picked up the phone. He called the publisher of Paris Match – a certain Arnaud Lagardere, who also happens to manage the largest magazine empire in the world. Shortly thereafter, the editor-in-chief at Paris Match responsible for running the photo was looking for a new job. It is also convenient that with Europe 1, Lagardere owns one of the most listened to radio stations in France, where Sarkozy was recently invited for prime-time interviews, often at short notice, whenever he seemed to be in trouble. An entrepreneur and wealthy heir, Lagardere is also a minority shareholder in the respected daily newspaper Le Monde, but this is hardly noticeable. Furthermore, he also owns magazines (Elle), the Sunday newspaper Journal du Dimanche and various regional newspapers. (...) Another of Sarkozy's groomsmen, Martin Bouygues, is the director of TF1, the former public broadcasting channel that was privatized in 1987. At the same time, he also owns the third largest French mobile service provider. Bouygues is the godfather of Sarkozy's son. (...) Sarkozy's second groomsman, Bernard Arnault, not only owns such illustrious brands as Louis Vuitton, Kenzo and Givenchy, through the luxury group LVMH, the fact of the matter is that he also owns the business journals La Tribüne and Investir.[28]

Notwithstanding, there is much more going on than just groomsman journalism. *Bild* also retains politicians in a completely different way, and very cleverly at that. This is how they did it with the SPD politician Rudolf Scharping:

SPD politician Rudi Scharping and "Bild am Sonntag" shared a particular affinity. He introduced his new girlfriend to the public in BamS and he even shaved off his beard exclusively for BamS. As the SPD faction leader, he also wrote for BamS about his greatest passion – besides politics – the Tour de France. Every Saturday afternoon,

"Reporter Rudi," as he was called in the editorial office, handed over his report, which was crafted into a journalistically pleasing article by sports boss Bodo Müller. For his efforts, Scharping also received a respectable fee, mostly in cash.[29]

What Makes Kai Diekmann Tick?

The *Bild*'s recipe for success is simple – day after day, this newspaper squeezes all the facets of human life onto just a few pages. This is all written in a narrative style that, like in a cheap novel, doesn't make any great demands on the reader. Love and hate, devotion and betrayal, happiness and despair, deadly diseases, crime and politics portrayed as power struggles and showdowns – all this is presented in an emotionalized, personalized, simplified and extremely confrontational way. For *Bild* readers, what's important isn't what's objectively important; instead, anything that moves them emotionally is important. At most, the classic journalistic message in the *Bild* functions as an alibi. When it comes to reporting on boring political news like a local political party's conference or a governmental report, they seek out emotional elements and personalize complex issues. By means of pseudo-revelations, the reader's attention is steered away from what's objectively important and diverted to what's trivial. In this way, the reader is diverted away from contemplating the real problems in politics and society. The *Bild* newspaper is like a mythical cornucopia: Every day the whole world falls out of it – in easily digestible tidbits. On a day when *Der Spiegel* publishes matter-of-fact accounts of a military coup in Thailand, the Spanish king's resignation and NATO war games against Russia, the *Bild* asks their readers in giant letters: "Who else has Angela Merkel's mobile phone number?"[30] And then, for their readers' future reference, the *Bild* goes on to list everyone who does have Merkel's number:

She can be reached directly by office manager Beate Baumann (50), consultant Eva Christiansen (44), government spokesperson Steffen Seibert (53), Chancellery Minister Peter Altmaier (55) and some consultants such as Christoph Heusgen (59, foreign policy), Lars-Hendrik Roller (55, economics) and Nikolaus Meyer-Landrut (54, Europe), who all can send her information via text messages during important negotiations. Important: The Chancellor doesn't appreciate it at all if her number is given out or if confidants state that they have Merkel's number. On May 7, she even changed her number and sent a bilingual message (German and English) with her new extension ("I have a new mobile number" ...) – also because she wanted to narrow the circle of her mobile phone friends once again.

Of course, the *Bild* also has a number they can use to reach the Chancellor. Of course, the editor-in-chief can get in contact with her very quickly – but the readers aren't told this. Since January 2001, Kai Diekmann has been the chief editor of the *Bild* and publisher of the *Bild* and *Bild am Sonntag*. While I was researching this book, I stumbled across an interesting caption. Under a photo of the *Bild* editor-in-chief and Angela Merkel it said:

Bild stands for power. And that means when the newspaper holds its Summer Festival (here 2008) even Angela Merkel comes...[31]

Diekmann and Merkel know each other well. Very well. Both are members of the Atlantik-Brücke, and Diekmann is even a member of the board.

The German Journalists Association (DJV) has made a clear statement regarding such activities. In the summer of 2014 the Association announced:

In the current debate on journalists' membership in lobbying organizations, the German Journalists' Association has emphasized the role of journalists as observers. DJV Federal Chairman Michael Konken stated, "The independence and credibility of journalism requires that journalists do not play an active role in the organizations that they report on."[32]

Diekmann appreciates Merkel. And Merkel appreciates Diekmann. With Diekmann at the helm, the *Bild* newspaper writes everything about Angela Merkel, just nothing negative. Like the fact that Angela Merkel is Germany's most powerful nail biter. Yes, the Federal Chancellor chews her fingernails. Just like the former British Prime Minister Gordon Brown did. Or the late FAZ editor Frank Schirrmacher at big editorial conferences. This information would have been perfect for the *Bild* newspaper, but for some reason they remained silent.[33]

Merkel probably learned just how important the *Bild* newspaper is for a Chancellor from the powerful Helmut Kohl. Kohl, who was the Chancellor of Germany from 1982 to 1998, got to know Diekmann when he was a Bundestag correspondent for the *Bild* in the late 80s, when the West German capital was still in Bonn. At first, Kohl didn't like Diekmann because he had long hair and wore it in a ponytail. When Kohl wanted a reporter to interview him for the *Bild* in those days, he let everyone know he meant Diekmann when he said, "Send me one, but not that long-haired one!"[34] Michael H. Spreng, a media consultant and lead editor for the talk show *Menschen bei Maischberger* (People with Maischberger), writes in his blog about how this situation evolved:

Over the years, Diekmann wormed his way in deep, earning Kohl's trust, and is now closer to the former Chancellor than his own sons are – at least when it comes to taking part in family celebrations. Diekmann is so tactful, he rarely mentions the absence of Kohl's sons at weddings or birthdays, and if he does, he doesn't make an issue out of it.[35]

Under Kai Diekmann, many politicians have been raised to great heights – and then shot down again. An example of this was Theodor zu Guttenberg, Germany's Minister of Defense for a little while. He was featured striking a Top Gun pose for the front page of the *Bild* newspaper. His wife was the ambassador for the *Bild* charity action "Ein Herz für Kinder" (A Heart for Children). Hardly a day went by without "Gutti" appearing in the *Bild*. Even when he faced criticism for his wife's trip to Afghanistan, the *Bild* wrote: "We think she's good" (using gutt with two t's). An editor for the *Bild am Sonntag*, Anna von Bayern, wrote a heart-warming Guttenberg biography. Guttenberg introduced the new book by Nikolaus Blome, the head of the *Bild*'s Bundestag office. In those days, one of Guttenberg's relatives, Karl Ludwig von Guttenberg, was even deputy chief of the *Bild*'s national edition. Many readers aren't aware of the fact that Guttenberg did an internship with Springer publishing (*Die Welt*). There's no doubt: Guttenberg was extremely close to Springer's *Bild* – and the *Bild* was extremely close to Guttenberg. As an outsider, you could only wonder who was actually orchestrating it. It was a give and take: Guttenberg made the *Bild* very happy, feeding them a Ministry of Defense advertising campaign worth millions and recruiting volunteers for the German military[36] – even though the *Bild* doesn't have very many young readers. Exclusive contracts like this one, one that got the taxpayers' money flowing, were only signed with Springer. On the flip side, the *Bild* sang Guttenberg's praises. The *Bild* made Guttenberg into a political celebrity. The closeness between the *Bild* and Guttenberg was virtually indescribable. One example of this was the "Gorch-Fock Affair," which revolved around corruption allegations stemming from the restoration work on a tall ship used for sailing training by the German Navy. At first, Guttenberg warned of a "rush to judgement" – and then he relieved the commanding officer of his duties after a phone call from a *Bild* editor.

In 2013, journalist Michael H. Spreng reported on the "rather unusual corruption" between the *Bild* and politics:

Also in the relationship between politicians and journalists, there are different forms of corruption, but none of them have anything to do with money. And none of them are of any interest to the criminal justice system. Here, the situation is different: the politician allows access and provides confidential information or stands in as the figurehead for a newspaper or a publishing house's project. In return, the newspaper gives him positive coverage, gives him meaning, importance. Normally, business relationships like these remain secret, only their consequences can be seen publicly. Sometimes, however, a careless act tears apart a network of relationships like this – in this case, the embarrassing photo of the BILD's boss Kai Diekmann and FDP Minister of Economic Affairs Philipp Rösler. It shows them in an exuberant embrace, a politician and a journalist poised like two lovers, finally reunited after a long absence. Also true in this case: A picture is worth a thousand words. Our critical *public immediately wanted to know the history behind it. For weeks, the BILD has been praising the four-percent-party (FDP) chairman as "Mr. Cool" or "Minister Cool," while Rösler has been playing the role of the advertising prankster and opening doors for Springer's attempts to bring the publishing house into closer connection with the start-up scene. One could imagine this as a win-win situation. Alas, the photo turned this into a lose-lose situation. Two men, who should be greeting each other with critical, professional deference, are falling into one another's arms. Thanks to the photo, both suffered a loss of professional credibility. The photo will haunt both of them for a long time and continues to catch up with them – when the BILD publishes their next flattering report on Rösler or the next time Rösler makes an appearance to support Springer publishing. Just like Karl Theodor zu Guttenberg is haunted by his arrogant Times Square photo. Guttenberg used the BILD to accelerate his career – and the BILD used him. The rest is history.*[37] (For more information on Guttenberg's subsequent fall from grace, see: "Guttenberg plagiarism scandal").*

In 2011, the Frankfurter Rundschau tried to clear up the question of how this proximity functions. After many attempts at an explanation, they boiled it all down to a few sentences:

Unlike other newspapers, where the chief editors give their senior editors and department heads freedom, the Bild *works according to the bottleneck principle: Everything has to go through the chief editor's office, the* Bild *is the product of Kai Diekmann. The Bild is Diekmann.*[38]

So, how does Kai Diekmann tick? I personally met him several times, and during conversations in the *Bild* editorial offices, he came across as a likeable and utmost reliable person, but also as a very powerful person – and as a conservative, through and through. Diekmann is a member of the Franconia Burschenschaft (student fraternity) in Münster.[39] Diekmann became a Franconian in 1983, left the fraternity in 1985 and later rejoined it.[40] Even if he wanted to, Diekmann could not join the SPD. Because these two organizations are mutually incompatible: SPD members are forbidden from being a member of a fraternal organization.[41] Anyone who is in a fraternal organization is automatically a member of a gigantic network. Many politicians and business leaders are or were in similar fraternal orders: The CSU politician Markus Söder is with the Nuremberg Teutons, the CDU politician Bernhard Vogel is with Arminia in Mainz, the Austrian FPÖ politician Heinz-Christian Strache is with Vandalia Vienna, the CSU politician Hans-Peter Uhl is with Arminia-Rhenania in Munich, the Green politician Rezzo Schlauch is with Saxo-Silesia in Freiburg, the CSU politician Peter Ramsauer is with Franco-Bavaria in Munich, the CSU politician Edmund Stoiber is a member of the Catholic German student fraternity K.D.St.V. Trifels Munich, the former head of the Federal

Intelligence Service (BND) and Foreign Minister Klaus Kinkel is a member of the Catholic Students' Association A.V. Guestfalia Tübingen, the former Prime Minister of Baden-Württemberg and current EU politician Günther Oettinger is a member of the National Brotherhood of Ulmia Tübingen and the former Chairman of the Supervisory Board of Allianz (insurance), Henning Schulte-Noelle, got the big scar on his face, his dueling scar, from a fraternity beating.

Elite researcher, Stephan Peters, says that nobody brags in public that they're in a fraternal organization, but it's a well-oiled network – with tens of thousands of members.[42]

Connections are important. So, what connections does Diekmann the journalist have in addition to his old fraternity? As of 2004, he has been on the advisory board of the Turkish daily newspaper *Hürriyet*.[43] You have to understand his love for Turkey if you want to know why the *Bild* newspaper sometimes publishes entire articles in Turkish. Diekmann wants Turkey to become a member of the EU. He states:

I regularly spend my holidays in Turkey with Turkish friends. My personal assistant has Turkish roots. (...) Frankly, I could claim that I am the most Turkish editor-in-chief in the history of the Bild *newspaper.*[44]

Springer publishing, Diekmann's employer, has financial interests in Turkey. This is all information that you can look up for yourself. However, it might be much more interesting to take a look at the information, often kept secret from us, that shows how an elite network is pulling the strings behind the scenes here. Let's read an article on this from the *Frankfurter Allgemeine Zeitung* published on February 24, 2011, under the headline:

Zu Guttenberg, "Bild" and the Atlantik-Brücke[45]

Klaus-Dieter Frankenberger, head of the FAZ's foreign policy desk, reported in the article on the confusion over an appeal to the "Young Leaders" alumni of the elite network, the Atlantik-Brücke. (Incidentally, the Atlantik-Brücke advertises through Klaus-Dieter Frankenberger, something he doesn't share with the readers of his FAZ biography).[46] A former managing director of the association, Beate Lindemann, asked to take part in the *Bild* newspaper's telephone action and to speak out in favor of the "Young Leader" alumnus Karl-Theodor zu Guttenberg remaining in office as the Minister of Defense. Beforehand, the *Bild* had appealed for a "Guttenberg Decision!" on their front page. After this, though, the board of the Atlantik-Brücke once again distanced itself from the appeal. The article I mention here is completely irrelevant, both for us and for history, but the really intriguing part is an interesting fact that was left out of the article: Kai Diekmann himself is a member of the Atlantik-Brücke. And, just like Guttenberg, he was also a participant in the "Young Leaders" Program – namely in 1995.[47]

This Atlantik-Brücke that Diekmann is a member of, is also called a "secret lodge."[48] And it is considered to be "close to the CIA." In a report on this by Markus Kompa, he writes:

Their proximity to the CIA is not even played down, seeing that the Atlantik-Brücke officially presents the Vernon Walters Award – in honor of a deputy CIA director who was involved in extremely dirty coup d'états like in Iran (1954), Brazil (1964) and Chile (1973), and who was involved in subverting trade unions in Italy in the 1960s. Eastern intelligence agencies consider Walters, the sworn communist-hater, to be the mastermind, bar none.[49]

The same report also discusses whether certain journalists' proximity to the Atlantik-Brücke could have an influence on their reporting. It goes on:

Anyone who wonders why the Bild newspaper and Spiegel write so enthusiastically against Russia and reflexively identify any opinions differing from the US view as "anti-Americanism" will probably find their answer if they look into its membership list. Since it bestows honors on prominent journalists, is isn't surprising that there are hardly any critical reports on the Atlantik-Brücke in the press at all.[50]

Is it pure conspiracy theory if you believe that people like Kai Diekmann are caught up in a network of elites that influences their reporting? To find out, let's take a closer look at this elite network, where journalists, politicians and businessmen meet discreetly and the public is often denied access entirely. Will we find "corruption by association" here? Before we go any further, I can't omit the fact that I used to belong to parts of this network myself – and I was corrupted by it.

Bridge over the Atlantic

In 2014, Tina Hassel, director of the ARD studio in Washington D. C., was nominated to succeed Ulrich Deppendorf in mid-2015 and become the first woman editor-in-chief to head up the ARD studio in the US capital.[51] To this, ARD's chairman said, "Tina Hassel has exactly the credentials that the director of the ARD studio in the American capital should have"[52] He named many reasons for their decision, including her previous posts as a correspondent and her leadership qualifications. Other well-known journalists also spoke up and referred to Tina Hassel's qualifications. Interestingly enough: Nobody mentioned her connection to the Atlantik-Brücke, the Atlantic Bridge. Nevertheless, in the 2011/2012 Atlantik-Brücke Annual Report, she shows up in their official documentation at a meeting of the Rhine/Ruhr regional group and, in the 2010/2011 Annual Report, in the USA working group.[53]

Karl-Theodor zu Guttenberg, Kai Diekmann, Tina Hassel – so many famous names are found in connection with an organization that is virtually unknown to the public. An organization that is also referred to as a "secret lodge" and "close to the CIA".[54] The closer you look, the more amazing it becomes: Claus Kleber, director from 2003-2009, and anchor of the ZDF *heute-journal* since 2003, is a member of the Atlantik-Brücke Foundation's board of trustees.[55] The journalist Stefan Kornelius, director of the SZ's foreign policy desk, admitted in an NDR interview that he was a member of the Atlantik-Brücke.[56] The newspaper had an interest in him being in the organization and even paid for his membership. He calls this proximity a "part of my business."[57] Uwe Krüger, a communications scientist, had accused people like Kornelius of being close to the Atlantik-Brücke and claimed that the journalists who have been members there had adopted its way of thinking. Kornelius rejected this assertion. The US correspondent for the *Süddeutsche Zeitung*, Christian Wernicke, was present on a trip to Washington for members of the organization in 2012.[58] The well-known ZDF host Cherno Jobatey is also listed there.[59] The influential journalist Constanze Stelzenmüller[60] also shows up in connection with Atlantik-Brücke,[61] as well as the ZDF man Theo Koll.[62]

So who is hiding behind this peculiar association? And who is exercising influence on whom? Certainly, after seeing all of the names listed here, you might imagine that we're simply dealing with an association of or for journalists. Far from it. Here, it's all about the power of opinion, and the authority over opinions.

The "Atlantik-Brücke e.V." was described in the January 29, 1958 issue of *Der Spiegel* as a "society of former occupation force functionaries in post-war Germany." Knowing this, it's no longer surprising to learn that the "Atlantik-Brücke" published the English-language brochure, "Meet Germany," for the US soldiers stationed in Germany from 1957 to 1970. Ultimately, it is a propaganda organization of a "former" occupation force. So, why are people like the boss at the *Bild* newspaper, Kai Diekmann, members there?

The Atlantik-Brücke is an officially registered association (e.V. or *eingetragener Verein*).[63] There are about 600,000 registered associations or clubs in Germany.[64] Among all the pellet-gun clubs and rabbit breeders' associations, rowing teams and gardening societies, a quick glance at the list of people close to the Atlantik-Brücke, not to mention its membership, shows us that there is something very special about this organization.

Sitting on the board of this illustrious association we find the former CDU treasurer, Walther Leisler Kiep, as its honorary chairman. He was also a member of the Supervisory Board at Volkswagen and the Atlantik-Brücke's Chairman of the Board from 1984 to 2000. The current chairman of the Atlantik-Brücke is the CDU politician, Friedrich Merz, who is also a member of the Trilateral Commission,[65] a lobbying organization founded by David Rockefeller. The Vice-President of the German Bundestag, Edelgard Bulmahn (SPD), is the Vice-Chairman. She is also at the same time a member of Rockefeller's Trilateral Commission, a private association representing the interests of the financial sector. Management consultant Burkhard Schwenker is also a Vice-Chairman of the Atlantik-Brücke. Their treasurer is Andreas R. Dombret, a German-American bank manager who was a partner at Rothschild and is in a leading position at the Bank of America. Today, he is a board member at the Deutsche Bundesbank.[66] Richard von Weizsäcker, the German Federal President from 1984 to 1994, is an honorary member. The Atlantik association's home page lists additional board members: Kai Diekmann, Axel Springer SE, Berlin (Europe's largest publisher); Jürgen Fitschen, Deutsche Bank AG, Frankfurt; Angelika Gilford, Hewlett-Packard GmbH, Böblingen; Dr. Eng. Jürgen R. Grossmann, Georgsmarienhütte Holding GmbH (GMH Gruppe), Hamburg; Dr. Ingrid Hengster, KfW Bankengruppe (formerly the Credit Institute for Reconstruction, formed as a part of the Marshall Plan), Frankfurt; Prof. Dr. Michael Hüther, German Economic Institute, Cologne; Wolfgang Ischinger, Allianz SE, Munich; Eckart von Klaeden, Daimler AG, Berlin; Alexander Graf Lambsdorff, MEP Alliance of the Liberals and Democrats for Europe (ALDE), European Parliament, Brussels; Secretary of State Christian Lange, MB (SPD), Federal Ministry of Justice and Consumer Protection, Berlin; Philipp Missfelder, MB (CDU/CSU), German Bundestag, Berlin; Omid Nouripour, MB (Alliance 90/The Greens), German Bundestag, Berlin; Lawrence A. Rosen, Deutsche Post AG, Bonn; Karsten Uhlmann, Frankfurter Brauhaus GmbH, Frankfurt (Oder); Michael Zissis Vassiliadis, Industriegewerkschaft Bergbau, Chemie, Energie (IG BCE), Hannover und Max M. Warburg, M.M. Warburg & CO, Hamburg.[67]

Before we get into these illustrious members any further, a brief overview of the Atlantik-Brücke should give you an idea of what's going on there: The Atlantik-Brücke was founded as a private organization in 1952, at the suggestion of the former World Bank President John McCloy. At the time, McCloy was the chairman of Rockefeller's Chase Manhattan Bank. McCloy had been the first to be appointed by the US President as the High Commissioner of Germany (USHCG), i.e. the ranking representative of the American occupation forces in West Germany. The journalist, Marion Gräfin Dönhoff, co-editor of the weekly newspaper *Die Zeit*, was one of the founding members of the Atlantik-Brücke, whose aim of influencing public opinion with all means at the media's disposal was taken for granted. Officially, at least according to its statutes, the association had the stated aim of "pursuing educational, scientific, cultural and charitable purposes, as well as the promotion of international understanding." However, the truth is that, from the very beginning, its purpose was organizing a personal network of senior leaders who would be able to shape public opinion. In 1981, the

Frankfurter Allgemeine Zeitung called the Atlantik-Brücke an "elitist co-determination group" and called its work for democracy questionable from a purist's point of view.[68]

Today, the FAZ doesn't seem to fear rubbing elbows with this elitist group anymore. The head of the FAZ's foreign policy desk, Klaus-Dieter Frankenberger, is mentioned in this context on page 129 of the Atlantik-Brücke's 2009/2010 Annual Report from 10 June, 2010. There it states:

79th Meeting of the USA working group: "Security Partnership with the United States: Implications and Consequences for Germany and the EU," introduces: Hans-Ulrich Klose, MB, Coordinator for German-American Cooperation in the Foreign Office, Berlin, Stéphane Beemelmans, Department Head for Fundamental Issues EU and International Affairs; New Federal States, Federal Ministry of the Interior, Berlin, and Klaus-Dieter Frankenberger, Head of the Foreign Policy Desk, FRANKFURTER ALLGEMEINE ZEITUNG, Frankfurt; "Report from Washington," Ambassador (ret.) John C. Kornblum, Magnus-Haus, Berlin.[69]

In the 2006/2007 Annual Report, Frankenberger's photo at an event is on page 98.[70] Additionally, the Atlantik-Brücke advertises with Klaus-Dieter Frankenberger, which he does not share with anyone who reads his FAZ biography.[71] This is not an isolated case of the proximity that renowned journalists have to this controversial institution: In the years between 2006 and 2012, 88 journalists are mentioned in their annual reports, 26 of them alone working for state-run, publicly-funded media outlets. In other words: Journalists don't seem to see a need for keeping their distance. This pro-American, and certainly non-neutral organization, keeps creeping further and further into the forefront of the German media's reporting.

Now, "pro-American" is not necessarily a dirty word. We're not talking about good or bad here, but primarily about a value system that is operating in the background. So, who does Germany and the German media share a common value system with? Certainly, with countries like the Netherlands, Austria, Switzerland and Spain. Certainly not with NATO. And Germany certainly doesn't share a common value system with Erdogan's Turkey. What about the USA? Here, too, the answer is clear. Germans and Americans share many common values such as democracy, freedom of expression and the freedom of the press. However, we already run into major differences of opinion when it comes to questions of international law and the rule of law itself. The war in Iraq, Guantanamo Bay or drone executions are absolutely incompatible with German law. That our freedom is clearly being restricted by American espionage, something that violates the privacy of German citizens on a daily basis, is the clearest proof that we do not share a common value system with the United States and that we certainly don't see eye-to-eye with Washington. Thus, when German journalists debase themselves by associating with pro-American organizations like the Atlantik-Brücke, are present at their events or even support them at all, they are effectively abandoning our modern German value system. In doing so, these journalists become partial advocates and/or lobbyists for a foreign value system.

On March 12, 2010, in cooperation with the television station Phoenix, German public television broadcast its first Atlantik-Brücke event. On March 10, 2010, the Atlantik-Brücke had organized a discussion at the University of the German Federal Armed Forces (Bundeswehr) in Hamburg with former Chancellor Helmut Schmidt and the then Federal Minister of Defense Karl-Theodor zu Guttenberg on the subject of "Bundeswehr Mission: Flashpoint Afghanistan." The discussion was moderated by Friedrich Merz, chairman of the Atlantik-Brücke. To understand this properly, you have to know that Helmut Schmidt is a member of the Atlantik-Brücke and Guttenberg was one of the Atlantik-Brücke's "Young Leaders." So, viewers got to see a nice little chat among this club's members – and that, on German public television.[72]

The *Bild* newspaper, whose boss Diekmann is also a member of the Atlantik-Brücke, proffered the headline: "Former Chancellor and Defense Minister Discuss in Hamburg – What Guttenberg Can Learn from Schmidt."[73] We should also remember that Diekmann and Guttenberg were also good buddies at the time. Were the television viewers and newspaper readers aware of all this? I don't think so. It was a textbook example of: How to influence public opinion. A few opinion makers who all think alike meet, "discuss" – and their subservient media reports on it.

The proximity of this association to German politics is also quite conspicuous when you consider the address of the Atlantik-Brücke's current headquarters: It is literally located in the building adjacent to Chancellor Angela Merkel's private apartment. This was confirmed by a managing director of the Atlantik-Brücke in an interview – and also, that Angela Merkel is likewise a member.[74] Now, who still finds it surprising that Angela Merkel continues to sing the Atlantik-Brücke's praises?

That said, what does this association want? A former chairman of the association, Arend Oetker, put it this way, "The USA is run by 200 families and we want to have good contacts with them."[75] So, apart from their above-mentioned influence on the media, is this really all that they want?

The Atlantik-Brücke – as mentioned – presents the Vernon A. Walters Award. This prize is "awarded to persons who have rendered extraordinary service to German-American relations." The prize is named after the former US ambassador to Germany (1989-1991), Vernon A. Walters, who accompanied the reunification of Germany from the American side. Previous recipients of the award: Liz Mohn (Bertelsmann Foundation, 2008), Dr. Jürgen R. Großmann (Georgsmarienhütte Holding GmbH, 2007), Dr. Dieter

Zetsche (DaimlerChrysler AG, 2006), Dr. Michael Otto (Otto Group, 2005), Wolfgang Mayrhuber (Lufthansa AG, 2004), Dr. Bernd Pischetsrieder (Volkswagen AG, 2002), Dr. Manfred Schneider (Bayer AG, 2000), Dr. Henning Schulte-Noelle (Allianz AG, 1999), Dr. Thomas Middelhoff (Bertelsmann AG, 1998), Dr. Rolf-E. Breuer (Deutsche Bank AG, 1997), Jürgen E. Schrempp (Daimler Benz AG, 1996), Jürgen Dormann (Aventis Hoechst AG, 1995), Eberhard von Kuenheim (BMW AG, 1994), Louis R. Hughes (General Motors, 1993)."[76]

Alas, the Atlantik-Brücke is forgetting one tiny detail in this description: Vernon A. Walters (1917 - 2002) was a foreign intelligence coordinator for the USA and one-time Director of Central Intelligence. He consistently described the Vietnam War, despite its millions of victims, as "one of the most noble and selfless wars the United States has ever waged."[77] Also, it was precisely this agency man, Vernon A. Walters, who lay the foundations for the secret Gladio network in Europe. Vernon Walters began his service with the US Armed Forces in 1941, and occupied positions in American intelligence services from the very beginning of his career. He was significantly involved in subversive activities in all of the political hot spots throughout the second half of the 20th century, including: the Korean War (1950-1953), the coup d'état against the democratically elected Prime Minister of Iran, Mohammad Mossadegh (1953), the intelligence operations to prevent communist success in Italian elections (1960-1962), and the bloody military coup in Brazil (1964). He was Director of the CIA and, in this capacity, responsible for the CIA operation "Centauro," which provided comprehensive support for the military coup in Chile (1973), and in the activities used to stifle the Carnation Revolution in Portugal (1974). He can be traced to the violent subversion of democratic developments in Angola, Guatemala, and Nicaragua, and the years of human rights violations by the military regimes in South America (Operation "Condor"), in which hundreds of thousands of people were murdered, abducted or tortured there. Today, without mentioning any of this, the Atlantik-Brücke still awards a prize that honors this agency man.[78] And people like the German Chancellor Angela Merkel and the *Bild's* boss Kai Diekmann are members there. Even the FAZ seems to feel at home there.

One thing you need know regarding the transatlantic organizations mentioned here with journalists among their membership: They are always repeating a variation of the same theme over and over again at their numerous transatlantic meetings. The most important being the assumption of shared values, a transatlantic value system whose common, fundamental values are so self-evident they don't ever need to be discussed. Through constant repetition, this assertion has long since developed a life of its own. It is like a form of brainwashing. Only the German participants don't usually notice that they're getting a pro-American brainwashing. On closer inspection, however, it's plain to see that Germany has many values that stand in official opposition to America's official policy. These range from the death penalty and extrajudicial drone executions in distant lands to military deployments in foreign wars. All of these are rejected by the majority of Germans. All the pro-American mainstream media presented in this book, however, support German participation in foreign wars alongside the USA, and they support extrajudicial executions implemented by drones. This includes when they report on behalf of the arms lobby at the Munich Security Conference. This alone shows the effects of their brainwashing. And always there in the background: the intelligence agencies.

In truth, all of these transatlantic organizations are only dedicated to bolstering support for NATO, getting their direction from the USA. Germans are merely vassals in this equation. The historian and NATO expert Daniele Ganser is convinced that Germany, thanks to its integration in this military alliance, is nothing more than a "vassal state of the USA." He states:

NATO has NATO ambassadors in all NATO member countries. These are the ambassadors that every country sends to get updated on what NATO wants next. These channels function in such a way that NATO – and the USA in particular – says: That's the way it is and now you must do this. (...) Then, the Europeans often simply obey.[79]

Now, you should know that the Atlantik-Brücke organizes annual, confidential, high-ranking talks with the US European Command.[80] The purpose of these discussions is to create a confidential (!) forum where the commanders of the American branches of their armed forces stationed in Europe – the Army, Navy, Air Force and Marines – and the Inspector General of the German Armed Forces, together with his generals and admirals, can exchange information with other experts on current security policy issues. "The talks with USEUCOM (U.S. European Command) bring together high-ranking representatives from the U.S. European Command and the Bundeswehr with defense experts from government, industry and the media."[81] That is a direct quote from the Atlantik-Brücke's 2013/2014 Annual Report.

There is no transparency there whatsoever. These are exclusive events where ordinary citizens have absolutely no access. Just try getting inside one of the Atlantik-Brücke's events yourself, one where our alpha journalists naturally have a seat reserved for them. All of this is truly a scandal of the first order, because USEUCOM (U.S. European Command) is planning wars in Europe and the media is expected to cover their flanks with propaganda. This was easy to see after the crash of a Malaysian airliner in Ukraine in the summer of 2014. The *U.S. European Command* was planning a major NATO exercise in Ukraine for September of 2014. A newspaper report on this stated:

The US Army Europe and the Ukrainian army will lead the maneuver, in which about 1300 soldiers from 16 nations should be participating. It will take place on the almost 400-square-kilometer military training area near Yavoriv, not far from Lviv. In addition to Armenia, Azerbaijan, Bulgaria, Canada, Georgia, Great Britain, Latvia, Lithuania, the Republic of Moldova, Norway, Poland, Romania, Spain, Ukraine and the USA, Germany is also expected to send military personnel.[82]

Now do you understand why the German "quality media" discusses wars (which they play down as "security architecture") in "expert talks" with the U.S. European Command? Upon closer inspection, are these journalists anything more than biased NATO propagandists? If you are a journalist and you attend these "expert talks" with the U.S. European Command and then afterwards, you write everything from a NATO perspective... I'm sorry, but this doesn't have anything to do with "independent" journalism anymore.

In the Stranglehold of the Intelligence Agencies

Ever since the revelations of the whistleblower Edward Snowden at the latest, we now know: There is a Big Brother out there, he's the United States, and he knows everything about us. About every single one of us. As long as we do what he wants, he's a very kind big brother. However, when we disagree with him, certain things happen that would have been the stuff of conspiracy theories in the past. Professor Werner Weidenfeld is more familiar with this Big Brother than many others. After all, he was the German government's coordinator for German-American cooperation for many years. On the talk show *Beckmann*, he told us how this "friendship" between Germany and the USA functions in practice:

I can tell you, that in my 12 years as America Coordinator, I have experienced three behaviors from the American government. The moment you agree with them, they're your best friend, they hug you, you start worrying about your ribs they hug you so hard. When we disagree on secondary issues, then the American government always says, and this is happening to us, 'Where is your historical gratitude? We conquered and preserved the freedom and security of the German people.' When we have a different opinion on a serious question, however, then they put intelligence agency materials on the table that would incriminate Germany and either you play ball or you're next. (...) The Americans have a very clear understanding of their interests. (...) And it is implemented accordingly. That is the reality.[83]

What's clear: Since the 1950s, American intelligence agencies have founded and financed a wide range of private, charitable foundations in Germany. All of them have one primary goal: The establishment of intelligence agency outposts operating under the guise of philanthropic institutions. Here, agent handlers can be accommodated as alleged employees of these foundations. Their purpose is then to exert pro-American influence on the future German elite and, wherever possible, make them susceptible to blackmail.

So, let's take a closer look at the relationship some of these American foundations have to US intelligence services. Whenever German journalists, politicians and business leaders have a large meeting under the auspices of US think tanks, it's entirely possible that the CIA or other American agencies are sitting right there at the table with them. I have also participated as a fellow at such organizations' events. For example, I was once invited on a six-week, all-expenses-paid trip to America by the German Marshall Fund (officially approved by the FAZ). During trips like these, getting an invitation to meet with BND station chiefs and even being introduced to American agency employees seemed like it was just par for the course. It's no secret that the German Marshall Fund maintains impeccable relations with intelligence agencies: In June of 2014, when the former heads of the Saudi and Israeli military intelligence agencies met, naturally, this took place at the German Marshall Fund.[84] Karen Donfried, the first female president of the Marshall Fund, was previously a special assistant to the President in Obama's National Security Council, responsible for European affairs.[85] There are former, senior GMF employees who are also represented as having close ties to intelligence agencies.[86] Suzanne Woolsey, wife of the former CIA Director James Woolsey, is a director and member of the board of trustees of the German Marshall Fund.[87] And yes: I got my contact to her husband, the CIA boss James Woolsey, through the German Marshall Fund.

As I already described, the German Marshall Fund's behavior toward those of us on that trip was similar to the billionaire Sultan of Oman's behavior. The Marshall Fund gave each of us an envelope full of cash to facilitate our stay in the US. I got my choice of air-conditioned rental cars, gas included of course, just like the hotels, laundry service and meals were included. As you already know from my experiences with the nice billionaire from Oman, there were also gifts. You may recall that the Sultan paid for a private diving instructor so I could complete the training and become a PADI-certified rescue diver. Well, while visiting an American company during my first-class, transatlantic trip paid for by the German Marshall Fund, I was astonished to receive the most important components of a scuba diving set as gift. The Americans obviously had exact knowledge of the bribes I had previously accepted in Oman. Afterward, I was allowed to test out the new equipment at a depth of almost 60 meters with a US Navy SEAL team near San Diego. This was the journey where the German Marshall Fund (as I already mentioned) surprised me with an honorary citizenship certificate from the State of Oklahoma. At some point during this trip through the USA, I lost complete track of who was really only representing the German Marshall Fund and who was more likely a direct employee of one of the various US intelligence services. The only thing that was clear, and they made no secret of it, was that there were very close connections between the two. Today, I suspect that this is the case with many of the transatlantic organizations that were founded by or with the help of US intelligence agencies.

When I was on assignment in the Middle East for the *Frankfurter Allgemeine Zeitung*, in light of the "agreements" I had made in earlier, purely coincidental, "intelligence-related talks," there were certain situations where I made sure to report to the intelligence services first and the FAZ last. During my trips abroad, I would pass on important, new pieces of information to the "military attaché" of the German embassy (usually a BND man) and the local Americans before I finally submitted anything to my employers at the FAZ.

I don't know whether such agreements were or are made on the fringes of invitations from the Atlantik-Brücke, say, over the course of their "Young Leaders Program." I can only imagine that these candidates go through a similar, initiation-like process to the one I did throughout the series of invitations I accepted. (Could this also take place without the Atlantik-Brücke's direct knowledge)? On page 145 of her book, *Krieg, Atom, Armut. Was sie reden, was sie tun: Die Grünen (War, Nuclear, Poverty. What they say, what they do: the Greens (not available in English))*, Jutta Ditfurth describes how young German politicians visiting the USA are instrumentalized in very general terms for pro-American purposes. She writes:

> *Although the evening ended in an unresolved dispute, our host from the American Institute for Contemporary German Studies remained surprisingly calm and asked me if I was ready to write a research paper on my party. I rejected the offer. To persuade me, he gave the names of Green party members who were more willing to cooperate. One was Lukas Beckmann, the other, Otto Schily. We knew Petra Kelly well. My answer remained no. I learned a lot during this time about what "additional training" German politicians are offered when the Americans consider them to be useful leaders. Eleven years later, I was reminded of this when I read, we know Fischer well. This is their usual, conventional manner of speech, as you can see it again today in the Wikileaks documents, for example, the ones on Defense Minister zu Guttenberg.*[88]

I have had similar experiences to the ones Jutta Ditfurth describes having in the USA, both in the USA and in Germany. Therefore, I can say from my own experience that you don't even feel their embrace, particularly that of the intelligence services, for many years. Here, I would like to take a moment to flashback to one of my own early experiences. This is what happened when the BND were making their first delicate attempts at initiating me – at the time, I had no idea that I would become a journalist one day:

At the beginning of the eighties, I was studying law and politics in Freiburg im Breisgau. The 1979/80 spring semester was almost over, and the summer break was approaching. A trip to Italy was in the works. Since I still had to finance my upcoming semester, I planned to work on a construction site or as a waiter when I got back from vacation. Making money had always been a part of my semester breaks and I didn't want to skip a single opportunity. At the time, I had about as much knowledge of the Federal Intelligence Service (BND) as anyone else. It didn't play any role in my studies, and I didn't have any special interest in what their agents did. This didn't change until much later. Back in those days, professors were still persons of respect and, as a student, you didn't just immediately dismiss any of their suggestions without giving them a little thought. So, after a lecture right before the semester break, when one of these respected elders handed me a leaflet, it was only natural that I listened politely and attentively to what he had to say. At first glance, it looked like it was some kind of a flyer. It was an invitation. "You should definitely take part in this. Afterwards, tell me how you liked it," the law professor said. A respected man. A distinguished man. And a man with a double life. I have no idea whether he approached or invited other students, but it wouldn't surprise me. In and of itself, there was nothing unusual about getting an invitation to an extracurricular educational seminar. The professors knew their students, those who stood out were encouraged to do more. That's how it still is today. So, I didn't have any reason to think it was anything out of the ordinary.

Looking back, I am sure the honorable professor was a recruiter for the BND. How deeply he was tangled up in the net – I'm not so sure. I also don't remember having had any follow-up discussions with him about these initial meetings. His flyer was an invitation to a "Seminar on Conflict Research." The main focus: "Introduction to the Problematic Nature of the East-West Conflict." At the time, I couldn't have imagined anything more boring. I was still thinking of how I could politely express my lack of interest to the professor when he said, "There is a daily allowance of 20 marks, the cost of the train to the conference venue in Bonn will also be reimbursed. And naturally, there will be a hotel room waiting for you there. Finally, you will also get 150 marks for books." It was like music to my ears. The professor suddenly had my undivided attention. Working eight hours of construction, I could earn 50 marks at the most. On the other hand, with the prospect of a free hotel room, warm meals and a little extra financial icing on the cake – I suddenly wondered why I hadn't ever felt such a strong inner desire to attend a "seminar on conflict research" before. Now, I was simply unable to suppress this deep desire any longer. The professor was visibly pleased when I accepted his offer. The "Studiengesellschaft für Zeitprobleme" (Study Society for Contemporary Problems) – which no longer exists anymore –

was located at 88 Ubierstrasse in Bad Godesberg, an upscale suburb of Bonn, the former West German capital. It was financed by the Ministry of Defense. Today, it's a well-recognized fact that this organization was connected to the BND. The BND critic Erich Schmidt-Eenboom described seminars like these and the practice of recruiting students many years later in his 1998 book, *Undercover – Der BND und die deutschen Journalisten (Undercover – the BND and the German Journalists (not available in English))*. On February 25, 1980, I met about 20 other students in the old, two-story, bourgeois villa-style building at Ubierstrasse 88. The students hadn't only come from all over Germany, but from all over the world, and now they were finally getting their chance to delve into the true origins of the East-West conflict. In lectures that bored us to tears, we learned a lot about the Soviet Union and East Germany. We acted out role-plays in which we criticized or defended communism. In discussions with the other students, I learned that they too had also found their way to the then West German capital in a similar way – they had been recommended for an extracurricular training seminar. One thing that was perhaps a little strange was the fact that we were forbidden from going upstairs in the old building. The stairs leading up to the mysterious second floor were off limits. At the time, none of us had a clue that we were being observed. A man who we occasionally met in the house spent a lot of time upstairs, but we weren't aware of his role in all this. He called himself Schulte – I don't know if that was his real name or not. As it turned out, Mr. Schulte was quite well informed about each and every one of us. The role-plays and endless discussions were nothing other than a well disguised series of attitude tests by the German intelligence services. It never dawned on any of us. According to Schmidt-Eenboom, Rudolf Rothe, the managing director of the Studies Society at the time, subsequently stated that he knew nothing about Mr. Schulte's work.

Later, during my trips to the USA, I had several more experiences with scenarios of exactly the same nature. When a large and generous organization financed the trip, they would carefully observe every second of what we participants did or didn't do in a variety of different situations. When Jutta Ditfurth reports on the "additional training" she was offered during her trips to the USA – then I can confirm that. This is also the main reason you should avoid getting involved with organizations like these: It's easy to lose any backbone you might have there.

So why is the Atlantik-Brücke considered to be close to the CIA? Are there also things happening there in secret? Like I experienced in another form at the Studies Society for Contemporary Problems? There are people who have changed their minds and turned their backs on the Atlantik-Brücke. This includes the Green Party politician, Katrin Göring-Eckardt. At first, she was somewhat naive and said:

I am, like some of the other GREENS, a member of the Atlantik-Brücke association. The Atlantik-Brücke is an association that – as it's written in its mission statement – serves to promote international understanding. It is a registered association, which operates on the basis of association law (so, it is just as democratic as a sports club or the like), and it offers conferences and off-the-record discussions on foreign policy issues, transatlantic relations in particular. These are topics that are important to us GREENS and for this, we should keep the lines of communication open with journalists, people from the world of business and our political competitors, in this or in other contexts.[89]

In 2009/2010, she was even a member of the board there. In the meantime, she has reportedly cancelled her membership.[90] Claudia Roth, who was in the Atlantik-Brücke from 2005 to 2010, has also announced her departure in the meantime.[91] Cem Özdemir also states that he has nothing to do with it anymore.[92] However, in a more recent Atlantik-Brücke brochure, Cem Özdemir is named as one of the most prominent graduates of the "Young Leaders" program.[93] When an interviewer asked him about the Atlantik-Brücke and the "Young Leaders," Özdemir declared that the reporter must be a conspiracy theorist and needed medical help.[94] In the interview, Özdemir says in all seriousness, "Conspiracy theories are something that should be treated medically, so coming from politics, I am the wrong person to be talking to. (...) I would be more interested in what your therapist says about that." Mind you, on page 47 of the Atlantik-Brücke's 2010/2011 Annual Report, Cem Özdemir is pictured and mentioned by name in connection with the "Young Leaders" program. Perhaps Cem Özdemir will sue the Atlantik-Brücke association for listing him as one of their most prominent new recruits in the "Young Leaders" program.[95]

The *Berliner Zeitung* once wrote about the peculiarities and secrecy of the Atlantik-Brücke:

"The fact that little is known about the Atlantik-Brücke's activities is intentional. It is not the kind of club that wants to make waves. Rather, they act in silence, which sometimes gives the association the image of being a secret society – and the reputation of an elite club. One does not apply for membership in the Atlantik-Brücke, one is invited to do so. Its influence is considered significant. The Atlantik-Brücke is supported by all the major German corporations. The names of the board members (...) reads like a Who's Who of business and politics. And, on the other side of the Atlantic, the partners in this dialogue are no less influential."[96]

Today the Atlantik-Brücke has about 500 members. Half of them are from industry, about 100 are from politics and the rest are from science, social organizations, trade unions and, above all, the media.

The Names: Controversial Contacts

Journalists disinform and manufacture opinion. This means that they surely have an influence on politics, but who has an influence on our journalists? Who manufactures their opinions? Certainly, the Atlantik-Brücke belongs in this category. Its members make sure that public opinion is wholly influenced in the pro-American spirit of the association. In this respect, we can observe well-known journalists also being regularly invited to events organized by the Atlantik-Brücke or discussions with its members. Going through their annual reports from 2006 to 2012, you will find the names of 88 journalists. Among them there are also many well-known journalists who work for state-run, taxpayer-funded, public broadcasting companies. The following is a list of these journalists. This list does not claim that they are or were members or "Young Leaders" of this association. Only the contacts that were published by the Atlantik-Brücke in their 2006/2007 to 2011/2012 annual reports and in other Atlantik-Brücke documentation are listed here:[97]

Last Name	First Name	Media Affiliation
Schönenborn	Jörg	ARD – Chief Editor for WDR Television
Deiß	Matthias	ARD – Main Studio
Roth	Thomas	ARD – Correspondent in New York
Mikich	Sonia	ARD – Director of WDR's domestic programming group - Monitor
Wabnitz, Dr.	Bernhard	ARD – Host Weltspiegel
Hassel	Tina	ARD – Washington studio since 01 Jul 2012
Zamperoni	Ingo	ARD – Tagesthemen, Nachtmagazin
Ehni	Ellen	ARD – WDR Television – Program Group Director – Economics and Law
Jahn	Frank	ARD – London Correspondent
Wilhelm	Ulrich	Bavarian Broadcasting (BR) – Artistic Director
Schoeller	Olivia	Berliner Zeitung, Frankfurter Rundschau – Director of the Panorama Dept., former USA Correspondent
Diekmann	Kai	*Bild* Newspaper – Chief Editor
Kallen, Dr.	Paul-Bernhard	Burda Media – Chairman of the Board
Pleitgen	Frederik	CNN, previously ZDF, RTL, n-tv
Feo de, Dr.	Marika	Corriere della Sera – Germany Correspondent
Aslan	Ali	Deutsche Welle TV
Meurer	Friedbert	Deutschlandradio – Editorial Department Head - Zeitfunk
Stürmer, Prof. Dr.	Michael	Die Welt – Senior Correspondent, Die Welt – Chief Correspondent, Deutschlandfunk, Deutschlandradio Culture Author
Sommer	Theo	Die Zeit - Publisher, Editor-at-Large since 2000
Joffe	Josef	Die Zeit - Publisher
Naß	Matthias	Die Zeit – International Correspondent

Last Name	First Name	Media Affiliation
Brost	Marc	Die Zeit – Capital Office Director
Ross	Jan	Die Zeit - Editor
Stelzenmüller, Dr.	Constanze	Die Zeit – Editor, Director of the Berlin Office of the German Marshall Fund, Senior Transatlantic Fellow since 2009
Klingst	Martin	Die Zeit – US Correspondent
McLaughlin	Catriona	Die Zeit – Executive Secretary, Zeit online
Heckei	Margaret	fmr. Die Welt-Welt am Sonntag - Financial Times Germany Politics Director, freelance journalist and book author since 2009
Busse Dr.	Nikolas	Frankfurter Allgemeine Zeitung
Frankenberger	Klaus-Dieter	Frankfurter Allgemeine Zeitung - Editor
Wrangel, von	Cornelia	Frankfurter Allgemeine Zeitung - Editor
Kämmerer	Steffi	Freelance journalist, writes for Stern, Süddeutsche Zeitung, Spiegel, Spiegel online, Park Avenue
Seligmann	Rafael	Freelance journalist – published in Spiegel, B.Z., Die Welt, Bild, Frankfurter Allgemeine Sonntagszeitung, Jüdische Allgemeine, Atlantic Times
Schulte-Hillen	Gerd	Grüner und Jahr- Bertelsmann until 2003
Inacker, Dr.	Michael J.	Handelsblatt – Deputy Chief Editor
Steingart	Gabor	Handelsblatt Group – Management Board
Klasen-Bouvatier	Korinna	Jungle World
Marohn	Anna	NDR – Personal Secretary for Artistic Director Lutz Marmor
Diehl	Julia	NDR - Editor
Bremer	Heiner	n-tv – Host "Das Duell," Stern, Chief Editor
Kolz	Michael	Phoenix – Managing Editor, Ereignis 2 – Deputy Programming Manager
Augter, Dr.	Stefanie	Permanent Representative of the Federal Republic of German at the European Union, Brussels, Press Secretary for the Ministry of Family Affairs, Wirtschaftswoche, Handelsblatt
Arnold	Tim	ProSiebenSat1 - Senior Vice President of Political Strategy at ProSiebenSat.1 Group
Schremper, Dr.	Ralf	ProSiebenSat1 -CFO Digital & Adjacent
Ebeling	Thomas	ProSiebenSat1 - Chairman of the Board
Prochäzkovä	Bära	Respekt, Czech magazine
Krauel	Thorsten Wilhelm	Rheinischer Merkur – Dept. Head Domestic Policy
Ridderbusch	Katja	writes from Atlanta for Die Welt, Handelsblatt, Spiegel online, Deutschlandfunk, WDR, The European
Eloffmann	Christiane	Spiegel – Capital Office Director, FAZ
Hujer	Marc	Spiegel online
Trautmann, Dr.	Clemens	Springer Publishing – Döpfner Office Director
Klaeden von, Dr.	Dietrich	Springer Publishing – Director Government Relations

Last Name	First Name	Media Affiliation
Döpfner, Dr.	Matthias	Springer Publishing – Chairman of the Board
Gloger	Katja	Stern – Correspondent, Washington – fmr. wife of Georg Mascolo Chief Editor Spiegel
Wernicke	Christian	Süddeutsche Zeitung - US-Correspondent
Klüver	Reymer	Süddeutsche Zeitung - USA-Correspondent
Kornelius	Stefan	Süddeutsche Zeitung Foreign Policy Dept. Director
Dewitz von	Ariane	Tagesspiegel
Schäuble	Juliane	Tagesspiegel
Marschall, von	Christoph	Tagesspiegel - Correspondent Washington - Commentator Deutschlandfunk, Deutschlandradio, Cicero, Atlantic Times
Rohwedder	Cecilie	Tagesspiegel - Editor
Rimscha, von	Robert	Tagesspiegel until 2004, FDP, 2011 Ambassador to Laos
Karnitschnig	Matthew	Wall Street Journal – Germany Office Director
Hombach	Bodo	WAZ-Media Group – Managing Director, Bonner Akademie für Forschung und Lehre Praktischer Politik - University of Bonn (BAPP)
Koll	Theo	ZDF – Main Editorial Office Foreign, Domestic, Social and Educational Policy
Burgard, Dr.	Jan Philipp	ZDF – Capital Studio, Morgenmagazin
Kämpen van	Udo	ZDF – Director Brussels Studio
Kleber, Dr.	Claus-Detlev	ZDF – Host Heute Journal (German weekly version of the Daily Show)
Schmiese, Dr.	Wulf	ZDF – Host Morgenmagazin
Jobatey	Cherno	ZDF - Morgenmagazin
Theveßen	Elmar	ZDF – Deputy Chief Editor – Managing Editor-in-Chief Aktuelles

You can also see the list at: http://spiegelkabinett-blog.blogspot.de/2013/03/journalisten-der-atlantikbrucke-in.html

Every reader should form their own opinion and decide for themselves whether the aforementioned journalists really report transatlantic issues in an independent and non-partisan manner, or whether they are possibly pushing a particular perspective in some of their reports, especially a pro-American one. The Atlantik-Brücke would certainly welcome the latter and probably thinks of it as perfectly normal.

But let's take a closer look at these Atlantik-Brücke contacts using a very specific example. The FAZ journalist Nikolas Busse appears in the above table. The readers here already know his name from the embarrassing story in the chapter, "Well-Greased: The Sleazy System of Journalism Prizes," where depleted uranium munitions were glossed over for the Ministry of Defense.

In his own biography at the FAZ, journalist Nikolas Busse writes: "In November 1998, joined the political editorial staff at the *Frankfurter*

Allgemeine Zeitung. 2007, sent to Brussels as NATO and EU correspondent. Since September 2014, Deputy Editor in charge of foreign policy at the central office in Frankfurt."[98] That said, this journalist has a very responsible position and should therefore take great pains to make sure he presents himself as being completely neutral.

Far from it. What's not included in Busse's official FAZ résumé is that in February 2003, in a large-format advertisement placed in the New York Times by the Atlantik-Brücke, this journalist made a vow of allegiance to the United States. At least this is the impression I get from a huge advertisement proclaiming: "A Message to the People of the United States of America" by friends and members of the Atlantik-Brücke, where his name also appears at the bottom.[99]

Before we get into the details of Busse's invocation and the Atlantik-Brücke, here are some things to keep in mind: This newspaper advertisement was published only a few days before the American invasion of Iraq in March, 2003, in violation of international law. The then US Secretary of Defense Colin Powell had just presented falsified "evidence" to the UN Security Council that Iraq allegedly possessed weapons of mass destruction. At the time, it wasn't only the German Government that was against the American war in Iraq. Millions of Germans took to the streets to demonstrate against this impending war of aggression and they did it together with politicians from across the political spectrum. It was precisely at this moment that Busse, the FAZ employee in charge of security policy, sent a "message" to the American people in the New York Times, via the Atlantik-Brücke. If you read the ad in its entirety, then at least from my subjective point of view, it's nothing more than an oath of allegiance to the transatlantic partnership. Moreover, they did this knowing it was likely that the USA would be conducting a war of aggression against Iraq in violation of international law, (which they consequently did). It was also in March of 2003, by the way, that my last article appeared in the FAZ after working for them for 17 years. I felt that the FAZ's pro-American warmongering was outrageous at the time, especially given the prospect of the so many dead and wounded to come. I was also dealing with the aftermath of a serious accident at the time, having suffered debilitating nerve damage in my right leg, so the FAZ offered me a severance agreement. But I'll touch on that later when I get into personal experiences.

Back to the advertisement's "proclamation," or its message to the American people. It was straightforward: Nikolas Busse, as one of the several who signed it right before the invasion of Iraq, was announcing with his signature at the bottom that he would "spare no effort" to "preserve the bond between Germany and America for future generations." The man emphasized his "solidarity with the United States," and he announced his will "to defend" the value system he shares with the USA. By "value system," though, I don't know whether Busse means the excessive American espionage in Germany that has been evident for many years, the extrajudicial killings carried out at the order of the US President without trial, or the barbarous executions in US prisons. As the author of this book, I am convinced that this so-called "value system" is, for the most part, only a product of American propaganda. As the millions of demonstrators on the streets in 2003 showed, when it comes to the USA asserting their interests for raw materials and power, not everyone approves of their warmongering. Against this background, I also find it shameful that a FAZ employee can later become a NATO correspondent, knowing full well that he made such an oath of allegiance. And that, directly before a war of aggression in violation of international law. In February 2003, at the behest of the Atlantik-Brücke, this advertisement didn't only appear in the New York Times, it was also printed in some of the leading German papers including the FAZ and *Die Welt*. Thus, it was not only a matter of record in the USA, but also in Germany through Busse's own employer.[100] At the time, Busse was already in charge of "security policy" at the FAZ.

Of course, as a journalist, you are free to sign declarations. However, I asked the press offices at the Russian and Chinese embassies in Berlin if Busse had ever signed any similar declarations in favor of Moscow (for example, during the Crimean crisis) or in favor of Beijing in any Asian disputes. He hadn't. So, he has unilaterally committed himself to Washington alone. This is something that the FAZ readers should know about Busse, their NATO correspondent. If you're aware of his Atlantic oath of allegiance to the USA before the US war of aggression in Iraq, you will never read Busse's reporting on NATO through the same eyes again. At any rate, I have personally regarded Busse as an extension of the NATO press office ever since.

Another thing you have to know about Busse: Nikolas Busse, a mainstream journalist, also took part in the creation of the controversial and much-discussed study, "New Power – New Responsibility." This was a joint initiative by the US lobbying organization, the German Marshall Fund of the United States, and the German Institute for International and Security Affairs. It was sponsored by the planning staff at the Federal Foreign Office and published at the end of 2013.[101] Critics see the study as advocating the return of German militarism – under pressure from Washington.[102] Busse writes from this perspective, just how the Americans like it.[103]

It's harrowing when someone like this also appears publicly on television or hosts events, playing a supposedly neutral role. This is exactly what Busse does, whether it's for the Deutsche Nationalstiftung (German National Foundation) on the topic of "Which Reforms Does Europe Need?" or on ARD. Incidentally, on the *Presseclub*, a news talk show on ARD, for example, he enjoys talking with the likes of Tina Hassel, someone whose connection to the Atlantik-Brücke is already familiar to the readers of this book.[104] There, these two friends of this transatlantic lobbying association can have a pleasant chat on television, which, as we have just seen from the example of the advertisement above, is also pure propaganda for Washington's wars – but the viewer doesn't know this.

Furthermore, before I forget: The oath of allegiance to the United States made by the friends and members of the Atlantik-Brücke in the advertisement mentioned above not only included the FAZ-NATO man Busse, but it was also signed by the ZDF man Theo Koll. So, if you're ever watching the *Auslandsjournal* (Foreign Journal) or another show hosted by Theo Koll, you know what it stands for. According to Atlantik-Brücke, he is "defending" the supposed value system that Germany shares with the USA. Moreover, this also goes for every time the USA starts another war in violation of international law for raw materials and power. Therefore, when it comes to ZDF, the second German public television station, it might be just a little more one-sided than we're led to believe. The Turkish-born German writer Akif Pirinci once formulated ZDF's alleged bias much more drastically than I have portrayed it here. Live on ZDF in 2014, he looked straight into the camera and said, "You can see things better with your asshole." Of course, ZDF immediately censored and edited this politically incorrect interview.[105]

For the ZDF man Theo Koll and the FAZ man Nikolas Busse, their expression of deep loyalty to transatlantic relations wasn't a one-time slip: In a large advertisement placed on page 6 of the daily newspaper *Die Welt* on April 17, 2002, both journalists expressly thanked the Atlantik-Brücke for "the great opportunities it has opened up for us in our professional and personal careers." At the same time, the following individuals also expressed their thanks in this Atlantik-Brücke advertisement: Christiane Hoffmann, who was the sitting FAZ correspondent in Teheran at the time, for the aforementioned career help, and also Katja Gloger (then with *Stern),* Malte Lehming (*Tagesspiegel,* US correspondent)*,* Rüdiger Löwe (Bavarian Broadcasting (BR)), Eckart Stuff (lead instructor at the CRC), Christian Wernicke (Europe correspondent for the *Süddeutschen Zeitung* in Brussels)*,* Sabine Ulbrich (correspondent for N24 and SAT1 in Washington), Margaret Heckei (*Financial Times Deutschland*), Matthias Nass (Deputy Chief Editor of the *Die Zeit*) and Anke Plättner (journalist, Cologne). Supporting the Atlantik-Brücke for "the great opportunities and possibilities it offers, that it has opened for ... [the aforementioned journalists for their] professional and personal careers," somehow sounds to me like they should also be thanking the Atlantik-Brücke for their jobs. As a neutral third party, how does this sound to you when you read it? Do transatlantic organizations help journalists with their "professional careers?" What is really going on here behind the scenes?

Back to the Atlantik-Brücke. Maybe the journalists mentioned by name in the table above simply have no idea of whose company they're keeping. After all, there are also journalists out there who consider the UPI "news agency" to be a completely normal news agency. Yet, it belongs to Sun Myung Moon's Unification movement.[106] Many journalists simply have no idea. It is possible that Germans can easily be deceived and lulled to sleep with innocent, German-sounding names like the "Atlantik-Brücke."

Taking a look at organizations like the Atlantik-Brücke in 2013, the *taz* published a report under the title: "Journalists under the Influence – Bad Connections." There they write: "Are Germany's alpha journalists biased because they keep company with the political elite? One study now claims: Yes."[107] Their report features a doctoral thesis by Uwe Krüger that examines the influence the elites have on reporting and shows how important people in business, politics and journalism are networked. The Atlantik-Brücke was also listed among these networking organizations. According to the study, instead of representing an open marketplace of ideas, journalists often represent the positions of the people presiding over these networks. In Uwe Krüger's words, the conflict of the "elite against the people" is coming to a head everywhere, in Europe and all over the world. All too often in this conflict, journalists are standing on the side of the elite.

Embarrassing Adulation

Now, we should use the *Bild* newspaper to show what coverage of the Atlantik-Brücke looks like in the real world, where, of course, everything happens purely by coincidence. Let's take a look at their Winners/Losers column. This elite organization, the Atlantik-Brücke, which is otherwise virtually invisible to ordinary citizens, has been repeatedly smuggled onto the "winners" side in the *Bild*. A few examples from over the years:

Bild from April 12, 2002: **Winner**

A symbol of German-American friendship is celebrating its 50th anniversary: the Atlantik-Brücke. To the association's credit: promoting dialogue between the two countries, deepening political and cultural understanding. Chairman Arend Oetker (63, photo): "It is a bridge that needs continuous maintenance." The BILD's take: Friendship is all that matters.

Bild from April 18, 2002: **Winner**

A man who builds bridges: Former US President George Bush (77) received the Eric M. Warburg Prize yesterday in Berlin's Charlottenburg Palace. Foreign Minister Joschka Fischer delivered the congratulatory speech. The prize was awarded by the Atlantik-Brücke Association for

Bush's services to German-American relations. The BILD's take: Transatlantic!

Bild from May 5, 2003: **Winner**

Anyone who talks about German-American relations cannot overlook Dr. Beate Lindemann (60). She can reach anybody in Washington on the phone. The managing director of the Atlantik-Brücke association is currently working to maintain a good relationship with America. An important task, which she masters with a lot of wisdom and charm. The BILD's take: Transatlantic!

Bild from February 3, 2004: **Winner**

An airline captain who builds bridges: Lufthansa boss Wolfgang Mayrhuber (56) is receiving the Vernon A. Walters Award in New York today for his services to German-American partnership. The prize is awarded by the renowned Atlantik-Brücke association. The BILD's take: Above the clouds, friendship must be boundless. (See: the popular Reinhard Mey song).

Bild from June 11, 2004: **Winner**

CDU politician Walther Leisler Kiep (78) is the new honorary chairman of the Atlantik-Brücke association. The general meeting (including Otto Graf Lambsdorff, Hilmar Kopper, Rudolf Scharping) unanimously praised Kiep's services to German-American understanding. The BILD's take: Well-deserved honor!

Bild from June 16, 2005: **Winner**

Now the Atlantik-Brücke is getting wings: Dr. Thomas Enders (45), CEO of the European aerospace group EADS, will be the new chairman of the association. America's friend Enders studied in Los Angeles, succeeds Dr. Arend Oetker after five years. Since 1952, the non-partisan Atlantik-Brücke e.V. has been committed to the friendship between Germany and the USA. The BILD's take: Wishing you success!

Bild from October 1, 2005: **Winner**

Three high honors in two months for Michael Otto (62): First the Bertelsmann Prize for Youth Development, then the 2005 Environmental Award and now the Vernon A. Walters Award from the Atlantik-Brücke in New York. The 54,000 employees of the largest mail order company in the world can be proud of their boss. The BILD's take: Otto – find' ich gut! (i.e. I like 'em! a spin on a well-known advertising slogan).

Bild from October 10, 2005: **Winner**

She builds bridges between Germany and America. For this, Dr. Beate Lindemann was awarded the Federal Cross of Merit, First Class, today in

Berlin. The vice-chairman of the "Atlantik-Brücke" association has, among other things, set up an exchange program that has enabled more than 3000 East German high school students to spend a year in the USA since 1990. The BILD's take: Honor where honor is due.

Bild from May 15, 2007: **Winner**

In 1990, during the negotiations between the victorious powers of the Second World War and the two German states, Condoleezza Rice (52) played a decisive role in German unity. For this, the acting US Secretary of State will receive the Eric M. Warburg Prize from the Atlantik-Brücke e.V. on May 31. Her congratulatory speech will be held by former Chancellor Helmut Kohl. The BILD's take: Der Price ist Rice! (i.e. The Price Is Right gameshow in Germany is called Der Price ist heiss, (The Price Is Hot)).

Bild from June 1, 2009: **Winner**

Honorable assignment for Friedrich Merz (53): The controversial politician is the new chairman of the prestigious Atlantik-Brücke. Merz takes over the office from the Airbus boss Enders. The Atlantik-Brücke is an association of business leaders and politicians, among others, in Germany and the USA with the aim of promoting German-American friendship. The BILD's take: Top man for a top job!

Bild from June 30, 2010: **Winner**

The old and new chairman of the Atlantik-Brücke is Friedrich Merz (54). The lawyer and economic expert was re-elected with a large majority yesterday at the association's general meeting. Since its foundation in 1952, the Atlantik-Brücke has been committed to German-American friendship. The BILD's take: Bridge builder!

You can keep adding more and more to the list. As a very visual newspaper, the *Bild* does a lot of their reporting in the form of captions in and around photos of all sizes, so it's even more interesting when you study their photos.

On February 27, 2009, there was a photo on page 2 of the *Bild* that included a caption reporting on an Atlantik-Brücke declaration made in Mumbai. However, in publishing the photo, they didn't print the whole group photo. The man on the very left of the original photo is Kai Diekmann, editor-in-chief of the *Bild* newspaper and member of the Atlantik-Brücke – but he was cropped out of the photo printed on page 2.[108] As a reader, what would you make of such a "coincidence?" By the way, Kai Diekmann is by no means the only Atlanticist in the executive offices at the *Bild* newspaper. Today's Deputy Editor-in-Chief of the *Bild*, Bela Anda, who used to be the Director of the Federal Press Office, once admitted in an interview that he was a member of the Atlantik-Brücke.[109] How did that report in the *Berliner*

Zeitung start again? The one on the power of the Atlantik-Brücke? It had the headline: "Their Contacts Extend into the White House":

> *Government spokesman Bela Anda is on a first-name basis with her and Bild editor-in-chief Kai Diekmann is too. Former German Chancellor Helmut Kohl likes to be photographed with her and the former US President George Bush, the elder, always calls her "Dear Beate." Beate Lindemann isn't a politician, she doesn't run a business and she's not a publisher, yet she often stands next to the powerful: Beate Lindemann is the Executive Vice President of one of the most influential networks in this republic, the Atlantik-Brücke. Founded in 1952, the Atlantik-Brücke's primary aim is to foster and strengthen the German-American friendship.*[110]

By the end of this chapter, it will be hard to deny the impression that these kraken-like organizations such as the Atlantik-Brücke, with their controversial ties to intelligence agencies and the likes of Kai Diekmann sitting on their boards,[111] have an influence on our media, and that's putting it mildly. "Quality journalism is false advertising: Journalists as lobbyists" – that's at least how the trade journal *Meedia* views the activity of this organization. They ask, "Journalists don't allow their readers to dictate their opinions – but do they allow organizations?"[112] Evidently, there is only a very fine line between being a journalist and being a propagandist.

Undercover Power: Classic Propaganda Techniques

The aforementioned scientist, Uwe Krüger, wrote his doctoral thesis on the influence the elites have on German journalists. Krüger illustrates the networks connecting the important people in business, politics and journalism. According to his thesis, instead of taking part in an open marketplace of ideas, certain journalists often represent the positions of those in power. In an interview with Michael Voregger, Krüger said:

> *I was a journalist myself and, at the university, I was fed the high ideals – of independence, criticism and control. Then, when I worked as a media journalist, that is, I reported on journalism and journalists, I came across a secret conference – the annual Bilderberg conference. Leading representatives from politics, the military, business and journalism from North America and Western Europe all meet together there. At the time, hardly anything was known about this conference, the journalists that were invited there didn't report on it. So, I began searching for clues to find out what is really going on behind the scenes.*[113]

When he was asked about how close journalists come to the elites of our society and which media have particularly good contacts, the scientist answered:

I've been able to chart journalists' contacts to the elites across the board. There were 64 journalists involved in 82 organizations where elites from politics and business were also active. Particularly striking were the networks of four foreign policy journalists: Stefan Kornelius, the head of the foreign policy desk at the Süddeutsche Zeitung, Klaus-Dieter Frankenberger, editor-in-chief of the foreign policy desk at the FAZ, Michael Stürmer, chief correspondent for Die Welt, and Josef Joffe, co-editor of Die Zeit. They were involved in foreign and security policy think tanks, associations with affinities to the US and NATO and confidential rounds tables, in some of which they always met the same people.[114]

Krüger confirmed statements that have been considered conspiracy theories up to this point, for example, he said:

Journalists obviously enjoy great personal benefits from all this: background information, orientation, exclusive contacts, high-ranking interview partners. However, I see only a limited benefit for readers and viewers. They don't get this knowledge given to them in the form of reports and accounts from inside these closed-door meetings. Instead, they only get the information and the perspectives that the elites want them to have. This is reflected in the comments and editorials that we believe are being written by critical and independent journalists. This can also be absolutely counterproductive when journalists are an integral part of a confidential, policy planning process and they are committed to keeping it secret. This is because the elites solve their problems in these confidential settings and form a consensus before the public discussion even begins. The journalist, though, is an advocate for the public.[115]

Krüger says that certain journalists and media have distanced themselves from their function as a control mechanism:

The closer they get to the decision-makers and the powerful, the further they move away from criticism and control. This proximity is usually bought with conformity. At this point, we have to discuss how great the distance between journalists and elites should be. Do we want our largest and most influential media to have a strong bias towards the elites, or do we want to have neutral observers, critics and controllers – who then might not always be able to serve up the hottest scandals and the latest insider information from within elite circles?[116]

In the interview, Krüger speaks of a "partisanship" among the journalists he examined. He also points out that the renowned *New York Times* has a paragraph in its code of ethics stating that journalists themselves are not allowed to get involved in organizations that carry out newsworthy activities or that have connections to business and politics. Krüger says: "You are not allowed to sit on advisory boards or boards of trustees. They are only allowed to engage in journalistic training and further education. This is a purity law that I would also like to see anchored in Germany."

Albrecht Müller, former head of planning at the Federal Chancellery, has carefully studied and analyzed the above statements by Krüger. He speaks of the "US-like, organized standardization of the important leading media" in Germany.[117] The influential Müller demands:

It is important to shed light on the organized standardization of many media. It is important to shake up the credibility of these media in this way. (...) Therefore, the heartfelt plea: Expose the dependence that many German media have on the ruling elite and a military-oriented ruling ideology, which, incidentally, always has a domestic and socio-political side. Name the names. Because this system isn't running anonymously. It is organized and carried out by people. The credibility of these people must be shaken to the core.[118]

Below is a table with the names of influential German journalists who were or are involved in transatlantic-oriented, foreign and security policy organizations of the elite. This table is an excerpt from Uwe Krüger's book (pp. 119-122):

Media	Name	Organization, in which the journalist was involved between 2002 and 2009
ZEIT	Josef Joffe	American Academy in Berlin, American Council on Germany, American Institute for Contemporary German Studies, Aspen Institute Deutschland, Atlantik-Brücke, Bilderberger, Europe's World, Goldman Sachs Foundation, Hypovereinsbank, International Institute for Strategic Studies "International Politics", Munich Security Conference "The American Interest", Trilateral Commission
ZEIT	Matthias Nass	Atlantik-Brücke, Bilderberger
ZEIT	Marc Brost	Atlantik-Brücke
Süd–deutsche Zeitung / SZ	Stefan Kornelius	American Institute for Contemporary German Studies, Federal Academy for Security Policy, German Atlantic Society, German Council on Foreign Relations, "International Policy", Körber Foundation, Munich Security Conference
ZDF	Claus Kleber	Aspen Institute Deutschland
ZDF	Peter Frey	Federal Academy for Security Policy, Körber Foundation
BILD	Kai Diekmann	Atlantik-Brücke
FAZ	Klaus-Dieter Franken–berger	Atlantic Initiative, Federal Academy for Security Policy, Institute for European Politics, Munich Security Conference, Trilateral Commission

FAZ	Günther Nonnen–macher	Center for Applied Policy Research, German Council on Foreign Relations, International Institute for Strategic Studies International Politics, Valdai Discussion Club, Walter Rathenau Institute
FAZ	Frank Schirrmacher	(d. June 2014) Flerbert-Quandt Foundation, M100 Sanssouci-Colloquium
WELT	Michael Stürmer	German Council on Foreign Relations, European Council on Foreign Relations, German-British Forum, Munich Security Conference

According to the revised version of Uwe Krüger's doctoral thesis (*Meinungsmacht* (*Opinion Power*) not available in English)), the individuals listed above have been involved with those corresponding institutions in various ways over recent years. This includes: through their membership in associations, advisory boards or boards of trustees or, for example, participation in conferences, press conferences or confidential discussions.

Basically, the media scientist Krüger noticed that FAZ journalists are among the best networked opinion makers in Germany. Co-editor Nonnenmacher (politics) is in 3rd place on the list, FAZ foreign policy chief Frankenberger is in 5th place and FAZ co-editor Schirrmacher (features), who died in June 2014, is in 9th place, while former Federal Chancellor and *Die Zeit* co-editor Helmut Schmidt is only in 15th place.[119]

FAZ editor Günther Nonnenmacher is, for example, a member of the "German Council on Foreign Relations" (DGAP), which is listed in the Bundestag's official lobbyist register ("Lobbyliste").[120] According to information from Lobbypedia and Nonnenmacher's own biography, this organization is part of the lobbying network known as the *Transatlantic Policy Network*.[121] Lobbypedia writes: "*The Transatlantic Policy Network* (TPN) is a lobbying organization for large European and US-American corporations as well as networks with close ties to business. It influences transatlantic politics on behalf of their economic interests through the involvement of European and US politicians."[122] Therefore, in my view and also from the perspective of both the Bundestag and Lobbypedia, the FAZ's editor Nonnenmacher is an active member of a lobbying organization (although the DGAP itself denies being a lobbying organization).[123] Naturally, in light of this information, it isn't surprising to learn that the FAZ and the DGAP coordinate joint events together. On the DGAP homepage it reads: "The DGAP Frankfurter Forum was founded in 2010 at the initiative of our executive board members Herbert J. Scheidt and Prof. Dr. Günther Nonnenmacher. Under the title 'DGAP in Dialog' the forum holds high-profile events at the offices of the Frankfurter Allgemeine Zeitung (FAZ) in cooperation with the FAZ and Bank Vontobel."[124]

One of the lobbyists in the FAZ offices is foreign policy chief Klaus-Dieter Frankenberger, who was awarded the Steuben-Schurz-Gesellschaft

(Steuben-Schurz Society) media prize in 2008 for his transatlantic reporting. (On the website it says that he has "furthered German-American understanding").[125] Frankenberger also sits on the advisory board of the Atlantic Initiative.[126] The latter is, in my personal opinion, probably more of a violation of his professional journalistic role of merely being an observer.[127]

After all, this organization is also on the Bundestag's "lobby list."[128] So, as far as I can tell, the FAZ's foreign policy editor Nonnenmacher and foreign policy department head Frankenberger are lobbyists. Knowing this, you could come to the conclusion that they pursue the very specific interests of an elite network. Now, read what the FAZ says about itself when they're promoting their own newspaper: "Since its foundation in 1949, the F.A.Z. has placed the greatest importance on its independence."[129] More and more readers are turning their backs on this type of "independence." At any rate, the once so prestigious FAZ is rapidly losing its popularity, and long-time readers are simply cancelling their subscriptions to this biased paper. Fewer and fewer people want to continue spending their money on this kind of "journalistic quality,"[130] since its proximity to elite networks may very well be influencing its reporting as well.

One of the most important questions in Krüger's study is: Are their connections to the elite also reflected in the reporting of these top journalists: Klaus-Dieter Frankenberger (FAZ), Stefan Kornelius (*Süddeutsche*), Josef Joffe (*Die Zeit*) and Michael Stürmer (*Die Welt*)? To this, Krüger says:

Yes, I also began my research under the premise of the "cognitive appropriation" of journalists by the elites. And, when I examined the articles of these four, I actually came to the conclusion: These journalists were very much in line with the elites and even used classic propaganda techniques.[131]

So, according to the conclusions of this scientist, journalists from the FAZ, *Süddeutsche*, *Die Zeit* and *Die Welt* use "classic propaganda techniques." Can someone please tell me how this is compatible with a free press? Krüger goes on to mention quite a few other suggestive examples from the past:

In my study, I found the head of a foreign policy desk sitting on the German Atlantic Society's board, a lobbying association for NATO. There were also foreign policy directors and a ZDF, capital-city studio director sitting on the German Federal Academy for Security Policy's advisory board, advising the federal government on security matters. If this was no longer possible, if such honorary posts were declared taboo for journalists, then we would be making a big step forward.[132]

At this point, I think we would all like to know who is ignoring the safe distance needed between journalism and the elites, the buffer that is required to insure journalistic integrity. Who is this head of the foreign policy desk who was sitting in a NATO lobbying organization? According to Krüger's information, this was Stefan Kornelius, the foreign policy chief at the *Süddeutsche Zeitung*.[133]

And who is this head of the foreign policy desk who sat on the advisory board of the Federal Academy for Security Policy and advised the German Federal Government on security issues? According to Krüger, the FAZ man Klaus-Dieter Frankenberger was the very conspicuous director of that foreign policy desk.

At first, the journalists in question didn't want to answer Krüger's questions, even though the scientist had simply drawn up a detailed list of how these journalists are affiliated with various groups. Krüger writes:

The four journalists were informed of the study and invited to present their view of these facts in separate articles to be included in the publication of the book. All four refused.[134]

Kallmorgen and Bohnen – Dubious PR Experts and Prestigious Newspapers

According to those same statements by Uwe Krüger, FAZ man Klaus-Dieter Frankenberger was also a member of the Atlantic Initiative's advisory board, a member of the Institute for European Politics' board of directors[135] and a member of the Trilateral Commission.[136] I took a closer look at all of this.

The term lobby refers to the lobby of a legislative building. This is where the representatives of various groups (lobbyists) originally reminded the people's representatives that there was always a possibility of them being voted out of office. In this way, they exercised a certain form of control over legislators and could also promise distinct advantages that rewarded specific behavior. The President of the German Bundestag keeps a public list were all the associations that want to forward their interests vis-à-vis the Bundestag or the German Federal Government can register themselves. The list is publicly available and known as the "lobby list."[137] The Institute for European Politics is registered on this lobby list.[138] Therefore, the journalist Frankenberger was active in a group officially listed by the German Bundestag as a lobbying organisation.[139] Also on the official lobby list: the Atlantic Initiative.[140] The FAZ's foreign policy chief Frankenberger is still a member of their advisory board to this day.[141]

Let's take an even closer look. In my view, the Institute for European Politics is a lobbying group for the EU, based on its "strategic partnership" with the European Commission. On their homepage it reads: "The Institute for European Politics (IEP) is a strategic partner of the European

Commission and is financially supported by it."[142] Moreover, it is a lobbying organization for those German government circles that want to further strengthen European "integration" – i.e. EU enlargement,[143] under the guise of research and integration projects, something that is rather unpopular amongst the German population in general.

The Trilateral Commission, also mentioned in connection with Frankenberger, is a private interest group representing the financial sector, but we will get into that in a separate section. Also, the Atlantic Initiative is a controversial, pro-American lobbying organization,[144] co-founded by the owners of the PR agency and management consultants Bohnen Kallmorgen & Partner.[145]

Now, let's take a little closer look at the two founders of the Atlantic Initiative. Our dear Mr. Kallmorgen, according to his own bio, directed "the Transatlantic Relations Program at the German Council on Foreign Relations (DGAP) until the end of 2007. After graduating with a degree in history and political science, he completed a master's program in international relations at *Georgetown University* in Washington, DC. During this time, he worked for various management consultants and the World Bank. From 2000 to the beginning of 2003, he worked for the banking house Goldman, Sachs & Co. Kallmorgen is a member of the Young Leaders Program of the Atlantik-Brücke e.V."[146]

According to *LobbyControl*, the former Goldman Sachs investment manager Kallmorgen is also a lobbyist with "a lobbying platform for financial investors and hedge funds," which "operates at the same business address as Bohnen Kallmorgen und Partner."[147]

Additionally, our dear Mr. Bohnen "is a founder and honorary chairman of the Atlantic Initiative. He studied at *Georgetown University* in Washington, DC (Master of Science) and received his doctorate in international politics in Oxford. After working for, among others, the American think tank CSIS, the German Bundestag and the Bertelsmann Foundation, he worked as press spokesman for a state political party and as a speechwriter for the Federal Minister of Education and Research."[148]

According to *LobbyControl*, another lobbying organization founded by Kallmorgen und Bohnen engages in "a shady style of lobbying (...) in which it sells itself as something it isn't: It sells itself as a non-profit initiative, mainly supported by scientists and members of civil society, but it is in fact the invention of a lobbying agency; it deceives the public about its true objectives and its members; and it ultimately remains unclear as to how it finances itself."[149]

Let's summarize: The Atlantic Initiative was therefore founded primarily by people who are very certainly – to put it extremely politely and cautiously – controversial: According to *LobbyControl*, these are lobbyists who are working underhandedly and who have deceived the public about the true aims of their lobbying work in the past, moreover, with the help of the media.

The Swiss magazine *Saldo* reported in 2011 under the title, "Journalists in the Service of PR Agencies," on how the renowned FAZ and *Süddeutsche Zeitung* – independent of the Atlantic Initiative – got Kallmorgen and Bohnen to do their PR legwork for them.[150] In the article, they say that a new study now suggests that articles from the FAZ and *Süddeutsche* "spread the stylized message of a PR firm." What they meant was Kallmorgen, Bohnen and their lobbying network. Furthermore, regarding the uncritical copy published by the PR-agency's prestigious media outlets, the report says: "These antics show just how easily PR-companies can get journalists to do the legwork for their own ends." Kallmorgen and Bohnen have already been warned by the PR Council (DRPR) in 2011 for their misleading behavior.[151] They also present "dubious" organizations as "charitable initiatives" for the purpose of generating consulting jobs. Self-interest instead of public interest. A sleazy business model.[152]

So, we have the FAZ's head of foreign policy, Frankenberger, sitting on the advisory board of an organization founded by these lobbyists, the Atlantic Initiative, which is listed in the Bundestag's lobby register.[153] He obviously feels comfortable around lobbying organizations (like his colleagues with the other interest groups mentioned above). When it comes to journalists like this, Albrecht Müller, former planning director at the Federal Chancellery, says, "Their proximity to the elites and their political orientation also pays off in terms of these journalists' careers." They are "also successful professionally, thanks to their ideological orientation and their ties to powerful elite circles."[154]

Just a reminder: When referring to journalists like these, the former planning director of the Federal Chancellery speaks of the "important leading media's organized, self-imposed conformity with US interests" in Germany.[155] So, if you have a copy of the *Frankfurter Allgemeine Zeitung* or any other ostensibly prestigious media in front of you – then you know how you should probably be interpreting some of their reports: classic propaganda techniques, in line with the elites. There, it seems that journalists are clearly being intellectually appropriated by the elites.

If a reputable media outlet suddenly realized and could prove that any of their journalists were compromised by the interdependencies outlined here, they would probably dismiss them without notice. The reason that this doesn't happen is fairly easy to understand: The people up in the executive offices who are responsible for these decisions are also members of the same dubious networks themselves. Thus, they would have to sign their own termination notices at the same time. Instead, they just continue applauding their network associates. Realizing that we're the ones who are also paying for this "information," I honestly feel like the joke's on us.

Obama's Trolls: America's Fifth Column

In Germany, we are led to believe that we have a broad selection of newspapers, television stations and other media, basically covering the whole spectrum of opinion. From the far right all the way to the far left. The journalists are independent of the things and the people they report on. They have an exclusive commitment to the objective truth. And in reality? In reality, this freedom of expression is evidently only a facade.

Since the end of the Second World War, US lobbying organizations have metastasized within Germany on a massive scale. As a result, more and more ministers in German government agencies owe their careers to the protection they're provided through American old-boy networks. As we have seen and will continue to see, European journalists have also been intellectually appropriated by US lobbying organizations in increasing numbers.

In 2014, I read the following passage in the renowned *Neue Zürcher Zeitung* about the allegedly evil people who lie and cheat the public on a daily basis:

> *Half a year ago, an article in the Russian newspaper "Novaya Gazeta," which is critical of the Russian government, reported that an "agency for Internet studies" in St. Petersburg offers 650 francs a month and free food for people who regularly post comments on the Internet in support of the Kremlin. The agency's operators come from the nexus of youth organizations that are loyal to the Kremlin ...*[156]

That's moving. That hits close to home. The evil Russians in the Kremlin are paying young people to post propaganda on the Internet for the Russian government. It's a scandal. Poor Russians are getting free food and a few euros in return for posting propaganda. In the news, something like this spreads around the supposedly free world like wildfire. This villainy. But wait: What about the countless German-speaking journalists who – in return for favors – willingly write propaganda for pro-American organizations, for companies or for politicians? Why isn't this a scandal, but rather "self-evident?" Almost all pro-American or intelligence-related organizations mentioned in this book have blogs where German journalists are regular contributors. These same journalists are often seen in photos at invitational-only banquets held by these organizations – is this anything different from the "free meals" mentioned above that the Russians offer? What's more, these loyal, line-toeing journalists are often invited on trips to the USA. When they're there, they're even permitted to give (paid) lectures. And the circle is completed. There is absolutely no difference between this and the report in the *Neue Zürcher Zeitung*, a report that might rub you the wrong way when you first read it. This is just what happens when reporting is up for sale – it happens in the East and in the West. It's only become so "normal" and so widespread here that we hardly perceive it. We simply take it for granted.

In this department, the *Süddeutsche* has even provided us with a very special treat: In June of 2014, they published an article on "Putin's Trolls," about alleged Russian propaganda in the German media. It reads: "Hundreds of paid manipulators try to influence opinion in social networks and comment areas worldwide, including at *Süddeutsche.de*, on behalf of the Kremlin."[157] Reading the article, you get the impression that most comments being posted on German mainstream media websites are from Russian loyalists and propaganda agents controlled by Moscow. If there are any undesirable comments under an article, then it must have been the work of Moscow's fifth column. Uh – say that again? The long arm of the NATO press office is writing under the guise of German journalists. They also spread biased, pro-American articles in the *Süddeutsche*.[158] The latter has been scientifically proven in studies out of Munich and Leipzig. And Moscow's fifth column then counters in the comment sections below the articles? No, because in their bizarre analysis of this matter, which hasn't been scientifically proven, the *Süddeutsche* primarily refers to anonymous sources if anything. Accompanying said article, the *Süddeutsche* featured a large propaganda photo of a "Reporters Without Borders" billboard in which Russian President Putin is depicted "flicking off" the viewer. We can assume that this is suggesting to the *Süddeutsche*'s impartial readers that Putin doesn't give a damn about press freedom. They also failed to mention who finances these "Reporters Without Borders" and thus who they work for: In the past, for example, they have been financed by the US State Department and the US billionaire George Soros.[159] Reporters Without Borders' mission, according to the newspaper *Junge Welt*, is primarily spreading pro-American disinformation.[160] None of this was shared by the *Süddeutsche*. This reminded me of the "classic propaganda techniques" already covered in this chapter. As an average citizen reading this, you get the feeling that they're treating you like a child – or they're just trolling you.

Before we forget: According to the information from whistleblower Edward Snowden, British intelligence can manipulate content on the Internet at will. Therefore, this isn't being done by hackers, it's being done by a state, a European "democracy." They even change the results of internet polls. We used to think that this was the stuff of conspiracy theory. Today it's our reality. Their programs can not only change votes and traffic numbers on the net, but it can also censor videos. The journalist Glenn Greenwald describes these programs as "some of the most amazing methods of propaganda and deception on the Internet."[161] Now, British intelligence is a close partner of US intelligence and whatever the British are able do in this field,[162] the Americans have been able to do for a long time. Not only are they able to do it, they do do it.[163] They censor and manipulate the Internet, especially comments.[164] All throughout history, mass surveillance like this has only ever had one goal: the elimination of political opponents.[165] Uh, say that again? So, will the *Süddeutsche Zeitung* start calling the Americans who carry out this kind of manipulation on the Internet "America's Trolls" from now on? Or will America's fifth column just continue to whip up a frenzy over "Moscow's Trolls?"

Rockefeller's Ghost – The Trilateral Commission

Private citizens have a fundamental right to join private, elite associations. This also applies to organizations that are exclusively made up of influential, very influential people. At the same time, it is remarkable that there is so little public knowledge of the existence of these organizations. This only adds fuel to conspiracy theories, and makes you wonder what journalists are even doing in some of these organizations run by the power elite.

One of the most important organizations of the Western power elite, apart from the Bilderbergers, is undoubtedly the Trilateral Commission. Founded in 1973 under the aegis of David Rockefeller, it can be regarded as another mysterious offshoot of the Bilderberg family.[166]

According to Smilja Avramov, an international law expert from Belgrade who has written a book on this organization, the Trilateral Commission is "nothing more than a world government on hold. At their meetings, they negotiate the current problems in the world and decide on corresponding courses of action ..."[167] She maintains that the break-up of Yugoslavia must have been decided at a Trilateral meeting a few years before it happened. You could consider this a conspiracy theory, but many other experts also report similar things in connection with the Trilaterals. These include assertions like: The decision to impose the financial consequences of the European economic and financial crisis on Europe's citizens came from elites among the ranks of the Trilateral Commission. This is, for example, what the Argentine economist Adrian Salbuchi writes in a piece I can personally recommend entitled, "Socializing Losses: Trilateral Takeover of Europe?"[168] According to this, the Trilaterals have been working on this in the background for many years now, their primary concern being saving the wealth of the world's super-rich. Also, that the leading media should use Orwellian "Newspeak" to ensure that the citizenry swallows it all like good children. From this perspective, the media, writing or reporting in their interest, are nothing more than the Trilateral Commission's puppets. The media scientist from Leipzig, Uwe Krüger, describes the Trilateral Commission as an organization in which the elites can negotiate their "interests, before they come into public view."[169]

Excluding the press and thus the public from these Trilateral meetings is usually justified with the explanation that Commission members can only exchange their insights and ideas freely and openly under these conditions. This is just like in the Mafia. Thus, reliable information on the speeches and conversations taking place at their meetings generally doesn't reach the outside world. As a logical consequence, however, this secrecy also leads to a host of speculation, which must be met with a corresponding degree of skepticism. Smilja Avramov, for example, the international law expert from Belgrade mentioned earlier, says this about the Trilateral Commission:

For the Trilateral Commission, global governance, by the way, means governance without governments, world domination without (elected) governments. This is how you manage the worldwide destruction of government functions and create, via so-called non-governmental organizations, the instruments for bypassing existing governments to control the destinies of nations.[170]

After all this, you could conclude: The current crises are not happening by accident, they are deliberate. Moreover, they are also being induced by arcane organizations like the Trilateral Commission and are meant to serve the goals of the New World Order, a dictatorship of the elites.

An indication of the importance of their meetings is further demonstrated by the locations where their conferences are held: After all, the Trilateral Commission's 1977 annual meeting in Germany was held directly in the Chancellor's Office. The West German Chancellor at the time, Helmut Schmidt, had extra chairs brought in so that the powerful figures present could all have a seat at his table.[171] Since then, not much has changed. The 2013 annual meeting of the Trilateral Commission took place in Berlin. Just like in Bonn in 1977, the founder David Rockefeller took the place of honor.[172]

At its 2010 meeting in Brussels, the Trilateral Commission decided that EU citizens should hand over more of their decision-making power to the EU functionaries in Brussels. As the Reuters news agency later made it palatable for us, this dismantling of national state sovereignty should lead to "economic union."[173] More authority to make decisions was to be ceded to Brussels. Were the citizens, the tax-payers, the voters in agreement with this? How could they be, when they aren't even informed about the decisions being made behind closed doors? When they don't even know what the organizations, meeting in secret like at the Trilateral conference, are agreeing to behind their backs?

Lobbypedia, a project of *LobbyControl*, calls the Trilateral Commission a "lobbying organization of the economic elite."[174] Always happy to attend: FAZ foreign policy chief Klaus-Dieter Frankenberger.[175] This journalist was already attracting attention while I was at the FAZ by wearing a suit with

American cowboy boots and smoking fat cigars. He is obviously proud of being a member of a lobbying organization for the financial elite that is surrounded in mystery. In his official résumé for the *Frankfurter Allgemeine Zeitung* he writes: "Since the beginning of 2001: Responsible for foreign policy. Member of the Trilateral Commission."[176]

So, the FAZ journalist Frankenberger is sitting there, together in an organization with billionaire David Rockefeller, Bilderberger Mario Monti and Jean-Claude Trichet, former President of the European Central Bank, alongside Deutsche Bank CEO Jürgen Fitschen and former US Secretary of State Madeleine Albright, former US Secretary of Defense John Deutch, next to former US Secretary of State John Negroponte and Henry Kissinger.[177] Is this the right place for a journalist who, according to his earlier understanding of a properly functioning media, should have a control function above all else?

How can someone be in a lobbying organization for the economic elite and the US billionaire David Rockefeller, which comes across as rather conspiratorial to say the least, and still be considered a leading German journalist? What's more, this journalist then even writes about it, say, on the occasion of the organization's 2013 annual meeting in Berlin.[178] In the secondary headline it says, "There is no lighthouse – or maybe so?" And the piece begins with the words, "40 years ago, David Rockefeller called the Trilateral Commission into being." Does the reader even suspect that what we have here is an association member writing about his own association?

From my perspective, when I look into the FAZ archives, it seems like Frankenberger has written many articles on the Trilateral Commission and David Rockefeller that are reminiscent of the flattering reports you would expect to see coming from the court of a feudal lord. In April 2003, for example, Frankenberger began a column ("America's New Playmate") with the words, "Thirty years ago, David Rockefeller had a good idea: Wasn't it high time to create a forum..." In March 2013, Frankenberger began his FAZ article "World in Unrest" with the words, "40 years ago, David Rockefeller called the Trilateral Commission into being. It was the answer to the New York banker Mäzen's ..." The good billionaire Rockefeller with the good ideas, the good Trilateral Commission? Do you remember what I wrote at the very beginning of this book about another billionaire and Frankenberger's (and my!) noble court reporting in the FAZ: the other billionaire's name was Sultan Qabus and he sponsored dream-like, luxury trips for Frankenberger and me, which we both raved about among our colleagues for a long time afterward. We willingly let ourselves be "bribed" for the noble court reporting we submitted to the FAZ. Frankenberger has obviously maintained his intimate proximity to the elite. How close can journalists get to the financial and political power elites? How much involvement are journalists allowed to have in lobbying organizations?

I have already mentioned my former colleague Klaus-Dieter Frankenberger several times in this book. Not because I don't like him. Just the opposite. It is precisely my experiences with him over the years, up close and personal, that have made one thing clear to me: You can make a good comparison between alpha journalists like him and Russian matryoshkas. What I mean are those nesting dolls that always have another smaller one inside. Just when you think that you've found the last aspect of their character, hidden somewhere in the shadows... the next one suddenly appears. For Frankenberger it used to be the Advisory Board of the Atlantic Initiative, then it was the Directorate of the Institute for European Politics, then came participation in the Munich Security Conferences or membership in the controversial Trilateral Commission. Journalists shouldn't be matryoshkas, leaving us guessing whose interests they might possibly be pushing – when, where and how. The Trilateral Commission is and remains an offshoot of the Bilderbergers. It is also an organization, in my personal opinion, that journalists shouldn't have anything to do with.

The German sociologist Rudolf Stumberger speaks of a tendency towards neo-feudalism. He means this in the sense of our world's increasing reliance on self-proclaimed elites and their organizational structures. He sees these structures emerging parallel to official structures – in other words, he is describing the phenomenon we call shadow governments or the deep state and their goal of exercising comprehensive, total control and power over as much of the globe as possible.

It is time that the public learned about these structures and their objectives. However, since the public has deliberately not been informed of this situation, it's going to have to get with the program. In light of these new perspectives, the public must be ready, willing and able to accept the reality of these hidden organizations that make up this "kraken." The Trilateral Commission is only one of the many elite organizations that have swallowed up German leaders like a kraken.

Therefore, when it comes to German foreign policy, for example, it isn't at all surprising that the statements made by various politicians, along with the representatives of big business and the press, are almost always identical. Among the highest circles of German foreign policy, in fact, this is easier to see than anywhere else. The media scientist Uwe Krüger has done a good job in describing how transatlantic organizations have created networks that are exclusively aligned with NATO interests. Today, according to Krüger, these pro-American networks have an absolute character to their opinion making. Within them, differences of opinion don't stand a chance. Differing opinions are denigrated. Along with the billionaire Rockefeller's Trilateral Commission, other organizations that also have a major influence on Germany are: the *American Academy*, the *American Jewish Committee*, the *Aspen Institute*, the Atlantik-Brücke, the Atlantic Initiative, the German

Atlantic Society, the German Council on Foreign Relations (DGAP) and the billionaire George Soros' *European Council on Foreign Relations* (ECFR).

The following persons in particular have belonged to the networks of these and similar organizations and their sphere of influence:

Last Name	First Name	Organization	Position
Baring, Prof.	Dr. Arnulf	Atlantic Initiative	Historian
Berger, Prof. Hon. Dr.	Roland	Atlantik-Brücke, German Council on Foreign Relations DGAP, European Council on Foreign Relations ECFR	Roland Berger Strategy Consultants
Brok	Elmar	German Council on Foreign Relations DGAP	European Parliament
Brzezinski, Dr.	Mark	Atlantic Initiative	McGuireWoods
Bütikofer	Reinhard	American Jewish Committee, Aspen Institute, Atlantik-Brücke, German Council on Foreign Relations DGAP	European Parliament
Chrobog	Jürgen	Atlantic Initiative	BMW Foundation Herbert Quandt
Cromme, Dr.	Gerhard	European Council on Foreign Relations ECFR, Aspen Institute	Advisory Board Chairman, Siemens AG
Diekmann	Kai	Atlantik-Brücke	Bild Newspaper
Dohnanyi, Dr., von	Klaus	German Council on Foreign Relations DGAP	former Mayor, City of Hamburg, SPD
Dombret Dr.	Andreas	Atlantik-Brücke	Board Member, German Central Bank
Döpfner, Dr.	Mathias	American Academy, Aspen Institute, American Jewish Committee	Springer Publishing
Enders	Thomas	Atlantik-Brücke, German Council on Foreign Relations DGAP	European Aeronautic Defense and Space EADS
Fischer	Joschka	Atlantik-Brücke, European Council on Foreign Relations ECFR	former Foreign Minister

Fitschen	Jürgen	Atlantik-Brücke	Deutsche Bank
Frey, Dr.	Peter	American Jewish Committee	ZDF
Gauck	Joachim	Atlantik-Brücke	German President
Genscher, Prof. Hon. Dr.	Hans-Dietrich	German Council on Foreign Relations DGAP	former Foreign Minister
Graf Lambsdorff	Alexander	American Jewish Committee, Atlantik-Brücke, Atlantic Initiative, European Council on Foreign Relations ECFR	European Parliament
Graf Lambsdorff	Hagen	German Council on Foreign Relations DGAP	Diplomat
Großmann Dr.	Jürgen R.	Atlantik-Brücke	Georgsmarienhütte
Guttenberg zu	Karl-Theodor	Atlantik-Brücke, European Council on Foreign Relations ECFR	former Defense Minister
Holbrooke	Richard C.	American Academy	US Ambassador 1993, decd. 2010
Inacker, Dr.	Michael	American Academy, German Council on Foreign Relations DGAP	Handelsblatt
Ischinger	Wolfgang	American Academy, American Jewish Committee, Atlantik-Brücke, Atlantic Initiative, European Council on Foreign Relations ECFR	Allianz SE, Chairman Munich Security Conference
Joffe Dr.	Josef	American Academy, Aspen Institute	Die Zeit, Publisher
Kempe Dr.	Frederick	Atlantik-Brücke	The Atlantic Council of the United States
Kiep	Walther-Leisler	Atlantik-Brücke, Atlantic Initiative	Politician
Kissinger	Henry A.	American Academy	former US Secretary of State
Klaeden von	Eckart	Aspen Institute, German Council on Foreign Relations DGAP, Atlantik-Brücke, Atlantic Initiative	Daimler

Klose	Hans-Ulrich	American Jewish Committee, Atlantik-Brücke, Atlantic Initiative, German Council on Foreign Relations DGAP	Politician, SPD
Koch-Weser	Caio	Atlantik-Brücke, European Council on Foreign Relations ECFR	Deutsche Bank
Kornblum	John C.	American Academy, Atlantic Initiative	US Ambassador 1997 – 2001, Chairman, Lazard Germany
Lange	Christian	Atlantik-Brücke	Bundestag, SPD
Lindemann	Beate	American Jewish Committee, Atlantik-Brücke Atlantic Initiative	Executive Vice President, Atlantic Forum
Maltzahn Freiherr von	Paul	German Council on Foreign Relations DGAP	Diplomat
Maltzahn von	Nina	American Academy	
Missfelder	Philipp	Atlantik-Brücke, Atlantic Initiative, German Council on Foreign Relations DGAP	Bundestag, CDU
Müller	Kerstin	German Council on Foreign Relations DGAP	
Murphy	Philip D.	Atlantik-Brücke	US Ambassador
Naumann, Dr.	Michael	American Jewish Committee	former Minister of State
Nouripour	Omid	Atlantik-Brücke, German Atlantic Society	Bundestag, Green Party
Nowak	Wolfgang	American Jewish Committee	Alfred Herrhausen Society
Oetker, Dr.	Arend	American Jewish Committee, Atlantik-Brücke, German Council on Foreign Relations DGAP	Dr. Arend Oetker Holding GmbH & Co. KG

Oppenheim, Freiherr von	Christopher	German Council on Foreign Relations DGAP	Sal. Oppenheim
Pflüger, Prof. Dr.	Friedbert	Atlantik-Brücke, German Council on Foreign Relations DGAP	former Secretary of State
Polenz	Ruprecht	Atlantic Initiative, European Council on Foreign Relations ECFR	Bundestag, CDU
Primor	Avi	Atlantic Initiative	former Israeli Ambassador
Robbe	Reinhold	American Jewish Committee, German Atlantic Society	former Bundestag member, SPD
Sandschneider, Prof. Dr.	Eberhard	Atlantic Initiative, German Council on Foreign Relations DGAP	Director of the DGAP's Otto-Wolff Research Institute
Sommer, Dr.	Theo	German Council on Foreign Relations DGAP	former Die Zeit
Teltschik, Prof. Hon. Dr.	Horst M.	Aspen Institute, Atlantic Initiative, German Council on Foreign Relations DGAP	former Chairman Munich Security Conference, Advisor to Helmut Kohl
Vassiliadis	Michael Zissis	Atlantik-Brücke	IG Bergbau, Chemie, Energie
Voigt	Karsten D.	Aspen Institute, Atlantic Initiative, German Council on Foreign Relations DGAP	former Bundestag, SPD
Warburg	Max M.	Atlantik-Brücke	M. M. Warburg & Co. Private Bank
Weizsäcker von	Richard	American Academy	Former German President
Wenning	Werner	Atlantik-Brücke	Bayer AG
Wowereit	Klaus	American Academy	former Mayor, City of Berlin

You can also see the list at: http://spiegelkabinett-blog.blogspot.de/2014/06/das-atlantische-netzwerk.html

When you see the billionaires Rockefeller and Soros pulling strings behind the scenes in organizations like these, for example, then things start to come into focus. One example: The celebrated, left-liberal British weekly, *New Statesman*, has been around since 1913. In a detailed 2003 report, they revealed who the billionaire George Soros was entrusting with management tasks in the allegedly non-profit organizations he co-finances: Often, these positions are filled by former employees of American intelligence agencies, intelligence-related organizations or the military.[179] "Soros," wrote the *New Statesman*, "may not, as some have suggested, be a fully paid-up CIA agent. But that his companies and his NGOs are closely wrapped up in US expansionism cannot seriously be doubted."[180] Soros, Rockefeller and transatlantic think tanks have, mainly for strategic power and economic reasons, accompanied and sometimes even sparked upheavals in the former Eastern bloc countries, the Middle East and North Africa.

With the *European Council on Foreign Relations* (ECFR), the billionaire George Soros' modus operandi are always the same: An event, like an election result that is disagreeable to his own economic interests, is publicly discredited as manipulation. Otherwise, an incident such as the one in Tunisia – the alleged self-immolation of a produce vendor – is taken as an occasion for sustained protests and demonstrations, organized through the new media, until the incumbent government gives up and resigns. The intention is that a government will come to power that is sympathetic to the USA and which adheres to Soros' neoliberal economic interests.

The newspaper *Der Freitag* writes on Soros' overthrow machine:

Soros, however, is known for admitting his involvement in "regime changes" and revolutions only when it isn't dangerous for him. When the situations he has engineered have faded into history, as in the case of Solidarnosc in Poland in the 1980s and his overthrow of the Milosevic government in Serbia, which was planned long in advance and financed with hundreds of millions of dollars, he gladly admits his authorship and even boasts about it. In the case of the Rose Revolution in Georgia, where the Soros machine also struck and brought Sakashwilli to power with the billionaire's blessing, Soros has been a little more cautious. In the turmoil of the Egyptian power struggles and the Jasmine Revolution, however, you won't see any "claim of responsibility" from the self-proclaimed philanthropist with a passion for destroying whole states and societies.[181]

Are German media representatives playing their part in the press campaigns behind these, possibly out of pure ignorance? Let's just take a look at one report by the journalist Peter Riesbeck, which appeared in the July 2013 *Frankfurter Rundschau* and the *Berliner Zeitung*. It is on alleged pro-European unrest in Bulgaria.[182] He begins with the words, "Dimitar Bechev knows the situation in Sofia." And then the reader learns, "Bechev works in Sofia for the *European Council on Foreign Relations* (ECFR), a European research institute with offices in Sofia, Berlin and London."

Thus, the billionaire George Soros' ECFR is being sold to the average reader as a scientific "research institute." Not a word on George Soros and the demonstrations that he sparked in his own interest by means of the ECFR. Thus Bechev, who not only works for the ECFR, as Riesbeck claims, but even heads the office in Sofia,[183] has "sometimes even taken to the streets himself," and this only "out of his mere interest as a social scientist." Yet, how noble are the motives of the demonstrators in Sofia? "We are interested in real democracy," the piece tells us. As with the protests in the Arab world, it paints a picture of young, well-educated and allegedly, totally Western-oriented demonstrators. Furthermore, it calls for European intervention on behalf of the demonstrators. All of this sounds like an orchestrated press campaign.

Out there in the real world, whole countries are being transformed by "revolutions" or demonstrations, just how the U.S. and some of the super-rich need it to achieve their goals. This is the same thing that happened during the "revolutions" that took place in the Eastern bloc states, as well as the "revolutions" in North Africa. It was always about raw materials or the geopolitical interests of NATO and the world's superpower, the USA. Of course, these efforts need financiers – and financiers are easy to find when these "revolutions" also serve moneyed interests – first and foremost, the billionaires of the Rockefeller and Soros families. As George Soros himself said, "My foundations contributed to the regime changes in Slovakia (1998), Croatia (1999) and Yugoslavia (2000) and mobilized civil populations to oust Vladimir Meciar, Franjo Tudman and Slobodan Milosevic from their offices." As a rule, these Soros-financed foundations were there, all throughout the recent past, whenever foreign governments were being overthrown with the help of demonstrations and uprisings. The intellectual seeds of these events are germinated in transatlantic think tanks. And alpha journalists in the mainstream media have always accompanied these upheavals and military interventions, from Afghanistan to Egypt, Syria, Iraq and the Ukraine. Certainly, none of these events have ever served the interests of the general population in the affected countries, but they have always served Washington's strategic interests and the economic interests of a few billionaires.[184]

In Memory of FAZ Chief Schirrmacher: Tank Driver in the Civil Service

How do you actually become an alpha journalist? As an alpha journalist, you can do just about anything you want to do in the German-speaking world – you only have to be bold enough to lie through your teeth.

You want to be successful in life? You also want to network with the elite? Then all you have to do is analyze the lives of the journalists who've been successful up to the present. Albeit, you may have to leave the highroad from time to time. Especially if you want to be a really successful journalist. One tip in advance: First of all – depending on your needs – be sure to have a couple of different résumés on hand. When it seems appropriate, claim that you did civil service instead of serving in the army. On other occasions, it might be better to say you were a tank driver in the army. After all, you just might realize: At the end of the day, none of it even matters at all. You can still land at the top of the heap and reap your accolades.

Let's select a person from recent history whose name was mentioned almost daily in the media until his fatal heart attack in June of 2014. Today, from the vantage point of an average German citizen, he still seems above all reproach. Let's take a closer look at the long-time co-editor of the *Frankfurter Allgemeine Zeitung*, Frank Schirrmacher. I was able to observe him very closely, right from the beginning. As young editors, we talked a lot, especially on the fringes of big editorial conferences.

When Germany's powerful came together in the Chancellery, Frank Schirrmacher was also there. For example, he was at Deutsche Bank CEO Josef Ackermann's 60th birthday party in 2009.[185] We can't list all the prizes Schirrmacher won here, so here are just a few from that long list: The Ludwig Börne Prize, The Jacob Grimm Prize, The Golden Quill (Goldene Feder). Were the people awarding him all these prizes also paying tribute to this man's past?

When others refer to Schirrmacher today, it's surprising that they only mention his good side. However, the multifarious career of this celebrated editor may have been best described with the following words published in *Der Spiegel* in 1996:

The boundaries between truth, embellishment and free invention are pleasantly fluid when it comes to this highly gifted man. Some details are so bizarre that the editors at the FAZ must be asking each other whether their boss has lost all touch with reality when he describes the speedy development of his career.[186]

I will never forget how we all looked at each other, walking into the FAZ's political editorial offices the day after the article I just quoted appeared in *Der Spiegel*. It was infinitely embarrassing to have a colleague who *Der Spiegel* continued describing with:

He astounds even his close confidants when he tells them he was kidnapped as a child in Ethiopia and grew up under the eyes of men who were ready to kill him at any moment. And now, the newspaper staff is puzzled. Did their editor do civil service, as he claimed at first, or did he really drive a tank, as he has been telling others in the meantime?[187]

Take a deep breath. Are you thinking this might be the April Fools' Day edition? Don't stop now. Read a little more, because it's just getting good. Here's another story about Schirrmacher:

Some tall tales obviously come from a moment of fancy. Otherwise, there is no other explanation for why Schirrmacher would suddenly point to a particularly beautiful photo, while leafing through a picture book of stately villas from the turn of the century, and begin to explain that he grew up in such a house. In reality, little Frank grew up in a row house in Wiesbaden. Some of his factual mistakes, however, are also clearly calculated. Apparently, to ingratiate himself with Joachim Fest's office, when Fest was still the co-editor-in-chief at the FAZ, Schirrmacher once told him that he had been asked by the Harvard University Society of Fellows to give a lecture on Fest's book on Adolf Hitler. (...) In the Society of Fellows office at Harvard, however, no one can remember that Schirrmacher ever delivered any speech in public. This respected society of doctoral students and donors is mainly concerned with the awarding of scholarships. "We organize dinners, but not lectures," the responsible secretary explained.[188]

These are just a few of the many bizarre excerpts from an article in *Der Spiegel* on the life of a man who obviously didn't always take the truth very seriously. Despite the embarrassment, Schirrmacher was still quite sure of himself and became, for example, the vice-chairman of the board of trustees for the Herbert Quandt Foundation.[189] The man earned honors. Back then, he somehow earned appreciation as a strange successor to Baron von Münchhausen. Although, this was a time before we suspected many elites in Germany of plagiarizing or even falsifying their biographies and/or academic titles. Needless to say, Schirrmacher found himself in good company. The details on how Schirrmacher plagiarized *himself* in his doctoral dissertation, regurgitating large parts of his master's thesis to gain his doctorate at the university, can also be found in the article in *Der Spiegel* quoted above. Just to be clear: To this day, the people in Schirrmacher's circles obviously still seem to find this type of behavior completely normal. That's just the way it is in a world characterized by a decline in values: Where our forefathers would have probably been tarred and feathered, now, we simply dress the ugly stains on someone's character in lily-white gowns, applaud them and award them prizes. Is this really the kind of journalism that we want to have? Apparently it is.

When Schirrmacher's book *Ego: Das Spiel des Lebens (Ego: The Game of Life)* was published, Joachim Rohloff pointed out in the monthly magazine *Merkur*, in reference to the numerous examples of grammatical, stylistic and content-related mistakes in *Payback* (Schirrmacher's previous book), Schirrmacher is basically saying, "Dear reader, I don't give a damn about the garbage I dish out, because I know you'll eat it."[190]

In 2013, *Wirtschaftswoche* (Business Week) titled an article about the FAZ's editor: "Schirrmacher between infantilism and megalomania."[191]

And the Berlin *taz* knows how to report on Schirrmacher:

Our society believes in this biography artist, his personal entry on Wikipedia, the online encyclopedia, has been embellished at times – sometimes with awards that were later deleted again.[192]

In the many years that have passed since *Der Spiegel* article quoted at the beginning came out about the man who drove a tank during his time in the civil service, nothing seems to have changed about this journalist. He spoke in front of elite networks.[193] If you were invited to an evening with him, they said, "Dr. Frank Schirrmacher has been co-editor of the 'Frankfurter Allgemeine Zeitung' since 1994. In this position, Frank Schirrmacher established himself as one of the most influential opinion makers in Germany…"[194] An opinion maker, reminiscent of the Baron von Münchhausen, who mingled with the elite. Well, it seems that if you're an alpha journalist, you can do just about anything you want. All you have to do is lie through your teeth enough.

Buying Contacts with Big Names? Nobility Eradicated

When you work for an important newspaper, you're surrounded by interests that will ruthlessly try to appropriate you. This just comes with the territory, especially when you're reporting from the courts of the "modern nobility." If you copy the press releases from EU politicians, you are still churning out court reporting, just like anyone who regurgitates the press releases of political parties, associations and foundations via copy & paste or accepts their requests for courtesy interviews. Back in the Middle Ages, court reporting entailed informing a lord's subjects of the events that took place in their lord's court via public announcements (e.g. weddings, births, agreements between nobles, peace treaties, etc.). Court reporting is always complaisant. It is also selective. Evidently, the times have hardly changed since the Middle Ages. One example: On May 19, 1914, the *Dresdener Nachrichten / Dresdener Allgemeine* published a report in the typical style of a noble court report:

"His Royal Highness Prince Johann Georg celebrated his Name's Day on Saturday. On this occasion, His Royal Highness's family banquet took place at 1 o'clock in the afternoon, in which the princes and princesses of the Royal House took part."

Exactly 100 years later, in the *Frankfurter Allgemeine Zeitung* on May 18, 2014, there was a brief in the political section that read:

"Anton Andreas, Count of Faber-Castell celebrated his wedding with the Australian Kate Stahl in the family's Franconian castle on Saturday.

Some 300 guests gathered for the wedding ceremony in the Luther Church in Stein near Nuremberg."

As we can see, the FAZ still publishes classic "court reporting," i.e. they publish announcements pertaining to the personal events in the life of the nobility.

Nobility and journalism, do they go together? Sometimes journalists are "bought" primarily for their good contacts. I personally experienced this in connection with Alexander, Count of Schönburg-Glauchau. He is the brother of the billionaire[195] Gloria von Thurn und Taxis and also of Maya Flick (who allegedly couldn't manage on the 20 million she got after a divorce).[196] When I was still with the *Frankfurter Allgemeine Zeitung*, Schönburg, who claims to have grown up in humble circumstances, had a job working in the FAZ's *Berliner Seiten* (Berlin Pages) section. The feature editor from the FAZ whom I described in the last section, Frank Schirrmacher, once proudly told me that he had "bought" Schönburg for the *Berliner Seiten* in the FAZ. Later, Schönburg and I worked for one of the largest publishing houses in Europe together, Gruner + Jahr. There, the former FAZ man Holger Christmann and I were editing the classy *Park Avenue* magazine when Gruner + Jahr brought Count Alexander on board. Kress media reported on the occasion:

Von Schönburg, who was bought by G+J, not least because of his excellent contacts (he is the brother of Princess Gloria von Thurn und Taxis)...[197]

There it was again: that word "bought." People buy themselves a person. In this case, it was because of his contacts. Their first concern wasn't his skills. The scientists Stephan Weichert and Christian Zabel wrote the following lines about Alexander, Count of Schönburg-Glauchau and his work at *Park Avenue*:

This kissy-kissy high society, in declaring social opportunism to be a supreme virtue, has even flushed a rich and noble member of the elite, long believed to have been vanquished by journalism, back out onto the surface of media society. Here, for example, the brother of Gloria von Thurn und Taxis has been appointed as the editor-in-chief of a high society magazine, just because it seems to be fashionable again to have prominent aristocratic titles in the imprint – even if the person in question has little idea about putting together a magazine. It was already too late when the publisher admitted that their designated boss at Park Avenue was only suitable as a member of its publicity staff, and not its intellectual spokesman – which is why they later fired him ...[198]

To summarize, that sounds a little like: nobility eradicated. At the time, Count Schönburg was rather short on ideas. This was also noticed by others. The media journalist Stefan Niggemeier commented on this in 2011:

Six years ago, Alexander von Schönburg became the momentary laughingstock of the media industry. Schönburg was then editor-in-chief of a noble new Gruner+Jahr magazine called "Park Avenue." In search of topics and ideas, he asked in the online community "A Small World" for tips, and in return he offered fifty, three-month free subscriptions. When word of this got out, Thomas Knüwer commented on the "Handelsblatt" blog (...): "In our journalism school, one of the first rules was: 'The poorest person under the sun is a journalist without anything to write about.'" Thus, this made the editor-in-chief of "Park Avenue," Alexander von Schönburg a journalistic beggar – in the truest sense of the word.[199]

Alexander, Count of Schönburg-Glauchau, who so loved reporting from aristocratic circles, later ended up with the *Bild* newspaper. In 2007, he became the nobility expert at the *Bild*.[200] There, his attempt to succeed by means of his alleged insider knowledge of the high nobility just went from bad to worse. In describing the course of a Christmas Eve with the Windsors he wrote:

The English Royals have all gathered in Sandringham Castle. Their schedule for the day: walking or riding in the morning. At 3 o'clock in the afternoon, they all gather in front of the television to listen to the Queen's Christmas address.[201]

That was embarrassing. Count Schönburg didn't even know the Queen's Christmas address wasn't broadcast on Christmas Eve, it always aired on the 25th of December.[202] This aristocratic court reporter, who used to get ideas in exchange for free subscriptions, seemed to be quite out of touch with the world of the high nobility. Nevertheless, he went on to write a play about Otto von Habsburg for the *Bild* entitled, "The Man Who Would Be Emperor Today" (Der Mann, der heute Kaiser wäre).[203] In this brief historical summary, he wrote:

Franz Joseph's son, the young Emperor Charles I, only reigned for two years before the Habsburgs were deposed.

However, Emperor Charles I was not the son of Emperor Franz Joseph. Charles was very much the son of the Archduke Otto and Princess Maria Josepha of Saxony. He became the heir to the throne because Franz Joseph's only son, Crown Prince Rudolf, had killed himself in 1889, whereupon Franz Joseph's nephew, Franz Ferdinand, became the heir to the throne. He, as we all know, was assassinated by the Serbian nationalist Gavrilo Princip in Sarajevo in 1914. Through these events, the succession to the throne then went over to Franz Ferdinand's nephew Charles I. Alas, can you really expect any detailed knowledge about the high nobility from an aristocracy expert for the *Bild* who himself admitted that he gets "sore muscles in his brain" when he reads demanding books?[204]

I can't forget his non-fiction book, *The Happy Non-Smoker: How to stop smoking in a good mood.* Schönburg never had any problem smoking cigarettes around me. Hitting rock bottom in society, he bummed cigarettes off of other people.[205] Today he is writing headlines for the *Bild* newspaper like, "Royal Succession in Spain – Can Letizia Be Queen?"[206] (when she was the wife of the Crown Prince). At the same time Schönburg, head of the once respectable House of Schönburg, is penning lines like: "Germany the Land of Poets and Thinkers? Ridiculous! How often have YOU looked a 'cow in the ass' today? Or figuratively, 'had your golden prick blown?'"[207] That certainly doesn't sound very noble to me.

The *taz* once wrote about him: "Descending socially without perishing is his secret..."[208] His sisters have married into billions and millions – and Count Alexander Schönburg is allowed to write in the Bild newspaper about the "golden prick" and once in a while, "Can Letizia Be Queen?" Back in 1995, the *Bild* newspaper ran a front-page headline, "The Greedy Mrs. Flick" with a photo of Maya Flick, a sister of the Bild newspaper's illustrious Count. Meanwhile, he's now working at the *Bild* newspaper himself. Called a "multi-purpose noble"[209] in industry lingo, Schönburg, writes in *Bild* these days, "I was once laid off by the FAZ. Compassionately and obsequiously. But it still felt like sh… ."[210]

Does the "all-purpose noble" Alexander von Schönburg still remember what he once said about his readers: "Perverse is that we are ultimately serving exactly that public which we despise. That's why we find ourselves in a closed loop of prostitution, which of course, like the Happy Hooker, is a lot of fun for us."[211] As a writer, do you really have to despise your audience so much?

Count Schönburg likes to include the fact that he is related to the British Queen in his reports. When he told me this, as far as I can remember, it sounded like he was traipsing in and out of their house regularly. The truth: His wife's grandmother was Princess Sophia of Greece. Thanks to this, Schönburg is a great nephew of Prince Philip, the Queen's husband. So, he is a very distant relative – through marriage, twice removed. As a fan of the "multi-purpose nobility," you'd wish that Schönburg would write about some of the Royals' secrets.

The Spanish king Juan Carlos, who has retired in the meantime, is said to have shot his 14-year-old brother Alfonso in 1956 when he was 18. To this day, the police still haven't been allowed to investigate this family drama. So why doesn't Alexander von Schönburg reveal the true reasons behind this to us, if he's in so good with the high nobility? After all, Juan Carlos's wife, Queen Sofia, is also a Princess of Greece like Schönburg's wife's grandmother, and moreover, she speaks fluent German. I would also like to read about his in-law, Queen Elisabeth II, in the German media. Like what the lady studied to do for a living: She trained as an auto mechanic and can repair vintage car engines. There's nothing dishonorable about that. The Grease Monkey Queen, I'd love to read those details in the *Bild*. Also, the Norwegian Queen Sonja once did a tailoring apprenticeship and tapped beer before she met Crown Prince Harald and married him. Silvia of Sweden used to work as a hostess. Queen Maxima of the Netherlands was born out of wedlock in Latin America. From the Trigger-Happy King Carlos to Sonja the Barmaid, Schönburg could surely reveal a lot of exciting stories – if he really knew what was going on behind the scenes. I guess I'll just have to keep waiting for the *Bild* headline, "Nobility Expert Reveals: How King Juan Carlos Killed His Brother." Not to mention the shocking revelations behind all of King Carlos' paternity suits.[212]

One of Count Alexander's books begins with the sentence *"Je suis superflu mais irremplaçable."* I am superfluous, yet irreplaceable. This is what Alexander von Schönburg showed us in his brilliant, 2012 masterpiece in the *Bild*, his interview with Fredrick the Great – 226 years after the King of Prussia's death. The headline read: *Bild* Interview with "Old Fritz."[213] That's just how it goes when you can buy contacts with a great name. In the meantime, I guess the really important contacts are being made somewhere else.

The Power of the Bilderbergers: Conspiracy Theory or Reality?

These days, there is hardly any other name that stands for alleged conspiracy theories as much as the name "Bilderberger." For some, Bilderberg Meetings are only informal, private meetings of influential people from politics, business, the military, the media and the aristocracy. For others, it is a conspiratorial group that is plotting world domination. When it comes to the Bilderbergers, who Wiki-Leaks has published many documents on,[214] the same conditions apply to the *Council on Foreign Relations*, with their similar orientation and discretion: No one is allowed to report any concrete account of what exactly is going on there and who said what. This is exactly what makes it difficult for outsiders to form a neutral opinion about the group – and practically invites all this speculation from conspiracy theorists.

Mind you, the media themselves also refer to the Bilderbergers as a conspiratorial group in their own reporting. The BBC has published the headlines, "Inside the Secretive Bilderberg Group," "Bilderberg: The Ultimate Conspiracy Theory," and "Elite Power Brokers Meet in Secret." The *Asia Times* described the group as the "Masters of the Universe" in a 2003 article of the same name.[215] In 2005, the *Münchner Merkur* reported on a "Secret Meeting of the Powerful," also in an article of the same name. The *Ottawa Citizen wrote in 2006, "The World's Elite Slip into Town for Secret*

Meeting." And CBC News asked in 2006 whether the Bilderberg meeting would be an "Informal Forum or Global Conspiracy?"

So, are the Bilderbergers the "Masters of the Universe" – like the *Asia Times* claimed? Not long before they were making headlines, anyone who even mentioned the conference was considered a wild conspiracy nut. Today it's different. These days you're at least allowed to mention that they exist.

The first time the conference was held was in May of 1954, at the invitation of Prince Bernhard of the Netherlands. It took place at his Hotel de Bilderberg in Oosterbeek in the Netherlands. Thus, the name Bilderberger was taken from the location of the first meeting. Although, since the very beginning, the fact remains that the Bilderbergers have received substantial financial contributions from both the American government and the CIA, as well as from private sources through the American Committee for a United Europe (ACUE) and other institutions. Therefore, it is by no means a neutral organization. Instead, the argument can be made that it is an interest-driven, pro-American institution, working in the shadows for Washington and American interests.

The Bilderberg Group is an elitist circle that has brought together top elites from Europe and the USA since 1954 – business leaders and strategists meet with hand-picked politicians and journalists. Bilderberg Meetings aren't simply about politicians' personal careers, they have more to do with the structural proximity to elite networks. This is why the representatives of Germany's "most popular parties," the CDU/CSU (Union) and the SPD, are regularly in attendance. Generally, only around 130 people take part in a Bilderberg Meeting, two thirds coming from Western Europe and one third from North America. About two thirds of the invited participants come from the financial sector, industry, universities and the media, and about one third from governments or political institutions.

The following excerpt is from the organization *LobbyControl*, writing on the 2014 Bilderberg Meeting in Copenhagen:

For many years, the weekly newspaper "Die Zeit," traditionally the second pillar of the Bilderbergers in Germany, was represented alongside Deutsche Bank in the "Steering Committee" of the meetings. This year, Mathias Döpfner from Axel Springer was now there instead of someone from Die Zeit. According to media journalist Stefan Niggemeier, Die Zeit has permanently given up its place at the Bilderberg Meetings. In an article on Die Zeit's code of ethics in March, he wrote, "Allegedly, however, there is an increasing awareness of questions of transparency and distance within the editorial staff. One consequence of this is that "Die Zeit" has given up its place at the infamous Bilderberg conference that it has held for many decades – 'irrevocably,' it is said. This seat has now been taken by Springer Chairman Mathias Döpfner." It's nice to hear that Die Zeit has gotten out. That Axel Springer is taking over, not so much. When it comes to the subject of the Bilderbergers, the media in Germany are still not doing themselves any favors. We need more critical publicity and reporting on these conferences, because these silent, high-ranking meetings play an important role in advancing common perspectives among the elites. They stand for the problem that democratic structures are being superimposed by nontransparent, informal connections.[216]

In 2007, the media scientist Uwe Krüger titled one of the few reports that appeared on the Bilderbergers in Germany: "Alpha-Journalists Embedded." In it, Krüger wrote:

Journalistic curiosity or even an eagerness to enlighten the public cannot be sensed in the established media. There is some evidence that this isn't a coincidence. In 1967, a memorandum was discovered in England in which the head of the Newspaper Proprietors Association, Cecil King, "reminded" his fellow publishers that "on no account should any report or even speculation about the content of the conferences" in St. Johns College, Cambridge be published (...) When US activist and filmmaker Alex Jones flew to Ottawa in 2006 to document the Bilderberg conference there, he was detained for 16 hours at the airport by Canadian immigration officials (...) Bilderberg author Daniel Estulin from Spain tells us of his ten-hour interview by the German intelligence agents at the airport in Munich when he was on his way to Rottach-Egern in 2005. Also, his little hotel in Rottach-Egern, where he later stayed, was full of intelligence agents.

Krüger continues:

While some journalists are ramming their heads up against the Bilderberg's ramparts, others are sitting comfortably inside, in a conference room of a five-star hotel, filled with heads of state, ministers and corporate board members. Questions must be asked: What are they doing there when they can't even report on it, especially since they're obliged to secrecy? What about Hajo Friedrich's call to always keep a critical distance and not to debase oneself, not even for a good cause? Doesn't the motto, "Be everywhere, without belonging there," apply to Bilderberg journalists? (...) Josef Joffe, co-editor of Die Zeit, answers a request for an interview succinctly in an e-mail: "Sorry, confidentiality is agreed to and adhered to."

But not only the controversial Josef Joffe, a litigious party pooper,[217] has sat at the Bilderbergers' table in the past. Even *Die Zeit* editor-in-chief, Theo Sommer, along with the journalists Matthias Nass (*Die Zeit*) and Christoph Bertram or the publisher Hubert Burda and Springer boss Mathias Döpfner had no fear of coming in contact with the Bilderbergers.

The Munich-based media sociologist and publicist Rudolf Stumberger said of the 2010 Bilderberg conference: He could not understand "that responsible editors of the weekly newspaper *Die Zeit*, for example, have been closely intertwined with Bilderbergers for many years and yet, like all other journalists taking part, have never written a single line about the conferences."

It is clear that important political or economic decisions are being made at the Bilderberg Meetings, in which democratic institutions are either not involved at all or only partially. Thus, the Trilateral Commission (another pro-American lobbying organization) already mentioned in this book, was founded at a Bilderberg conference based on Rockefeller's recommendations. According to a Belgian entrepreneur and honorary chairman, Etienne Davignon, the introduction of the euro also goes back to a Bilderberg conference.[218] Also, according to the former US ambassador to Germany, John McGhee, the Bilderberg conferences played an "important role" in drafting the Treaties of Rome, which established the European Economic Community (EEC).

But the Bilderbergers are just one of many similar elitist circles. In the book, *Superclass: The Global Power Elite and the World They Are Making*, David Rothkopf deals with the approximately 6,000, globally-active, top executives from governments, international corporations, financial conglomerates and the media who, due to their highly concentrated power, "basically hold the key to the planet in their hands." His research is characterized by the fact that, as a former Deputy Secretary of State for International Trade Relations in the Clinton administration, he had a glimpse into these circles himself. His presentation clearly shows that the Bilderberg conferences are only one of many forums where these types of meetings take place. David Rothkopf supports the view that:

> *The individuals who take part in these institutions ... probably do not have secret designs for world domination, but most likely do have common interests. They share similar goals and in many cases a similar view of the direction it should take. In linking together with one another, they aim not to conspire as a group but to enhance their own power by advantageous associations.*

Media expert Uwe Krüger clearly says what he thinks about the proximity of some journalists to the Bilderbergers and the secrecy surrounding these conspiratorial meetings:

> *This can be explained by a combination of several factors. First: Most ordinary journalists may have never even heard anything about Bilderberg until recently. Second: The alpha journalists with good contacts in the highest circles may have known about it, but they probably do not consider confidential meetings among the elite as scandalous, but*

rather normal, and do not want to jeopardize their contacts. Third: Journalists from the Springer, Burda and Holtzbrinck publishing houses disqualify themselves as whistleblowers because Mathias Döpfner, Hubert Burda and Matthias Nass (Die Zeit is a product of the Holtzbrinck-Publishing Group) are Bilderbergers and no one investigates the hand that feeds them. Fourth: For a good story, you need a good source. In the Bilderberg's case, there aren't any good sources: All participants are sworn to secrecy; all non-participants don't have any concrete knowledge. Seen normatively, however, the Bilderberg Meetings should come more into the public's focus, because this is where "soft power" comes from, and this is where global elites are socialized and networked.[219]

Powerful decision-makers from all over the world meet every year with a few select journalists and spend three days together in seclusion. The importance of these meetings to us, the citizenry, is a combination of such a concentration of power with the possible decisions and agreements that can be made at conferences like these. The oath of secrecy speaks contrary to an assumption that these conferences are merely for exchanging pleasantries. All participants are figures relevant to contemporary history and the public has a justified interest in what they are doing. The reason their actions continue to be deliberately concealed is unclear.

So, are the Bilderberg Meetings conferences for the "Masters of the Universe" as the *Asia Times* wrote? The French intellectual Thierry Meyssan, president and founder of the Voltaire Network and the Axis for Peace International Conference, has focused his attention on the Bilderbergers and their history like hardly anyone else before. He comes to a completely different conclusion: The Bilderbergers are a lobbying organization created by NATO that is meant to manipulate public opinion for pro-American purposes.[220] Also, journalists don't have any business being there.

Chapter 4. Buy a Journalist – See How Money Talks

Everyone named in this book denies having intimate, Velcro-snug contacts to elite organizations. Moreover, they deny being lobbyists. They also deny being "corrupted" by their proximity to the elite. And, they deny having lost their journalistic edge, working as they do in such close proximity to the aforementioned powers that be. They deny that this proximity has any influence on their reporting.

The German PR consultant Hasso Mansfeld advertises on his homepage: "We complement your media business at the highest levels – by arranging interviews, placing name articles…"[1] etc. Mansfeld, who originally studied to be a gardener,[2] probably isn't setting up these interviews for free. He also isn't the only one. Accordingly, there are many journalists and PR consultants out there who openly regard services like these as "perfectly normal." They don't see a conflict of interest when the public is presented with media reporting that, on closer inspection, appears to have been bought for a neutral third party. This sentence from Mansfeld the PR man's homepage is similar to ones used by many other PR agencies. Personally, when I read it, I feel it could just as easily say, "Buy yourself a journalist!"

As we will see, there are many Mansfelds out there who want to stuff us full of ethically questionable PR. Evidently, there are also even more journalists who want to get in on the action, or at least give PR reps like Mansfeld a stage. However, your average media consumer still thinks that credible journalists steer clear of PR-agencies like this, ones that openly advertise their ability to "arrange interviews" for the media. As vigilant citizens, we should see red flags going up when a plain[3] journalist like Stefan Faurin, for example, who sometimes writes for *Welt am Sonntag*, for *Cicero* and also for the financially struggling *Ruhrbarone* blog,[4] interviews the PR man Hasso Mansfeld about the future of the media.[5] In conducting this 2014 interview, Faurin not only condescended to doing PR legwork for Mansfeld, he was also plugging for Mansfeld's agency in the process. Yet, let's forget this trivial example and take a look at where it really gets disturbing – when the most important and influential media outlets start doing the legwork – when politicians, financial moguls and the top names from our public broadcasting channels and prestigious newspapers directly engage in the PR.

Two in Three Journalists are for Sale

While he was still alive, the publisher Axel Springer not only paid his editors good salaries, he also gave them Christmas presents. In addition to their holiday bonuses, every editor also received a gift (a television set or the like) and a large box full of delicacies from Michelsen's gourmet foods in Hamburg. For the publishing house's jubilee, all his employees received a gold coin. So, to receive gifts like these, what did Springer's journalists have to do? Here's one example: In February of 1983, the *Bild am Sonntag* started a smear campaign against Hans-Jochen Vogel, the SPD's candidate for chancellor at the time. The newspaper ran a front-page story that "revealed (…) the Nazi Party history of the chancellor candidate, Dr. Vogel." He was a "former Nazi cultural officer." It quickly turned out, however, that this SPD politician's alleged Nazi past consisted of him being a squad leader in the Hitler Youth when he was 16. Furthermore, this so-called exposé was managed directly out of Axel Springer's office in Berlin. Some journalists, who pleased Axel Springer exceptionally well, even received the keys to a new car. Today, these days are over. Today, many journalists and their publishing houses are simply fighting for survival. Today, all of the boundaries are blurred.

A 2014 decision by the German Federal Supreme Court clarified the situation: Purchased reports must be clearly and unambiguously labeled with the word "advertisement" and printed in a clearly distinguishable format for the reader.[6] In reality, however, this isn't the case. In 2014, the business magazine *brand eins* told us what it's really all about these days. In giant letters on the cover: "KAUF, DU ARSCH" (BUY, YOU ASS).[7] Around the coffee machine, journalists discuss how far you can let them bribe you as an editor,[8] and then they get back to work. The "dossiers" and "specials" these days are rather audacious too. Here is a January 2014 example from *Capital*. The topic: "Your personal pension plan." Sole advertiser: The ERGO Insurance Group. Concept: "ERGO Pension Guarantee" and "We can advise you." The aim: customer acquisition. This is enough to make your stomach turn.

According to industry experts, Wolfram Weimer, a colleague of mine at the *Frankfurter Allgemeine Zeitung* from 1990 to 1998, has perfected the business of purchased reports. Since founding the Weimer Media Group in 2012, he has been publishing business magazines.[9] One of them is called *Börse am Sonntag* (Stock Market on Sunday). It features "guest contributions." Consequently, the advertising expert Dr. Thomas Levermann has written some ugly things about my former FAZ colleague and his product, *Börse am Sonntag*. He tells us they have:

… "guest contributions" in the Wolfram Weimer publication "Börse am Sonntag." These stand out because of their particularly critical interviews. Quote: "BaS: ActivTrades is one of the most successful CFD brokers. In your opinion, what are the most important reasons for the company's strong growth?" This works in three ways: The first method is where contributions like these are paid for directly (another example from the Börse am Sonntag here[10]), but not indicated as such, so these are the worst of all. With the second type, the contributions are paid for indirectly, because there is also an advertisement in the same or in the

next issue, (sorry Börse am Sonntag, one of yours[11] *again in the Wikifolio example). The third is when the contribution is not identified as an "advertisement," but labeled instead as "in cooperation with."*

Perhaps all this is technically legal – but it certainly isn't ethically sound from my point of view.

Markus Wiegand, editor-in-chief at *Wirtschaftsjournalist* (Business Journalist), has had nasty experiences with the alpha journalist Wolfram Weimer. He writes about the authorizing of a front-page interview with Weimer for *Wirtschaftsjournalist* in 2014:

The conversation with the publisher and long-time top journalist, Wolfram Weimer, in a restaurant in Munich's English Garden was fairly normal. (...) However, its subsequent authorization was much more laborious than seldom before. Weimer lengthened the conversation by a third (...), relativized several statements and honed many of the formulations with his own, ambitious PR-style. All of it verged on the limits of acceptability. This award-winning journalist, however, also went over the line when he lent his hand to the exact way in which the questions were asked during the interview. Original question: "Your last position, with 'Focus,' was a failure according to public accounts. Did your transition to the publishing side have something to do with this?" Question after it was authorized by Weimer: "At your last position, with 'Focus,' you weren't as successful as usual. Did your transition to the publishing side have something to do with this?" For the printed version, Weimer didn't want to be asked why his publishing house's offerings were "hardly being noticed" and that the impression was being created from the outside that he was now "in the third league." Weimer found these passages ranged from being "outrageous to humiliating" and changed them. In turn, I didn't want to accept this.[12]

Media enterprises and their employees are first and foremost companies with business interests. Put simply: They have the goal of maximizing their profits. The goal of publishers and journalists is also to earn money. As everywhere, this interest in making money has a significant influence on the business itself. Anyone who pretends that journalists and publishers are good Samaritans, whose first concern is a commitment to pure truth and the common good, is lying to themselves. They also don't understand why journalists are becoming more and more compromised, especially in a time that is becoming increasingly difficult for the industry financially.

Public officials who take a bribe of a few euros are considered corrupt. They get dismissed and may face criminal charges. With journalists, however, bribery seems to be a given. It is even considered to be standard business etiquette. The more journalists allow themselves to be corrupted, the greater their chances of moving up the career ladder. Anyone can become a government or corporate spokesman. All you have to do is be willing to regurgitate the wishy-washy talking points coming out of political or corporate marketing departments. If you can convincingly pass these off on the public as "news," you're in business. We are about to meet many more examples of corrupt journalists.

Two out of three journalists in German-speaking countries can be bought – and they consider this to be completely normal. From the 45,000 full-time journalists and a further 40,000 freelance journalists in Germany, around 73,000 regularly take advantage of press discounts. In plain language: They're personally capitalizing on these advantages. Another verifiable figure: 74 percent of all German journalists can be bought willingly.[13] On the homepage of a major German portal for journalists, visitors are greeted with the words: "Press discounts of up to 50 percent included: The largest press discount database on the Internet helps journalists save money: Over 1700 press discounts from airline tickets, fitness equipment, coffee machines and teddy bears to personal lubricants ensure market transparency. Together with 10,000 tips from industry insiders, Germany's largest press discount database offers the best tips on everything affecting the press."[14]

Journalists are also active and assertive when they're demanding discounts from companies. Dominik Stawski wrote his dissertation on it and he comes to some astonishing conclusions.[15] He said, "I was stunned by what the companies had to say. Some of their press representatives said that journalists put them under a lot of pressure to get a discount. This goes as far as to threatening companies with negative reviews."[16]

The European Union, for example, pays journalists for positive reporting on Brussels. So far, German journalists alone have secretly received almost one million euros for this.[17] In order to get the money, they even sign a formal obligation stating, among other things, "I affirm that I will not damage, directly or indirectly, the image of the European Union, its policies and its institutions." In plain language: Critical reporting is unwelcome. So, the journalists toe the line with their reporting – for a fee, of course. We live in a giant theatre. The play presently on stage is called "democracy." As we can see, the so-called "freedom of the press" in this play is only a well-acted illusion.

It's not just about getting paid either. Every week, I receive e-mails from PR agencies that offer to discreetly and inconspicuously network journalists with PR departments. That's not illegal, but I don't think it's morally appropriate. I never answer them, so you shouldn't be able to find me in one of these databases through any fault of my own. Why don't I do it? Because my readers wouldn't know which PR agency is "supporting" my reporting from behind the scenes. Just so you can get an idea of these offers, I will quote a typical e-mail. This is one I received in July of 2014:

Subject: Request for inclusion in the Cision Journalists Database

Dear Ladies and Gentlemen,

My name is... and I work as a media researcher in the editorial department of Cision Germany GmbH, a leading service provider for the PR industry. We are currently expanding our journalist database in the fields of daily news and health and would like to add new members to our (...) editorial staff. The aim of our database is to facilitate a topic-related dialogue and exchange of information between media representatives and PR professionals, specifically focused on the subject areas of the journalists, bloggers and media listed with us. From our clients – PR agencies as well as small and large companies – you would receive press releases as well as invitations to press events and further information relevant to your field of journalism. Naturally, there are no costs associated with your inclusion and we guarantee that the data will not be made publicly accessible in any way. (...) Thank you very much. Best regards, (...) Media Researcher DACH, CISIONGermany GmbH, Hanauer Landstraße 287-289, 60314 Frankfurt/Main

According to my earlier experiences, when you're in databases like these, you do get many lovely invitations. You will be courted as a journalist. Then, at some point down the line, you won't even know how cleverly you're being manipulated anymore.

Favoring Favors: How to Bend the Media's Knees

Increasingly, money is no longer an object when it comes to buying journalists. For four days in 2008, around thirty German automotive journalists took up Volkswagen's invitation to travel to the Olympic Games in Beijing – at a cost of up to 25,000 euros per person. The way I see it, VW's goal was to bribe them. As a PR man from the car company explained during an in-house tax audit in July 2008, they wanted to invite select journalists to the Olympic Games in Beijing in August, "In order to guarantee positive reporting in the media." The Games were sponsored by VW and the journalists were used to pay homage to Volkswagen's generosity. The then deputy editor-in-chief of the *Autozeitung* (Auto Magazine), Walter Eschment, let himself be corrupted in this way. He went with them to Beijing. As to the revelations that were later published about this soft form of bribery, he let everyone know, "I think it's extremely stupid when journalists investigate each other." Also present in Beijing, Stefan Anker, head of the automotive desk for the Springer paper *Die Welt*, and, surprise surprise, an employee of the *Frankfurter Allgemeine Zeitung*[18] also accepted VW's offer.

This type of purchased reporting can be found right where the average reader expects it least: in the most prestigious media establishments. The most prominent of these include formerly respectable gazettes like the

Frankfurter Allgemeine Zeitung. Yours truly worked for the FAZ for a long time. A portion of my business trips, which I had to go on behalf of the various FAZ editorial departments, were paid invitations from companies, governments or even factions involved in civil wars. As a FAZ journalist at the head office in Frankfurt at the time, I was made aware of a few things. One, for example, was that accepting invitations to go on paid trips and then composing hymns of praise for whomever had invited you was just the nature of the business. In my 17 years with the FAZ, such – in retrospect – dubious journalistic practices were simply a part of everyday life. I also witnessed many of my colleagues doing the same thing.

Nothing seems to have changed since I left. In 2012, for example, there was a headline in *Focus* that read: "The FAZ allowed ThyssenKrupp to invite them on an expensive trip." In the report they wrote: "The ThyssenKrupp steel conglomerate has apparently invited journalists on luxury trips that included a broad spectrum of leisure activities. Awkward, embarrassing: even the renowned FAZ accepted invitations – shortly thereafter, a flattering article appeared."[19] According to the article, the FAZ editor flew in the ThyssenKrupp corporate jet from Düsseldorf to Munich, and then in first class to Beijing with Lufthansa. There, the reporter spent the night in 5-star hotels at ThyssenKrupp's expense. The total cost of the trip that ThyssenKrupp spent on the FAZ man: allegedly around 15,000 euros. *Deutschlandfunk* (German public radio) later reported that the trip's purpose was not only to get a courtesy article printed in the FAZ, but also making him amenable and getting a permanent commitment from this FAZ journalist. In an exposé by *Deutschlandfunk*, *Die Welt* journalist Jörg Eigendorf provides a quote on the FAZ's bribery by ThyssenKrupp, saying: "To be honest: It isn't about the article afterward at all. That's not the one that matters. This is about creating a close connection, getting access and getting journalists on board, like helping them into a boat they can't get out of by themselves anymore. You create a certain dependency here and you also put the journalist in a situation that, afterwards, makes it difficult for him to act in a way that's undesirable or to write anything disagreeable."[20]

The FAZ later announced that it found all of this to be completely normal. Therefore, the FAZ was basically stating that the newspaper's independence remained intact, regardless of whether their editors accepted such invitations or not.[21] This statement didn't surprise me in the least. After all, my experience wasn't any different when I was working at the FAZ. In the 1980s, I went on one of my first foreign assignments for the FAZ – to Namibia and South Africa. This was financed, not by the FAZ, but by the South African apartheid regime, which was still in power at that time. One of my next luxury trips to southern Africa, on assignment for the FAZ's political desk, was financed by a South African gold industry association, and further trips followed at short intervals. The FAZ even accepted an invitation to Iraq by the Iraqi dictator Saddam Hussein in the summer of

1988. They sent me as a pro-Iraqi reporter to the battlefields on the Iraq-Iran border in July of 1988, where Iranians had just been gassed with German-manufactured chemical weapons. What I want to say here is: It didn't matter if it was for luxury trips in 5-star hotels or to battlefields where poison gas was still lingering in the air, if the invitation was all-inclusive, my bosses had no qualms about accepting the offer. Just so that this is perfectly clear to the reader, that actual invitations were extended to media outlets to send journalists to report on a poison gas attack on the battlefield: This wasn't a place where you could just rent a car at the airport and go see the battlefield as a tourist. This was a war zone. These were very well-organized invitations.

Media professionals are apparently a particularly greedy segment of the general population. The financial benefits seem to be an integral part of their way of thinking. A Daimler-Chrysler employee reported: "If we give a journalist a car to test for a month, we wind up getting complaints that he can't keep driving it for another half a year."[22] Freeloading journalists can't seem to get enough.

"As an automotive journalist, you would have to be really stupid to ever buy a car," remarked Franz Danner's lawyer in a study by *Transparency Deutschland*.[23] Danner was a former marketing manager at Mazda. When it comes to working with journalists, Danner's work provides a deep insight into the lobbying work done by a car company. In automobile journalism, it is standard practice to order one new test car after another. Danner sometimes handed journalists the keys to a test car and let them use it until the next model came in. The gala presentations of new car models were often only a "facade for luxurious trips to enticing locations," the study says. For example, when he organized test drives in Vienna, the journalists he invited also received tickets to attend the spectacular Vienna Opera Ball and a custom-tailored evening tailcoat. In 2013, Danner stood before the 6th Criminal Chamber in the Cologne District Court after being charged with criminal breach of trust. He was accused with not only having bribed many journalists, but also to cheating Mazda out of a total of 41 million euros.[24] In his trial, he frankly stated what it looks like when a car manufacturer is dealing with journalists. "Media landscaping" is what it's called. How he influenced the media was reported in the *Berliner Zeitung*.[25] "It was my job," Danner said, "to ensure that written and broadcast reports about the cars were as positive as possible." In detail, this means:[26]

To make automotive journalists "pleasantly agreeable," Danner says there is a relatively simple formula. The PR expert listed the following: "Super destination, super hotel, super service, super gifts." A German car manufacturer, for example, once invited journalists to Sardinia for the presentation of a new car. They then had a private jet for 40 people waiting at the airport to fly them to their destination: an exclusive hotel on Sardinia's Costa Smeralda, (Europe's most expensive resort area). *Other companies would go to Cape Town and combine the presentation of a new model with a trip through the desert to Namibia. "The more attractive the location, the better the press," said Danner.*

According to Danner, Mazda is said to have organized about ten such events for automotive journalists. As to the accommodations, the ex-PR man described them rather drastically:

"Every automotive journalist was free to drink the minibar dry, order champagne at the hotel bar until sunrise, and take advantage of all the services a five-star hotel has to offer at our expense."[27]

The annual budget for Mazda's PR department at their European headquarters in Leverkusen was between 15 and 16 million euros. The expenses earmarked for influencing journalists were subject to a simple cost-benefit analysis:

"We had a very simple calculation: The average journalist taking part in one of our events costs us three to five thousand euros. All they had to do was give us a return of at least 15,000 euros on our investment. They never let us down."[28]

Danner's people in the Mazda PR department even measured whether this business goal had been achieved: How long a column about a car was in a newspaper, how many seconds a vehicle was shown on television, how much coverage it got on the Internet.

"If you consider what an advertisement in a newspaper or even television commercials cost, the journalists' automotive reports were almost cheap in comparison, despite the average event costing around two million euros."[29]

An additional positive effect of influencing reporting like this was that journalistic articles come across as much more credible than simply paid advertising – although in reality, it's the same thing.

The Mazda Group did not want to comment on the details and, according to its own statement, assumed that Danner had implemented all these actions "in compliance with our code of conduct." What's also telling is how little coverage the Danner trial received, given the journalistic practices that were exposed throughout it. Danner also said during the trial:

"There was a well-developed culture of looking the other way." He continued, "Everybody knew it was my job to keep the journalists happy by whatever means necessary. And you wouldn't want to know the exact details of these means."[30]

For many years now, top German lawyers have been pointing out that there is no threat of punishment for corruption among members of the media in Germany. Professor Dr. Ulrich Sommer, a well-known lawyer specializing in criminal corruption, admonishes us, "We must ask ourselves if we finally want to change the fact that journalists can act like they're beyond the law." Michael Loer is the senior public prosecutor in the Frankfurt public prosecutor's office (he heads the anti-corruption department for the financial crimes division). Loer warns us of a legal situation that is still far from satisfactory, "We cannot guarantee credibility through legislation, rather, this must be the focus of professional ethics. If this were the case, more corrupt practices would certainly come to light."[31]

Coming from the USA, there is a new trend that is now attracting more attention in Germany: Buy yourself a journalist. On the www.spot.us[32] website, users (mostly corporations) can suggest topics to journalists and openly pay for reporting. This is called "community funded reporting." Yes, in all seriousness, the business model is: Buy yourself a journalist.

Also in Germany, the boundary between PR and journalism is becoming increasingly blurry. In a research paper on marketing, it was said that this increasingly results in a "win-win situation":

Product PR and journalism always find themselves in a win-win situation if both sides have an interest in publicity. Finally, that cooperation is not always initiated from the product PR side can be demonstrated by using the "car" example again, where daily tabloid media like to compete to be the first outlet to publish so-called "production mule photos." If we speak of this situation as a "secret" win-win situation, this can be taken in two ways. The first meaning being the reciprocal contacts, the personal relationships, which take place behind closed doors and thus in "secret places." The second aspect of this secret win-win situation is related to the debate surrounding journalism. This is because journalists are essentially taking on the role of marketing agents in publicizing a product. If this wasn't kept secret, it could create the impression that journalists are being partisan and that isn't readily compatible with our classic expectations of a journalist's role in society.[33]

Journalists are thus increasingly becoming "marketing agents." Is the average citizen aware of this?

Now, to use an old German adage, one crow doesn't peck another's eye out. Among journalists, we're expected to stick together, and even if we fight, we shouldn't compromise each other's chances of career survival. This is why this book will quickly become the object of the entire industry's hatred. Just like a doctor who is forbidden from talking about malpractice within the medical establishment and will become an outcast among colleagues when they violate this unwritten rule, a journalist is expected to see no evil when it comes to corrupt reporting. We are supposed to leave all the filthy evidence behind the closed doors of our so-called "elites." German journalists find self-criticism extremely difficult. This is also confirmed by the study, "Little Prudes? How German Journalists Deal with Criticism," by the Erich Brost Institute for International Journalism at the Technical University of Dortmund.[34] Around 1800 journalists from twelve European and two Arab countries answered questions on self-criticism and self-control in their own professional lives. The result: One third of German respondents said they never or almost never criticize colleagues themselves, while two thirds reported never or almost never being criticized by colleagues. This has become something like an iron rule: Dish it out, but don't take it. The editor of *Wirtschaftswoche*, Sebastian Matthes, once broke this iron rule. He wrote in his blog:

There has been a lot of discussion in recent years about doctors and luxury travel financed by pharmaceutical companies. Never anything about German reporters taking business trips to Miami, Barcelona or Dubai, where car manufacturers are sometimes merely presenting the latest cosmetic changes to popular models. Naturally, their flights are always at the car manufacturer's expense, with seats in the business class or better. No wonder so many automotive journalists have long enjoyed Senator status with Lufthansa. (...) If doctors aren't allowed to accept an invitation to see the presentation of a new painkiller on a tropical island in the South Pacific because this may influence their decision when choosing a medication for their patients, how can journalists remain objective after a trip to Miami? We also hear stories about managing editors at large newspapers who let their paper's automotive editor enjoy driving a Porsche over a long weekend. (...) Frankly, we need to start talking about this situation as soon as possible. (...) Why is this hardly discussed? Because it involves so many.[35]

Bribery in journalism is one of the best kept secrets of the whole profession. The other is the secrecy surrounding their proximity to power. Nearly all of the prestigious German-language media outlets, as we have already seen, have very close connections to the movers and shakers within business and politics.[36] They never mention this to their customers – the public. There is good reason for this – they are also being corrupted from above. In the end, the result is what more and more citizens are rejecting every day: bought and manipulated disinformation that only serves the interests of a small clique.

But it's even more horrifying that that. In the past, the advertising departments of media companies also offered their customers the opportunity to influence the scope and choice of topics of their reporting in secret talks.[37] From the *Westdeutsche Allgemeine Zeitung* (WAZ), which belongs to the SPD, the Social Democratic Party, to the *Frankfurter Rundschau* (FR), which today belongs to the *Frankfurter Allgemeine Zeitung*, advertisers were able to exert direct influence on reporting. At least this was the way things worked in the past. Logically, any assertions that a separation of journalism and its advertising business has somehow developed in the meantime are often pure fiction. For example, with regard to the Bauer Media Group, Andreas Eickelkamp, a lecturer at the Free University of Berlin, says:

Among the Bauer Media Group, there were many cases of surreptitious advertising, especially in their low-priced women's magazines. There, it was primarily pharmaceutical companies that had exerted their influence on editorial reporting. This behavior was reprimanded by the Press Council several times. This is a classic example of what it looks like when a publishing house has weak editorial policies. The pharmaceutical industry in particular is subject to remarkably strict advertising guidelines – and if it still is able to infiltrate editorial texts, this is a clear indication of a poor publishing culture.[38]

The media world used to be clearly structured and rather straightforward. There were PR agencies that did lobbying. There were journalists who were committed to certain principles. Today these boundaries are rapidly dissolving or are long since gone. This is what they say in *medienforum*:

Public relations' increasing encroachment on journalism is hardly being noticed by the public. In addition to their journalistic offerings, large publishers have already been publishing PR magazines for a long time. Grüner + Jahr, for example, publishes corporate promotional materials including the customer magazines for Deutsche Bahn (DB mobil) and Volkswagen AG (VW Magazin). In view of this proximity, it can't be easy for the editorial offices of the publisher's journalistic titles to keep a critical distance from Deutsche Bahn and Volkswagen.[39]

Anyone compiling facts like these will quickly be branded as an enemy – simply for being the messenger. When the example of an exclusive safari trip was used to reveal how corrupt some media houses are, there were legal threats. A media portal reported:

Journalists from the Süddeutsche Zeitung, Tagesspiegel, NRZ and Rheinische Post were on a safari in South Africa in March 2011. "The trip provided the expected background information about the company," reports Tagesspiegel editor-in-chief Stephan-Andreas Casdorff to Welt am Sonntag. The other newspapers also made similar arguments. The SZ pointed out that the reporter in question is a freelancer. The NRZ even threatened the WamS indirectly: "Please understand that we will subject any other reporting about our house to a legal review" (...).[40]

People don't like to talk about it. The South Korean company Samsung, for example, invited journalists to the Olympic Games in London – and used them for courtesy reporting. Samsung did the same at the Internationale Funkausstellung Berlin (Berlin Radio Show, (IFA)) in Berlin.[41] Travel expenses were paid for and nice reports were expected.

Exposed: The Side Hustle

In Germany, every resident must register their address with the government (*Meldepflicht*), and in turn, every address is required to pay a fee for public broadcasting (*Rundfunkbeitrag*). What everyone paying this mandatory tax has always suspected is now official: Quite a few of the journalists employed in public broadcasting companies make a lot of money on the side. Elected government officials who are financed by taxes must publicly report any additional income. Personalities working for public broadcasters, which are essentially financed by additional taxes, do not.

News anchors from public broadcasting channels receive up to 20,000 euros for talking to a private audience.[42] The NDR (Northern German Broadcasting) media magazine *Zapp* reported on the lucrative additional income being made by prominent television journalists for side jobs such as corporate appearances. Their list included names like the ARD's Tom Buhrow, Michael Antwerpes and Anja Kohl, as well as the ZDF's Claus Kleber, Peter Elahne and Petra Gerster. Former ZDF editor-in-chief Nikolaus Brender said that the additional income made by journalists with any claim to credibility should be transparent. He said, "A journalist who wants to carry out activities on the side should publicly report what they do, who pays them and what their fee is."

In an NDR report from 2009, they asked, "...can you really still carry out a critical interview with a bank director if that same bank already paid you a lot of money to moderate a panel discussion? Is it possible to report independently on a company today when you did advertising for them yesterday?"[43] Clearly, journalists don't make corporate appearances for free. These appearances have their price and the only people who learn this information are the ones actually trying to book journalists for their events. In 2009, the NDR magazine *Zapp* listed these speaking fees to an astonished public. They reported, "Still: after many discussions, Zapp got the price lists from the agencies. For a presentation or a lecture by Petra Gerster they charge about 14,000 euros, for Tom Buhrow around 20,000 euros, the same amount for Claus Kleber, Anja Kohl allegedly comes for about 6,500 euros, Peter Eiahne for around 10,000 euros, and the agency price for Michael Antwerpes is about 8,000 euros. What remains unclear is how much the journalists themselves receive – neither the agencies or the journalists were willing to divulge that informaiton."[44]

Anja Kohl is an ARD presenter who regularly covers the stock market and financial news for ARD. After one of the NDR broadcasts, her appearances became rather controversial. *Zapp* explained: "Because she moderates and speaks at events that are also financed by banks and corporations whose shares are traded on the stock exchange. Her face and her advice graces company brochures and she also receives fees for her appearances at energy company events. For some critics, this poses a conflict of interest."[45]

Professor Christian Schicha, media scientist at the Düsseldorf University of Applied Sciences, said, "It upsets me when journalists, in addition to their work, look for additional opportunities to make a name for themselves, to earn income that they only get because of their popularity. This doesn't necessarily have anything to do with having expert knowledge, but it does have a lot to do with having celebrity status. So, it upsets me when this popularity is then used to literally open the doors of opportunity in these areas."

The highest paid journalists, the ones already sitting at the head of the conference table, don't do too badly either. According to press reports, the former nightly news anchor, Tom Buhrow, received an annual salary of over 3,500,000 euros from WDR in 2013.[46] The head personnel at ARD and ZDF earn more than our heads of government – and they also pocket cash on the side.

Brainwashing: Power Scissors in Your Head

Brainwashing is psychological manipulation toward automatic self-censorship. It is used in an attempt to control someone's consciousness and it is a hallmark of totalitarian states. When the North Korean media publish coordinated reporting in praise of their beloved leader, this is a form of brainwashing. If the mullahs in Tehran get hundreds of thousands out on the streets and everyone is chanting slogans like "Death to the USA," then we are also seeing brainwashing in action there. In totalitarian states like North Korea or Iran, no journalist is allowed to report anything other than the official line. The result: unanimous public opinion. In democracies, on the other hand, we are told there is no brainwashing taking place. After all, in 1975 the United Nations banned all forms of brainwashing and consciousness control used on populations or population groups. So, how should we refer to what the "quality media" is producing these days in the German-speaking world? Where pluralism and different opinions once argued with each other, today we have a climate of fear.

Evolution has given humans eyes to see their world – and a brain to process these impressions. Human beings are also susceptible to delusions. Knowing this, politicians and also the media like to paint a picture of our world that is often completely different from what we can see for ourselves upon closer inspection. While this picture may indeed be politically correct, we are now afraid of the truth. There are taboos among journalists.

An older, yet very good example: On June 5, 2008, Maybrit Illner hosted a panel discussion on ZDF television about the spying scandal at Deutsche Telekom (T-Mobile). Prior to the broadcast, the public had found out that

Telekom's management had illegally compared telephone connection data from supervisory board members and journalists between 2005 and 2006. They did this to find out who had leaked internal corporate information from supervisory board meetings to the media. In the panel discussion to debate the issue, there were top politicians such as Wolfgang Bosbach and journalists including Hans Leyendecker (*Süddeutsche*). However, even though the scandal was also about the failings of the new Telekom CEO René Obermann (head of the mobile division at the time), his name was never mentioned once. How could this be? Possibly because Maybrit Illner, the segment's moderator, and René Obermann were seeing each other in private at the time? (They married in 2010). This obvious blind spot made it clear for everyone to see that there are taboos when it comes to reporting. Over the course of the discussion, the panel seemed to discuss every possible aspect of this serious spying affair. Still, they somehow forgot to mention the name of someone with direct responsibility for it. Neither Wolfgang Bosbach (CDU) nor Hans Leyendecker, nor Sabine Leutheusser-Schnarrenberger, the Minister of Justice, or even the managing director of the Federal Association of German Detectives (BDD) broke this unspoken taboo.

From a culture once known for its poets and thinkers, Germany is now a land full of cowards. Free thought, the key to our former prosperity, is now considered indecent. We are the victims of brainwashing by the media. Politically correct journalists, who willfully redact their own work, are dictating our thinking – just like in a totalitarian dictatorship. For the average citizen today, being politically correct means you have accepted the brainwashing and dutifully swallowed the lies coming from politicians and the media. So, what really distinguishes us from Iran or North Korea?

In Germany and elsewhere in the Western world, we are tangled up in such a dense network of taboos and political correctness, we are no longer allowed to even address this situation openly. The mere suspicion of having violated political correctness can brand someone as an idiot for the rest of their life (like the former German President Heinrich Lübke). Others are shunned as outsiders. Everyone knows this. And now, just like in a dictatorship, everyone simply obeys, in strict compliance with thought and language requirements. Anyone who can think clearly and steps outside the bounds of political correctness is quickly branded as an evil "populist." We're even afraid of being called "populist." Why is this? After all, the word "populist" literally comes from the Latin "populus" (people) and denotes a familiarity with the people. As a citizen, is it really taboo to be close to the people?

In the old days, executions used to take place in public, in the market squares. Today, the media plays the role of executioner for all those who still defy this prescribed political correctness. Established on what is assumed to be the moral high ground, the media has been given the prerogative to interpret all language. Anyone daring to question this authority will quickly disappear – if they haven't already been hanged in the media by a politically correct lynch mob.

Anyone who doesn't believe in the future of the euro, for example, is portrayed in the German-language media as an enemy of Europe and eternally living in the past. If you have any doubts as to the degree of human involvement in this alleged, anthropogenic climate change, you get booed and hissed. Even worse are those who look for the cause of poverty and other social problems among the afflicted themselves. They are accused of being hard-hearted and lacking any sympathy. When it comes to Christianity, things are completely different. It seems like everyone is free to badmouth Christians and Christian values as much as they want these days. For some reason, the situation is completely different when the subject is Islam. While criticism of the church is considered to be progressive, a critical view of Islam is regarded as xenophobic, practically worse than anti-Semitism.

Looking at the paternalism we see in our thought and speech, the patronizing attitude taken toward the public in the German-speaking world, a people who once thought so freely, it gives you the unmistakable feeling that journalists have taken over the role of the block wardens. These were the Nazi Party functionaries responsible for the local political supervision of a neighborhood. When journalists exemplify these rigid thought patterns better than anyone else, how else can we describe them? They have herded the public into a cage of fear. We now have a new language, *Schönsprech* or beautiful speech, that makes everything nicer. We now call ugly people "aesthetically challenged" and the stupid "intellectually challenged." We say "generation 60 plus" instead of retired and "differently abled" instead of disabled. And no politician wants to "admit" anything anymore, they are much more likely to "acknowledge." All this conforms with the conversational tone of political correctness.

In recent years, editorial offices have been very busy. Imperceptibly, they have been replacing thousands of old words with new ones. Usually, the average citizen doesn't even notice it. Those in the media who are entrusted with the prerogative to interpret our language, they are the ones who are changing our thinking by predefining these new, politically correct terms for us. We now call killing civilians "collateral damage" and a layoff is now a "release." When he wrote his 1949 masterpiece, *1984*, George Orwell called this surreptitious transformation of language "Newspeak." In the novel, he explains that "Newspeak" was developed to reduce the variety of thoughts people could have. In plain language: to unify the thinking of the masses through brainwashing. An example: Millions of Germans listen to the ZDF anchorman Claus Kleber read the news on a daily basis. In the late summer of 2013, when the discussion was about whether Western troops should intervene in the Syrian civil war or not, Claus Kleber explained what war is and literally said, "Although, to round things out, we must also say that nobody is talking about war at the moment. They are talking about the possibility of a limited military strike as a punitive measure."[47] So, when we're talking about – like the Western countries were at the time – invading a foreign country and bombing it, then this doesn't have anything to do with war. No, Claus Kleber was "rounding things out" and spoke of a "limited punitive measure." At the same time, *Bild* called the planned operation a "limited deployment" – journalists avoid the word "war." This is how the politically correct manipulation of the masses works, by using new patterns of words, which predefines the way the masses of people out there think.

In Germany, we're still waiting on a constitution, but the "Basic Law" of the land guarantees the freedom of expression. The Basic Law permits more than what this political correctness allows us. The Allensbach Institute for Public Opinion Research proved this in 2013.[48] According to this institution, the number of social taboos and strict language regulations is increasing. A considerable segment of the population definitely feel that they may be subject to social pressures if their views deviate from the societal consensus. Increasing numbers of people have the feeling that they are no longer allowed to say certain things. They don't want to "say the wrong thing," because there are real punishments for having differing opinions. The gatekeepers of political correctness – intellectual journalists – decide what can and cannot be discussed in public. It doesn't even have anything to do with healthy common sense anymore. Political correctness wants to condemn differing opinions as immoral. This is why no one criticizes dissenting opinions anymore – they simply hate them. Anyone who contradicts these conventions will not be refuted. Instead, they are silenced. The new Jacobins, touting the editorial offices' one true opinion, claim that many of these dissenting opinions are a shameful violation of honor and decency. In Germany, claims like these are quickly followed by accusations of inciting the public. People are afraid of this. This has created a situation in Germany today where our freedom of thought only exists on paper. Political correctness in the media's editorial offices is nothing other than a modern form of censorship. Banned speech and censorship have given rise to a sordid conformism.

The average citizen has been enduring this for a long time now. We have participated in it ourselves. We have become its molded followers. Indeed for a long time, we didn't even notice how stupid we were, letting journalists rape our language with unspeakable new creations. The following example is specific to the German language, but the trend is similar elsewhere. Today, the most common of these disparaging developments to the German language is the capital I, now being inserted into the middle of words. It is used to denote gender inclusivity. In German, when referring to any one group of people, instead of simply saying, for example, activists and politicians, we now say activists and activist*Innen* and politicians and politician*Innen*. And, if German words weren't long enough to begin with, heaven help you if you'll have to talk about professionals like development aid experts, because now you're obliged to say *Entwicklungshilfeexperten und EntwicklungshilfeexpertInnen*. All this must make an unassuming housewife (*Hausfrau*) feel pretty stupid, not having any special way to demonstrate her femininity through how she spells the title of her occupation. Perhaps we could adapt the English "homemakers" to *Heimmacher und HeimmacherInnen*. Regardless, we Germans are still proud of the advanced state of our media down-dumbing. Even the less gifted must notice that women sure do like to attach importance to the feminine plural ("*Innen*") when it comes to professions such as professors, doctors, journalists, authors, teachers and all other terms that aren't masculine (in the grammatical sense) in the first place. However, as strange as it may sound, you never see this in the media when it comes to murderers, thieves, terrorists and other criminals. They don't want to have anything to do with that, that's purely a man thing. Furthermore, we haven't seemed to have discovered gender equality in descriptive appellations like monster*Innen*, slacker*Innen* or jackass*Innen* yet either. The politically correct, feminist language policy of our intellectual journalists simply hasn't taken this into account.

One man who has recognized the everyday madness of journalists is Jacob Appelbaum. He could be compared to whistleblower Edward Snowden, who gained international notoriety thanks to his revelations about the extent of the NSA's spying. Jacob Appelbaum is an American journalist. In 2014, he received the Henri Nannen Prize for investigative journalism. Afterward, he publicly declared that he intended to melt down his prize, a bronze bust of Henri Nannen. Appelbaum pointed out that Nannen, the founder of the German weekly *Stern* magazine, was a member of an SS propaganda company for the Third Reich, working in the "Südstern" (Southern Star) unit. Nannen had close connections to the Nazi regime and was a stadium announcer for the Nazis at the 1936 Olympic Games in Berlin. The "Südstern" unit insignia used by the SS would later inspire Nannen's logo for his *Stern* magazine, which he founded after the war. In 2014, Appelbaum published texts which, according to his research, shine a whole new light on Hitler's diaries. He wrote, "After the war, Henri Nannen was later involved in attempting to present the Hitler Diaries to the public as a fact." Appelbaum says of Nannen, "we know that he was involved in key meetings regarding the decision to publish the Hitler Diaries. It is often forgotten that the Hitler Diaries were actually a whitewash of Adolf Hitler; they presented him as being against Kristallnacht, of wanting peace with England and opposing the Holocaust."[49] Appelbaum continues, "Nannen bears a responsibility for the attempts at whitewashing one of the greatest fascist mass murderers in history." And moreover, Nannen "was not just a Mitläufer (fellow traveler), but clearly and directly a Mitgestalter (co-creator)."

For the record: The Hamburg publishing house Gruner + Jahr and the *Stern* magazine, which it publishes, want to promote and cultivate quality journalism in the German-speaking world and at the same time they keep Henri Nannen's memory alive, the founder of *Stern*, by awarding the Henri Nannen Prize. Nobody there seems to have any problem with the fact that Henri Nannen worked in the SS "Südstern" unit. That's not headline-worthy in the *Stern*. In the case of the actor Horst Tappert, the *Stern* journalists sang a completely different tune: "Five years after his death, a dark secret from his past came to light."[50] In doing so, they're keeping the difference between Henri Nannen and Horst Tappert in the shadows.

How far are we willing to go with all this? This "united thought front" has become a threat to our democracy. The same circles, composed of journalists and media outlets, politicians and business leaders, are meeting together over and over at conferences, seminars, workshops and at balls or parties. There, they determining their prerogative to interpret our lives. They agree on the new thought patterns and catchphrases, which are then dutifully regurgitated by the media. They're taking away our ability to think. They cook up their prize winners, be it in journalism, politics or science (without ever asking the people), and they almost exclusively occupy all positions of moral authority. There is only one way to escape this totalitarian brainwashing: Boycott the mainstream media and put their employees out of work.

Voting with Our Wallets: Turning Journalists into Welfare Recipients

Imagine what would happen to a country if 25 percent of its population emigrated within the space of a few months – and nobody else paid taxes anymore – and the trend wasn't just temporary. This country would collapse faster than you could see it happening, and this is exactly what's happening right now to Germany's mainstream media. The people who are financing their work are turning away in droves. They're voting with their wallets. In July of 2014, a trade magazine reported on the dramatic, second quarter losses in newsstands sales. They were hard to believe:

Percentwise, the FAZ, Die Welt *and* Handelsblatt *all took double-digit losses at the newsstand.* Die Welt *and* Handelsblatt *lost a fifth of their customers and* TAZ – *a whole quarter!* Handelsblatt *can still get rid of 5000 copies in retail sales, while the* TAZ [Berliner Tageszeitung] *is down to less than 4000.*[51]

This development continues uninterrupted. The people have given up on the mainstream media. Put simply: The "quality media" are choking on their own vomit – and this doesn't have anything to do with the Internet as they often claim. The masses could keep subscribing to the electronic editions of these "quality media" if they wanted to, but they aren't. They've finally had enough of the subversive propaganda published by those outlets.

In the nearly 15 years since the turn of the millennium, the German media landscape has experienced its largest wave of layoffs in history, more than any other similar time period. As early as 2012, the German Federal Employment Agency even admitted that it was completely helpless when it came to all of the "quality journalists" who were lining up in the street, thanks to one media house after another going bankrupt.[52] The forecast: From now until 2022, every seventh journalist will lose their job.[53] The editorial offices have already been shaken up vigorously in the process. Newspaper journalists, like the cobblers and saddlers before them, are members of a dying profession. Today's journalists will be tomorrow's welfare recipients.

The *Rheinische Merkur* was discontinued in 2010 after running up losses into the millions. Then, one after another started to fall. The *Financial Times Deutschland* (FTD), founded in 2000 by the Hamburg media house Grüner + Jahr, was one of the most renowned German business papers, from the elites' point of view. This politically left-leaning paper was actively interfering in politics and, while calling itself a business newspaper, was still making election recommendations, like for the Bündnis 90/Die Grünen in the 2009 European elections. This was apparently only being read and cheered on by the left-wing establishment – in reality, the work done by the FTD journalists was more likely to be found in a trash can than someone's hands. By 2012, they couldn't avoid the inevitable – it was all over. 300 FTD journalists lost their jobs. The business paper *Capital* (founded 1962), also published by Grüner + Jahr, still had a circulation of 293,000 issues in 2000. By 2014 it was down to about 137,000 – far less than half its previous circulation. The future isn't looking very rosy there either. Another business magazine, *Impulse*, founded in 1980 and also published by Grüner + Jahr, was just sold in January. The *Financial Times Deutschland* alone racked up losses of 250 million euros for Gruner + Jahr.[54]

At this point, we should remember that journalists and media outlets are in the business of making money, not burning it. But this is exactly what the majority of them have been doing for years now. The *Frankfurter Rundschau*, founded in 1945, and on the political left since its inception, recorded a loss of around 19 million euros in 2012, even though they had already lost 20 million euros in 2011.[55] It seems that the concept of running a newspaper coupled to the SPD political party has turned out to be a failure.[56] In 2011, after 66 years, the FR's history as a national newspaper came to an end (afterward, the extra-regional part was continued in Berlin[57]), and then by 2013, its final demise and takeover was inevitable.[58] In between, there had been massive layoffs. Only a handful of editors survived the transition – the rest ended up on the street. Even the once renowned FAZ can only boast

208,000 paid subscribers. Its bottom line has plunged into the red and salary increases have also been cancelled. The FAZ stands at the edge of the financial abyss.[59]

The *Abendzeitung Nürnberg* was discontinued in 2012 after 93 years – 35 employees were affected.[60] The *Münchner Abendzeitung* – also a paper with a long tradition – filed for insolvency in the spring of 2014. It had heaped up losses totaling 70 million euros.[61] Overnight, 115 employees faced an uncertain future.[62] In January 2013, the WAZ Media Group announced that it would be completely closing the editorial offices of its newspaper, the *Westfälische Rundschau*, by February 2013. Within five years, it had incurred losses of 50 million euros. The *Bonner General-Anzeiger* closed its correspondents' office in Berlin on the last day of 2013 – in order to save around 400,000 euros a year. Three correspondents lost their jobs.[63] In March, 2014, the *Westdeutsche Zeitung* (WZ) announced its intention to halve the number of its editorial employees from 100 down to 50.[64] In May, 2014, 36 editorial positions were cut at the *Leipziger Volkszeitung*.[65]

None of the journalists affected by these mass layoffs gave any thought to why all this was happening. Everyone was thinking about how the old system could be forced back onto the population – for example, with a "newspaper revival law," according to which "quality media" journalists would receive subsidies from the state's general fund.[66] Even the heads of these media companies can't seem to comprehend what's going on here. A particularly glaring example of this is provided by the FAZ's co-editor Werner D'Inka. He shared his fundamental view in a commentary on the closure of the *Frankfurter Rundschau*, stating, "And when the last decent newspaper has finally disappeared, all that will remain is gibberish."[67]

So, according to an editor at the FAZ, if it's not printed, it's "gibberish." What is this other than an antiquated world view from the last millennium? As a young FAZ editor in the 1980s, I stood next to my then colleague D'Inka in the FAZ editorial offices when they were still setting lead type. We experienced the end of the "Lead Age" together. Since then, the media landscape has undergone drastic changes. Alas, for D'Inka, journalism is obviously only journalism if it is (also) printed. Managers like this aren't adequately preparing their employees for the digital revolution. They aren't facing up to this change themselves; they simply want to ignore it and hope it doesn't happen. That's not going to work. Can you go forward in reverse? No, of course not. So who's surprised that the once wealthy *Frankfurter Allgemeine Zeitung* is also heading straight off a cliff when it has executives like this?

Additionally, many journalists apparently don't even have a very positive opinion when it comes to their own work. At least, they aren't even prepared to pay a penny for it themselves. An online portal reported the results of a survey taken by 1300 journalists:

What's surprising, however, is that many journalists are not convinced of the value of their work or the media outlets where they are full-time employees. 38 percent say they wouldn't pay money to read the online edition of their own medium, only 44 percent "signaled willingness to pay" – as they said: for their own medium. 17 percent don't know or didn't answer.[68]

So, if journalists themselves are not convinced of their own work and aren't prepared to pay for it, how can they expect that from their customers? The future looks bleak for journalists in the German-speaking countries. Yet they're still bragging. If you want to know what's in store for Germany's "quality journalists," all you have to do is take a quick look at the United States. A buzzword that is (still) strange for Europeans is: Robot journalism. As a media portal reported in 2014:

Automated journalism has long since established a foothold in the USA. Forbes, for example, has an entire blog that is populated by the US company Narrative Science. The computer autonomously writes reports on balance sheet expectations for companies. Recently, the Los Angeles Times also tried out a new project. The so-called Quakebot publishes earthquake reports almost in real time, as soon as they exceed a certain strength. Automated journalism seems to be most popular in sports reporting. Statsheet.com specializes in basketball news. Northwestern University is implementing a similar project for baseball.[69]

What sounds like something out of a science fiction novel for many journalists has long since been in its test phase behind the scenes in Germany. Robot journalism is also on the march here. A Stuttgart-based communications agency has developed software that can formulate articles on the basis of large amounts of data without any editors getting involved. The machine will soon be competing against the established news media.[70] When it's ready, you'll only need a few alpha journalists to set the tone of the articles – then, the rest will be done by machines.

Nonpartisan? The SPD's Media Empire

In 2013, the rather conservative *Frankfurter Allgemeine Zeitung* took over the more left-leaning *Frankfurter Rundschau*.[71] By the end of 2012 though, the *Frankfurter Rundschau*, the media flagship of the German Social Democrats, had already filed for bankruptcy. Yes, you read that right. The FR was closely intertwined with the German Social Democrats. Through the SPD-owned holding company, Deutsche Druck- und Verlagsgesellschaft (DDVG), the SPD comrades Sigmar Gabriel, Peer Steinbrück, Gerhard Schröder, Andrea Nahles and Co., held a 40 percent share in this impending bankruptcy. However, the FR wasn't the only newspaper the SPD had a stake in. At the time, the Social Democrats held shares in the renowned

Westfälische Rundschau, the magazine *Öko-Test* and the *Nordbayerischen Kurier*. Many regional daily newspapers are still in the Social Democrats' portfolio, along with radio stations, printing houses and bookstores. They also have a hand in travel companies and marketing agencies. The Social Democrats even wanted to make money on cruise ships. A few years ago, they began to market vacation packages on the "MS Princess Daphne" through their own SPD-Reiseservice GmbH. No, that's not a joke. The SPD brought a love boat on board.[72] The SPD is a business enterprise. Sitting at the helm of this business was the former treasurer for the Social Democrats, Barbara Hendricks, who is now the Minister for the Environment in the black-red (CDU-SPD) coalition. On the party's supervisory board, she was supported by veteran comrades in the media and the cruise ship business. Today, Dietmar Nietan, a Member of the Bundestag for the SPD, is steering the business. Most Germans have probably never heard of him, but he is one of the biggest publishers in Germany.

Thus, the SPD also generates revenue through their participation in media outlets. So far, the SPD's investments have also paid off in terms of party politics. During the 2002 Bundestag election campaign, the research institute "Medien Tenor" studied the journalistic work of the *Sächsische Zeitung*, in which the DDVG held a 40 percent share at the time. The researchers discovered the obvious. The reporting in the *Sächsische Zeitung* was significantly tamer and friendlier toward Schröder's SPD government than it was to the CDU-led opposition at the time. The DDVG also manages other important investments via the Madsack GmbH in Hanover, a company in which it has voting rights. Through this circuitous route, the SPD has possibly also made political use of Madsack's access to numerous local newspapers, such as the *Leipziger Volkszeitung* and the *Hannoversche Allgemeine*, as well as to the television production companies *AZ Media* and the *TVN Group*. Both TV companies produce reporting, documentaries and tasteless mass entertainment for all major broadcasters, private and public. The former SPD treasurer Inge Wettig-Danielmeier explained, "Even where we only have 30 or 40 percent, as a rule, nothing can happen without us." Therefore, you shouldn't let the SPD's holdings in the DDVG deceive you, even though they are purported to be quantitatively small stakes and therefore insignificant. Many German children read the stories about "Oscar the Balloonist," (available in video and video game formats in English) and "Paula Pünktchen" or "Heini Hummel" (the lady bug and bumble bee characters from the author Hallmark picked up for *Tall Tales from the Magical Garden of Antoon Krings*). DDVG also holds shares in the children's book publisher Tivola, which publishes these stories. It seems that political conditioning can't begin early enough. Through its subsidiary Vorwärts, DDVG holds shares in Parthas-Verlag, which is primarily responsible for publishing books originating from ARTE, a state-owned broadcasting channel. In addition to these and other commitments in the mostly local print sector, the SPD invests a great deal of money through the DDVG in supposedly private radio stations. In this way, they also have additional access to an audience of up to 10 million potential voters a day. Can the editorial offices of so-called "private" newspapers and broadcasters still work independently under these business conditions?

Also asking himself these questions is Wolfgang Storz, the former editor-in-chief of the *Frankfurter Rundschau*. In a 2005 letter, the then SPD treasurer Inge Wettig-Danielmeier "recommended" the publication of a text describing "an interesting aspect of the relationship between the SPD and Die Linke (The Left Party). (…) I would be delighted if this article could soon be made accessible to a larger readership via the 'Frankfurter Rundschau.'" Editor-in-Chief Storz did not follow up on her recommendation. His reply to this loyal party member was that he was "firmly convinced that this would affect editorial independence." However, in her view, "my request was justified in this special case, because with Mr. Storz as editor-in-chief, the 'Frankfurter Rundschau' had been becoming a propaganda rag for The Left Party for weeks." In 2006, Wolfgang Storz had to vacate his post. As managing director Peter Skulimma is said to have confirmed at the time, the dismissal was connected with differences in opinion over content, in regard to the future political orientation of the newspaper.[73]

So let's take a look at the concentration of media power in the SPD's own holding company, the Deutsche Druck- und Verlagsgesellschaft (DDVG): The DDVG held stakes in the following publishing houses (naming here the most important holdings and media products): Oliva Druck- und Verlagsgesellschaft, which in turn holds stakes in the Cuxhaven-Niederelbe Verlagsgesellschaft (*Cuxhavener Nachrichten, Niederelbe-Zeitung*). The DDVG owns the Berlin-based vorwärts Verlagsgesellschaft (*Vorwärts, Demokratische Gemeinde*), the vorwärts-Buch Verlagsgesellschaft and also Presse-Druck. Via the latter, it has a majority stake in the newspaper publishing company Zeitungsverlag Neue Westfälische, Bielefeld *(Neue Westfälische)*. The DDVG has shares in Tivola Publishing (edutainment, learning software and children's books), is majority owner of the Öko-Test Holding, has a stake in the Öko-Test Verlags GmbH, in the Bayreuth Druck + Media, in the Nordbayerischen Kurier Zeitungsverlag *(Nordbayerischer Kurier),* in the Dresdner Druck- und Verlagshaus *(Sächsische Zeitung, Morgenpost Sachsen)*, in the Frankenpost Verlag, Hof *(Frankenpost)*, in *the Suhler Verlagsgesellschaft (Freies Wort, Südthüringer Zeitung)*, in the Druck- und Verlagsanstalt 'Neue Presse' *(Neue Presse Coburg)* and, through further layers of investment, in the *Hannoversche Allgemeine Zeitung, Neue Presse Hannover, Göttinger Tageblatt, Peiner Allgemeine Zeitung and Märkische Allgemeine Zeitung*, as well as in the Leipziger Verlags- und Druckereigesellschaft *(Leipziger Volkszeitung, Dresdener Neueste Nachrichten)* and in the private radio broadcasters FFN, Hit-Radio Antenne and Radio 21 as well as Rheinland-Pfälzische Rundfunk

GmbH & Co KG (RPR1). Furthermore, they have shares in printing houses like Dräger + Wullenwever print + media Lübeck and Hildesheimer Druck- und Verlagsgesellschaft. You could keep on going with this list.

The interconnectedness of party politics and the media can hardly be shown any more clearly. It is also clear that the SPD has not used its media power for solely editorial purposes throughout the past either. In December of 2013, *Der Spiegel* reported that the DDVG undermined the minimum wage agreement for newspaper and letter delivery companies reached by the SPD and the CDU/CSU's grand coalition. The DDVG had an indirect stake in this decision, because delivery personnel are paid according to the number of items delivered rather than according to hours they work.[74]

The Social Democrats have now been active in the newspaper publishing business for 140 years.[75] During the Second German Reich (1871-1918), the SPD papers were financed by the countless pennies the German proletariat managed to save working long hours in the factories, and they still saw themselves as a counterweight to the mostly authoritarian, bourgeois newspapers of the day. Today, the combined holdings of the DDVG are not the remnants of this small, once-proud workers' press. It has become a media force that can no longer be overlooked by anyone. Used cleverly, it can influence large masses of people at any time.

In 2008, Torben Stephan wrote an interesting book about this history *(Medienmacht Sozialdemokratie (The Social Democratic Media Powerhouse (not available in English))*. It shows the circumstances in which the SPD rapidly expanded its media empire: While Chancellor Gerhard Schröder refused to give interviews to the *Bild* newspaper in early 2004 because of the alleged campaigns against him, another part of the SPD was busy buying up more newspapers. At the same time, the then SPD Minister of Economic Affairs, Wolfgang Clement, worked on easing the merger regulations regarding the press – naturally, to the SPD's advantage. The coincidence in the timing of the three events briefly outlined here led many observers to think there must be a conspiracy. There were accusations that the SPD was making the media compliant. For this reason, questions arose surrounding the Social Democrats' media strategy and the goals they were pursing with their minority shareholdings in German publishing houses. The author Torben Stephan examined the individual aspects and tried to find an answer to the question of why the Social Democrats were expanding their media involvement. His thesis: It was no longer about merely bolstering the SPD's campaign finances; their primarily strategy was for holding onto power by exerting influence on the media.

The FAZ has written about the SPD's media holdings:

The holdings were and are controversial, because the media should report on the SPD – and they should do it independently.[76]

The reality in German editorial offices looks like this: As communications expert Mathias Kepplinger explained, according to a representative study, 34 percent of journalists are close to the Greens and another 25 percent are close to the SPD. So, if around 60 percent of German journalists lean to the left (without even bringing The Left Party into the equation), and the SPD is increasingly a media conglomerate to be reckoned with – how does this dangerous proximity between politics and media representatives play out?

In 2014, we were given a glimpse of how outrageously the SPD promotes its media power through its own holding company, the Deutsche Druck- und Verlagsgesellschaff (DDVG): To compensate for the additional costs that came with the new statutory minimum wage, publishers were to be granted a discount on the social security contributions they must make on behalf of their delivery personnel. According to the plan, about 60 percent of the costs resulting from the minimum wage increase would now flow back to the newspaper publishers. The state would be chipping in upwards of 135 million euros for this special arrangement. This "horse trade" was negotiated by the Labor Minister, Andrea Nahles, a well-known member of the SPD. However, the Social Democrats might not just have a political interest in the newly found compromise. As a party, they may also have an economic interest in it.

As I mentioned, most newspapers in Germany are suffering from declining circulation. This is not only due to the increasing relevance of electronic media, but it's also linked to an increasing self-awareness among readers. They no longer want to be served the same politically-correct mush from left-leaning editors anymore and they're cancelling their subscriptions in record numbers. In times of crisis like these, the political establishment is in urgent need of submissive journalists who can either disguise the seriousness of the situation or make it sound like everything's okay. Therefore, this 135-million-euro concession to the publishers is also in these old parties' political self-interest.

Besides, there could have been concrete economic reasons playing a role in the agreement – at least when we consider the SPD. This organization is not only a political party, but as I just described in detail, it is also the owner of Deutsche Druck- und Verlagsgesellschaft. The majority of the DDVG's profits are paid out to the SPD as a shareholder and, in turn, they state that these funds contribute to the financial independence of the party. As a publishing group, the DDVG's daily newspapers alone have a combined total circulation of around 435,000 copies. Most copies are delivered directly to their subscribers, brought to their door every morning by an army of newspaper couriers. Consequently, the DDVG and thus the SPD both benefit from their minister's gift to Germany's newspaper publishers. These are the kind of deals that are negotiated discreetly, behind closed doors.

Chapter 5. Case Histories from the Propaganda Front

Everyone named in this book denies a sticky, sleazy coziness with elite organizations. Moreover, they deny being lobbyists. They also deny being "corrupted" by their proximity to the elite. And, they deny having lost their journalistic edge, working as they do in such close proximity to the aforementioned cabal. They deny that this proximity has any influence on their reporting.

My friend, Peter Scholl-Latour, who I met in many war zones, was asked in 2014, a few weeks before his death at the age of 90, about the experiences he had had throughout his life with media synchronization and censorship. He answered:

Paul Sethe, who was an incredibly conservative editorialist and wrote for Die Welt and the FAZ, once wrote many years ago, "The freedom of the press in the West is the freedom of 200 rich people to publicize their opinions," in the meantime it isn't 200 anymore, in the meantime it's only 4 or 5 people.[1]

Thus, according to Peter Scholl-Latour, only four or five people determine the prevailing opinion these days. Diversity of opinion is now a thing of the past. Incidentally, the Paul Sethe that Peter Scholl-Latour mentioned was one of the founding editors of the FAZ (from 1949-1955), who was later dumped by the FAZ because he wasn't toeing the line.[2] The Federal Chancellery and the other top editors were the ones exerting this pressure. The business community helped keep up the pressure by withholding ads from the FAZ until he was out. The head of Salamander AG at the time, Alexander Haffner, sat on the FAZ's funding committee and stated very openly, "The newspaper was founded by the business community ..." And their interests must be reflected in it.[3] So, Sethe, the FAZ's publishing editor-in-chief, got the boot. How a FAZ publisher gets "kicked out" was even outlined during a session of the Bundestag, (the 116th session).[4] This is also what happened to FAZ publisher Jürgen Thern. The same thing happened to Hugo Müller-Vogg after 24 years with the FAZ (13 of which as co-editor-in-chief). On a Tuesday afternoon, he was surprised with a termination notice. To this day, he still hasn't gotten any explanation for why he was thrown out. The lasting impression from this book: There is sometimes a corrupt presence, as we have seen, lurking in the background at the FAZ. Evidently, it's also being promoted and protected, because it certainly hasn't been terminated. From my subjective point of view, the FAZ is not as impartial, neutral and independent as it pretends to be. You can also say this about all of the leading media in Germany. Anyone who causes friction or has a different opinion will be escorted to the door. This goes for editors, section chiefs and even publishing editors-in-chief. This is standard practice throughout Germany's mainstream media. Even alpha journalists have to stay strictly on course – or otherwise they'll get the ax.

People are beginning to recognize the constant deception by the "leading media" in all areas. This is because, behind it all, there is a (fraudulent) system, the likes of a shell game. Our mainstream media are pulling the wool over our eyes so the financial elite can rake in lots of money. That's at least the realization I've come to a thousand times over and it's one you can prove with countless, concrete examples of manipulative reporting.

Let's just take a quick look at the 2014 European elections. In the German-speaking world at the time, established politicians were afraid that the new political parties could become a future danger to them on the European level. There's no question about that. So, what do you resort to when you're in a situation like this? What else? Propaganda. And who spreads the propaganda? Who else? The mainstream media. While every citizen knows that the EU is in dire financial straits and that ailing, bankrupt, EU states were only being kept alive on life support with constant infusions of cash, EU-friendly politicians were still feverishly building Potemkin villages with the help of the mainstream media, right up to the elections.

For example, Greece, – sorry, please don't laugh yet – whose government has been long since bankrupt, was given a quick makeover and it became a bastion of financial security overnight. On April 10, 2014, *ZEIT online* headlined: "Investors are fighting with each other over Greek bonds."[5] On the same day, *Die Welt* claimed: "After the state bankruptcy, Greece is returning to the capital market – and can hardly meet the demand for bonds."[6] In those heady days, the FAZ spoke of Athens' "comeback" on the financial market.[7] These are all examples of economic headlines from about six weeks before the European elections. Needless to say, it was all a gigantic bluff, a big stage show that was easy to see through. Why? What was going on behind the scenes?

The German Chancellor Angela Merkel needed positive news. To these ends, she arranged a trip to Athens and encouraged the Greeks to issue a government bond with a whopping 4.75 percent interest rate. This was at a time when Germans were only getting a measly 0.1 percent interest on their own savings. Thus Greece, which had a debt exceeding 300 billion euros, managed to quickly raise a whole 3 billion euros on the capital market. Not even a drop in their Aegean Sea of debt, but the mainstream media in Germany was ecstatic. This corrupt farce, portraying the Greek state as allegedly healthy right before the EU elections, was sure to take the wind out of the Eurosceptics' sails. Angela Merkel was enthusiastically celebrated by the German media even before she even left Athens. All of it was a staged act – easy to see though from the beginning, all the way to its predictable end.

Nevertheless, it worked: In the subsequent EU elections, the Eurosceptics in the German-speaking world didn't get the huge surge in votes that the established political ranks had so desperately feared. And what about the 4.75 percent interest rate that was promised in the corrupt farce I described above? The German taxpayers are primarily responsible for that now. That's one side of the story. The other: Three months after this boondoggle, one which caused so much delirious rejoicing among our mainstream media, Greece was back out on the street looking for someone to buy another one of their government bonds. By then, however, there was nothing but silence in the German mainstream media. In reality, Greece hadn't experienced any "comeback" on the capital market at all. On the contrary, the situation was exactly the opposite: In July of 2014, Athens could only get rid of half of the government bonds they were urgently seeking buyers for.[8] Of course, our leading media basically remained silent on this. After all, the EU elections and the propaganda show were over. Reading this one example, you can see how German citizens are manipulated, treated like fools, lied to and cheated by our mainstream media. Afterwards, as the taxpayers, German citizens still wind up footing the bill for all the damage this causes. Our mainstream media are primarily in the business of generating moods.

Do you want to know the truth? When it comes to the media in general and the German media in particular, it's like this: The desire for personal recognition mixed with missionary zeal, along with a penchant for arrogant posturing – that is the heart and soul of a journalist's work. In talk shows, news broadcasts, books, newspapers and on the radio, all of it always follows the same formula: They all serve to fuel a particular, predetermined mood, handed down from a few public opinion lords. In this process, the truth is completely irrelevant.

Over the course of my career, I must have appeared on television several hundred times. Of all those appearances, I still remember the time I was invited onto the Sabine Christiansen show on April 18, 2004, as a "security expert." Sitting around me were the ex-Foreign Minister Hans-Dietrich Genscher (FDP), the EU's Enlargement Commissioner Günter Verheugen (FDP), Saxony's Prime Minister Georg Milbradt (CDU), the Slovak President Rudolf Schuster and other illustrious guests.[9] The show's topic was the upcoming, enormous eastward enlargement of the EU: "The fateful question – Will Germany's future be decided in the East?" I had obviously been invited on the show so that the others could butcher me alive on camera. I was to be an example of the evil, stupid German who was crazy enough to warn against opening the borders to so many terribly poor countries. On the show, I predicted that the borders would close again after a few years anyway because of crime, for example. Then, I was executed right there on live TV. After the broadcast, the Berliner Tagesspiegel wrote: "The viewers got to see Dr. Ulfkotte get butchered live. Now they can form a picture of how political bodies work for themselves. Always at the expense of the weak."[10] In the meantime, the situation has changed. The ones we can thank for this EU insanity and the record-breaking increases in crime accompanying it – they seem to be ones who are increasingly losing touch with reality.

On May 1, 2004, the EU expanded by admitting ten new member states. Three years later, another two joined: Bulgaria and Romania. Leading up to this, our politicians had only emphasized the theoretical advantages of the EU's eastern expansion, completely ignoring its major pitfalls. Anyone who pointed these out (like me) was considered to be "right-wing." Now, however, no one can ignore the reality of the situation anymore: The prosperity gap between the new and the old member states was and is considerable, the social systems of the new EU states were and are in poor condition. Poverty and freedom of movement has led to cross-border crime, and the citizenry was not informed about the possibility of this in 2004. I brought all of this up on the *Sabine Christiansen* show in 2004 and I was led to the slaughter – by Genscher, by Verheugen and their ilk. So when are we going to finally "butcher" the Genschers, the Verheugens, the Milbradts and all the others who brought this upon us? Were they too stupid or too incompetent to anticipate these developments? Or, were they acting with malice aforethought? Today, they live off our tax money like it's their birthright and they want to go down in the annals of history as great politicians.

Let's look at another example: Since the 1990s, economic researchers haven't made a single accurate prognosis when it comes to predicting economic crises. The IMF economist Prakash Loungani has proven this, year after year, from the 1990s up until 2012. The economists have always missed the target with their forecasts.[11] This is an undeniable fact. Nevertheless, our media still scramble to publish these economic researchers' forecasts every week. Their accuracy could only be rivaled if you handed out rifles to blind people at a shooting match. Strangely enough, these economists still manage to make it onto our mainstream news programs time and again, even though they usually just spout nonsense.

For the average citizen, trusting these expert forecasts and, heaven forbid, adjusting your investments accordingly would spell certain disaster. You can see this if you track the price forecasts for gold, for example, that have been published in the media. Let's look at some of the forecasts so we can expose the absurdity found in some of these statements. In December 2010, when the price of gold stood at 1,400 dollars per troy ounce, the renowned American economist James Turk's forecast was published in the German media: "An ounce of the precious yellow metal will soon cost 3,500 dollars." At the same time, the former chief economist for the HypoVereinsbank, Martin Hüfner, said, "The gold price will drop from

1,400 dollars per troy ounce to 500 dollars. There will be a panic among gold owners. They'll be trying to get rid of their gold stocks come hell or high water." The reality: The price of gold rose from 1,400 dollars in December 2010 to 1,800 dollars in August 2011. Not one of the forecasts was right. In point of fact, there were tangible interests driving these forecasts from behind the scenes. They didn't have anything to do with the truth.

Still, journalists keep running with this nonsense. Why? They are manipulating us, lying to us and cheating us. In May of 2014, the TV listings magazine *Hörzu (Listen Up)* was conducting a survey for the new ZDF rankings show, *Deutschlands Beste (Germany's Best)*. They were collecting viewer nominations to rank the top 100 living Germans, 50 women and 50 men. Readers had until May 24, 2014 to send in their suggestions to the editors. They announced: "Dear readers, the winner is up to you." However, the readers could have saved themselves the effort, because the forsa Institute (for Social Research and Statistical Analysis) had long since determined the Top-50-Germans for ZDF. Additionally, ZDF announced that everyone could also vote online. In the end, neither the *Hörzu* readers nor those who took part in the ZDF vote online had any say in the matter.[12] It was all just a grand illusion. The readers' and viewers' participation in the result was purely simulated.[13] As a reader or viewer, it was easy to feel like you were getting jerked around, because ZDF, a public broadcasting channel, was then presumptuous enough to boldly announce that Angela Merkel was the greatest living German woman. This, even though she didn't fare well among the respondents, not even nearing their top choices. Among the other women at the top, there were also names like Helene Fischer and Ina Müller (both pop singers and media darlings).[14] At the time of the survey, two thirds of Germans were already fed up with Angela Merkel. Possibly fearing a reaction from those who took the time to respond, the results were only published broadly in Austria.[15] So what did our quality media do to spin the fact that only 24 percent of Germans would like to see Angela Merkel serve another term as Chancellor? Are you sitting down? The headline read: "One in four wants another 10 years of Merkel."[16] Three quarters are against it and our media spins it into a positive talking point. That's how disinformation functions in the Synchronized Age.

There are some things that a German journalist would never dare to write. Nevertheless, these things are important for Germans' understanding of the outside world. In 2009, for example, in order to make the precarious situation and the ever-worsening crisis in the heart of Europe comprehensible to every UK citizen, Lord Mandelson, the British Minister for Economic Affairs, made the following remark, "The banks are f**d, we're f**d, the country's f**d!"[17] This didn't need to be translated for the German public. It doesn't get any clearer when you're describing the situation of the British citizens' savings – and that, coming from an English lord and high-ranking member of the British government. In German-speaking countries, nobody wants to hear anything remotely like that at the moment. In Germany, we prefer to see the light at the end of the tunnel everywhere we look, even though we haven't even entered the tunnel yet. In Germany, the "quality media" will be churning out propaganda right up until the moment everything collapses. Our best journalists lie on command, whenever the politicians want it. You think this sounds like a conspiracy theory? Well, why don't we prove it.

The Higher Goal: Amputating Germany's Identity

The following sections of this chapter will deal for the most part with German politicians, the media and the euro. Why? The idea of the euro, as already mentioned and this isn't a conspiracy theory, was hashed out at a Bilderberg conference. Even the *Frankfurter Rundschau*, which certainly isn't a purveyor of conspiracy theories, has also reported in the meantime: "And according to the honorary chairman of the circle, the Belgian entrepreneur Etienne Davignon, the euro can also be traced back to Bilderberg."[18] As we have already seen, elitist circles like the Bilderberg conferences are certainly not democratic institutions, but rather propaganda and lobbying associations that pursue very specific interests and these are the interests of pro-American high finance. How can it be that politicians – Angela Merkel has also appeared among the Bilderbergers – and journalists let themselves do the legwork for the Bilderbergers and other similar organizations, creating propaganda to serve their interests? On the following pages, we will explore which German media outlets have been propagandizing the euro and have even answered the politicians' call to lie to the public.

Did you know that there was a higher goal, one that coupled German politics with the introduction of the euro? The goal is the destruction of nation-states and nationalist thinking – especially any nationalistic thought in Germany. Before the introduction of the euro, the SPD politician Olaf Schwencke explained it to us like this: With the introduction of the euro, the EU will become the world's largest capital and financial market of the future. This will have cultural repercussions. Schwencke said that if national currencies no longer exist, then nation states would effectively come to an end. In Schwencke's words, "Its most important material proper, monetary policy, being the core of state sovereignty, will thus be abandoned and the European legal and economic community will assume this function." The diversity of cultural expressions in Europe could be eliminated in an increasingly powerful, commercial World Culture – also referred to as "McWorld."[19]

Put simply: It was and is about the destruction of our cultural and national identity. Today, the ones who are overwhelming us with the gigantic costs of the euro currency union are claiming that there is no way they could have foreseen any of this beforehand. These liars are hoping that the citizenry is forgetful. Still, there were many who warned them, but their opponents were ridiculed at the time. Forgotten and erased from our memories are the large nationwide initiatives in the 1990s including "Yes to the DM – No to the euro = teuro" (expensive-o), "Europe yes, but euro no!" and "Who will stop the euro madness?" Also forgotten are the lawsuits brought against the euro in the 1990s. These were filed with the German Federal Constitutional Court by numerous euro critics. The media and politicians at the time disparagingly called the euro's opponents "pompous" and "scaremongers."

How did the euro sceptics reply to these attacks? Specifically, how did the professors Wilhelm Hankel, Wilhelm Nölling, Karl Albrecht Schachtschneider and Joachim Starbatty respond in their book: *Die Euro-Klage – Warum die Währungsunion scheitern muss (The Case against the Euro – Why the Monetary Union Will Fail ((not available in English))*, published in February of 1998? They wrote: "Those who do not see real lurking dangers or minimize them are not responsible politicians; those who point out real lurking dangers are not scaremongers or populists, but realists." Do you know what politicians and the media often called these four professors in the 1990s? – "Gang of Four,"[20] "self-proclaimed representatives of the people" or "anti-euro senior citizens."[21] *Die Zeit* editor-in-chief, Theo Sommer, a Bilderberger and lobbying group networker, wrote an article in 1998 entitled: "The fair exchange – Germany, in particular, needs the euro." In it, he lashed out at the euro critics, saying, "Now they're making a terrific racket: professors, politicians, pseudo-prophets. (...)." Theo Sommer continued: "Unproven and unprovable is, after all, the assertion that (...) large transfer payments would be due to weaker countries – German transfer payments, mind you." Oh, if only Theo Sommer had to eat his words from back then, all that nonsense, letter for letter, every single word. In his article, Sommer called euro critics, the likes of professors Hankel and Schachtschneider, the "standard bearers of the upstanding four" (aka the Gang of Four), "who stagger toward Karlsruhe" (the seat of Germany's highest court) "on their shaky legs to try to prevent the new currency."[22] How does someone feel when they're vilified as a "pseudo-prophet?" Have *Die Zeit*, Theo Sommer, now a convicted tax evader, or any of the other Bilderbergers who absolutely had to have the euro against the will of the people – Have any of them ever apologized for the nonsense they were spewing at the time? No!

Merkel's Fairy-Tale Hour: How the German Government Lies to Its Citizens

At the time of the euro crisis and its looming financial crash, the Chancellor openly called on the German media not to inform the public about this truthfully. This is an undisputed fact, and in the meantime, this incident has even been mentioned in passing by the "quality media" in Germany. Notwithstanding, a coming generation will one day ask the German people why they put up with all of this, tolerating it for so long. What follows are a few facts that you can evaluate for yourself, but if you have any German friends or acquaintances, you should definitely pass it on to them. With any luck, they will use this information to their advantage – by always immediately withdrawing their money from the bank. Otherwise, they will join the ranks of those fools who believed the Chancellor and have possibly lost a lot, if not everything.

It is an undisputed fact that the Chancellor has openly called on Germany's media establishment to lie in order to conceal the real situation. Allegedly, this was done in the public's own interest – to avoid panic. Yet, at some point, the truth always comes to light, sometimes sooner, sometimes later. The German Chancellor, Angela Merkel (CDU), can't be happy that a rather unpleasant episode in her career as Germany's top political leader finally became public: Strangely, it already seems like a long time ago that she called most important editors-in-chief in Germany into her office and asked them to no longer report the truth about the country's situation. October 8th, 2008 was a sunny autumn Wednesday. On short notice, Merkel invited the most important media representatives and publishing directors to an evening meeting at the Chancellery. Three days before that, Merkel had made a bold claim in front of the television cameras: "We are saying to the depositors that your savings are secure. This is also assured by the Federal Government." But the fact of the matter was that the situation was, and still is, anything but secure when it comes to German citizens' savings. This is why, on behalf of Germany's Chancellor, journalists and publishing directors were asked to say anything but the truth in the German media.

Merkel told these journalists from the "quality media" who were marched up in front of her that the German media plays an "important role" in the economic and financial crisis. Moreover, for reasons of the state's very own raison d'être, the citizenry should by no means learn the full truth about how dire the situation was with regard to public finances and the developing economic crisis. The media should show restraint and concentrate on bringing the people positive news instead. Angela Merkel insisted that journalists must use caution when reporting on the actual situation. Otherwise, the country might spiral out of control. Avoiding a panic was now in the journalists' hands. Her challenge for them to distract the public from the reality of the situation was unmistakable. *Die Zeit,*[23] the *Süddeutsche* and the *taz* all reported very briefly on this meeting and about the call to distract the population from the reality of the situation.

Die Zeit began their corresponding article with the words:

On the 8th of October 2008, the crisis was still young, you might almost like to say: innocent. That Wednesday evening, the Chancellor and her Finance Minister invited the heads of the most important newspapers to the Chancellery to pass a new development on to them. It was: Although we don't exactly know what will happen in the next two to three weeks, we would like to sincerely ask you for your trust and, above all, that you don't generate a detrimental atmosphere, because the situation is much too serious.[24]

In another paper, we also read:

A few months before, on the 8th of October 2008, there had been a strange meeting that should be mentioned in this context. On that day, the Chancellor had invited the most powerful chief editors of the most powerful media outlets. It was at the moment when the great financial crisis was breaking out. You won't find any detailed report published about this meeting and only a few mentions of it are in the archives at all, only a partial sentence here and there, a brief remark. In one article, in a few words, you can read what was going on in the Chancellor's office that evening: Merkel asked the journalists to report cautiously on the crisis and not to fuel any panic.

They did what they were told, these top editors. Even into February 2009, four months later, the taz was wondering about the media: "They keep the citizens in a good mood, so they don't make a fuss. How much money has already been pumped into the banks, how many billions in guarantees have been made (and how many months of Hartz IV (welfare) "wages" this is), all of this isn't stated in the newspaper. The Süddeutsche from the 15th of January, for example, hides the announcement that Hypo Real Estate will, for the fourth time in four months, need billions in cash and guarantees in an article titled, "When Steinbrück knocks on the door." The Bild newspaper even received a prize for having reported so "responsibly." A prize that is awarded by journalists.[25]

So, the journalists obey when the politicians whistle. Someone who knows about all of this from up close writes about it:

Merkel spoke to the journalists as if they were employees in one of the departments of the Chancellor's Office. And when you really think about it, you come to the conclusion: Yes, that's how more and more journalists see themselves as well. And, when it continues like this, then the fact is, you don't need journalists anymore.[26]

Angela Merkel, an East German secretary trained in propaganda work, was simply bringing the heads of the German media into line at this (8 October 2008) meeting and similar ones after that. The synchronization of the German press has been confirmed (see the examples above) by a few independent, contemporary witnesses. If there had been a free, independent press, there would have been an outcry heard throughout the entire Republic. Like a Russian autocrat, Merkel called the heads of German journalism together and made them swear to keep a common line. This is similar to what you would otherwise experience in banana republics, when revolutionaries occupy the radio stations so they can deliver THEIR truth to the people. However, instead of an outcry coming from German journalists, there was only silence and government-compliant reporting.

The former ZDF editor-in-chief Nikolaus Brender (2000 to March 2010) is one of the few to make a clear statement on this development. He also speaks of an informer system found among the ranks of the state-run public media, like in the days of the Stasi, the East German secret police. Shortly before the end of his tenure, Brender spoke of "unofficial employees" from political parties at ZDF, "really comparable with the informal collaborators (IM) in the GDR." There, a "finely spun network of dependencies," had arisen "from which career opportunities as well as obligations could be derived." Personally, he had "tried to keep such spies away from, at least, posts with real responsibility."[27] Previously, a Union (CDU/CSU) majority among the ZDF board of directors had managed to assure that Brender's contract wouldn't be extended there, because he didn't want to dance to the Chancellery's tune.

Peter Voss saw the situation similarly, with regard to the parties' influence on the public broadcasting stations, and this is why he left the CDU in 2009 after 35 years.[28] Today, Klaus Bresser, founder of *heute-journal* and predecessor of Nikolaus Brender as the ZDF's editor-in-chief, has also lost any illusions he had about the absolute independence of the journalists at ZDF.

Only a few journalists have a spine like Brender's – and can resist the embrace coming from the political ranks. Some "quality journalists" don't have the slightest scruples against switching sides from public broadcasting to politics – and continuing their careers by regurgitating political talking points. Steffen Seibert, who had been with ZDF since 1989 and anchored the *heute-Nachrichten* (daily news) from 2003 to 2010, became a government spokesman and head of the German Government's Federal Press Office with a civil service rank equivalent to a State Secretary.[29] In plain language: Seibert is the head of the German Ministry of Propaganda. Thus, it's easy to see how interchangeable these systems are and how close they are to one another. The *Süddeutsche* wrote:

For the government spokesman who is now making the switch to public broadcasting, there is a top journalist coming from public broadcasting into the press office. The systems replace each other.[30]

Battle of Lies: The Propaganda Spiel of Sabine Christiansen and Ulrich Wickert

Let's take a closer look at how broadly this influence is exerted, namely, using the euro as our example. The majority of Germans definitely didn't want the euro. However, that definitely didn't fit the bill, so the politicians decided to make it fit with advertising. The information campaign to indoctrinate the masses into supporting the euro cost nine million euros (17.6 million German marks). It was financed with money from the Federal Press and Information Office's budget. In plain language: The taxpayers had to pay for their own brainwashing. What's more, they had to do it twice: first, with taxes and the second time with their mandatory public broadcasting contributions (GEZ).

The advertising campaign began in 2000 and was to accompany the euro's dash to the finish line in five phases, leading up to the euro's cash premiere on January 1, 2002. The campaign was never aimed at informing the public on the issue. It's primary purpose was to elicit "positive emotions" among Germans with regard to the new currency. The funds were spent as follows: 7 million euros went to advertising and PR campaigns (ads, TV commercials, billboards), 750,000 euros for PR partnerships with non-governmental organizations and state governments and, finally, 1.2 million euros went for ongoing campaigns (service centers, public info tents, distribution).

The first advertising phase focused on pure advertising campaigns. Phase two included advertisements featuring well-known public figures. Phase three introduced leading figures from the various sectors of society who supported the euro. And in phase four, in the summer/autumn of 2001, not only celebrities but also "average Germans" were featured in advertisements expressing their support for the euro. For example, there were full-page advertisements with Berti Vogts, the then coach of the German National Soccer Team. His advertisements read, in thick, bold letters: "The euro is the long pass into the next century." It went on: "In Team Europe, Germany has to be a starting player economically. With the euro, we'll be successful in global competition. The single European currency is the best hedge against the risks of currency fluctuations. The German economy, a strong exporter, must be fit for the challenges of the next century. We have to work hard to create opportunities – in soccer as with the euro. Only those who seize their opportunities are successful."

In the course of this campaign, euro-critics were kept off the field of debate, speaking from the sidelines if they were even allowed to speak at all. The CDU printed and distributed a propaganda brochure entitled, "Euro: The currency for a secure future." In it, the German population was taken for a ride. With nothing but an outrageous pack of lies, the German citizens were persuaded that the D-Mark would lead to a future of mass unemployment and the dismantling of the German industrial base, but the euro would have everyone living in the lap of luxury.

As far as the federal government was concerned, money didn't seem to be an object in the propaganda battle for the euro. Otherwise, how else can we interpret this press release from June 5, 2000?

Publicis in Frankfurt has been commissioned by the Aktionsgemeinschaft Euro (Euro Action Group), consisting of the Federal Press Office, the EU Commission and the EU Parliament, to implement the euro information campaign in Germany. (...) The appearance of the new currency has been funded with a budget of 28 million marks for the years 2000 and 2001. In addition to the budget provided by the European Central Bank, which is managed by Publicis PR in Berlin, the Publicis Group also has an additional budget for the introduction of euro cash.[31]

On June 18, 2001, the German Federal Government then announced, "The Euro Action Group, in which the European Commission, the European Parliament and the Federal Government are working together to introduce the new European currency in cash, is starting (...) a first wave of television spots on the introduction of euro cash. As up to this point in newspaper and magazine advertisements and on billboards, four well-known individuals will be used as unpaid euro ambassadors: Sabine Christiansen, Richard von Weizsäcker, Helmut Schmidt and Ulrich Wickert. In these two months, the Euro Action Group will allocate more than three million marks for these television spots. As with all PR and advertising activities within the framework of the euro information campaign, half of these are financed from the budget of the Federal Government's Press and Information Office and half from European Commission funds. Ulrich Wickert will be the first to appear "on air" for the euro. Following him, in order, will be Christiansen, von Weizsäcker and Schmidt."[32]

At the time, the former Chancellor Helmut Schmidt raised eyebrows with his rather embarrassing statements about the euro. Either way, they proved that, although he might be knowledgeable on many topics, he certainly wasn't when it came to currencies. Schmidt said, "The outward stability of the euro, against other major currencies, will be greater than that of the German mark up to this point. This can be attributed to the larger volume of the new currency." Peter Odendahl, the then CEO of Aurecon Vermögensberatung GmbH (investment consulting), replied, "Top German politicians represent the view that a larger currency zone will make the euro more resilient than the D-mark currently is. Now – if these politicians believe that the size of a zone is a criterion of resilience – Russia is more than two hundred times larger than Switzerland. It would therefore be interesting to examine whether these gentlemen would prefer to invest their savings in rubles rather than in Swiss francs in the future." With that, Helmut Schmidt was publicly humiliated. Helmut Schmidt went on to spread a lot of nonsense about the euro, writing in the *Welt am Sonntag* on June 29, 1997: "The euro will be – in all likelihood – a hard currency, one whose external value cannot easily be manipulated by speculators in the financial markets or by political decisions in Washington or Tokyo."[33]

Now, let's take a closer look at two other euro spokespersons: Were Ulrich Wickert and Sabine Christiansen even legally allowed to prostitute themselves in an advertising campaign for the euro? This campaign in which our government advertised the euro on billboards, in print ads and on TV was pretty shady at the very least – if it wasn't in fact illegal. At the time, the German Interstate Broadcasting Agreement prohibited "appearances in television commercials by persons who regularly present news programs or programs on current political events." Media law expert Christoph Degenhart from the University of Leipzig also considered these celebrity appearances to be "problematic" because the authority these ARD journalists exercised over the public was "purposefully" exploited for political propaganda purposes.[34]

Sabine Christiansen, a television presenter born in 1957, explained in August of 2001 why she prostituted herself for the euro, "The euro's prospects are good. Even though it is weakening at the moment, experts see the great potential it has to become more stable than the mark."[35] She also said, "I get repeated requests from financial circles to do more broadcasts about the euro, but unfortunately, many of the CEOs from banks or large companies don't want to appear as guests." When "financial circles" make requests, people like Mrs. Christiansen obviously like to do their bidding. Alas, Sabine Christiansen wasn't able to enjoy the euro euphoria for very long. By November 30, 2003, the topic on her talk show was: "Germany bankrupt? Euro in danger?" On the broadcast, the constitutional lawyer Hans Herbert von Arnim commented on the development of the euro, "In my opinion, this is a nuclear meltdown. What's going on here is absolutely fatal. The confidence is now being gambled away, and the same thing goes for domestic policy. What we have done here is sacrifice long-term goals in the interests of short-term politics."

If you take a thorough look into Sabine Christiansen's broadcast archives, even the most skeptical won't be able to avoid noticing just how much her state-run television program was misused for euro propaganda. You don't even need to watch each individual show in its entirety. All you have to do is look at the facts: The euro-skeptic (who filed legal action against the euro), Professor Wilhelm Hankel was initially invited and then uninvited to the very first Sabine Christiansen broadcast on January 4, 1998. While the editors blamed "conceptual reasons" and offered him a 500-euro cancellation fee for their mistake, Hankel suspects there was intervention by Wolfgang Schäuble (CDU). ARD denies this.[36]

When it comes to other broadcasts, a quick glance at the glaringly lopsided guest lists is enough to get a good impression. Also, if you keep in mind that the presenter was one of the official euro propagandists, the picture becomes even clearer. In September of 2001, Christiansen headlined her talk show with the theme: "Deutschmark Ade! Euro tut weh?" (Deutschmark adieu! Euro hurts too?) In it, the euro pioneer Theo Waigel, euro propagandist in government employ Ulrich Wickert, euro proponent Hans Eichel and euro-supporting, whodunit author Horst Ehmke never gave the euro critics a chance. It wasn't any different in her broadcast, "The End of an Epoch – Bye-Bye Deutschmark!" from December 2001. There, sitting alongside Sabine Christiansen was the euro campaigner Hans Eichel, euro champion Egon Bahr ("... the historic, unique opportunity to realize a united Europe without war") and on behalf of the euro campaigner and former chancellor Helmut Kohl, his right-hand man, Lothar de Maiziere. The actor Heinz Schenk was allowed to impersonate the backward and euro-skeptical average German. On Sabine Christiansen's 250th show, on the 29th of June 2003, CDU politician and Union faction leader Friedrich Merz described how important Sabine Christiansen's talk show has been in influencing the population, "First, I think we should congratulate you on this program. In the meantime, this program has come to determine the political agenda in Germany more than the German Bundestag."[37]

Referring to Sabine Christiansen, the FAZ once wrote: "Over the years, it has become hard not to notice that Christiansen, with her substitute parliament, has lost sight of the rest of the world. (...) To be measured by your own words, especially by your deeds, being confronted with the consequences they have on others – this isn't something that happens to Christiansen."[38] She was simply someone who echoed the words of the mighty. She was a tool of the powerful. Every year, the ARD spent almost ten million euros of our mandatory public television fees on this panopticon, the Sabine Christiansen show (1998-2007), presented by a woman who trained to become an airline stewardess – adding up to almost 200,000 euros per broadcast. In a portrait of Sabine Christiansen, the glamour magazine *Park Avenue* once wrote, "With shallow questions, Sabine Christiansen became one of the most powerful women in Germany. Her talk show is the barometer of the country's political mood."[39] Perhaps it really was a barometer for the political mood, but certainly not for the mood among the public. If the average citizen had been looking to her for a return of the D-Mark, they were looking in vain. She also hasn't been ashamed to cash in on her popularity with the best of them: According to media reports, Christiansen charges 30,000 euros to appear as a speaker under a corporate logo.[40] For comparison: The former Labor Minister Norbert Blüm pads his retirement by 15,000 euros per speech. According to media reports, this also is the fee for Ulrich Wickert, the ex-*Tagesthemen* presenter,[41] who appeared on billboards along with Sabine Christiansen to advocate ditching the D-Mark in the run up to the euro's introduction.

So, it was precisely this woman who was taking the wind out of the euro critics' sails and making an unappetizing euro palatable to the German citizenry. On May 7, 2001, *Focus* wrote: "Now it's up to the celebrities to decide. ARD talk show host Sabine Christiansen, her colleague Ulrich Wickert, former Federal President Richard von Weizsäcker and former Chancellor Helmut Schmidt – all four of them have been smiling for the new euro money since last Tuesday. On 4000 billboards and in countless advertisements, this quartet is explaining to Germans why they should finally accept this unpopular new currency wholeheartedly. One of the mottos of this sympathy campaign that's costing us millions: The euro – our future."[42] Today, are Mrs. Christiansen and Mr. Wickert embarrassed about the part they played in this unbelievable propaganda campaign?

You can recognize a good journalist by the fact that they don't get in bed with any cause, not even with a worthy cause. As I already mentioned, this journalistic principle was once expressed by Hanns Joachim Friedrichs, an evening news anchor with the *Tagesthemen*. If anything, his successor Ulrich Wickert, (who is married to Grüner + Jahr CEO Julia Jäkel), got into bed with one cause in 2001: the introduction of the euro. In 2011, the NDR moderator and former *Tagesschau* presenter Eva Herman published an informative article on Ulrich Wickert and his commitment to the euro. In it, she wrote:[43]

In television commercials, in newspapers and on billboards, the political journalist Ulrich Wickert always wore a confident face while advertising the introduction of the euro. In another instance, he was pictured biting on a euro coin, signalizing that the future currency is a "hard currency."

However, for millions of Germans, this was making them feel increasingly sick to their stomachs: They wanted to hold onto their stable deutschmark. Nevertheless, Wickert, along with Sabine Christiansen, Günther Jauch, Helmut Schmidt and Richard von Weizsäcker, put their concerns to bed by means of carefully prepared testimonials. In advertising, and also in numerous interviews, he constantly emphasized the supposed advantages of the euro: How great it would be not to have to exchange money before going on vacation. How immense the economic benefits of the euro would be (this point, though, was hardly ever sufficiently explained in any detail by the TV journalist). And, how it could only be a blessing when "we" had finally given up on our foundational myth surrounding the DM.

No, it was at this point at the latest that a large segment of the German population – with all due sympathy – could no longer comprehend Mr. Wickert. This was also confirmed by a study conducted by the University of Hamburg on "The influence and effect of euro advertising on the observer:"[44] Six out of eight respondents had seen the advertisements for the euro featuring Wickert. When asked what was on their minds when they looked at the advertisement, the respondents agreed on a number of points, mentioning things like seriousness, intelligence, sympathy and their association with the "Tagesthemen" (his evening news broadcast). However, this obviously didn't amount to much. The investigation went on to state: When it came to the term EURO, all of those interviewed could only come up with almost exclusively negative points: skepticism, uncertainty, price increases, cheating to fulfill the criteria for the adoption of the currency. When asked what they thought of the currency changeover, they also answered negatively and repeated themselves in their statements.

Despite all their sympathy for the Tagesthemen newsman Wickert, the planned coup had already backfired from the start: The people realized that something was rotten. Nevertheless, this didn't seem to deter any of the numerous, pro-euro fiscal policymakers from carrying out their plans. They were looking for a suitable public figure and they hit the jackpot: Wickert seemed likeable and he served as a kind of bridge between politics and the citizenry, between above and below, between France and Germany. This, because people in Germany weren't going to get excited about someone who came across like a cardboard cutout: The German economy was doing relatively well, despite the recent reunification, and this had been made possible by the stability of the deutschmark, a currency with worldwide recognition. The D-Mark had basically become an object of envy for many countries around the world in terms of stability, reliability and sustainability. But this German mark was to take a fall for the euro, without a peep, forever. The doubts that surrounded this plan were more than justified.

At the time, Wickert had long since established himself as a daily news anchor, like an amusing, agreeable weatherman. He had written intelligent books on morality and decency, and on the crux of this life we're living. He had posed that everyone who wants to remain genuine and honest in the face of material seduction always winds up playing the fool in the end. True words. Over more than 270 pages, Wickert had expressed his moral philosophy concerning the loss of value: And now, as an anchorman on the German national news, he personally participated in mercilessly uprooting the D-Mark, Germany's greatest material asset.

Yes, ten years ago, Ulrich Wickert was exactly the right superstar for the euro. As a cosmopolitan gentleman, he knew his way around the world very well. Having spent time in many foreign countries, he had become familiar with a wide range of political mindsets, their currencies and the people who represented them. After all, he had been an ARD correspondent in Washington for years, but first and foremost, he had worked as a journalist in France, the country that had initiated the euro.

Citizens paying any attention suddenly learned a whole lot about Wickert's international résumé: Little Ulrich was born in distant Tokyo, where his father Erwin, a respected diplomat, worked for a long time as a radio attaché at the German Embassy. Wickert was also able to refer to the time he spent as a schoolboy in Paris, where his family spent several years thanks to his father's assignment to Germany's NATO delegation. In the sixties, Ulrich Wickert studied political science and law in Bonn, which was still the West German capital at the time. He also spent several years in Connecticut on an academic scholarship. At the end of the sixties, he began his journalism career at West German Broadcasting (WDR) in Cologne. A storybook celebrity for the introduction of the euro.

Wickert played ball willingly. Why he didn't seem to have any moral or ethical concerns throughout the whole process is still a matter of speculation. Perhaps he really believed in the ultimate success of the euro, without realizing any of the political intrigues behind this momentous decision, but that hardly seems possible. If so, this means we would be accusing him of being utterly naive. Perhaps, however, his employer was also to blame for his agreement, the state-funded and politically correct North German Broadcasting (NDR). With a similar devotion, this broadcaster also took part in the comprehensive advertising campaign and they also lent out their full-time employee to take part, something that is technically illegal according to the German Interstate Broadcasting Agreement.

From today's point of view, one simply wonders: How was all of this even possible, everything that was going on during the great euro euphoria? Apart from the fact that almost all media was reporting in lockstep with the euro and that euro critics were often slandered and silenced from the very outset, the fundamental question arises: Wouldn't ARD, funded with compulsory public contributions, have to be much more critical when dealing with such clearly political decisions? Was NDR really allowed to lend out the best horse it had in its stable for such an all-encompassing and life-changing European economic and monetary initiative? Or, did the even more powerful West German Broadcasting (WDR), where Wickert earned his first journalistic stripes and was their France correspondent for many years, help conceal these plans? Furthermore, was WDR also the company behind the advertising deal? Regardless, the idea of the euro was born in France: In 1988, a committee drew up the so-called "Delors Report" on the creation of the currency, named after the then French President of the European Commission, Jacques Delors. This report ultimately paved the way for the three-step creation of European Economic and Monetary Union. Germany, led by CDU Chancellor Helmut Kohl at the time, was initially reluctant: In Bonn, they knew what lay ahead for Germany in the course of the planned East-West reunification. Regardless, France wasn't going to take no for an answer: The French President François Mitterrand is said to have made his support for German reunification conditional on the introduction of the euro into Germany. Outside observers never tired of repeating that Germany had regained its old strength after its reunification, but this was of hardly any interest to the modern world, including other European countries. However, by depriving Germany of its strong Deutschmark, this theoretical problem could be solved fairly quickly. And Ulrich Wickert was right in the middle of it!

One can only speculate as to how big the circles were at the time the decision was made to get Wickert to do the legwork. Wickert, a fluent French-speaking Francophile, was the European bridge between Germany and France. It just seemed like a coincidence that the public got to know how much Wickert liked the Provence, French cheeses and red wines: He was a regular connoisseur of the region's specialties.

His role as a serious anchorman on the evening news naturally helped as well: Even today, it feels almost like it's time for the official government announcements – when you hear the fanfares of the Tageschau or the Tagesthemen and they begin presenting the news of the day. It has only been in recent days that more and more citizens have started experiencing a growing unease and have had any doubts about what news gets selected and how it's shaped by the editorial staff. In those days, however, the advertising that accompanied the introduction of the euro in Germany received an additional, highly official stamp. A guy like Wickert from the evening news, he could never be wrong! Could he?

In September of 2011, Wickert's new book came out. The title: *Redet Geld, schweigt die Welt (When Money Talks, the World is Silent (not available in English))*. Ahead of its release, the publishing house Hoffmann und Campe gave us an idea of its content: "Is it mere greed that makes people lie, cheat and deceive? Was this the reason for the biggest financial crisis since the Second World War? Are we justified in denouncing bankers as scoundrels? Ulrich Wickert names the culprits by name and demands that they finally assume responsibility and that action be taken." But what about Ulrich Wickert himself? What about his responsibility? Why doesn't he refer to himself and Sabine Christiansen as accomplices? After all, they were heavily involved in the euro hysteria. Did he already forget that? This man, who endorsed the euro and has certainly benefited from the economy much more than any ordinary citizen, had the gall to write a book in 2011 entitled:

When Money Talks, the World is Silent. Promotional events featuring Wickert were advertised with the following: Ulrich Wickert warns us, "We have to learn that everywhere in the world, as well as in business, only those who understand ethical values and align their actions accordingly will have lasting success."[45] Seriously? Here's a question: Did Wickert ever have the decency to humbly apologize to the German people for what he did to them a decade before he wrote this book? No? I never heard anything.

Wickert, someone who allegedly stands for ethical values and decency and criticized those greedy banks, really began to stand out for his hypocrisy in 2011. Ulrich Wickert advertised for a bank. He also caught hell from an investor protection group for it.[46] The *Association for Investor Protection e.V.* (SfA) issued a press release which wasn't exactly flattering for Wickert, the moral crusader. The release from August 23, 2011 reads:

"We hereby call on the former Tagesthemen presenter and author Ulrich Wickert to terminate his advertising contract with the Cooperative Financial Group." This announcement was made in Bremen today by Angelika Jackwerth, Managing Director of the Association for Investor Protection (SfA). When Wickert is quoted in the current advertisements for the group, to which DZ Bank, Volksbank and Raiffeisenbank belong, with the words: "What one alone cannot do, many can do," for investors, this sounds like they're being mocked. Although, Wickert is right when he says this, because around 1000 Volksbanks and Raiffeisenbanks recommended DG funds to their customers in the '90s. 15,000 investors then invested more than 500 million euros in these closed-end real estate funds. But now (...) the investors stand facing the prospect of losing everything and for many of them, the provisions they made for their retirement are no longer secure. (...) Wickert cannot seriously be representing cooperative banks that have treated their customers like fools.

Yes, Wickert can. Wickert also treated the entire German population like fools when it came to the euro. Afterwards, he went on to stand at the side of banks that treated their customers like fools. The average citizen's point of view is completely irrelevant – whether he continues to do this over and over again out of stupidity, negligence or it's intentional – because he's one of the ones cashing in on it. What was the title of his book again? *When Money Talks, the World is Silent.* So Wickert still hasn't stopped slaving away for the financial sector. One bank's website states: "On the 10th of December, 2012, the 'Wickert meets...' campaign begins. The Heimat Berlin ad agency has produced a series of spots with an unusual format for this on behalf of the Cooperative FinanzGruppe Volksbanken Raiffeisenbanken. Ulrich Wickert, who was already representing the values of the Cooperative Banking Group as their brand ambassador in 2011, will now meet Bill

Kaulitz, Andrea Petkovic and Hannes Jaenicke."[47] Now honestly, can anyone still trust this Ulrich Wickert, the unscrupulous poster boy who advertised for getting rid of the perfectly stable D-Mark at the time? On the other hand, perhaps it really was a father-son conflict that led Wickert to talk the Germans into the lousy euro after all. Wickert's father was in the euro opposition camp, trying to prevent its introduction, standing at the side of Professor Karl-Albrecht Schachtschneider.

There is an interview from the summer of 2001 (that has become legendary in the meantime) between one of the first euro-skeptics, constitutional law Professor Karl Albrecht Schachtschneider (a close compatriot of Nölling and Hankel), and the *Tagesthemen* anchor Ulrich Wickert. Its title: "Why do you believe in the euro, Mr. Wickert?"[48] This took place when Wickert the journalist was actively hawking propaganda for the single currency. In their conversation, Schachtschneider, who had filed several lawsuits against the Stability and Growth Pact with the German Federal Constitutional Court, countered Wickert with the claim that the euro would endanger Germany's stability. Among other things, the university professor warned that the euro would take German economic policy out of German hands. This is Wickert's exact reply: "No, we can determine tax policy, and we determine wage policy just as well." This alarming assessment was only one of countless misperceptions that the journalist Wickert had regarding the euro. Among other things Wickert also said in the 2001 interview was this gem: "... the euro has already set a lot in motion. The plan alone, to create the euro, has led to great budgetary discipline among the member states."[49] It makes your jaw drop. It is precisely this lack of budgetary discipline on the part of the southern EU states that has finally brought us to the edge of the abyss. In contrast, Schachtschneider was truly the visionary in the interview, telling Wickert, "Capital will flow outward because the euro cannot promise stability. This is reflected in the current inflationary trend. We no longer have a community based on stability."

It is time for the euro propagandists, the likes of the Sabine Christiansens and Ulrich Wickerts out there, to be held publicly accountable for what they have done. They took on a great responsibility – and sided with the losers. In the history books, this is why we are going to have to place them alongside the ones who are responsible for this misery.

Soap Commercials for the Euro: The Mannstein Advertising Agency

In retrospect, the unscrupulous way they wanted to make the euro palatable to German citizens through the media is truly incredible. At the time, they even used psychological tricks to get to German parents through their children: By distributing packets to school children, the

Aktionsgemeinschaft Euro (Euro Action Group), the German Bundesbank (central bank) and the state school boards directly influenced third and fourth grade pupils in all schools nationwide. With small gift packets, the children were to familiarize themselves with the new currency. As with any successful lottery, the people's desire to participate needs to be encouraged. These gift packets, which were designed in a playful way, were also distributed to retirement homes as well as refugee centers and homeless shelters. The distributors were aided by the employees of participating organizations. The aim of the campaign was for pupils to pass on their "knowledge" about the euro to their parents. For the elderly, the homeless and asylum seekers, they would have something politically correct to talk about. Euro critics, armed only with objective arguments, had no chance against this concentrated propaganda and the financial means behind it. Looking down over all of this was the Mannstein advertising agency.[50] The good Mr. Mannstein (who also came up with the "red sock campaign" which successfully humiliated the SPD to the CDU's benefit), together with the Federal Ministry of Propaganda ("Federal Press Office"), sold the euro to Germany's citizens like a trendy new gadget. Mannstein said, "The time has come to set a new course." The euro had to be given more of an emotional quality by communicating, to young people in particular, that the euro means "more fun" and "more freedom."[51] I already noted that the Federal Government was making sincere claims that the euro would allow young Germans to "live it up" in the future. The sad reality today: There has never been as much mass unemployment in Europe among the younger population as there is now.

All the while, the Mannstein advertising agency was cajoling us with live-it-up politics like they were marketing laundry detergent. This agency had been marketing Helmut Kohl and the CDU for years in the Bundestag elections and had also increased brand recognition for the Korean car company Daewoo in Germany. Now, this agency was also responsible for the German government's euro campaign. Mannstein worked out a precise timetable, placed advertisements, held seminars for journalists, distributed brochures and put up billboards – "The euro – as strong as the mark" (*stark wie die Mark*). "Education providers," that is teachers, were given training courses and trade unions were brought on board. At the same time, the European Monetary Institute (the future EU central bank) hired its own advertising agency and the European Commission spread 100 million marks across the continent, hiring 130 marketing experts to prepare for the great raid on the D-Mark.

Still, the Federal Press Office and the Mannstein agency were evidently completely overwhelmed by the task. At any rate, they were still having trouble selling the euro to the German citizenry. As the weekly newspaper *Die Zeit* wrote about it at the time:

Those responsible have apparently not yet recognized the significance of the task. After all, they are charged with getting the Germans ready to say farewell to their national treasure, the D-Mark – an undertaking that, in light of the population's fears and concerns, places the highest demands on communication. Instead, they have opted to follow the well-worn path of traditional marketing: a little advertising, supplemented by PR campaigns. Sparkasse Bank President Horst Köhler seems to have shouted his warning – "Please no laundry detergent ads!" – into the wind. Anyway, this is what the advertising created by von Mannstein's agency for the Federal Press Office suggests: With tired slogans like "Europe – because it makes sense" or "Euro – bright(er) future," the majority of the population's concerns are unlikely to be dispelled. Not wanting to place the euro at the center of their advertising also goes to show how little the strategists in Bonn are convinced of this monetary union themselves. Instead, they are planning a so-called sandwich campaign: The economic arguments are to be packaged between political ones – the Big Mac for Europe.[52]

According to a doctoral thesis from 2007, the advertisers continued to demand more and more money from the federal government. They pointed out that the industry would normally spend twice as much money on advertising to introduce a new brand of yoghurt than what they were spending on advertising for the euro. The Henkel AG & Company even spent 160 million euros on the market launch of the Persil Megapearls laundry detergent before the desired market saturation had been reached.[53]

The audacity with which the then federal government and the Mannstein agency wanted to manipulate the population with euro propaganda was highlighted by Jens Peter Paul in his 2007 dissertation. In it, he states:

Von Mannstein's agency was also awarded the contract because it offered the German government the prospect of comprehensive and extremely cost-effective cooperation with newspapers, radio and television stations. The BPA (Federal Press Office) hoped that this would allow them to get a lot moving, even with a small budget. Addressing an audience of millions could be achieved by means of "themed placements by means of casual and personable presentations in popular entertainment programs such as Wetten, dass ..." (Bet That ... (an extremely successful German TV show)), *as it was stated in the – then victorious – von Mannstein presentation. It goes on to talk about "new TV productions like, e.g. 'The Euro-Festival – for the euro's birthday' or 'The Euro – The European Game Show' with well-known presenters / artists / stars from different EU countries." Boulevard Bio and Hans Meiser, Talk im Turm (Talk in the Tower) and Harald Schmidt – there wasn't a popular talk show that von Mannstein didn't want to use for his euro advertising. The government was promised product placement on an unprecedented scale at minimal cost. And with a view to the mass communications medium of radio, the BPA was also sold a supposed nationwide cooperation with German radio stations.*[54]

Before this campaign, propaganda in its pure form like this had probably only existed in dictatorships like those of East Germany or among Third World regimes. Especially perfidious: Young journalists were to have the honor of being awarded a hyped-up media prize "for outstanding reporting" on the euro.[55] Reviewing the work by Mannstein's agency, you get the impression that entire nations are ultimately nothing other than unwashed masses who need to be sold a laundry detergent; with sufficient means, they can be influenced at will to support the interests of whoever's in power.

Looking back at their own advertising work for the euro, Mannstein's agency reported, "As we know from hindsight, the introduction of the euro took place without any problems, both physically (technically) and in terms of mass psychology. This (the work we performed up to 1998) will certainly also ... have a long-lasting contribution."[56]

When Helmut Kohl was honored in 2012 for his "life's work" with a postage stamp (five million of which were sold), the Mannstein agency was once again responsible for the graphic design. They proudly referred to the Kohl stamp as, "A symbol that stands for his vision and his great achievements."[57] It remains to be seen if any of the euro-sceptics like professors Schachtschneider or Hankel will also be honored with their own stamp one day. As opposed to Kohl, their visions haven't turned out to be illusory, they have become reality.

So, now we're familiar with the propaganda measures used to usher in the euro. A giant machine was set in motion. On the other side, isolated individuals stood their ground, trying to fight this machine made up of the state's propaganda apparatus and its willing accomplices. These individuals were spied on, beaten down and ridiculed. What's harrowing, though, is that some of them truly went through an experience that most of us would like to think only happens to regime critics living under Third World dictatorships.

Democracy Failed

SPD politician Liesel Hartenstein was never suspected of being a right-wing radical or a populist. Born in 1928, she had gone through a lot in her lifetime. Her great merit as a politician was that she wasn't a conformist. She wasn't afraid to open her mouth when others were following the party line and only paying attention to party interests. From the German Bundestag's point of view, Liesel Hartenstein was a rather irritating woman. In 1998, she dared to publicly indict the Bundestag and the politicians represented therein. Mrs. Hartenstein said that the Bundestag had never held an open, public discussion on the decision to abandon the D-Mark. Euro-critics had been effectively muzzled by a "spiral of silence." The introduction of the euro by political means was "not a heroic act of democracy."[58]

This was also Elisabeth Noelle-Neumann's view, the former head of the Allensbach Institute for Public Opinion Research. In 1997 she pointed out that in interviews – in surveys among the average population – only 21 percent of German citizens definitely wanted the euro. However, what were to be published were only the results of the survey conducted among the country's so-called elites. These included executives from politics, business and the media. In 1995, 61 percent of these elites were in favor of the euro. By 1997, this number had climbed to 87 percent. The silent majority of the population – put on ice – had no voice to represent themselves in politics or the media. The worst thing about it: The German-language media had slept through the entire development phase of the euro's introduction, only waking up after all the facts had already been manufactured. At least some of them did finally realize what was going on, but this was when the point of no return had already been reached in terms of international law. Rolf-Dieter Krause, WDR's correspondent in Brussels, said that journalists had been "asleep for a long time" leading up to the Maastricht summit. The media had been preoccupied with the German reunification and its consequences. Krause said of his journalist colleagues' behavior at the time, "We deal with it by pushing anyone who expresses any doubts about the meaning of the euro into the nationalist corner (...). Manfred Brunner was once considered a liberal but has since been assigned to the right-wing camp. He was shoved into it because he dared to express doubts about the euro."[59]

According to Axel Bunz, then head of Germany's representation in the European Commission, the political agenda in the 1990s didn't want the media, let alone the population, discussing the euro at all – it was a taboo subject. Bunz said, "The population was deliberately left out because it didn't concern them." Additionally, the Bavarian Green Party MEP, Gerald Hefner, reported that the spiral of silence surrounding the euro had an extremely influential impact on his political environment. He said, "People, including parliamentarians, were afraid to clearly express their concerns. Critical attitudes towards the euro, often even questions, continued to be considered as nationalistic, chauvinistic, dull, unmodern, un-European, anti-European." Does this sound anything like a democracy? When politicians are afraid to properly inform themselves on the most crucial issue in decades? When they're not allowed to ask questions because it's considered "nationalist?"

In 2007, Jens Peter Paul wrote a doctoral thesis on this topic at Frankfurt's Goethe University entitled, "Result of Failed Communication." He sent a questionnaire to 1086 members of the Bundestag, the European Parliament and State Parliaments asking, among other things, whether the euro had been pushed through "from above," that is, imposed on the citizenry. 78 percent of the MEPs agreed with this statement in its entirety or at least partially.[60]

Jens Peter Paul also quoted the then president of a state central bank (Landesbank), who was asked in an off-the-record conversation about the monetary union: What kind of currency devaluation could the Germans expect with the euro? In his thesis he reports: "He said that he assumes that it will be between 15 and 20 percent, but that he would deny saying this if anyone was to quote him."[61] Thus, the disinformation encompassing this allegedly wonderful euro was pre-programmed. Is that still democracy?

In his doctoral thesis, Paul writes that journalists who didn't toe the line experienced problems: "Among the journalists based in Brussels, who were naturally the first on the scene and thus the best informed about plans at the EU level, there had been a code of conduct since the 1980s that had only allowed a critical attitude towards a European monetary union within very narrow limits. Anyone who crossed the line was led to understand that they were considered out of place, or at least disoriented."[62] One person who clearly felt this was Winfried Münster, the *Süddeutsche Zeitung*'s correspondent in Brussels. He describes the pressure on him like this, "A few weeks before the Maastricht summit, Dietrich von Kyaw (the German ambassador in Brussels) called me a 'rat.' He stood in front of me, 'If you continue writing like this, you will destroy the German economy, because then the monetary union won't pass!' And crap like that. The pressure was immediately enormous. Then there were officials in the Brussels delegation who wouldn't speak to me anymore. And also, some of my colleagues too. That hurt the most. That I'm a European, there's never been any doubt. For me, the whole thing was so disappointing because the monetary union wasn't going to bring European integration any further along. Regardless, I was (...) designated as being a right-winger within a matter of weeks."[63] During those days, Chancellor Kohl took Münster off to the side during a journalists' conference and told him not to submit any of his euro criticism to his editors. Kohl personally rebuked him, saying he could "poison" the atmosphere. On another occasion, Kinkel, the Foreign Minister at the time, also told Münster that he shouldn't write so "destructively" about the euro anymore.[64]

In his doctoral thesis, Jens Peter Paul draws the following conclusion regarding the German media: "The journalists followed the other members of the German elite who (...) aligned themselves with the pro-euro course. (...) The euro remained an elite project. (...) In the end, failed attempts at communication can be recognized on both sides. Seldom have the rulers and the ruled faced each other with such a lack of understanding."[65]

All of this certainly doesn't have anything to do with the core principles of democracy anymore. What you've read in this chapter is much more reminiscent of sinister dictatorships and the fallen regimes of the past.

Nonetheless, this is just a tiny glimpse of what is happening behind the scenes.

The public broadcasting channels ARD and ZDF receive more than 7.5 billion euros annually through compulsory funding. This is an incredible amount of money. They receive it first and foremost because they are fulfilling a public mandate: namely, to provide the information the German democracy needs for political and social discourse. When more and more newspapers are only serving the standard newsroom slop, when the diversity of opinion is drastically dwindling, when more and more editorial offices are being merged and journalists are being dismissed in such numbers that the remaining ones hardly have any time left to do research, then this is when the public broadcasters' mission statement becomes even more important – and this is exactly what they aren't living up to anymore. Just the opposite: They allow themselves to be bought. And they are churning out propaganda.

The average viewer, let's say someone who follows a drama series produced by a public broadcasting channel, hardly suspects that the dialogues created for their favorite show are also for sale. These popular, prime-time shows with millions of viewers are, as I mentioned, funded by the mandatory contributions of German citizens (GEZ). On top of that, these broadcasters also generate revenue through surreptitious, paid advertising, bought with the intent of influencing the opinions of their mass audience. A past example of this includes a lobbying association for employers, the "Initiative Neue Soziale Marktwirtschaft" (New Social Market Economy Initiative (INSM)), that inserted hidden PR into dialogues they purchased in the prime-time ARD series Marienhof.[66] The message they wanted to have anchored in the minds of the viewers through these manipulated dialogues: "Up your work hours." The price to insert the employers' hidden, surreptitious advertising into seven episodes: 58,000 euros.[67] So even when we just want to relax by watching a meaningless television series in Germany, we are still being subjected to clever psychological manipulation. That was how it was when we said goodbye to the D-Mark, and that's the way it is every day. We're being disinformed around the clock.

Crime Scene Editorial Suite: the Shady Side of the Media

If you've managed to read this far, then you probably haven't garnered a very favorable impression of the German media. However, I know for a fact that the situations and interrelationships described in this book are only a small handful of excerpts from a very colorful reality. That being said, personal impressions only compose a portion of our reality. I began this book by sharing some very personal accounts. I related how I didn't use to think twice when it came to cashing in on press discounts, that I accepted all-expenses-paid invitations to 5-star hotels and I went on buddy-buddy trips with top politicians. I also noted that I accepted positions in foundations, associations and organizations that are closely related to intelligence agencies. Looking back, I also have to say that I produced very well-bought reports in exchange for those privileges, especially in the FAZ. I did all of this with the backing of my bosses. Now, at the end of this book, I will also tell you about the price I paid for doing all this. The price has been extremely high, and it certainly isn't something anyone should aspire to.

For many young people, being a professional journalist is their idea of a dream job. That's also how I thought of it back then, even before my first day of work. You can imagine how delighted I was, fresh out of college, with a generous job offer as a foreign policy editor with the *Frankfurter Allgemeine Zeitung*. However, my first day of work turned out to be completely different than I imagined it would be. It was the first day of October 1986, a Wednesday. On that day, the former US President Jimmy Carter turned 62. The violinist Andre Rieu turned 37 on that day too. Klaus Wowereit, who would later become the SPD Mayor of Berlin, was also celebrating his 33rd birthday. I was excited to go into work that day, so much so, I arrived at the FAZ offices an hour before I was told to arrive – and then I got my first assignment. It wasn't even 10 a.m. yet when the news editor at the political desk sent me to a corner store in Frankfurt's Gallus quarter. He gave me a 10 mark note and told me to get him a bottle of schnapps ("Obstler") and a pack of cigarettes.

At the time, the *Frankfurter Allgemeine Zeitung* was still one of the top addresses in the German-language media business. That day, I was full of awe as I entered those supposedly hallowed halls. And then, I learned pretty damn quick that my direct superior was an alcoholic. He was and certainly is a wonderful person. I'm only mentioning this to say that waking up to my new reality was pretty brutal. The next thing I learned was that any time a correspondent paid a visit to the editorial offices, they had to bring a bottle of schnapps or buy a case of beer for everyone. No one coming back from a trip for the paper ever showed up empty-handed. It was referred to as, "*Eine Molle geben*," Berliner slang for buying a round at the bar. The FAZ's network of correspondents was rather large and they were taking a lot of trips on the company dime. Suffice it to say, there was also a lot of alcohol going around. If the readers would have known how much of it was being imbibed in the FAZ's political editorial department, there would have been more than just an uproar.

At the time, the FAZ was promoting itself to the outside world with the pithy slogan, "There's always a clever mind behind it." However, sometimes these allegedly clever minds were so preoccupied with themselves that they totally missed the important things going on around them. On one of my first trips to Africa, I came down with the malarial strain *Plasmodium falciparum*. Considered to be the deadliest of all,it kills hundreds of thousands every year. I'm only mentioning this because my former employer didn't bother reporting to the employers' liability insurance association that I picked up this parasite while I was on the job. In the 17 years I worked for the illustrious FAZ, I experienced several occasions where they violated the obligation they have to report things like this to the authorities. I also suffered a lung contusion while on assignment in a war zone in southern Iran – and the FAZ didn't report anything to the professional association responsible for occupational illnesses – nothing. That seemed to be their unofficial official policy.

Unbelievable and incomprehensible: As I have already mentioned, I am probably the only Western observer still alive who witnessed a chemical weapons attack on Iranians. Particularly, those who were gassed in southern Iran in July of 1988 with German-manufactured poison gas (mustard gas). The FAZ sent me there and then they published a report of mine in the newspaper along with a photo I took of a poison gas victim. It never dawned on my former employer that I might have suffered any health-related effects (as they also failed to notice in so many other cases) from the poison gas on the battlefield. Simply put: The FAZ also didn't report this to the Employers' Liability Insurance Association for Trade and Goods Logistics (Berufsgenossenschaft (BG) Handel und Warenlogistik or BGHW). Due to the serious, long-term damage to my health (I got cancer, among other things), the doctors who treated me in the clinic after I returned were sure that I only had a few days to live. Thanks to the poisoning, they were sure I was going to be another casualty of war and they encouraged me to get married as soon as possible. They thought it would be a waste if I didn't pass on any of my benefits to my partner. So, at least from the view of the doctors who were treating me at the time, I can thank the FAZ for a wedding without wedding rings, without a wedding party and without anything else you would expect at a wedding. To the doctors' amazement though, I survived the effects of the mustard gas, along with the effects of all the other wars I've witnessed.

After 25 years, the BG finally recognized a whole series of serious occupational illnesses and accidents I racked up while employed at the FAZ. This, even though I came back from a FAZ assignment as a war correspondent in southern Iraq and was officially diagnosed with "occupational illness (BK) 1311 (mustard gas)." Processing these work-related accidents with the BG has taken more than 25 years and the FAZ wasn't much help at all. Just the opposite. Dear reader, even if you have an idea of the German bureaucratic system (or the evasive tactics of American health insurance providers, for example), you would still be hard pressed to imagine all the hurdles you have to get over as a German journalist to be officially recognized as a victim of chemical weapons poisoning. At the BG, they hadn't dealt with a case like mine for at least several decades. In December 2013, I sent a letter with the following question to the FAZ publisher who had been responsible for me at the time: "Would you please explain to me once again in retrospect why, for example, despite having definitive knowledge of the use of poison gas in this war, you sent me there as a war correspondent and (like with so many other assignments that had health consequences) you did not report this to the BGHW? After all, it was obvious that exposure to mustard gas would have health-related consequences." Two months later, I received a letter from the offices of a Frankfurt law firm. They explained that as far as the FAZ was concerned, the matter was already settled.

Once again, I'm not sharing this experience here to disparage the FAZ. I am sharing it in the hopes that the next generation will think twice before they risk their lives to spread somebody else's propaganda. Generally speaking, and this statement doesn't have anything to do with the FAZ in particular, life-threatening journeys like these will sometimes result in an exciting story for a journalists' employer. Of course, exciting stories can provide a big spike in short-term circulation. The correspondent who risked their life, on the other hand, well, they're going to be the one paying the final bill at some point. On assignment in the deepest African bush, a colleague of mine at the *Süddeutsche Zeitung* got a good look at how a soldier, glassy-eyed and obviously on drugs, held a submachine gun to my head and was ready to pull the trigger. This colleague did a good job describing the scene in an article he wrote about it afterward. However, when I made it back to the FAZ's editorial offices after having experiences like these, I was never greeted with any compassion or understanding. Nope, the first thing they did was heap "late shifts" lasting until 11 p.m. on me, because I had the privilege of travelling abroad and got to "experience" something.

Once, on my way to the FAZ offices, I suffered a basilar skull fracture. It was terrible. It took a few months before I was able to walk entirely on my own again. Do you think that anyone from the FAZ came to see how I was doing? A few months after my exposure to poison gas, I was diagnosed with cancer and spent several months in various clinics. I never got a visit from anyone at the FAZ at any of those clinics either. After six weeks, I also stopped receiving a paycheck. That was brutal. Meanwhile at the FAZ, they'd already posted a want ad for my job – and this wasn't the last time they would do this while I was still alive. I survived and came back to the editorial offices severely disabled. And then, despite my severe disabilities, they kept sending me to war zones over and over again. Why? Why not? That's what they're in the business of doing. In 2003 I had another serious accident and nerves in my right leg were severed. The result: The FAZ presented me with a severance agreement, no pun intended. From my point of view, to put it politely, this was rather unpleasant. As far as this subject is concerned, I think I'll just stop right here.

Having seen it from the inside, I don't understand why the FAZ has a reputation of being noble, truthful and sincere. It probably has something to do with their marketing. However, the drastic decline in their circulation numbers shows that the FAZ's shiny logo is losing its appeal to more and more people. I've written some ugly things about the FAZ in this book – and I won't be the last. It is all true – even if the folks at the FAZ don't like hearing it and would rather not be reminded of it.

What Should We Do?

Over the course of this book, we have seen how noticeable is the integration of prominent alpha journalists into elitist power circles. Their proximity to specific milieus in politics and business obviously has an influence on the extent to which various elite agendas affect reporting in the media. Given the situation, it may even be difficult for journalists who strive to be unbiased and neutral to escape this influence. They have long since become a part of a complex communication system of self-regulating mutual bias, in which "newsworthy" issues are determined and shaped ahead of time. For the most part, these highly questionable networks, where influential journalists rub elbows with international organizations and government institutions, remain hidden from newspaper readers, television viewers and radio listeners. Nevertheless, the interrelationships that have had a past influence on Josef Joffe (*Die Zeit*), Stefan Kornelius (*Süddeutsche*), Michael Stürmer (*Welt*), Günther Nonnenmacher and Klaus-Dieter Frankenberger (*FAZ*) as well as Kai Diekmann (*Bild*) have already been worked out in a scientific study by Uwe Krüger. The once so distinguished newspapers, the FAZ, *Süddeutsche*, *Welt* and *Die Zeit*, not to mention the *Bild*, certainly haven't received a boost in prestige thanks to these revelations.

Under the title, "Journalists under the Influence," the *taz* once wrote:

Of the media representatives surveyed, Krüger selected four journalists who had close ties "to the US and Nato-affiliated milieu": Stefan Kornelius (Süddeutsche Zeitung), Klaus-Dieter Frankenberger (Frankfurter Allgemeine Zeitung), Michael Stürmer (Die Welt) and Josef Joffe (Die Zeit). All four regularly took part in the Munich Security Conference. They were also involved in the Atlantik-Brücke and in the "secret Bilderberg Conference, where North American and European elites exchanged ideas." (...) So do these four alpha journalists write with a one-sided bias? (...) Krüger found 83 relevant articles from the journalists Joffe, Frankenberger, Kornelius and Stürmer. In them, he discovered a correlation between their NATO and US-related networks and their argumentation: "They extensively used the 'extended security concept' and argued for stronger German military engagement, especially in Afghanistan, which is desired by NATO and the USA but rejected by the majority of the German population." In 2008, for example, 53 percent of citizens were of the opinion that Germany should stay out of these conflicts. This attitude among the citizenry had been partly disparaged and the federal government was recommended to do a better job of persuasion. "There was no discussion of the objections and the criticism."[68]

Simply put: Journalists from the mainstream media have, at least in the past, been "entirely in line with the elites."[69] Moreover, it appears that sometimes, when they meet in those many isolated circles where ordinary citizens have no access, they are likely to be intellectually appropriated by powerful individuals from politics and high finance. In light of this, it's no wonder that scientific studies examining journalists like these come to the conclusion that the journalists reporting for leading media outlets have a bias and want to influence their readers with their "intellectual attitude."[70] So, when journalists write "biased" reports, move in exclusive power circles, seek an intimate proximity to elites, omit all of this from their reporting and suggest to the reader that there is no influence on their reporting, then what we have in front of us is only a simulation of true reporting: Then everything that we read, hear or see is an illusion, a sensory illusion, and not a true reflection of reality.

When journalists from the leading German media walk in and out of lobbying organizations like the Atlantik-Brücke, the Trilateral Commission, the Munich Security Conference, the Bilderbergers, the *Aspen Institute* or the Federal Academy for Security Policy, or even become members as "media leaders," then a red line has been crossed – because some of these journalists are for sale. They let themselves be invited on 5-star vacations and afterward they publish uncritical reports praising their hosts. What we then find in the media is nothing other than corrupt reporting, the worst kind of journalism. At the beginning of this book, I admitted that I also practiced these very same methods in the past, that I had been corrupted with the backing of my employer. This admission doesn't excuse what I have done, but it can and should help to bring an end to these practices.

The reporting found in Germany's leading media today is, to put it politely, dishonest. But those journalists who are dishonest should no longer be allowed to enjoy our trust. This means: Anyone who buys any of the big newspapers is deceiving themselves and is financing a propaganda machine. As long as their standard operating procedure involves employing lobbyists, this isn't likely to change. For ethical reasons alone, leading journalists should not be allowed to carry out any duties on advisory boards, boards of trustees or political planning bodies. Furthermore, the heads of major foreign policy desks have no place in any association promoting transatlantic political relations. In reality, however, the situation is completely different.

Therefore, my recommendation would be: To reject all those who seek to manipulate and disinform us, be it on television, in the newspaper or on the radio. Turn it off and starting immediately, don't spend another cent on it. The more people who do this, the greater the pressure will be. Above all: Write to the newspaper publishers, editorial offices and media houses and tell them why you are not going to spend another cent on articles published in the "leading media" that are written by lobbyists aiming to disinform us. Cancel your subscriptions and ask your friends, relatives and acquaintances to do the same. In this way, you will quickly become a part of a rapidly growing, new movement that is simply pulling the plug on this unethical propaganda.

Instead, what we can do is keep ourselves informed free of charge on the Internet, through many of the freely accessible, alternative news portals.[71] The new leading medium is undoubtedly the Internet. Just as renting video cassettes and then DVDs went extinct with the advent of digital media and online stores, these antiquated, mainstream media outlets will also become a thing of the past. And, as much as they try to scare us, this definitely won't lead to the collapse of our culture. On the contrary, there is something very positive about this development.

The elites who are bent on manipulating us these days have lost touch with reality, and their ability to perceive injustice is near zero. Everyone reading this book has the ultimate power over the journalism I have described here. All we have to do is stop giving our money and our attention to these "leading media." When enough of us stop buying the products offered by these media houses, when we no longer click on their Internet articles and we switch off their television or radio programs – at some point, these journalists will have to start producing something of value for their fellow citizens, or they're going to be out of a job. It's that simple. If you take a close look, you'll see that this process actually began a long time ago: Every day, journalists are being laid off somewhere, not only in the German-speaking world, because customers no longer want their style of reporting.

In July of 2014, the German Bundestag held a hearing on the future of German "quality journalism."[72] The professional experts who testified at this hearing made it clear to all the participants that "quality journalists," the kind I have been describing throughout this book, are up against the wall financially. Heading into the future, it is entirely possible that only alternative forms of journalism will be able to survive. This includes, for example, "personal brands" or "citizen journalists," independent journalists who market themselves as individual brands. Consumers will only pay for information they receive directly from journalists they can trust. Alpha journalists influenced by foreign interests, as I have described abundantly in this book, are a model that is being phased-out, a relic of days gone by. More and more enlightened people will realize that alpha journalists simply cannot be trusted. Independent journalists who can earn money without publishers because they've earned the public's trust – they are the ones that have a future. In the German media sector, Stefan Niggemeier is one example.[73] Or Thomas Knüwer.[74] In the business sector, we have Markus Gärtner.[75] In the English-language news sector, Matt Drudge established a name that earned universal recognition.[76] You can find the work of several German-language "brand journalists" collected at Kopp's news site: *http://kopp-report.de*

At least you won't find any Bilderbergers, transatlanticists, billionaires, politicians or other obscure figures trying to sell biased reporting to you there.

Nevertheless, this book is only a momentary snapshot. Just like in the 1950s when West German citizens knew their televisions were a propaganda instrument and called it "Adenauer television." Shortly thereafter, state-run TV had to stand its ground against the explosive growth of other media. The propaganda journalists of the leading media today have the same problem. People are simply abandoning them and getting their information from other sources. However, taking a look into the (foreseeable) future allows us to see the severity of what's coming: When it comes to how Europeans gather their information, we are looking at fundamental changes happening within a few years' time. At least this is what we're due for according to a public statement by the British Ministry of Defense that dates back to 2007: Around 2035, it will be completely "normal" for our children to have a chip implanted in their heads for the transmission of information. No, this isn't an incoherent prophesy by some crazy cultists. This was an official statement by the British Ministry of Defense based on actual technical developments and the likelihood of their implementation, which was calculated by scientists on the British military's payroll at the time.[77] The Guardian reported this in 2007 under the headline "Revolution, flashmobs and brain chips. A grim vision of the future."[78] The British Ministry of Defense also released a 90-page report to the British public on the foreseeable and apparently realistic developments the British army was expecting in the security sector. Regardless of its spin or whether you think it's good or bad, you should at least be aware of this report.

On a sobering note, even if we don't want to admit it yet, these developments are quite plausible, even though they're rather unpleasant: the destabilization of Europe. As opposed to the classical wars between nation-states that fill the pages of European history, migration, meaning these masses of immigrants being ushered into Europe, will give rise to more and more internal conflicts between new, disparate population groups. Increasingly large groups of people who are bitterly opposed to one another will continue to be crammed into the narrow confines of European cities. We've seen it over and over throughout history. It has preceded so many of history's catastrophes: from Alexander the Great's attempt to create a world empire and the barbarian onslaughts of the Migration Period that ended the Roman Empire, to our modern history and the final failure of Yugoslavia's multi-ethnic state experiment. In the end there are always horrific wars, because completely different groups of people living side by side in a single territory have never managed to create a lasting peace, not even under dictatorial coercion. That is at least one side of the coin.

It is precisely in this context that the British Ministry of Defense is examining how people will acquire their information in the future. At any rate, the quality of news is expected to consistently decline from now on. In all likelihood, journalists will soon be made up almost exclusively of citizen bloggers ("citizen-journalists"). With the combination of this decline in the quality of information and the brain chips mentioned above, this will make it easy for governments, criminals or terrorists to mobilize crowds of people at any time, for their own interests, via interfaces implanted in people's brains. You could mobilize "flash mobs" according to your own ends, for example, stirring them up and getting them to engage in extreme acts against opposing population groups.

In plain language: According to the military's forecast for the future, anyone who masters the interfaces to networked chips in people's brains and can hack into them would also be able to take control over the increasingly diverse masses of people brought together by these migration policies. At first glance, this probably sounds absurd to the average person – just as absurd as it would have sounded thirty years ago if someone told you that today, a large segment of the population will be in constant, wireless communication with the world's information networks, regardless of what they were doing, by means of a tiny device in their ear. Back then, if somebody told you that, from the middle of a huge forest for example, a tiny device would let you to make free phone calls to friends on other continents, give you access to the world's libraries and pinpoint your position on the Earth to the nearest meter, you would have thought that person was crazy – even before they mentioned that all of these communications would be recorded, evaluated and permanently archived, 24/7 by the Americans.[79]

Today, we take all of this for granted. Every phone call made in Germany is automatically recorded, word for word, and permanently stored in distant countries like the United States. Imperceptibly, our freedom is becoming more and more restricted in this way. A generation ago, this realization would have been the stuff of science fiction. Today, we have a bunch of alpha journalists, members of various pro-American foundations and associations, who want to palm off the most absurd things on us as being supposedly positive: from the alleged "Euro: project for the future" and "enrichment through immigration," to the subject of "surveillance for our security." The only thing that these NATO and USA apologists always fail to mention is in whose interest they're doing all of this.

The Frankenstein monsters out there know about these developments and want to be the ones influencing their progress. They have a perfectly natural desire to get their fingers on the buttons in our brains. So, when we look at the report released by the British Ministry of Defense or the American military's vision of our future, even though it still sounds like it was written by Mary Shelley or Phillip K. Dick, it is by no means as absurd as it may seem at first glance. Why? Because we already live in an age where only a handful of people decide what information will get wired deep into our brains and thus, how we think. There is a small clique of alpha journalists from an elitist circle close to the arms industry and US policy who, on closer inspection, already function similarly to the Dr. Frankensteins described in the British military's dystopian vision of our future I just mentioned. However, these accomplices, seeking their rewards for manipulating our brains in the interest of the power elite, are still human beings. We can still report on how they operate. We still have time to hold their feet to the fire and possibly even stop these developments. And, there are still some sincere journalists among them, the ones who can't be bought and the ones who condemn these abuses. Journalists with a spine.

These include Ulrich Tilgner. This man has been reporting on the Near and Middle East since 1982. Born and raised in Bremen, he ran the ZDF office in Teheran since 2002. In 2003, for his coverage of the War in Iraq, he received the Hanns Joachim Friedrich Prize for Television Journalism. He, "preserved and proved his professional quality and journalistic independence under the extreme conditions of war reporting." Then he dropped his own bomb: Tilgner, a foreign correspondent who was a familiar face to all ZDF viewers, now only reports for Swiss television. He did not extend his contract as a special correspondent for the Middle East and the head of the ZDF office in Tehran. He justified his move by saying that he felt increasingly restricted in his work in Germany, "especially as far as reporting from Afghanistan is concerned, now that German soldiers are dying there." There were considerations involving the military alliance that were reflected in the channel's editorial independence. At the same time, politics was increasingly being pushed into niches. "In Switzerland, on the other hand, programs like the *Tagesschau* or *10vor10* are institutions." There, he hasn't yet experienced any interference with his work. Of course, ZDF didn't tell its viewers why their foreign correspondent Ulrich Tilgner suddenly disappeared. So, there are journalists with a spine out there.

What remains is the realization: Our alpha journalists report down to the German people. They aren't interested in what the average citizen has to say, rather, they try to shame the people into keeping their mouths shut or ignoring the issues in the interest of political correctness. This can be seen in the ongoing bias in reporting. More and more people are getting the impression that German media is patronizing their lives, their feelings and their opinions. That there is an aloof, corrupt elite who are arranging the world to please themselves and only themselves. That the only thing the media offers is the annoying drone of talking heads who think they know better and don't even give a damn anyway. However, there is a new zeitgeist emerging from the people and it's poised to upset the applecart.

Before I close, I would like to thank all the alpha journalists I named by name in this book. After all, they have provided an important service: In the future, they will provide journalism schools with an example of what not to do, serving as a warning and a deterrent to a new generation of up-and-coming reporters.

Everyone named in this book denies having close, intimate contacts to elite organizations. Moreover, they deny being lobbyists. They also deny being "corrupted" by their proximity to the elite. And, they deny having lost their journalistic edge, working as they do in such close proximity to the aforementioned groups. They deny that this proximity has any influence on their reporting.

Afterword

Carl Bernstein is the American reporter who exposed the Watergate affair and, in doing so, brought down President Nixon in 1974. Bernstein is a Pulitzer Prize winning journalist. He is a heavyweight among journalists. After leaving the *Washington Post* in 1977, he worked for six months on a single report: an article about journalists collaborating with the CIA. His report was published in *Rolling Stone*.[1] In it, Bernstein revealed that the CIA had about 400 American journalists working for them. The *New York Times* even had a contract with the CIA at the time, stipulating that its journalists could be "borrowed" by the CIA whenever they wanted them. According to the report, many of the day's most well-known columnists and contributors were on the CIA's payroll, including editors, chief editors – and foreign correspondents. Since this 1977 revelation at the latest, it has been clear that journalists and the leading staff at media companies worldwide are recruited by the CIA or handled as informants.[2]

What does this mean for Germany? One example: Manfred Lahnstein, SPD politician and German Finance Minister in 1982, worked for the media group Bertelsmann from 1983 to 2004, and most recently as its "Special Representative for the Executive Board." Lahnstein was a member of the Trilateral Commission, which I detailed earlier in this book. Additionally, he has been the Chairman of the Board of Trustees for the weekly newspaper *Die Zeit*'s foundation (Zeit-Stiftung) since the mid-1990s. Lahnstein's name appears in the files of the former CIA officer Robert Trumbull Crowley as a CIA informant. Lahnstein is just one of the 2,619 names of alleged CIA informants found in these files. Robert Trumbull Crowley died in a Washington hospital on October 8, 2000.[3] He was second in command of the CIA's Directorate of Operations and head of the covert operations division. It is entirely possible that the people on his list did not even know that they were listed as CIA informants.[4] In August 2014, I wrote to the weekly newspaper *Die Zeit* to ask Manfred Lahnstein whether he was aware that he – like other Germans – was on this list of CIA informants. Obviously, at the time when he was in charge of media at Bertelsmann, because his former address in Gütersloh is mentioned on the list. Lahnstein was noticeably surprised, answering, "Thanks for the heads up. I had and have no idea."

I am convinced that Lahnstein is telling the truth. According to my own past research, members of the Trilateral Commission are routinely added to CIA lists without their knowledge. When it comes to individuals who are close to US intelligence agencies or even actively support them, this happens automatically. Lahnstein could have therefore been added to this CIA informant list for simply having been a member of the Trilateral Commission at one point in time. In plain language: As a journalist, it's best just to steer clear of transatlantic organizations.

I find it inexplicable that German journalists still cozy up to networks like these. This is because, since 2006 at the latest, they should know exactly what they're getting themselves into. That was the year *Arte* broadcast the documentary, "Benutzt and gesteuert" ("Used and Controlled"). This astounded its audience by detailing how the CIA tries to influence the editorial staff of German publishers and broadcasters through various front organisations.[5] It revealed: Many writers, musicians and publishing house or public broadcasting employees – have been controlled remotely from Washington.[6] It also showed that magazines, like the literary magazine *Der Monat*, were co-financed by the CIA. When this became public knowledge in a *New York Times* article, *Die Zeit* simply bought out *Der Monat*.[7]

None of this was ever classified information. It's just that nobody ever wanted to see it. As early as 1996, the CIA publicly announced that it would be recruiting more journalists.[8] And where is the best place to make such contacts? Where could an alpha journalist be turned into one of "Frankenstein's monsters?" Of course, in one of the many transatlantic organizations. Because there, the CIA always has a seat reserved at the table.

Today, many of the people I have mentioned by name in this book may claim to not be aware of what is going on around them. They could claim that they are simply too stupid, too naive or too incompetent to know. However, we can easily see right through this: Because the individuals leading this transatlantic cooperation are sitting in the *Council on Foreign Relations* (CFR). The CFR has very close ties to the CIA.[9] The CFR also has many prickly offshoots, such as the *German Council on Foreign Relations* – better known to Germans as the Deutsche Gesellschaft für Auswärtige Politik (DGAP), which the CFR was instrumental in founding.[10] Almost all pro-American lobby organizations in the *Transatlantic Policy Network* (TPN) are affiliated with them. This network sees itself as a lobbying organization of large European and American corporations, media and think tanks and boasts member companies including the likes of:[11] Allianz, AT&T, BASF, Bertelsmann AG, Boeing, BP, Caterpillar Inc., Citigroup, Coca-Cola, Daimler AG, Dell, Deutsche Bank, Dow Chemical, Ericsson, Facebook, GE, Hewlett Packard, HSBC, IBM, JP Morgan, The McGraw-Hill Companies, Michelin, Microsoft, Nestle, Oracle, Pfizer International, SAP AG, Siemens AG, S.W.I.F.T., Syngenta and UPS. Furthermore, the following is a list of think tanks that are also united under the umbrella of the *Transatlantic Policy Network*,[12] together with the large corporations mentioned above: AmCham EU (*The American Chamber of Commerce to the EU*), *Aspen Institute – Berlin, Aspen Institute – Italy, Atlantic Council of the United States, Brookings Institution, BRUEGEL, Carnegie Endowment for International Peace, Centre for European Policy Studies* (CEPS), *Chamber of Commerce of the United States, Chatham House, Council on Foreign Relations, Center for Strategy and International Studies* (CSIS), Deutsche Gesellschaft für Auswärtige Politik e.V. (DGAP), *European Policy Centre*

(EPC), *European Round Table of Industrialists* (ERT), *European-American Business Council, European Institute, German Marshall Fund of the United States, Institut Français des Relations Internationales* (IFRI), *TransEuropean Policy Studies Association* (TEPSA), UNICE and the *US Council on Competitiveness.* The only ones missing are the Atlantik-Brücke and its partner organization, the *American Council on Germany,* as well as Mr. Rockefeller's Trilateral Commission.[13] High-ranking politicians are present in almost every one of the aforementioned organizations. So, there you have it, the network of major corporations, media outlets and think tanks that has ensnared so many mainstream media journalists, business bosses, politicians and scientists. Are they all really just involved for fun and games?

So, is it a conspiracy theory if I am personally convinced that the many individual cells of the *Transatlantic Policy Network* and their peripheral organizations are preparing brain massages for us of the utmost sophistication? When it comes to the members and friends, scholarship recipients and researchers associated with these many lobby organizations, are their perspectives so artfully shaped and refined that they become the perfect medium for propagating the ideas of these large corporations, intelligence agencies and US interests? Is this carried out so persuasively, that they even think these thoughts and strategies are their own ideas and logical conclusions? After all, the ideas generated in this way then go on to appear in the mainstream media, in an overwhelming number of publications and other formats, passed off as the original products of their own thought.

Against this background, it is absolutely crazy to see the leading German-language media functioning like this, publishing reports akin to those found in Iraq or other distant countries where they hardly enjoy any press freedom. There, the overwhelming majority of the media isn't independent and simply acts as a mouthpiece for political factions. Reporters Without Borders, financed by the US billionaire George Soros, also likes to shed light on abuses like these in far-flung countries – but not here in Europe.[14] However, in actuality, our German-language media are predominantly the mouthpieces for political factions and, as we have seen in connection with their transatlantic interdependencies, they are by no means independent. At ZDF, almost all of the editors and broadcasters with any influence are card-carrying members of various political parties. Today, you can even legally refer to ZDF as the most dependent broadcaster in the entire Federal Republic of Germany. This, because in March of 2014, Germany's Federal Constitutional Court reprimanded the influence politics has on our broadcasting bodies – and declared the "state contract" that ZDF has with the Federal Government to be unconstitutional.[15] This means: The influence that political groups have on the ZDF is so extreme that it has been declared unconstitutional! The situation in Germany can literally be compared to a banana republic.

What we have examined in this book is the nexus of the power politics the elites use to influence the system. Once you've seen it, you're no longer surprised that this is exactly where we find the origins of many of the buzzwords we take for granted today: From "globalization" to the "liberalization of world markets" and from the "fight against international terrorism" to the "Arab Spring," this list also includes the use of seemingly harmless words like "air strikes," for example, when what we're really talking about are brutal, often indiscriminate bombings. That said, the pro-American elites' transatlantic systems of influence are developing plans for war. From the Iran-Iraq War in the 1980s, the many lesser-known wars in Africa, the Gulf War in 1990, the Yugoslav Wars in the 1990s, the Iraq War in 2003, the ongoing War in Afghanistan, the civil wars in the Arab states to the Ukraine and back again to the Middle East, all of these wars are about raw materials and geopolitical power. And the German mainstream media have readily accompanied all of this with their propaganda.

After conducting extensive studies, what does the Austrian conflict researcher, Dr. Kurt Gritsch, call our mainstream, quality media? He refers to them as "warmongers" (*Kriegstreiber*).[16] And even Gabor Steingart, editor of the renowned *Handelsblatt* business newspaper, accuses his colleagues from the mainstream media (such as the alpha journalists at the *Frankfurter Allgemeine Zeitung*) of being war profiteers, and calls FAZ articles "intellectual draft notices." In the late summer of 2014, he even accused the FAZ of using false reports to reinforce their warmongering against Russia.[17] One day, dear readers, a future generation will ask you how long you supported these warmongers. Four-fifths of Germans reject German military operations abroad.[18] Federal President Joachim Gauck is quite different altogether.[19] He is a member of the elite transatlantic association, the Atlantik-Brücke.[20] Moreover, like a large segment of the leading media in Germany, he is very close to the provocateurs in the United States.[21]

Today, I am ashamed of having worked for these warmongers for a good portion of my former journalistic life. Others aren't ashamed at all. Just the opposite: Many alpha journalists are in contact with the American Ralph F. Goff. This man was active behind the scenes in many American organizations. According to Russian sources, Ralph F. Goff is said to have been the CIA's station chief in Germany until the summer of 2014.[22] Officially, he operated under the title of "Foreign Service Officer with the U.S. Department of State,"[23] thus disguising himself as a harmless diplomat. Much like his wife, Jennifer Goff, he is said to specialize in recruiting foreigners who participate in transatlantic talks for the CIA. His wife Jennifer is said to have been deported from another country in 2004.[24] All this is perfectly normal in American service circles. Even the world-famous whistleblower Edward Snowden worked for the CIA in Geneva for a long time disguised as a diplomat.[25]

Do you remember how I described the methods that the US intelligence agencies used to help found transatlantic organizations in Germany during the Cold War in this book? And how these organizations were designed to influence public opinion in Germany? Do you also remember the prizes these organizations named after US intelligence officials and the positions the US intelligence services occupied in German transatlantic foundations? Evidently, nothing in this whole system has changed up to the present day, because this Ralph F. Goff, who is said to have worked for the CIA in Vienna before working in Berlin (disguised as a diplomat) and who also counted many alpha journalists among his friends there, was compelled to leave Germany in the summer of 2014 due to his excessive intelligence agency-related activities. Thanks to his profiles on various social media platforms, it was easy to identify the relevant contacts he maintained as of the summer of 2014. Now they're probably all going to be deleted as quickly as possible. Why didn't any of Germany's alpha journalists report on this any earlier?

If you did actually wonder about that question, please flip back to "page one," because you should probably start over and read this book a little more carefully the next time…

Do you still remember what I covered on pages 56 and 57? About DU. Then take one last deep breath:

On January 31, 2000, the then 23-year-old German Armed Forces private first class Andre Horn died in the Prizren field hospital in Kosovo. He had been deployed as a member of the Kosovo Force (KFOR) in Kosovo since the end of November 1999. The Bundeswehr states that his official cause of death was a meningococcal sepsis. The truth, however, appears to be different. The scientists, Prof. Peter Horn, a biotechnology professor at the Ludwig Maximilian University in Munich and expert in isotope geochemistry at the International Atomic Energy Agency (IAEA), and the doctor and medical scientist Horst Günther Siegwart, came to the conclusion that private Horn could have died from the consequences of a severe uranium munitions poisoning (depleted uranium, DU), which he contracted in Kosovo. The ability to confirm this possible radiation poisoning by uranium munitions would still be possible today if Andre Horn's body was exhumed and a scientific analysis was carried out on its tissue. The family of the dead Bundeswehr soldier has made repeated requests for permission to exhume private Horn. They would like their son's mortal remains to be examined by internationally recognized experts, but all of their requests have been refused by the German Ministry of Defense. Attempts to go through the public prosecutor's office have also failed because the Ministry of Defense is needed to authorize the family's corresponding application. The Ministry continues to publicly claim that uranium munitions aren't dangerous and our alpha journalists support the statements made by the Ministry. Now, take a very good look at the documents reproduced on pages 56 and 57 of this book once again. Then you will get an idea of how unscrupulous these networks working behind the scenes can be. Do they dance on our graves too?

[Editor's note. Sadly, the author's last question was to be ironically prophetic, as he passed away in 2017. Accordingly, he could also not fulfill the intentions in the closing remarks that follow.]

To close, I only have one request I would like to make to the reader: This book is the first volume of an explosive three-part series on the media industry. So far, you've learned about the secret networks that control this flood of information. You have also gotten to know the proximity the German media has to the elites and the consequences this has. Every statement in this book has been documented, step by step. Reality has emerged from a "conspiracy theory." In a subsequent volume, we will learn the tricks that major media publishers use to cheat their advertisers. I have already given you a small sample of their methods in this book. If you, as a reader of this book, also have (verifiable!) tips directly from the industry, then I am already looking forward to receiving your contact request or letter. In a third volume, I will give a very concrete account of the PR industry, naming which journalists are on which internal lists. Yes, most of our reporting has already been bought and paid for these days. I have already revealed some of the names in this book. If you, as the owner or employee of a PR agency, have had any explicit experience with the demands from media houses or journalists or are responsible for a company's press discounts and would like to make verifiable information available, I would be eternally grateful for your contribution at: *info@ulfkotte.de* or I can be contacted directly via Twitter: *@UdoUlfkotte.* The people out there should finally become aware of the truth so they can defend themselves. You can also follow my reporting on the Internet at http://info.kopp-verlag.de/ and subscribe to the underlying information service at http://www.kopp-exklusiv.de, where I also publish my writings.

After the Afterword: the Editor's Last Word

This book has shown how today's German media are the propaganda arm of US imperialism, as thoroughly as the East German media were organs of propaganda and control by a Soviet-style dictatorship. What are the parallels for us in America? Who controls the agenda for us?

I don't watch TV, for reasons that will be clear, but I just happened to catch this scene from the "Great News" sitcom: Gorgeous blonde is telling her mother, "My body is a temple... and by that I mean I let a lot of Jewish guys in." There it is, in your face and straight from the horse's mouth. Our American media are prostitutes for you know who is running this country.

Notes

A note for doing source research: All of the links below [during the author's lifetime were] to be found on the Internet at *www.gekaufte-journalisten.de* under the heading "Quellen" (sources). Internet links are sometimes deleted or changed. Nevertheless, you may find the links with their original content at any time retroactively in the Internet archive at *https://archive.org/web/*, if you enter the link you are looking for there. [The author's website *http://ulfkotte.de/* is still online as of this writing.]

Notes to the Foreword

1. See for instance http://www.independent.co.uk/voices/comment/israelgaza-conflict-thesecret-report-that-helps-israelis-to-hide-facts-9630765.html
2. See http://meedia.de/2014/07/29/einstweilige-verfuegung-gegen-die-anstalt-zdfwehrt-sich-gegen-zeit-journalisten-joffe-und-bittner/
3. See http://www.focus.de/politik/experten/wolffsohn/steuerhinterzieher-theosommer-von-wegen-vorbild-wieder-ein-unmoralischer-moralist_id_3572472.html
4. See http://www.internet-law.de/2014/07/zeit-journalisten-gehen-gerichtlichgegen-das-zdf-und-die-anstalt-vor.html
5. From http://www.internet-law.de/2014/07/zeit-journalisten-gehengerichtlich-gegen-das-zdf-und-die-anstalt-vor.html
6. Concerning Joffe's network of contacts see https://dl.dropboxusercontent.com/u/64910762/Manuskripte/Kr%C3%BCger-Meinungsmacht_356-362.pdf
7. See Hans-Jürgen, *Bucher, Mediensprache, Medienkommunikation, Medienkritik*, Tübingen 1991
8. See for instance http://www.internet-law.de/2014/07/zeit-journalisten-gehengerichtlich-gegen-das-zdf-und-die-anstalt-vor.html
9. See for instance http://www.cicero.de/berliner-republik/die-liste-der-500/38015 and http://www.cicero.de/bilder/die-liste-der-500-wichtigsten-intellektuellen
10. See http://www.bundestag.de/dokumente/lobbyliste/
11. See https://lobbypedia.de/wiki/Hauptseite
12. See https://cablegatesearch.wikileaks.org/search.php?q=&qo=0&qc=0&qto=2010-02-28
13. See for instance https://www.freitag.de/autoren/soenke-paulsen/wie-man-den-neuenkalten-krieg-gewinnen-kann
14. See http://www.huffingtonpost.com/2009/02/06/ap-ceo-bush-turnedmilita_n_164812.html
15. See doctoral thesis "Meinungsmacht" by Uwe Krüger, Köln 2013
16. See https://cablegatesearch.wikileaks.org/search.php?q=&qo=0&qc=0&qto=2010-02-28
17. Das CIA-Dokument findet sich hier: http://file.wikileaks.org/file/cia-afghanistan.pdf
18. See http://file.wikileaks.org/file/cia-afghanistan.pdf and http://www.globalresearch.ca/the-cia-s-strategy-to-manipulate-european-public-opinion-onthe-afghanistan-war/18376
19. See http://www.coffeeandtv.de/2014/07/07/sack-reis-in-china/

20. Quoted from http://kress.de/tagesdienst/detail/beitrag/126900-
zeitungsforschervogel-zur-talfahrt-der-tagespresse-produktdifferenzierung-ist-die-
letzte-chance. html
21. See http://library.fes.de/pdf-files/akademie/10790.pdf and http://
katharinabrunner.de/2014/07/studie-andreas-vogel-fes-auflagenrueckgang-
tagespresse/
22. See for instance http://kreuzer-leipzig.de/2014/07/22/ab-und-zu-kommt-mal-
einpraktikant/
23. Quoted from http://uni.de/redaktion/wie-medien-uns-sprachlich-manipulieren
24. See http://meedia.de/2014/07/25/warum-das-zdf-schuld-daran-ist-dass-die-
fdpaus-dem-bundestag-flog/
25. See http://www.newsroom.de/news/detail/$IWCOHRFNMSFJ/kommentar_
stefan_ laurin_ber_den_derzeit_wohl_gefhrlichsten_mediepolitiker_und_seinen_
griff_in_ die_kasse
26. In addition to the information in this book, I recommend as further research the
dissertation "Meinungsmacht" by Uwe Krüger, Köln 2103; also Stephan Weichert
and Christian Zabel: *Die Alpha-Journalisten*, Köln 2007, and Philip Baugut:
*Politische (Nicht) Öffentlichkeit in der Mediendemokratie – Eine Analyse der
Beziehungen zwischen Politik and Journalisten in Berlin*, Baden-Baden 2009
27. Financial Times, 23. April 2009, The Blindness of Journalists, http://www.ftd.de/
meinung/kommentare/:Kommentar-Die-Blindheit-der-Journalisten/504082.
html?p=1, archived at http://web.archive.org/web/20111129183355/ http://www.ftd.
de/meinung/kommentare/:kommentar-die-blindheit-derjournalisten/504082.html
28. Concerning comments about the FAZ, see http://www.faz.net/aktuell/ feuilleton/
medien/troll-kommentare-meine-tage-im-hass-13038925.html?
printPagedArticle=true#pageIndex_2
29. See http://derstandard.at/1331207267450/Kurt-Gritsch-Gut-inszeniert-
dieMainstream-Meinung, Also the report, "Medien als Weichensteller zum Krieg",
on the Internet at http://www.ag-friedensforschung.de/rat/2003/loquai. html
30. See http://www.bild.de/politik/ausland/europaeische-union/eu-chefs-kuschen-
vorputin-36938114.bild.html
31. See http://diepresse.com/home/3842902/USA_Keine-Beweise-fur-
russischeMitwirkung-an-MH17Absturz?_vl_backlink=/home/3840315/index.
do&direct=3840315
32. See http://deutsche-wirtschafts-nachrichten.de/2014/07/25/amerikaner-werden-
nervoes-hat-die-ukraine-den-abschuss-von-mh17-ausgeloest/
33. See the dissertation "Meinungsmacht" by Uwe Krüger, Köln 2013
34. See http://www.faz.net/aktuell/politik/bundeswehr-in-afghanistan-feigheit-
vordem-buerger-1510966.html
35. See the report "Der Medien-GAU von Odessa" at https://www.freitag.de/
autoren/maennlicherlinker/der-medien-gau-von-odessa
36. See http://washington.cbslocal.com/2014/07/23/kerry-defies-faa-ban-flies-
intotel-aviv/
37. Quoted from http://www.newsroom.de/news/detail/$IWCOISLTIOKO/
38. See http://derstandard.at/1259281033038/Pressestimmen-Obama-versuchtworan-
Alexander-der-Grosse-scheiterte
39. See http://www.hrw.org/sites/default/files/reports/usnsa0714_ForUPload_0.pdf
and http://www.hrw.org/news/2014/07/28/us-surveillance-harming-journalismlaw-
democracy and http://www.asiantribune.com/node/83887

40. Those who are mentioned but not contacted or interviewed, I ask for your understanding. For the many hundreds of persons named, it was impossible for me to ask each individual to comment. I tried to prove each statement with a reputable source. If sources do not or no longer agree or statements are not true, I am always ready to change them. Send notes to info@ulfkotte.de. At the same time, I kindly ask for your understanding that, after more than thirty nonfiction books and millions of readers, I can not answer every other private inquiry on other topics.

41. Quoted from http://www.newsroom.de/news/detail/$IWCOISLTIOKO/

42. Internet links are sometimes deleted or changed. Nevertheless, you can find the more than 500 links listed in the footnotes of this book, including original content, when deleted by third parties, retrospectively in the Internet Archive at https://archive.org/web/, when you enter the link into the search engine.

43. See http://www.sprengsatz.de/?p=2986

44. See http://www.stern.de/gesundheit/naegelkauen-knabbern-bis-das-blutkommt-647394.html

45. http://www.sprengsatz.de/?p=3025

46. See http://www.hildegardknef.de/filmografie%20TV%201997%20B.htm

47. See for instance http://www.wiwo.de/erfolg/beruf/kein-bedarf-diese-jobs-sind-vomaussterben-bedroht/10208452.html?slp=false&p=7&a=false#image

Notes to Chapter 1. Fake Freedom of the Press: My Life as a Reporter

1. Quoted from http://www.tt.com/home/8573752-91/zitate-von-jean-claude-juncker.csp

2. See http://www.fr-online.de/politik/bilderberg-konferenz-geheimes-treffen-derelite,1472596,4471506.html

3. See: "Tendenziöse Attributierung in deutschen Printmedien: Putin vs. Obama – eine linguistische Analyse", Bachelor's thesis presented by by Mirjam Zwingli, SDI MUC / University of Applied Languages (Hochschule für angewandte Sprachen, Fachhochschule des Sprachen & Dolmetscher Instituts), München, 2012; p. 62ff.

4. See http://programm.ard.de/TV/bralpha/strippenzieher-und-hinterzimmer/ eid_284876038998330

5. See for instance http://www.youtube.com/watch?v=vo_ApLgdlSM

6. See John R. MacArthur: *Die Schlacht der Lügen. Wie die USA den Golfkrieg verkauften*. DTV, München 1993, or *Second Front: Censorship and Propaganda in the 1991 Gulf War*, University of California Press, 2004

7. For clarification: This does not mean the use of poison gas by Iraq against Kurds in Halabsha in March 1988, but in fact a completely separate later use of poison gas in July 1988, which hardly anyone knows about today, because it was downplayed by our media or not mentioned at all. I still have masses of color photos of the gassed Iranians that I took myself on the battlefield.

8. See http://www.faz.net/aktuell/feuilleton/kino/gekaufte-berichte-die-eu-bezahltjournalisten-um-ihr-image-zu-pflegen-1330793.html

9. See http://www.deutschlandfunk.de/gekaufte-stimmen.795.de.html?dram:article_id=119300

10. See http://www.schweizamsonntag.ch/ressort/medien/2484/

11. See http://www.aargauerzeitung.ch/aargau/kanton-aargau/artikel-125129229

12. Quoted from http://www.spiegel.de/spiegel/spiegelspecial/d-9157545.html See

220   UDO ULFKOTTE: *Presstitutes, Embedded in the Pay of the CIA*

also http://www.sueddeutsche.de/wirtschaft/werbung-klammheimliche-verfuehrer-1.
474417-2 and den Werbefilm unter http://www.youtube.com/
watch?v=l005GEY10Uw
13. Mirjam Zwingli, op. cit.
14. Ibid. p. 40
15. See Wolfgang Donsbach: "Wahrheit in den Medien", in: *Die politische Meinung*,
August 2001, p. 72
16. Quoted from http://www.ag-friedensforschung.de/rat/2003/loquai.html
17. See http://archive.today/RPOF#selection-255.0-255.306
18. Quoted from http://www.spiegel.de/spiegel/spiegelblog/ein-plaedoyer-
dafuerinterviews-autorisieren-zu-lassen-a-859433.html
19. See for instance http://www.haz.de/Nachrichten/Politik/Niedersachsen/
Wirbelum-McAllisters-Sommerinterview and http://www.taz.de/!39718/ and http://
www. vergabeblog.de/2011-01-20/kurioses-ramsauer-nennt-interview-uber-
zusatzlichemittel-fur-erhaltung-der-bundesfernstrasen-nicht-autorisiert/ and http://
www. abendblatt.de/politik/article119858929/Philipp-Roesler-gibt-Interview-mit-
der-taznicht-frei.html
20. See http://www.sueddeutsche.de/medien/heute-journal-moderator-claus-
kleberzu-kopf-gestiegen-1.1691417 and http://www.focus.de/kultur/kino_tv/kritik-
anard-sendung-zdf-mann-kleber-vergleicht-tagesschau-mit-nordkorea_aid_1007092.
html and http://www.bild.de/politik/inland/claus-kleber/claus-kleber-
vergleichttagesschau-mit-korea-30728574.bild.html, with this quote from Claus
Kleber: "A dry reading of the news is nowhere to be found these days except at 8 pm
on Korean TV."
21. Quoting Heise in "Grüne and Linke auf der Atlantik-Brücke", http://www.heise.
de/tp/ artikel/41/41551/1.html sowie http://www.taz.de/1/archiv/print-archiv/
printressorts/ digi-artikel/
?ressort=me&dig=2003%2F05%2F06%2Fa0139&cHash=30ef25c225
22. Quoted from Stefan Weichert: *Die Alpha-Journalisten*, p. 191;
23. See for instance http://meedia.de/2014/07/29/einstweilige-verfuegung-gegen-die-
anstalt-zdf-wehrt-sich-gegen-zeit-journalisten-joffe-und-bittner/
24. See for instance Friederike Beck: *Das Guttenberg-Dossier*, p. 132ff.
25. Quoted from Friederike Beck: *Das Guttenberg-Dossier, Das Wirken
transatlantischer Netzwerke*, p. 132.; See also http://www.taz.de/1/archiv/print-
archiv/ printressorts/digi-artikel/
?ressort=me&dig=2003%2F05%2F06%2Fa0139&cHash= 30ef25c225 and the book
Transatlantische Kulturkriege: Shephard Stone by Volker Rolf Berghahn, in which
Stone's involvement with intelligence agencies is described in detail.
26. See http://www.taz.de/Pressekonferenz-mit-Angela-Merkel/!142597/
27. Quoted from http://www.sueddeutsche.de/medien/zdf-mann-singt-fuer-
merkelzwischen-naehe-und-distanz-1.2050806
28. Quoted from https://www.wsws.org/de/articles/2014/07/15/korn-j15.html
29. See http://www.ludwig-erhard-stiftung.de/index.php?seite=8
30. See http://www.johanna-quandt-stiftung.de/index2.html#kuratorium
31. See http://www.hayek-stiftung.de/115.html
32. See http://www.hayek-stiftung.de/115.html, abgerufen am 11. Juli 2014
33. See http://www.faz.net/redaktion/holger-steltzner-11104375.html
34. Quoted from http://www.cicero.de/kapital/warum-man-die-marktradikalen-
zumteufel-jagen-muss/54265/seite/3

35. Quoted from http://www.cicero.de/kapital/warum-man-die-marktradikalen-zumteufel-jagen-muss/54265/seite/3

36. See http://www.washingtonpost.com/blogs/in-the-loop/wp/2014/06/17/supportu-s-eu-free-trade-the-embassy-in-berlin-wants-you

37. See https://docs.google.com/ document/d/1oLBKsA_4pmdzSrVlebl6buH6CFvES4JqKqfRwliANlE/edit?pli=1 On July 11, 2014, when I accessed the page where one could apply for funds, it said, "We've received many excellent proposals. Thank you."

38. See for instance https://es-la.facebook.com/kas.jona

39. See https://de-de.facebook.com/pages/FES-Journalistenakademie/173356906150424

40. See also the Parliamentary Investigative report (*Untersuchungsbericht des Bundestages*) which includes some names at http://webarchiv.bundestag.de/archive/2010/0304/bundestag/ausschuesse/ gremien/pkg/bnd_bericht.pdf

41. See https://www.wiltonpark.org.uk/

42. See http://de.wikipedia.org/wiki/Wilton_Park

43. See dazu: "Tendenziöse Attributierung in deutschen Printmedien: Putin vs. Obama – eine linguistische Analyse", Bachelor-Arbeit vorgelegt by Mirjam Zwingli, Hochschule für angewandte Sprachen, Fachhochschule des Sprachen & Dolmetscher Instituts München, 2012

44. Quoted from http://www.presseportal.de/pm/65649/2112879/studie-faz-steht-beilobbyisten-ganz-oben-auf-der-lektuereliste

45. See http://www.nordbayern.de/nuernberger-nachrichten/nuernberg/pilot-alsrisiko-1.1172849 and http://www.heise.de/tp/artikel/34/34655/1.html

46. See for instance http://www.gmfus.org/?s=frankenberger, danach schreibt Frankenberger für den GMF http://www.gmfus.org/archives/the-atlantic-imperative-in-an-eraof-a-global-power-shift/, hält Vorträge vor GMF-Fellows und nimmt an Veranstaltungen des GMF teil – See for instance http://www.bu.edu/european/tag/klaus-dieterfrankenberger/

47. See dazu taz vom 23. Mai 1997: "Die Folgen einer Dienstreise" and taz vom 3. Juli 1997: "Zuhälter and Prostituierte"

48. See http://www.faz.net/redaktion/werner-sturbeck-11104391.html

49. See dazu http://www.welt.de/wirtschaft/article110891981/Luxusreisen-desThyssen-Managers-auf-Firmenkosten.html

50. Über das Journalistenbüro by Renate Komes, welches vom Sultanat Oman finanziert wurde

51. See for instance http://www.cbsnews.com/news/the-worlds-enduring-dictators-qaboosbin-said-oman-19-06-2011/

52. See http://www.theguardian.com/commentisfree/2011/jun/15/oman-middle-eastuprising

53. See http://theweek.com/article/index/211722/5-dictators-the-us-still-supports

54. See http://www.middle-east-online.com/english/?id=67681

55. See for instance die Dissertation by Uwe Krüger: "Meinungsmacht", Köln 2013

56. See Mirjam Zwingli, op. cit., for instance on p. 37, where it gives an example how he tries to influence the readers's psychological attitude.

57. The judgement from July 1997 applied equally to me and the FAZ; and received a lot of attention in the media, and can be found also in publications such as the book by Christian Krüger and Matthias Müller-Hennig: *Greenpeace auf dem Wahrnehmungsmarkt*, Lit-Verlag, Berlin-Hamburg-Münster 2000, p. 224 f.; See also

the following excerpt from the Rheinischen JournalistInnen Büro (RJB) at http://www.rjb-koeln.de/ zensur.html#schmiere. Quote:

In late 1996, at an event held during the "KenSaro-Wiwa-week" in Cologne, Karl Rössel claimed that FAZ editor Udo Ulfkotte was "bribed" to give a friendly report by the oil company Shell, and that by printing his article, FAZ "prostituted for Shell". The background: Ulfkotte, like other colleagues from WAZ, FR, Welt and SZ, participated in a Shell-sponsored trip to Nigeria. After a round trip in a Shell helicopter over the Ogoni countryside, he reported that any sign of environmental pollution by the oil production was hardly to be seen. While his colleagues at least named Shell as the trip the sponsor in their reports, FAZ editor Ulfkotte concealed this fact, and Shell reprinted his articles as "objective reporting" in their advertising brochures.

In January 1997, the FAZ and Udo Ulfkotte sued Karl Rössel for slander, a retraction and 100,000 DM damages.

In response, the RJB teamed up with Mediawatch, an initiative to critically monitor Third World reporting, and compiled a comprehensive reader on Shell Group's attempts to manipulate public opinion in its favor. Just when Shell came under fire because of the Ogoni protests against environmental destruction and human rights violations, and the execution of the writer and civil rights activist Ken Saro Wiwa by the military regime in November 1995, the oil company tried to win over critics to its side, and launched counter-propaganda in the media.

In July 1997, the District Court of Cologne ruled that Rössel's characterization of the FAZ and its correspondent (me) was not "slander" but an "expression of opinion" that was admissible on the basis of the facts. The decision was well received in the media, once again focusing on the boundaries between journalistic reporting and PR work for companies.

58. See http://www.oman.de/oman-landeskunde/kultur-oman-handwerk-architektur/musiktanz/royal-oman-symphony-orchestra/ and http://www.spiegel.de/spiegel/print/d-81303008.html

59. There is a lot of discussion of this on the Internet, e.g. https://uk.answers.yahoo.com/question/ index?qid=20101221162251AAjFPPg

60. Regarding Anthony Ashworth, see John Beasant: *Oman – The True-Life Drama,* Edinburgh 2002; and Marc Valeri: *Oman: Politics and Society,* London 2009, p. 178; and Christopher Ling: *Sultan in Arabia*, Edinburgh 2004

61. See http://www.state.gov/j/drl/rls/hrrpt/

62. See http://en.rsf.org/oman-two-omani-bloggers-freed-after-18-08-2014,46810.html and http://muawiya1983.blogspot.fr/ and http://fr.rsf.org/oman-deuxblogueurs-dans-le-collimateur-17-07-2014,46648.html and http://en.rsf.org/omantwo-bloggers-detained-in-oman-for-18-07-2014,46652.html

63. See http://www.hrw.org/world-report/2013/country-chapters/oman and http://www.amnestyusa.org/our-work/countries/middle-east-and-north-africa/oman

64. Note: Renate Komes does normal (good) PR work for Oman, and to my knowledge she has nothing to do with the corruption that one encounters as a journalist in Oman. She will have heard a lot about it over the years, but she is certainly not responsible for it, nor the driving force.

65. FAZ, June 1995, PR-article paid for by Oman, printed in the politics section of the newspaper.

66. FAZ, April 1997, PR-article paid for by Oman, printed in the politics section of the newspaper.

67. FAZ, October 1998, PR-article paid for by Oman, printed in the politics section of the newspaper.

68. FAZ, November 2000, PR-article paid for by Oman, printed in the politics section of the newspaper.

69. See http://www.mediummagazin.de/aktuelles/pressereisen-affare-faz-schafftfortan-transparenz/

70. Quoted from http://www.mediummagazin.de/aktuelles/pressereisen-affare-fazschafft-fortan-transparenz/

71. Quoted from http://www.sprengsatz.de/?p=3523

72. The complete report of the general meeting of the Frankfurter Allgemeine Zeitung GmbH of June 26, 2014, which was sent to FAZ employees and which I have seen, shows a total of 280 million euros in costs for this company, which is struggling to survive. Many costs can not be reduced, as it says, for example: "Likewise, the costs of company pensions increased by 2.2 million euros compared to the previous year, to 13.6 million euros in 2013. The decline in interest rates on the capital markets resulted due to legal requirements, the need to increase pension provisions accordingly. "Elsewhere it says:" ... but unfortunately our result is still very much in the red. Against this backdrop, management and publishers have decided not to raise salaries this year. This is annoying for everyone, but unavoidable. Such a salary increase would add millions of dollars on top of the already existing losses. "

73. See http://www.dlg.org/fileadmin/downloads/food/DLG_Pruefbestimmungen_2012.pdf and http://www.dlg-verbraucher.info/

74. See for instance http://www.haz.de/Nachrichten/Wissen/Uebersicht/DiesenGuetesiegeln-koennen-Sie-trauen

75. See for instance http://www.augsburger-allgemeine.de/bayern/Mueller-Brot-DieErmittlungen-werden-langwierig-id18938661.html

76. See http://www.augsburger-allgemeine.de/wirtschaft/Das-sind-Guetesiegel-wertid19071936.html

77. Quoted from www.ndr.de/markt, Sendung vom 2. 4. 2012

78. Regarding this Journalism prize see http://www.hanns-joachim-friedrichs.de/ 78a Quoted from Karin Busch: *Der Einfluss der Tabaklobby auf das Bundesnichtraucherschutzgesetz – Analyse einer geheimen Strategie* (The influence of the tobacco lobby on the Federal Non-Smoker Protection Act – Analysis of a secret strategy), p. 56

79. See http://www.liberty-award.de/index.php/liberty-award/43-jury/372-theosommer

80. See http://www.focus.de/politik/experten/wolffsohn/steuerhinterzieher-theosommer-von-wegen-vorbild-wieder-ein-unmoralischer-moralist_id_3572472.html and http://www.spiegel.de/kultur/gesellschaft/ex-zeit-chef-theo-sommer-wegensteuerhinterziehung-verurteilt-a-944935.html

81. See http://www.zeit.de/2001/26/Uransyndrom_Die_Blamage_der_Alarmisten

82. See Uwe Krüger: Meinungsmacht, p. 21

83. See http://www.theosommer.de/index.php?seite=7&lang=d

84. See dazu http://www.derblindefleck.de/top-themen/top-themen-2008-2/top-6/

85. The literature on the possible health risks of depleted uranium is inconsistent. There is disagreement about the actual extent of the threat. Opponents of these weapons, such as the organization Physicians for the Prevention of Nuclear War, blame uranium ammunition for cancers, birth defects and consequential damage such

as Gulf War syndrome. They argue that statistics show an unmistakable rise in skin and lung cancers in affected war zones. According to studies of the World Health Organization (WHO) and the International Atomic Energy Agency (IAEA), there is no particular danger. Critics complain about the methodology and alleged lack of independence of these studies. The so-called Lloyd Report on health damage in British Gulf War veterans revealed the existence of Gulf War syndrome and investigated a number of potential triggers for it. Uranium ammunition was described as a potential trigger, but the study clearly pointed to the lack of certain facts about the risks. Particular emphasis was given to a previous report by the Royal Society, which estimated the danger of uranium ammunition for soldiers rather low according the current state of knowledge, but also called for long-term studies and further investigations. The cancer, child mortality and gender-related birth rate study by Chris Busby, Malak Hamdan and Entesar Ariabi by 2010 shows an increase in cancer and malformations in Fallujah, Iraq.

86. See http://www.liberty-award.de/index.php/liberty-award/43-jury/372-theosommer

87. See for instance http://deutsche-wirtschafts-nachrichten.de/2014/07/24/tabakkonzern-phillip-morris-spuelt-geld-in-die-parteikassen/

88. See http://www.focus.de/politik/deutschland/wende-in-der-teppich-affaereniebel-muss-seinen-teppich-verzollen_aid_769237.html and http://www. tagesschau.de/inland/niebel212.html and http://www.zeit.de/politik/deutschland/ 2012-06/niebel-teppich-affaere

89. Quoted from http://www.sprengsatz.de/?p=3512

90. See http://www.sprengsatz.de/?cat=3&paged=5

91. See http://www.kas.de/villalacollina/

92. See http://www.kas.de/villalacollina/de/about/

93. See http://www.rockefellerfoundation.org/bellagio-center

94. In the meantime, the CIA website has a report that lists the chemical weapons gas attack – the one with mustard gas that the FAZ sent me to in July 1988: https://www.cia.gov/library/reports/general-reports-1/iraq_ wmd_2004/chap5.html. The report is headed "Iraq's Chemical Warfare Program" and lists it thus: "July 1988 South-central border Mustard & nerve agent, 100s or 1,000s Iranian casualties". So the poison gas used im July 1988 (which was only the battle of Zubaidat, which I reported on) is a "Mustard & nerve agent." (*Senfgas* in German). In late August 1988 the Los Angeles Times also mentioned the gas attack on the Iranians at Zubaidat, see http://articles.latimes.com/1988-08-28/ news/mn-1725_1_poison-gas

95. FAZ vom 19. Juli 1988

96. There is is described thus, "July 1988 South-central border – Mustard & nerve agent, 100s or 1,000s Iranian casualties", Quelle: https://www.cia.gov/library/reports/generalreports-1/iraq_wmd_2004/chap5.html

97. See Hans Leyendecker: "Die Giftgaslieferungen an den Irak waren kein Zufall" (poison gas deliveries to Iraq were not accidental), at library.fes.de/gmh/main/pdf-files/gmh/1991/1991-03-a-200.pdf

98. See http://www.berliner-kurier.de/kiez-stadt/steffen-jacob-der-leise-tod-des-puffprinzen-vom-stutti,7169128,28124090.html

99. See http://www.alikepenek.com/

100. See for instance http://www.liveleak.com/view?i=01e_1175818014

101. See http://www.theguardian.com/world/2014/mar/11/journalist-shot-deadafghanistan-kabul

102. See http://www.aljazeera.com/news/africa/2013/11/two-french-journalistsexecuted-mali-2013112174124558898.html
103. See http://edition.cnn.com/2014/04/04/world/asia/afghanistan-journalists-shot/
104. See for instance http://www.spiegel.de/panorama/verdacht-auf-geheimnisverrat-razziabeim-terrorexperten-ulfkotte-a-293459.html
105. Quoted from http://www.stefan-niggemeier.de/blog/faz-was-wissen-professorenschon-vom-geldverdienen/
106. See http://www.stefan-niggemeier.de/blog/faz-was-wissen-professoren-schonvom-geldverdienen/

Notes to Chapter 2. Our Media: Lockstep, Obedient and No Questions Asked

1. See for instance http://www.n-tv.de/politik/21-Prozent-fuer-die-Gruenenarticle1440946.html
2. See http://www.taz.de/!57865/
3. See http://www.ksta.de/debatte/kommentar-zu-sarrazin-der-zwanghaftedemagoge,15188012,12644874.html
4. See http://www.deutschlandradiokultur.de/rechtspopulismus-sarrazin-will-antabus-ruehren-die-in.954.de.html?dram:article_id=278802
5. See http://www.tagesspiegel.de/weltspiegel/verstoss-gegenpersoenlichkeitsrechte-thilo-sarrazin-gegen-die-taz/8653894.html
6. Quoted from http://www.zeit.de/2010/36/01-Sarrazin
7. Quoted from http://www.heute.de/diskussion-um-armutszuwanderung-vielebulgaren-fuehlen-sich-von-der-csu-offen-angegriffen-31602446.html
8. Ibid.
9. See http://www.zdf.de/ZDFmediathek/beitrag/video/2060066/Rumaenen-undBulgaren-in-Deutschland#/beitrag/video/2060066/Rumaenen-und-Bulgaren-inDeutschland
10. See http://www.handelsblatt.com/politik/international/bulgaren-und-rumaenendie-voelkerwanderung-faellt-aus/9272340.html
11. See http://www.fnp.de/rhein-main/Begriff-Armutszuwanderung-als-Unwort-desJahres-vorgeschlagen;art1491,726636
12. See http://www.sueddeutsche.de/kultur/sprache-sozialtourismus-ist-das-unwortdes-jahres-1.1862368
13. See http://www.tagesschau.de/inland/unwortdesjahres114.html
14. Quoted from http://www.bild.de/politik/inland/hartz-4/bezieher-aus-rumaenienbulgarien-36201208.bild.html
15. See for instance http://www.derwesten.de/politik/zahl-bulgarischer-und-rumaenischerhartz-iv-bezieher-steigt-id9457712.html
16. Quoted from http://www.deutschlandfunk.de/es-entwickelt-sich-einezivilgesellschaft.694.de.html?dram:article_id=255262
17. E.g. http://meedia.de/2013/08/20/berufe-ranking-journalisten-weit-hinten/
18. See http://www.kontextwochenzeitung.de/macht-markt/152/streiken-im-keller2051.html and http://www.derwesten.de/panorama/politiker-sind-dieberufsgruppe-mit-dem-niedrigsten-ansehen-id3445294.html
19. See http://www.sueddeutsche.de/wirtschaft/reden-wir-ueber-geld-michelfriedman-ich-habe-mich-zu-wenig-selbst-geliebt-1.1079939-3
20. See http://medien-news.blog.de/2005/06/09/journalisten_haben_einen_

schlechten_ruf/
21. Ibid.
22. Quoted from *Krise der Printmedien: Eine Krise des Journalismus?*

Notes to Chapter 3. The Undercover Truth: Alpha Journalists Toe the Line for the Elites

1. See http://www.zeit.de/2014/07/deutsche-aussenpolitik-sicherheitskonferenz/komplettansicht
2. See http://www.swp-berlin.org/de/projekte/neue-macht-neue-verantwortung/mitwirkende.html
3. See http://m.heise.de/tp/artikel/42/42401/
4. Quoted from http://m.heise.de/tp/artikel/42/42401/
5. Quoted from http://www.internet-law.de/2014/07/zeit-journalisten-gehengerichtlich-gegen-das-zdf-und-die-anstalt-vor.html
6. See http://www.zeit.de/2014/07/deutsche-aussenpolitik-sicherheitskonferenz/komplettansicht
7. See http://www.youtube.com/watch?v=-NABdIPFvls
8. Quoted from http://www.heise.de/tp/artikel/41/41841/1.html
9. See for instance diesen Ausschnitt aus einem Brief Joffes, welchen er seinen Kritikern zukommen ließ unter http://www.heise.de/tp/bild/41/41841/41841_1.html
10. See http://www.stefan-niggemeier.de/blog/17162/die-zeit-erinnert-anti-lanzpetition-an-anti-juden-kampagne-der-nazis/
11. Quoted from http://www.internet-law.de/2014/07/zeit-journalisten-gehen-gerichtlich-gegen-das-zdf-und-die-anstalt-vor.html
12. Abgerufen am 2. August 2014 and Quoted from http://europe.stanford.edu/people/josef_joffe/
13. Quoted from http://www.handelsblatt.com/meinung/presseschau/presseschaugoldman-gottes-werk-und-bankers-beitrag/3302952.html , See also original source at http://blogs.reuters.com/felix-salmon/2009/11/12/goldman-sachssnot-very-charitable-foundation/
14. See http://www.bild.de/politik/inland/angela-merkel/zum-geburtstag-von-angelamerkel-leser-malen-die-kanzlerin-36838114.bild.html
15. See http://www.kn-online.de/Freizeit/KN-Forum-Wissen-2014/Prof.-Dr.-BrigitteWitzer-Die-Diktatur-der-Dummen
16. Quoted from http://wirbt-fuer-bild.de/wer.html
17. Quoted from http://www.boeckler.de/32365_35234.htm
18. See for instance http://www.spiegel.de/kultur/gesellschaft/a-921253.html
19. Quoted from http://www.sprengsatz.de/?p=3644
20. Quoted from http://link.springer.com/chapter/10.1007%2F978-3-531-90536-5_7
21. See for instance Bettina Wagner: "Bild – unabhängig • überparteilich". In: Oskar Niedermayer et al.: *Die Bundestagswahl 2005: Analysen des Wahlkampfes and der Wahlergebnisse*, 2005, p. 145–170
22. See http://www.welt.de/print-wams/article129161/Angela-Merkels-zweierleiWelten.html
23. See http://www.carta.info/73163/bild-studientrilogie-nicht-die-ereignissebestimmen-die-berichterstattung-sondern-die-eigene-vorhersage/
24. See http://www.stern.de/lifestyle/leute/kohl-hochzeit-mit-dem-bild-chef-alstrauzeugen-620216.html

25. See http://www.rp-online.de/panorama/bild-chefredakteur-diekmann-undkolumnistin-kessler-verheiratet-aid-1.2048046

26. See http://www.sueddeutsche.de/medien/bild-chef-kai-diekmann-bild-dir-deinemacht-1.998172-11

27. Quoted from http://www.eurotopics.net/de/home/presseschau/archiv/magazin/politik-verteilerseite/frankreich-2008-07/artikel_scalbert/

28. Quoted from SZ vom 17. Mai 2010, Michael Kläsgen: *Ein Netz von Freunden*, on the Internet at http://www.sueddeutsche.de/kultur/sarkozy-und-die-medien-einnetz-von-freunden-1.805499

29. Quoted from http://www.sprengsatz.de/?p=2580

30. http://www.bild.de/politik/inland/wolfgang-bosbach/wolfgang-bosbach-beiwer-wird-millionaer-wer-hat-eigentlich-merkels-handy-nummer-36244074.bild. html

31. Quoted from http://www.sueddeutsche.de/medien/bild-chef-kai-diekmann-bild-dirdeine-macht-1.998172-2

32. Quoted from https://www.djv.de/startseite/profil/der-djv/pressebereich-download/ pressemitteilungen/detail/article/unabhaengig-bleiben.html, See also http:// www.heise.de/tp/artikel/42/42430/1.html

33. See dazu http://www.sprengsatz.de/?p=2986

34. Quoted from http://www.sprengsatz.de/?p=3437

35. Ibid.

36. See http://www.fr-online.de/politik/eigenwerbung-der-bundeswehr-vertraegevorerst-nur-mit-springer,1472596,7504662.html

37. Quoted from http://www.sprengsatz.de/?p=4016

38. Quoted from http://www.fr-online.de/politik/nach-dem-ruecktritt-guttenberg-unddie-bild-zeitung,1472596,7504534.html

39. Zur Burschenschaft: http://www.franconia-muenster.de/

40. See http://www.taz.de/1/archiv/archiv/?dig=2006/10/28/a0203

41. See http://www.spiegel.de/unispiegel/studium/parteivorstand-hat-gesprochenentweder-sozialdemokrat-oder-burschenschafter-a-408440.html

42. See http://www.politik-kommunikation.de/ressorts/artikel/niemand-geht-damithausieren

43. See http://www.spiegel.de/spiegel/vorab/a-327652.html

44. Quoted from http://www.deutsch-tuerkische-nachrichten.de/2014/05/502462/kai-diekmann-erdogans-politik-fuehrt-tuerkei-in-eine-instabile-lage/

45. See http://www.faz.net/aktuell/politik/der-aufruf-zum-anruf-zu-guttenberg-bildund-die-atlantik-bruecke-1593253.html

46. See https://www.atlantik-bruecke.org/willkommen/analysen-und-kommentare/ Above the photo and article by Frankenberger is written: "Here you will find current publications and interviews from the Atlantik-Brücke's field of work on transatlantic topics." I have saved screenshots.

47. See http://www.atlantik-bruecke.org/service/dokumente/overtures-and-finalesgermany-and-the-united-states.pdf

48. See for instance http://www.heise.de/tp/artikel/41/41551/1.html

49. Ibid.

50. Ibid.

51. See http://www.dwdl.de/nachrichten/45406/tina_hassel_loest_deppendorf_im_hauptstadtstudio_ab/

52. Ibid.

53. See p. 46 http://www.atlantik-bruecke.org/w/files/dokumente/120628_

jahresbericht_2012.pdf

54. See for instance http://www.heise.de/tp/artikel/41/41551/1.html

55. See http://www.atlantik-bruecke.org/stiftung/

56. See http://www.ndr.de/fernsehen/sendungen/zapp/zapp7506.html and for instance http://www.atlantik-bruecke.org/w/files/dokumente/120628_jahresbericht_ 2012. pdf

57. See http://www.ndr.de/fernsehen/sendungen/zapp/zapp7506.html

58. The original page http://www.atlantik-bruecke.org/programme/mitgliederreisen-indie-usa/ has since been taken down, but still can be reached in the internet archive with the data from the slide show at https://web.archive.org/web/20140103013945/ http:// www.atlantik-bruecke.org/programme/mitgliederreisen-in-die-usa/

59. Ibid.

60. See http://de.wikipedia.org/wiki/Constanze_Stelzenm%C3%BCller

61. See http://www.atlantik-bruecke.org/w/files/dokumente/120628_jahresbericht_ 2012.pdf

62. See http://www.atlantik-bruecke.org/service/dokumente/where-thirst-forknowledge-meets-food-for-thought.pdf

63. See http://www.atlantik-bruecke.org/

64. Stiftung für Zukunftsfragen: Immer mehr Vereine – immer weniger Mitglieder: Das Vereinswesen in Deutschland verändert sich, Forschung Aktuell, 254, 35. Jg., 16. April 2014.

65. See for instance www.trilateral.org

66. See for instance http://www.atlantik-bruecke.org/ueber-uns/gremien/

67. Screenshot of the page from May 6, 2014 at http://www.atlantik-bruecke.org/ ueber-uns/gremien/

68. See Ludger Kühnhardt: *Atlantik-Brücke: Fünfzig Jahre deutsch-amerikanische Partnerschaft*, p. 11 and p. 37 and p. 71. In 1981 the FAZ devoted extensive publicity space to the Atlantik-Brücke. Alluding to the widespread system of private corporations in the United States, "who have no decision power but are nevertheless part of the decision-making background" and therefore an unheard of new experience in Germany, it was said that "a democracy purist could have misgivings about such elitist collaboration groups."

69. Quoted from p. 129 http://www.atlantik-bruecke.org/w/files/dokumente/jb-0910final.pdf

70. Gemeinsame Veranstaltung mit der Bundesakademie für Sicherheitspolitik, siehe p. 98 at http://www.atlantik-bruecke.org/service/dokumente/jahresbericht-deratlantik-bruecke-2006-2007.pdf

71. See https://www.atlantik-bruecke.org/willkommen/analysen-und-kommentare/ Dort heißt es über dem Foto and Artikeln by Frankenberger "Above the photo and article by Frankenberger is written: "Here you will find current publications and interviews from the Atlantik-Brücke's field of work on transatlantic topics." I have saved screenshots.
See also Frankenbergers self-presentation in the FAZ at http://www.faz.net/ redaktion/klausdieter-frankenberger-11104551.html. This connection is not mentioned for the reader there.

72. See http://www.phoenix.de/content/phoenix/bibliothek/442028

73. See http://www.bild.de/politik/2010/schmidt/diskutierte-in-hamburg-mitaltkanzler-schmidt-11791926.bild.html

74. See this Interview by Eveline Y. Metzen from Minute 6:35 at http://www.

tvbvideo.de/video/iLyROoafzSjA.html

75. Quoted from http://www.berliner-zeitung.de/archiv/ein-whos-who-der-politik-undwirtschaft,10810590,9990036.html

76. Quoted from https://www.atlantik-bruecke.org/programme/preisverleihungen/vernon-a-walters-award/

77. Quoted from Friederike Beck, *Das Guttenberg-Dossier*, p. 76

78. See the book by Ernst Langrock: "Der Drahtzieher. Vernon Walters – Ein Geheimdienstgeneral des Kalten Krieges"

79. Quoted from http://deutsche-wirtschafts-nachrichten.de/2014/07/14/nato-experteaus-sicht-der-usa-ist-deutschland-ein-besetztes-land/

80. See http://archive-org.com/page/1259165/2013-01-29/http://www.atlantik-bruecke.org/programme/konferenzen-und-expertengespraeche/expertengespraeche-mit-dem-us-european-command/20-expertengespraech-mit-dem-us-europeancommand/

81. Quoted from http://www.atlantik-bruecke.org/programme/konferenzen/expertengespraeche-mit-dem-us-european-command/21-expertengespraech-mitdem-useucom/

82. See http://www.neues-deutschland.de/artikel/940649.nato-bereitet-manoever-inukraine-vor.html

83. Quoted from Beckmann, "Der geheime Krieg," ARD on 28.Nov., 2013, 00:51:10-00:

52:10 at http://mediathek.daserste.de/sendungen_a-z/443668_beckmann/18361194_der-geheime-krieg

84. See http://www.srf.ch/news/international/stelldichein-von-einstigen-widersachern and http://www.srf.ch/player/radio/echo-der-zeit/audio/geheime-liaison-zwischenisrael-und-saudi-arabien?id=944e8419-117f-471a-8030-fb51130ccf5a

85. See http://www.rp-online.de/politik/deutschland/telefonierte-cia-chef-mit-kanzleramt-aid-1.4374517

86. See for instance http://www.voltairenet.org/article30085.html

87. She was appointed "Board Member", See for instance http://www.gmfus.org/?s=suzanne+woolsey

88. A Screenshot of the book's page is also here: http://1.bp.blogspot.com/-gGV7k8rOgxo/UUh-vBZO39I/AAAAAAAAAPA/hlohWIT48kk/s1600/Jutta+Ditfurth+USA.jpg

89. Quoted from http://www.gruene.de/partei/urwahl/frage-5-atlantikbruecke.html

90. See for instance http://www.heise.de/tp/artikel/41/41551/1.html

91. See http://www.gruene.de/partei/urwahl/frage-5-atlantikbruecke.html

92. See http://www.youtube.com/watch?v=4wBK7mjBcqg

93. See http://www.atlantik-bruecke.org/w/files/dokumente/yl-history-2011.pdf

94. See http://www.youtube.com/watch?v=4wBK7mjBcqg

95. See http://www.atlantik-bruecke.org/w/files/dokumente/yl-history-2011.pdf

96. Quoted from http://www.berliner-zeitung.de/archiv/ein-whos-who-der-politik-undwirtschaft,10810590,9990036.html

97. See the Annual Report http://www.atlantik-bruecke.org/service/dokumente/jahresbericht-der-atlantik-bruecke-2006-2007.pdf and http://www.atlantik-bruecke.org/service/dokumente/jahresbericht-2008-2009.pdf and http://www.atlantikbruecke.org/w/files/dokumente/jb-0910-final.pdf and http://www.atlantik-bruecke. org/w/files/dokumente/jahresbericht-2010_2011-final.pdf and http://www.atlantikbruecke.

org/w/files/dokumente/120628_jahresbericht_2012.pdf

and https://www. atlantik-bruecke.org/service/dokumente/a-message-to-the-people-of-the-unitedstates-of-america.pdf and

https://www.atlantik-bruecke.org/w/files/dokumente/ conference-report-daylk-2007. pdf and

https://www.atlantik-bruecke.org/w/files/ dokumente/yl-history-2011.pdf and https://www.atlantik-bruecke.org/programme/ konferenzen/deutsch-amerikanische-konferenzen/konferenz-ab-acg/?pic=15&gal= gal_0

98. Quoted from http://www.faz.net/redaktion/nikolas-busse-11104508.html

99. See https://www.atlantik-bruecke.org/service/dokumente/a-message-to-thepeople-of-the-united-states-of-america.pdf

100. See https://www.atlantik-bruecke.org/veroeffentlichungen/ weitereveroeffentlichungen/a-message-from-germany/

101. See http://www.swp-berlin.org/de/projekte/neue-macht-neue-verantwortung/ mitwirkende.html

102. See for instance https://www.wsws.org/de/articles/2014/05/08/mili-m08.html

103. See http://www.bmlv.gv.at/wissen-forschung/publikationen/beitrag.php?id=363

104. See for instance http://programm.ard.de/TV/Programm/Alle-Sender/?sendung= 287216448290044 and http://www.nationalstiftung.de/tagungen

105. See https://www.youtube.com/watch?v=A9Qi0R-6bFQ

106. News agencies are commonly regarded as the epitome of seriousness. But what should one think of an agency when it is owned by the "Moon sect" which is trying to take over the world? Founded in 1907 and merged with William Randolph Hearst's New Service in 1958, United Press International (UPI) was – at least in the past – a strong competitor to the Associated Press (AP). 159 employees in Washington, London, Latin America and Asia report on political and economic developments around the world. In May 2000, UPI was purchased by News World Communications Inc. – an asset of the "Unification Church" – better as "the Moonies." In the meantime, they own not only UPI but also a whole series of well-known newspapers. UPI is a traditional name in the news business, so in Germany UPI has many customers. Seen in this way it is frightening news reports come in from an agency, whose owners should be avoided like the plague, according to journalistic yardsticks. However, many journalists take over agency reports as their "own" without identifying them as such. How to figure out if the reporter's information isn't coming from the UPI ticker? In 2011, the official name of the Moon sect, founded by a Korean in Germany, was renamed to "Tongil-Gyo Unification Movement". 99 out of 100 German-speaking journalists do not know the backgrounds of the news agency UPI nor have they any idea about the name Tongil-Gyo. This pleases the backers who can thus spread their strange world view.

107. Quoted from http://www.taz.de/!114755/

108. The photos are on the Web at http://www.bildblog.de/20427/ kleine-bruecken-unter-freunden-2/

109. See http://www.mediummagazin.de/archiv/2012-2/ausgabe-092012/bela-andabild-mann-und-sonne-fan/

110. Quoted from http://www.berliner-zeitung.de/archiv/beate-lindemann-setzt-sich-mitder-atlantik-bruecke-seit-jahrzehnten-fuer-die-deutsch-amerikanische-freundschaftein-die-kontakte-reichen-bis-ins-weisse-haus,10810590,10058202.html

111. See https://www.atlantik-bruecke.org/ueber-uns/gremien/vorstand/ weiterevorstandsmitglieder/

112. See http://meedia.de/2014/05/02/qualitaetsjournalismus-fehlanzeige-journalistenals-lobbyisten/

113. Quoted from http://www.nachdenkseiten.de/?p=17471

114. Ibid.

115. Ibid.

116. Ibid.

117. See http://www.nachdenkseiten.de/wp-print.php?p=21155

118. Ibid.

119. Uwe Krüger, *Meinungsmacht*, p. 126f.

120. See http://www.bundestag.de/dokumente/lobbyliste/

121. See https://lobbypedia.de/wiki/Deutsche_Gesellschaft_f%C3%BCr_Ausw%C3%A4rtige_Politik and http://www.tpnonline.org/organisation/cooperating-institutions/

122. Quoted from https://lobbypedia.de/wiki/Transatlantic_Policy_Network

123. According to its own statements, the DGAP wants to actively influence foreign policy formation at all levels. So it's a lobby organization. The DGAP describes itself "as a private, independent, non-partisan and non-profit association; the DGAP is actively involved in shaping foreign policy opinion in Germany and providing policy advice at all levels." Quotation from the title page of "DGAP reports", by Markus Lux and Gereon Schuch, The Carl Friedrich Goerdeler Kolleg of the Robert Bosch Stiftung, (a one-year leadership study program) Berlin 2008; the author has a screenshot is available to the author. In my view, anyone who "actively" and just not passively participates in the formation of opinions and exerting influence, is a lobbyist.

124. See https://dgap.org/de/gesellschaft/dgap_regional/dgapforum_frankfurt

125. See http://www.steuben-schurz.org/projekte/medienpreis/medienpreis1.htm

126. See http://atlantische-initiative.org/ueber-uns/verein/

127. See also the remarks at http://www.heise.de/tp/artikel/ 42/42430/1.html

128. See http://www.bundestag.de/dokumente/lobbyliste/

129. See http://verlag.faz.net/unternehmen/ueber-uns/portraet/wissen-fuer-klugekoepfe-portraet-der-f-a-z-11090906.html

130. The FAZ advertises its "Independence" and "quality journalism", See http://verlag.faz.net/unternehmen/ueber-uns/portraet/wissen-fuer-klugekoepfe-portraet-der-f-a-z-11090906.html

131. Quoted from http://www.heise.de/tp/artikel/38/38515/1.html

132. Quoted from http://www.heise.de/tp/artikel/38/38515/1.html

133. See Uwe Krüger, *Meinungsmacht*, p. 133

134. Quoted from http://www.message-online.com/archiv/message-1-2013/leseproben/ die-naehe-zur-macht/

135. See http://archive.today/gysXX

136. See Uwe Krüger, *Meinungsmacht*, p. 131

137. See http://www.bundestag.de/dokumente/lobbyliste/

138. Ibid

139. See http://archive.today/gysXX

140. See http://www.bundestag.de/dokumente/lobbyliste/

141. See http://atlantische-initiative.org/ueber-uns/verein/

142. See http://www.iep-berlin.de/

143. See http://www.iep-berlin.de/erweiterungundnachbarschaft.html

144. See for instance http://spiegelkabinett-blog.blogspot.de/2012/10/ein-blick-in-

denberliner-lobbysumpf.html

145. See http://atlantische-initiative.org/team/ and See also http://
spiegelkabinettblog.blogspot.de/2012/10/ein-blick-in-den-berliner-lobbysumpf.html.
Here it is presented thus: "The Bohnen Kallmorgen & Partner Agency and the
Atlantic Initiative are located at the center of an immense network for holding by our
elites. The Bertelsmann Foundation, Atlantik-brücke, Initiative Neue Soziale
Marktwirtschaft, Goldman Sachs, CDU-Wirtschaftsrat, ZDF, Bildzeitung, Springer
corporation, the energy and arms industries, that is the mix that power and wealth are
made of."

146. Quoted from http://atlantische-initiative.org/team/
147. See die Studie by LobbyControl zur Schöpfung einer Lobbyagentur NTSA, p.
12, at https://www.lobbycontrol.de/download/NTSA-Dossier.pdf
148. See http://atlantische-initiative.org/team/
149. Quoted from "Die Non Toxic Solar Alliance – die Schöpfung einer
Lobbyagentur, LobbyControl", Seite 4, unter https://www.lobbycontrol.de/
download/NTSADossier.pdf
150. It should be expressly noted that here the newspaper editors and not the
aforementioned journalists are meant in person. The article from Saldo is found here
https://www.saldo.ch/artikel/d/journalisten-im-dienst-von-pr-agenturen/
151. See https://www.lobbycontrol.de/2011/07/pr-rat-mahnt-lobbyagentur-hinter-
dernon-toxic-solar-alliance/
152. See https://www.lobbycontrol.de/2011/07/pr-rat-mahnt-lobbyagentur-hinter-
dernon-toxic-solar-alliance/ and http://www.google.de/url?sa=t&rct=j&q=&esrc=
s&source=web&cd=3&cad=rja&uact=8&ved=0CDEQFjAC&url=http%3A%2F%2
Fdrpr-online.de%2Fwp-content%2Fuploads%2F2013%2F08%2FNTSA_BKP_
Ratsbeschluss_110728.
pdf&ei=PHbKU4yZO8v07AbJwICYBA&usg=AFQjCNEV7Hub
dE1W9bEH8jBsOf_vCBr-wg&bvm=bv.71198958,d.bGE
153. See http://atlantische-initiative.org/ueber-uns/verein/
154. Quoted from http://www.nachdenkseiten.de/wp-print.php?p=21155
155. See dazu http://www.nachdenkseiten.de/wp-print.php?p=21155
156. Quoted from http://medienblog.blog.nzz.ch/2014/05/02/rebellion-unter-den-
lesern/
157. Quoted from http://www.sueddeutsche.de/politik/propaganda-aus-russland-
putinstrolle-1.1997470
158. See also Uwe Krüger: *Meinungsmacht* and "Tendenziöse Attributierung in
deutschen Printmedien: Putin vs. Obama – eine linguistische Analyse", Bachelor's
thesis presented by Mirjam Zwingli, SDI MUC / University of Applied Languages
(Hochschule für angewandte Sprachen, Fachhochschule des Sprachen &
Dolmetscher Instituts), München, 201.
159. See for instance http://www.heise.de/tp/artikel/20/20052/1.html
160. See http://www.hintergrund.de/2007080165/hintergrund/medien/mission-
desinformation.html
161. See http://www.zerohedge.com/news/2014-07-14/new-snowden-docs-
britishspies-manpulate-polls-and-pageview-counts-censor-videos-the and https://
firstlook. org/theintercept/2014/07/14/manipulating-online-polls-ways-british-spies-
seekcontrol-internet/
162. See http://bazonline.ch/digital/internet/Der-Servicekatalog-des-
britischenGeheimdienstes/story/29902489

163. See http://www.washingtonsblog.com/2014/07/pentagon-admits-spendingmillions-study-manipulate-social-media-users.html

164. See http://www.washingtonsblog.com/2014/02/secret-playbook-social-mediacensors.html

165. See http://www.washingtonsblog.com/2014/06/spying-different-time.html

166. Quoted from http://info.kopp-verlag.de/hintergruende/deutschland/andreas-vonr-tyi/trilaterale-kommission-hauptversammlung-dieses-jahr-in-deutschland.html

167. Quoted from http://juergenelsaesser.wordpress.com/2009/05/21/bilderberger-undtrilaterale-kommission/

168. See http://rt.com/news/europe-debt-crisis-takeover-215/

169. See Uwe Krüger, Meinungsmacht, p. 148f.

170. Quoted from http://juergenelsaesser.wordpress.com/2009/05/21/bilderberger-undtrilaterale-kommission/

171. See http://www.zeit.de/1977/45/heimliche-herrscher-des-westens

172. See photo at https://compact-online.de/bilderberger-und-trilaterale/

173. See http://www.reuters.com/article/2010/05/17/us-eurozone-budgets-analysisidUSTRE64G12W20100517

174. Quoted from https://lobbypedia.de/wiki/Trilaterale_Kommission

175. See http://www.trilateral.org/download/file/TC_list_12-13(3).pdf

176. Quoted from http://www.faz.net/redaktion/klaus-dieter-frankenberger-11104551.html

177. See See http://www.trilateral.org/download/file/TC_list_12-13(3).pdf

178. See the FAZ article "Welt in Unruhe" ("World Unrest") at http://fazarchiv.faz.net/?q=frankenberger+ trilaterale+kommission+2013&search_in=q&timePeriod=timeFilter&timeFilter=& DT_from=&DT_to=&KO=&crxdefs=&NN=&CO=&CN=&BC=&submitSearch=Suchen&sext=0&maxHits=&sorting=&toggleFilter=&dosearch=new#hitlist

179. See http://www.newstatesman.com/economics/economics/2014/04/ns-profilegeorge-soros

180. See http://www.newstatesman.com/economics/economics/2014/04/ns-profilegeorge-soros

181. See https://www.freitag.de/autoren/soenke-paulsen/die-soros-maschine

182. See http://www.berliner-zeitung.de/politik/bulgarien--uns-geht-es-um-echtedemokratie-,10808018,23826154.html and http://www.fr-online.de/politik/bulgarien-proteste-bulgarische-mutbuerger,1472596,23816396.html

183. See http://www.ecfr.eu/content/experts and http://ecfr.eu/content/staff/dimitar_bechev/ ; ECFR names him on their Homepage: "Head of Sofia Office, Senior Policy Fellow"

184. See for instance http://nsnbc.me/2013/10/29/atlantic-council-energy-summit-inistanbul-and-regional-balkanization/

185. See http://www.zeit.de/politik/2011-04/gericht-kanzleramt-essen-ackermann; Schirrmacher sagt "Ich war dabei".

186. Quoted from http://www.spiegel.de/spiegel/print/d-8924245.html

187. Quoted from http://www.spiegel.de/spiegel/print/d-8924245.html

188. Quoted from http://www.spiegel.de/spiegel/print/d-8924245.html

189. See for instance Seite 11 der Sinclair-Haus-Gespräche, hrsg. by der Herbert-QuandtStiftung, Thema: Gesellschaft ohne Zukunft?, Bad Homburg, November 2004

190. Quoted from http://www.merkur-blog.de/2013/02/sorgfaltspflichten-wenn-

frankschirrmacher-einen-bestseller-schreibt/

191. See http://www.wiwo.de/politik/deutschland/bettina-roehl-direkt-schirrmacherzwischen-infantilitaet-und-groessenwahn/7840200.html

192. Quoted from http://www.taz.de/1/archiv/?dig=2006/06/24/a0014

193. See https://www.elitenetzwerk.bayern.de/elitenetzwerk-home/aktuelles/meldungen/2013/november-2013/enbforum5/

194. Quoted from https://www.business-rhein-neckar.de/portal/fep/de/dt.jsp?setCursor=1_434427&cursorPath=%7C434427%7C444798

195. See http://www.mittelbayerische.de/region/regensburg/regensburg/artikel/45minuten-bei-den-thurn-und-taxis/983218/45-minuten-bei-den-thurn-und-taxis.html

196. See http://www.welt.de/print-welt/article663344/20-Millionen-Mark-sind-nurrelativ-viel.html

197. Originalquelle http://kress.de/ and also hier zu finden: http://www.indiskretionehrensache.de/2005/09/armer-alexander-von-schoenburg/

198. Quoted from Stephan Weichert, Christian Zabel, Die Alpha-Journalisten, p. 25

199. Quoted from http://www.stefan-niggemeier.de/blog/11657/armer-thomas-knuwer/

200. See http://www.bildblog.de/2525/alexander-von-tuten-und-blasen/

201. Quoted from http://www.bild.de/leute/star-news/leute/royal-kolumne-schoenburg-3347564.bild.html

202. See for instance http://diepresse.com/home/techscience/internet/350508/Queenveroffentlicht-Weihnachtsansprache-auf-YouTube and http://www.managermagazin.de/unternehmen/it/a-525227.html

203. See http://www.bild.de/leute/2007/leute/otto-adel-kaiser-2059128.bild.html

204. See http://www.bild.de/unterhaltung/kultur/frank-schirrmacher/von-diesem-buchbekommt-man-muskelkater-im-gehirn-29221524.bild.html

205. See for instance http://www.taz.de/1/archiv/?dig=2005/04/11/a0162

206. See http://www.bild.de/unterhaltung/royals/letizia-von-spanien/kann-letiziakoenigin-36248272.bild.html

207. Quoted from http://www.bild.de/news/inland/arjen-robben/warum-polen-undhollaender-besser-fluchen-36523934.bild.html

208. Quoted from http://www.taz.de/1/archiv/?dig=2005/04/11/a0162

209. See http://meedia.de/2013/04/12/spiegel-wohin-segelt-muller-v-blumencron/

210. Quoted from http://www.bild.de/geld/wirtschaft/gruner-jahr/steife-brise-inhamburgs-blaetterwald-29951972.bild.html

211. Quoted from http://www.pop-zeitschrift.de/2014/05/09/ironie-und-product-placement-in-tristesse-royalevon-sonja-lesniak9-5-2014/ and http://www.wienerzeitung.at/nachrichten/archiv/66005_Ein-Dandy-sucht-sich-vergebens-selbst.html

212. See http://diepresse.com/home/leben/mensch/royal/3848885/Juan-Carlos-Aergermit-der-Justiz?_vl_backlink=/home/index.do

213. See http://www.bild.de/news/inland/interview/mit-dem-preussen-koenigfriedrich-dem-grossen-22221908.bild.html

214. See http://search.wikileaks.org/?q=bilderberg

215. See http://www.atimes.com/atimes/Middle_East/EE22Ak03.html

216. Quoted from https://www.lobbycontrol.de/2014/06/bilderberg-2014-eliten-untersich/

217. See for instance http://meedia.de/2014/07/29/einstweilige-verfuegung-gegen-

dieanstalt-zdf-wehrt-sich-gegen-zeit-journalisten-joffe-und-bittner/
218. See http://www.fr-online.de/politik/bilderberg-konferenz-geheimes-treffen-derelite,1472596,4471506.html
219. Quoted from http://www.heise.de/tp/artikel/34/34928/1.html
220. See http://www.voltairenet.org/article171339.html

Notes to Chapter 4. Buy a Journalist – See How Money Talks

1. Quoted from http://www.hassomansfeld.com/site/, Screenshot vom 8. Juli 2014, under "Dienstleistungen", Point C. Operative Medienarbeit.
2. See http://kress.de/kresskoepfe/kopf/profil/9063-hasso-mansfeld.html
3. I do not mean the word "plain" pejoratively, but only that he is not an "alpha journalist".
4. See http://druckstellen.info/organisation/jury/stefan-laurin.html?PHPSESSID= r0gf8paji12q6kuc957knppv16
5. See http://www.ruhrbarone.de/oeffentlich-rechtliche-schonkost-fuer-diemassen/ 82986#more-82986
6. See http://juris.bundesgerichtshof.de/cgi-bin/rechtsprechung/document. py?Gericht=bgh&Art=pm&Datum=2014&Sort=3&nr=66713&pos=1&anz=24& Blank=1
7. See http://www.brandeins.de/archiv/2014/werbung.html
8. See for instance http://www.journalist.de/ratgeber/handwerk-beruf/menschen-undmeinungen/umfrage-zu-native-advertising-darf-werbung-inhalt-sein.html
9. See http://www.weimermediagroup.de/Weimer_Media_Group/Weimer_Media_ Group.html
10. See http://www.boerse-am-sonntag.de/leben/refugium-der-woche/artikel/ hotelbuelow-palais-dresden.html
11. See http://www.boerse-am-sonntag.de/aktien/gastbeitraege/artikel/ein-neuer-typvon-anleger.html
12. Quoted from http://www.newsroom.de/news/detail/$IWCOISLTIOKO/
13. See http://blog.wiwo.de/ungedruckt/2012/02/20/die-anfalligkeiten-vonjournalisten-fur-kleine-geschenke/
14. Accessed on 27. Mai 2014 at http://www.journalismus.com/
15. Dominik Stawski, "Die Prozente der Presse. Bewertung von Journalistenrabatten aus Anbieter- and Nutzerperspektive", VS Verlag 2010
16. Quoted from http://www.mediummagazin.de/archiv/2012-2/ausgabe-032012/ journalisten-drohen-mit-negativen-berichten/
17. See http://www.faz.net/aktuell/feuilleton/kino/gekaufte-berichte-die-eu-bezahltjournalisten-um-ihr-image-zu-pflegen-1330793.html
18. See http://www.stern.de/wirtschaft/news/unternehmen/journalisten-lustreiseprassen-in-peking-652145.html and http://www.handelsblatt.com/ unternehmen/ management/strategie/gekaufte-berichterstattung-wenn-journalisten-verfuehrtwerden/8864088.html
19. See http://www.focus.de/finanzen/news/unternehmen/stahlkonzern-laedtjournalisten-ein-faz-liess-sich-von-thyssenkrupp-zu-teurer-reise-einladen_ aid_ 858010.html
20. Quoted from http://www.deutschlandfunk.de/thyssenkrupp-bezahlt-luxusreisen-fuerjournalisten.761.de.html?dram:article_id=227635
21. See for instance http://meedia.de/2012/11/12/thyssenkrupp-bezahlte-luxusreisen-

furjournalisten/

22. See http://www.welt.de/print-welt/article243562/Rabattjaeger-mit-Presseausweis.html

23. Quoted from https://www.lobbycontrol.de/2013/08/gefallen-an-gefalligkeiten-wiejournalisten-umgarnt-werden/

24. See dazu http://www.ksta.de/stadt-leverkusen/untreue-danner-nimmt-sein-urteildankbar-an,15189132,23520970.html

25. Quoted from http://www.berliner-zeitung.de/medien/beeinflussung-der-pressechampagner-bis-zum-abwinken-,10809188,22395994.html

26. Ibid.

27. Ibid.

28. Ibid.

29. Ibid.

30. Ibid.

31. Quoted from http://www.handelsblatt.com/unternehmen/management/strategie/gekaufte-berichterstattung-wenn-journalisten-verfuehrt-werden/8864088.html

32. See http://spot.us/stories

33. Quoted from Peter Szyszka, Produkt-PR and Journalismus

34. See http://www.sueddeutsche.de/medien/studie-zur-medienselbstkontrolledeutsche-journalisten-sind-wenig-selbstkritisch-1.1651105

35. Quoted from http://blog.wiwo.de/ungedruckt/2012/02/20/die-anfalligkeiten-vonjournalisten-fur-kleine-geschenke/

36. See for instance http://www.message-online.com/archiv/message-1-2013/leseproben/ die-naehe-zur-macht/

37. See for instance http://www.taz.de/!68411/

38. Quoted from http://meedia.de/2011/04/07/schleichwerbung-in-allen-bereichen/

39. Quoted from http://www.medienforum-archiv.de/nc/blog/liste/blog-post////pr-undjournalismus-problematische-beziehungspflege.html

40. Quoted from http://meedia.de/2012/11/12/thyssenkrupp-bezahlte-luxusreisen-furjournalisten/

41. See for instance http://www.welt.de/wirtschaft/webwelt/article108949078/WieSamsung-auf-der-Ifa-Tech-Blogger-erpresst.html

42. See http://www.fr-online.de/medien/nebenjobs-nachrichtensprecher-in-derkritik,1473342,3117896.html

43. Quoted from http://www.ndr.de/fernsehen/sendungen/zapp/nebenerwerb100.html

44. Ibid.

45. Ibid.

46. See http://www.mopo.de/politik---wirtschaft/tom-buhrow---co--das-verdienendie-oeffentlich-rechtlichen-senderchefs,5066858,23911640.html

47. See http://www.zdf.de/ZDFmediathek/kanaluebersicht/aktuellste/228#/beitrag/video/1971936/ZDF-heute-journal-vom-2608-2013

48. See http://www.faz.net/aktuell/politik/inland/allensbach-analyse-tatsaechlicheund-gefuehlte-intoleranz-12120753.html

49. The original text is at http://www.nachtkritik.de/index.php?option= com_content&view=article&id=9572:theater-der-welt-2014-jacob-appelbaumsopening-speech-&catid=53:portraet-a-profil&Itemid=83

50. See http://www.stern.de/lifestyle/leute/tv-kommissar-derrick-horst-tappert-warmitglied-der-waffen-ss-2002874.html

51. See http://www.dnv-online.net/medien/detail.php?rubric=Medien&nr=91387

52. See http://www.spiegel.de/kultur/gesellschaft/medienkrise-nie-zuvor-gab-es-soviele-entlassungen-in-der-presse-a-870402.html

53. See for instance http://www.wiwo.de/erfolg/beruf/kein-bedarf-diese-jobs-sind-vomaussterben-bedroht/10208452.html?slp=false&p=7&a=false#image

54. See http://www.faz.net/aktuell/wirtschaft/unternehmen/zeitungen-in-der-kriseden-wirtschaftsmedien-von-gruner-jahr-droht-das-aus-11957636.html

55. See http://www.faz.net/aktuell/wirtschaft/unternehmen/zeitungen-in-der-kriseden-wirtschaftsmedien-von-gruner-jahr-droht-das-aus-11957636.html and http://www.tagesspiegel.de/medien-news/;art15532,2370490

56. For the background of the FR as a newspaper close to the SPD, see Ute Volkmann: "Legitime Ungleichheiten. Journalistische Deutungen vom 'sozialdemokratischen Konsensus' zum 'Neoliberalismus'", VS Verlag, Wiesbaden 2006

57. See http://www.handelsblatt.com/unternehmen/it-medien/stellenabbaufrankfurter-rundschau-schrumpft-zur-lokalzeitung/4015702.html

58. See http://www.taz.de/!111694/

59. See Der Spiegel, 14. Juli 2014, p. 128–130

60. See http://www.merkur-online.de/aktuelles/bayern/nuernberg-abendzeitungnuernberg-2523059.html

61. See http://www.spiegel.de/kultur/gesellschaft/muenchner-abendzeitung-istinsolvent-a-957098.html

62. See http://mmm.verdi.de/medien-wirtschaft/02-2014/muenchener-abendzeitunggeht-in-die-insolvenz

63. See http://kress.de/tweet/tagesdienst/detail/beitrag/118847-zum-31-dezember2013-bonner-general-anzeiger-schliesst-berliner-buero.html

64. See http://mmm.verdi.de/medien-wirtschaft/03-2014/50-entlassungen-bei-derwz

65. See http://www.labournet.de/branchen/medien/medien-presse/medienverschiedenes/entlassungen-bei-der-leipziger-volkszeitung-madsack-konzernvernichtet-weiter-arbeitsplatze/

66. See for instance Vorschläge gegen Zeitungssterben: journalist 6/2009, S.53ff., 1/2010

67. Quoted from http://www.faz.net/aktuell/politik/kommentar-die-rundschau-amende-11959447.html

68. Quoted from http://www.heise.de/tp/artikel/41/41878/1.html

69. Quoted from http://meedia.de/2014/04/08/robotertexte-stuttgarter-agentur-plantvollautomatisiertes-sportportal/

70. Quoted from http://meedia.de/2014/04/08/robotertexte-stuttgarter-agentur-plantvollautomatisiertes-sportportal/

71. See for instance http://www.sueddeutsche.de/medien/nach-insolvenz-faz-darffrankfurter-rundschau-uebernehmen-1.1611595

72. See for instance http://www.stuttgarter-zeitung.de/inhalt.ms-princess-daphne-spd-legtsich-traumschiff-zu.27289134-7683-4cd4-ae6b-03e6441f1665.html and http://www.sueddeutsche.de/politik/sozialdemokraten-reisen-statt-presse-traumschiffspd-1.1122795 and http://www.abendblatt.de/reise/article1963482/KurswechselDie-SPD-wird-Kreuzfahrtunternehmen.html

73. See http://kress.de/kressreport/heftarchiv/details-des-kressreports/beitrag/62132.html?tx_ttnews%5Bedition%5D=10%2F2006&cHash=5a68913dbe2874ae83858eab8ab4b357 and http://www.spiegel.de/wirtschaft/fliegender-wechsel-vorkoettergeht-zur-frankfurter-rundschau-a-416426.html

74. See http://www.spiegel.de/spiegel/vorab/spd-medienholding-haelt-sich-nicht-angeplanten-mindestlohn-a-941082.html

75. See http://www.zeit.de/2004/13/FR_2fSPD

76. Quoted from http://blogs.faz.net/medienwirtschaft/2014/02/03/die-medienmachtder-spd-broeckelt-die-ddvg-ihre-zeitungen-und-dietmar-nietan-402/

Notes to Chapter 5. Case Histories from the Propaganda Front

1. Quoted from http://german.ruvr.ru/2014_07_03/Wenn-ich-mit-der-Hisbollah-redenwill-kann-ich-mit-der-Hisbollah-reden-5595/

2. See his letter at www.ifz-muenchen.de/heftarchiv/1975_1_4_soell.pdf

3. See http://www.taz.de/1/archiv/?dig=2003/05/17/a0288

4. See dipbt.bundestag.de/doc/btp/02/02116.pdf

5. See http://www.zeit.de/wirtschaft/2014-04/griechenland-staatsanleihe-emissionkapitalmarkt

6. Quoted from http://www.welt.de/wirtschaft/article126785396/Anleger-reissen-sichum-griechische-Staatsanleihen.html

7. See http://www.faz.net/aktuell/finanzen/anleihen-zinsen/comeback-amfinanzmarkt-riesiges-interesse-an-griechen-anleihe-12887760.html

8. See http://www.handelsblatt.com/finanzen/boerse-maerkte/anleihen/staatsanleihen-griechenland-holt-sich-weniger-geld-als-erwartet/10181086.html

9. See http://www.tagesspiegel.de/medien/kurzmeldungen/508682.html and http://f3.webmart.de/f.cfm?id=1378521&r=threadview&t=1979924&pg=1

10. See http://www.tagesspiegel.de/politik/von-der-rolle/509240.html and See also http://www.dasgelbeforum.net/30434/messages/267806.htm

11. See http://diepresse.com/home/wirtschaft/economist/3829231/Okonomen_Zielsicher-daneben?_vl_backlink=/home/index.do

12. See http://www.stefan-niggemeier.de/blog/18300/die-schein-abstimmungen-deszdf-fuer-deutschlands-beste/

13. See http://meedia.de/2014/07/08/das-zdf-als-adac-unter-den-sendern-umfragebluff-bei-den-besten-deutschen/

14. See http://www.derwesten.de/kultur/fernsehen/boehse-onkelz-wohl-zu-boesezdf-manipulierte-weitere-show-id9601359.html

15. See http://diepresse.com/home/politik/aussenpolitik/3839315/Noch-zehn-JahreMerkel-Zwei-Drittel-der-Deutschen-dagegen?from=gl.home_politik

16. See http://www.focus.de/politik/deutschland/umfrage-zur-kanzlerin-jeder-viertewuenscht-sich-weitere-zehn-jahre-merkel_id_3994455.html

17. See The Guardian, Jan 19. 2009, http://www.guardian.co.uk/politics/2009/jan/19/economy-banking

18. See http://www.fr-online.de/politik/bilderberg-konferenz-geheimes-treffen-derelite,1472596,4471506.html

19. See Schwencke, Olaf: Der Euro als Kulturfaktor: die neue Währung and die alte Welt, in: Zeitschrift für Kulturaustausch, Jg. 48/1998, H. 4, p. 102-106;

20. See http://www.spiegel.de/spiegel/print/d-8798815.html

21. See for instance http://www.freitag.de/autoren/tom-strohschneider/selbst-ernanntervolksvertreter and http://www.spiegel.de/wirtschaft/soziales/kampf-um-stabilewaehrung-die-euro-fighter-a-692289.html

22. Quoted from http://pdf.zeit.de/1998/09/euro.txt.19980219.xml.pdf

23. See http://www.zeit.de/2009/06/Ratlosigkeit/komplettansicht

24. Quoted from http://www.zeit.de/2009/06/Ratlosigkeit/komplettansicht

25. Quoted from http://www.sueddeutsche.de/medien/serie-wozu-noch-journalismusdas-ist-nicht-ihr-kanzleramt-1.63398-2 and http://www.freitag.de/autoren/ jaugstein/wozu-noch-journalismus-beitrag-zu-einer-serie

26. Quoted from http://www.sueddeutsche.de/medien/serie-wozu-noch-journalismusdas-ist-nicht-ihr-kanzleramt-1.63398-2

27. Quoted from http://www.spiegel.de/kultur/tv/einflussnahme-der-parteien-brenderprangert-spitzelsystem-bei-oeffentlich-rechtlichen-an-a-679247.html

28. See http://content.stuttgarter-nachrichten.de/stn/page/detail.php/2318415

29. See http://www.spiegel.de/kultur/tv/steffen-seibert-zdf-moderator-wird-merkelsneuer-sprecher-a-705773.html

30. Quoted from http://www.sueddeutsche.de/medien/seibert-wird-neuer-regierungssprecher-ein-wechselwaehler-spricht-fuer-angie-merkel-1.973028

31. See http://www.horizont.net/aktuell/agenturen/pages/protected/Publicis-holtEtat-der-Aktionsgemeinschaft-Euro_22704.html

32. Quoted from http://www.pressrelations.de

33. See *Welt am Sonntag*, 29. June 1997, Article by Helmut Schmidt, "Die Stabilität des Euro wird größer sein als die der deutschen Mark"

34. See http://www.focus.de/magazin/archiv/euro-kampagne-ein-biss-zu-viel_ aid_ 189848.html

35. Quoted from http://www.spiegel.de/wirtschaft/sabine-christiansen-ich-bin-eind-mark-kind-a-149299.html

36. Jens Peter Paul: "Bilanz einer gescheiterten Kommunikation", Dissertation 2007, p. 266

37. Quoted from http://www.rp-online.de/gesellschaft/fernsehen/sabine-christiansen-einrueckblick-in-zitaten-1.566907

38. Quoted from http://www.faz.net/aktuell/feuilleton/medien/sabine-christiansen-wieeine-unpolitische-politik-machte-1410151-p2.html

39. See http://www.parkavenue.de/persoenlichkeiten/stories/528

40. See http://www.rp-online.de/panorama/was-promis-als-redner-verdienen-1. 1838551

41. Ibid.

42. Quoted from http://www.focus.de/finanzen/news/wirtschaft-vorsicht-teuro_ aid_ 189022.html

43. 8. August 2011, Eva Herman: "Ulrich Wickert and die Einführung des Euro: Eine überfällige Betrachtung", on the Internet at http://info.kopp-verlag.de/hintergruende/ deutschland/eva-herman/ulrich-wickert-und-die-einfuehrung-des-euro-eineueberfaellige-betrachtung.html

44. On the Internet at http://www.kultur.uni-hamburg.de/volkskunde/Texte/Vokus/2002-2/hell.html

45. Quoted from http://www.heymann-buecher.de/ulrich_wickert_und_dr_michael_otto_im_gesprach

46. See for instance http://www.dasinvestment.com/berater/news/datum/2011/08/23/anlegerschuetzer-nehmen-bankwerbung-mit-ulrich-wickert-unter-beschuss/

47. See http://www.bvr.de/p.nsf/index.html?ReadForm&main=6& sub=1&ParentUNID =098E767340F7F77DC1257ACB002F910A

48. See http://www.welt.de/print-wams/article612939/Warum-glauben-Sie-an-denEuro-Herr-Wickert.html

49. Quoted from http://www.welt.de/print-wams/article612939/Warum-glauben-Sie-

anden-Euro-Herr-Wickert.html

50. See for instance http://www.welt.de/print-welt/article665221/15-Millionen-D-Mark-fuerden-Euro.html

51. Quoted from http://www.tagesspiegel.de/wirtschaft/dem-euro-fehlt-noch-dieemotionale-qualitaet/67660.html

52. Quoted from http://www.zeit.de/1996/08/Bitte_keine_Waschmittelreklame_

53. Jens Peter Paul: Bilanz einer gescheiterten Kommunikation, Dissertation, Frankfurt 2007, p. 111f.

54. Quoted from Jens Peter Paul, Bilanz einer gescheiterten Kommunikation, Dissertation, Frankfurt 2007, p. 114f.

55. Ibid., p. 115

56. Quoted from Ibid, p. 130

57. Quoted from http://nachrichten.rp-online.de/politik/verbeugung-vor-kohlslebenswerk-1.3011952

58. See Liesel Hartenstein: "Das Wagnis Euro", in: Festschrift für Wilhelm Hankel, 1999, Seite 45ff.

59. Comment by Rolf-Dieter Krause on 6. February 1998 at a Symposium of the EU Commission in Bonn on the theme of European public opinion, see "Das Europäische Meinungsbild", p. 88

60. See Jens Peter Paul: "Bilanz einer gescheiterten Kommunikation", Dissertation 2007, p. 230

61. Quoted from Jens Peter Paul: "Bilanz einer gescheiterten Kommunikation", Dissertation 2007, p. 49

62. Ibid. p. 51f.

63. Ibid. p. 52

64. Ibid. p. 52

65. Ibid. p. 56f.

66. See dazu https://www.lobbycontrol.de/download/insm-marienhof-bewertung.pdf

67. See for instance the Zapp report http://www.youtube.com/watch?v=Sj6hKKummk

68. Quoted from http://www.taz.de/!114755/

69. Quoted from http://www.heise.de/tp/artikel/38/38515/1.html

70. See "Tendenziöse Attributierung in deutschen Printmedien: Putin vs. Obama – eine linguistische Analyse", Bachelor's-Thesis by Mirjam Zwingli, Hochschule für angewandte Sprachen, Fachhochschule des Sprachen & Dolmetscher Instituts München, 2012, for instance on p. 37, where it gives an example how he tries to influence the readers's psychological attitude.

71. for instance http://info.kopp-verlag.de/index.html

72. See http://www.bundestag.de/dokumente/textarchiv/2013/42897964_kw08_pa_kultur/210904

73. See http://www.stefan-niggemeier.de/blog/

74. See http://www.indiskretionehrensache.de/

75. See http://blog.markusgaertner.com/

76. See http://drudgereport.com/

77. See http://www.theguardian.com/science/2007/apr/09/frontpagenews.news

78. Ibid.

79. See http://diepresse.com/home/techscience/internet/3832697/NSA-speichertDaten-aller-sieben-Mrd-Menschen-auf-Dauer

Notes to the Afterword

1. See http://www.rollingstone.com/music/pictures/rolling-stones-biggest-scoopsexposes-and-controversies-2-aa-624/journalists-exposed-as-secret-cia-operatives81185346 and http://www.carlbernstein.com/magazine_cia_and_media. php and http://cryptocomb.org/wp-content/uploads/2014/01/THE-CIA-AND-THE-MEDIA.pdf

2. See http://cryptocomb.org/?p=279#more-279

3. See http://sutherlandsalute.blogspot.de/2008/12/robert-crowley-former-ciaclandestine.html

4. See http://cryptome.org/cia-2619.htm

5. See http://www.arte.tv/de/244,em=033674-000.html and https://www.youtube.com/watch?v=5KxbQGQHjPo

6. See dazu http://www.heise.de/tp/artikel/24/24027/1.html

7. See http://de.wikipedia.org/wiki/Der_Monat and http://www.heise.de/tp/artikel/24/24027/1.html

8. See http://www.welt.de/print-welt/article655495/CIA-will-in-NotfaellenJournalisten-rekrutieren.html

9. One of many examples https://www.cia.gov/news-information/speechestestimony/2014-speeches-testimony/a-conversation-with-john-o-brennan.html

10. According to its own statements, the DGAP wants to actively influence foreign policy formation at all levels. So it's a lobby organization. The DGAP describes itself "as a private, independent, non-partisan and non-profit association; the DGAP is actively involved in shaping foreign policy opinion in Germany and providing policy advice at all levels." See also Note 123 to Ch. 3.

11. Quoted from http://www.tpnonline.org/organisation/business-members

12. Quoted from http://www.tpnonline.org/organisation/cooperating-institutions/

13. See Seite 33 unter www.atlantik-bruecke.org/w/.../ab_4250_interviewbroschuere_final.pdf

14. See https://www.reporter-ohne-grenzen.de/pressemitteilungen/meldung/rogbericht-zur-lage-der-pressefreiheit-in-der-kurdischen-region-kaum-unabhaengigeberichterstattun/

15. See http://www.heute.de/ZDF/zdfportal/blob/32482080/1/data.pdf

16. See http://derstandard.at/1331207267450/Kurt-Gritsch-Gut-inszeniert-dieMainstream-Meinung

17. siehe: http://www.horiz.net/aktuell/medien/pages/protected/Steingart-vs-FAZKleinkrieg-um-die-grosse-Krise_121899.html

18. See https://www.freitag.de/autoren/vorabmeldung/deutsche-gegen-militaer-einsaetze-im-ausland

19. See http://www.bundespraesident.de/SharedDocs/Reden/DE/Joachim-Gauck/Interviews/2014/140614-Deutschlandfunk-Interview.html

20. See http://www.cicero.de/berliner-republik/ein-praesident-fuer-die-eliten/48408

21. Ibid.

22. See http://ru-facts.com/news/view/37094.html

23. See http://www.linkedin.com/pub/ralph-goff/b/779/279

24. See http://ru-facts.com/news/view/37094.html and http://cryptocomb.org/?s=jennifer+goff

25. See http://www.neues-deutschland.de/artikel/935167.ein-buch-wie-der-nsaskandal.html

Index of Names

Ackermann, Josef, 139
Albrecht, Karl, 15, 16, 121, 126, 181, 194
Albright, Madeleine, 131
Alexander the Great, 22, 207
Al-Sabah, Saud bin Nasir, 29
Al-Sisi, 22
Altmaier, Peter, 92
Anda, Bela, 118, 119
Anker, Stefan, 154
Antwerpes, Michael, 161
Appelbaum, Jacob, 166
Arnault, Bernard, 91
Arndt, Marco, 80
Arnim, Hans Herbert von, 80, 187
Ashworth, Anthony, 45, 222
Avramov, Smilja, 129, 130
Bacia, Horst, 31
Bahr, Egon, 188
Barber, Lionel, 20
Baring, Arnulf, 133
Baumann, Beate, 92
Bayern, Anna von, 94
Bechev, Dimitar, 137, 138
Beck, Kurt, 64, 65
Beckmann, Lukas, 104, 106, 229
Beemelmans, Stephane, 100
Berger, Roland, 133
Bering, Klaus, 44
Bernstein, Carl, 211
Biedenkopf, Kurt, 25
Biskup, Daniel, 90
Bittner, Jochen, 83, 84, 85
Blome, Nikolaus, 94
Blüm, Norbert, 189
Böhm, Karlheinz, 25, 61

Bohnen, Johannes, 124, 125, 126, 232
Böll, Heinrich, 88
Bosbach, Wolfgang, 163
Bouygues, Martin, 91
Boyles, Roger, 82
Brandt, Willy, 70, 71
Brender, Nikolaus, 161, 184
Bresser, Klaus, 184
Breuer, Rolf-E., 102
Brok, Elmar, 133
Brost, Marc, 111, 121, 159
Brown, Gordon, 93
Brunner, Manfred, 198
Brzezinski, Mark, 133
Bücher, Hans-Jürgen, 15
Buhrow, Tom, 161, 162
Bulmahn, Edelgard, 99
Bunz, Axel, 198
Burda, Hubert, 110, 147, 149
Bush, George, 32, 116, 119
Busse, Nikolas, 56, 111, 112, 113, 114, 115
Bütikofer, Reinhard, 133
Carter, Jimmy, 201
Casdorff, Stephan-Andreas, 160
Christiansen, Sabine, 32, 92, 177, 178, 185, 186, 187, 188, 189, 192
Christmann, Holger, 142
Chrobog, Jürgen, 133
Clement, Wolfgang, 173
Cromme, Gerhard, 133
Crowley, Robert Trumbull, 211
Danner, Franz, 156, 157
Dau, Rolf-Wilhelm, 76
Davignon, Etienne, 148, 180
Degenhart, Christoph, 187

Delors, Jacques, 191
Deppendorf, Ulrich, 97
Deutch, John, 131
Diekmann, Kai, 33, 88-102, 110, 118, 119, 121, 133, 204
Ditfurth, Jutta, 106, 108, 229
Dohnanyi, Klaus von, 133
Dombret, Andreas R., 99, 133
Donfried, Karen, 105
Dönhoff, Marion Gräfin, 99
Donsbach, Wolfgang, 31, 82, 220
Döpfner, Mathias, 111, 112, 133, 146, 147, 149
Dormann, Jürgen, 102
Drudge, Matt, 207
Ehmke, Horst, 188
Eichel, Hans, 188
Eickelkamp, Andreas, 160
Eigendorf, Jörg, 155
Elter, Andreas, 17
Enders, Thomas, 117, 118, 133
Erodottu, Jason, 43
Eschment, Walter, 154
Estulin, Daniel, 147
Euler, Hans Wolfgang, 64, 65
Faber-Castell, Anton Andreas Graf von, 141
Fack, Fritz Ullrich, 62, 69
Ferres, Veronika, 87
Fitschen, Jürgen, 99, 131, 134
Flick, Maya, 142, 144
Frankenberger, Klaus-Dieter, 40, 44, 45, 47, 49, 62, 69, 84, 96, 100,

111, 120-126, 131, 132, 204, 221, 227, 229
Frey, Peter, 84, 121, 134
Friedman, Michel, 82
Friedrichs, Hanns Joachim, 189
Garrett, David, 87
Gärtner, Markus, 207
Gauck, Joachim, 83, 134, 214, 242
Genscher, Hans-Dietrich, 88, 134, 177, 178
Gerster, Petra, 161
Gloger, Katja, 112, 115
Goldman, Guido and Nahum, 39, 85, 86, 121, 125, 232
Göring-Eckardt, Katrin, 108
Gottschalk, Thomas, 87
Graham, Philip, 36
Greenwald, Glenn, 128
Gritsch, Kurt, 20, 21, 214, 218, 242
Großmann, Jürgen R., 101, 134
Guttenberg, Karl-Theodor zu, 94, 95, 96, 98, 101, 106, 134, 220, 229
Haffner, Alexander, 175
Hankel, Wilhelm, 25, 181, 187, 194, 197, 241
Hartenstein, Liesel, 197, 241
Hassel, Tina, 97, 98, 110, 114
Hayek, Friedrich August von, 35
Heckei, Margaret, 111, 115
Hefner, Gerald, 198
Helene Fischer, Helene, 179
Helmut Kohl, 61, 62, 90, 93, 118, 119, 136, 188, 192, 195, 197

Hendricks, Barbara, 171
Hengster, Ingrid, 99
Herman, Eva, 189, 240
Heusgen, Christoph, 92
Hoffmann, Christiane, 115, 192
Holbrooke, Richard C., 134
Horn, Andre, 60, 215
Horner, Nils, 73
Hüfner, Martin, 178
Hughes, Louis R., 102
Hunziker, Michelle, 87
Hussein, Saddam, 29, 30, 50, 155
Hüther, Michael, 99
Illner, Maybrit, 162
Inacker, Michael, 111, 134
Ischinger, Wolfgang, 99, 134
Jackwerth, Angelika, 193
Jacob, Steffen, 70, 139, 166
Jaenicke, Hannes, 194
Jäkel, Julia, 189
Jauch, Günther, 31, 189
Jobatey, Cherno, 98, 112
Joffe, Josef, 15, 34, 84, 85, 86, 110, 120, 121, 123, 134, 147, 204, 217
Jones, Alex, 147
Joschka, Joschka, 116, 133
Juncker, Jean-Claude, 27
Kaiser Franz Joseph, 25, 143
Kallmorgen, Jan-Friedrich, 124, 125, 126, 232
Kämpen, Udo van, 34, 112
Kaulitz, Bill, 87, 194
Kelly, Petra, 106
Kempe, Frederick, 134
Kepenek, Ali, 71
Kepplinger, Mathias, 174
Kerner, Johannes B., 82

Kerry, John, 22
Kiep, Walther Leisler, 98, 117, 134
King, Cecil, 145, 147
Kinkel, Klaus, 44, 61, 96, 199
Kirch, Leo, 90
Kissinger, Henry, 131, 134
Klaeden, Eckart von, 99, 111, 134
Kleber, Claus, 33, 98, 112, 121, 161, 164, 220
Klose, Hans-Ulrich, 100, 135
Knef, Hildegard, 25
Knop, Carsten, 47
Knüwer, Thomas, 143, 207
Koch-Weser, Caio, 135
Kohl, Anja, 161
Kohl, Helmut, 62, 70, 90, 93, 197, 199
Köhler, Horst, 196
Koll, Theo, 98, 112, 115
Kompa, Markus, 97
Konken, Michael, 93
Kopper, Hilmar, 25, 117
Kornblum, John C., 100, 135
Kornelius, Stefan, 32, 34, 84, 85, 98, 112, 120, 121, 123, 124, 204
Kornes, Renate, 47
Krause, Rolf-Dieter, 198, 241
Krebs, Diether, 43
Kretzschmar, Stefan, 88
Krüger, Uwe, 21, 55, 84, 85, 98, 116, 119-124, 129, 132, 147, 148, 204, 217, 218, 221, 223, 231-233, 251
Kuenheim, Eberhard von, 102
Kurat, Georg, 22
Kyaw, Dietrich von, 199
Lafontaine, Oskar, 89

Lagardere, Arnaud, 91
Lahnstein, Manfred, 211
Lambsdorff, Alexander Graf, 99, 134
Lambsdorff, Hagen Graf, 134
Lambsdorff, Otto Graf, 117
Lange, Christian, 99, 135
Lehming, Malte, 115
Leif, Thomas, 28
Levermann, Thomas, 151
Leyendecker, Hans ,, 54, 163, 224
Lindemann, Beate, 96, 117, 119, 135
Lindenberg, Udo ,, 25, 87
Loer, Michael, 158
Loquai, Heinz, 32
Loungani, Prakash, 178
Löwe, Rüdiger, 115
Lübke, Heinrich, 163
Maiziere, Lothar de, 188
Maltzahn, Nina von, 135
Maltzahn, Paul von, 135
Mandelson, Lord Peter, 179
Mannstein, Coordt von, 194, 195, 196, 197
Mansfeld, Hasso, 150
Mao Tse-tung, 86
Matthes, Sebastian, 159
Mayrhuber, Wolfgang, 102, 117
McCloy, John, 99
McGhee, John, 148
Meiser, Hans, 196
Menz, Konstantin Alexander, 22
Merkel, Angela, 18, 25, 34, 70, 86, 90, 92, 93, 101, 102, 176, 179-184, 220
Merz, Friedrich, 98, 101, 118, 188
Meyer-Landrut, Nikolaus, 92
Meyssan, Thierry, 149
Middelhoff, Thomas, 102

Mikich, Sonia, 110
Milbradt, Georg, 177
Milosevic, Slobodan, 137, 138
Mitchener, Brandon, 82
Mitterrand, François, 192
Mohn, Liz, 101
Monti, Mario, 131
Mossadegh, Mohammad, 102
Mubarak, Hosni, 22
Müller, Albrecht, 121, 126
Müller, Bodo, 92, 112
Müller, Ina, 179
Müller, Kerstin, 135
Müller-Vogg, Hugo, 175
Müller-Westernhagen, Marius, 87
Murphy, Philip D., 135
Nahles, Andrea, 170, 174
Nannen, Henri, 166, 167
Naß, Matthias, 110
Naumann, Michael, 135
Nayirah, 29
Negroponte, John, 131
Niedringhaus, Anja, 73
Nietan, Dietmar, 171
Niggemeier, Stefan, 74, 85, 142, 146, 207
Noelle-Neumann, Elisabeth, 71, 198
Nölling, Wilhelm, 181, 194
Nonnenmacher, Günther, 84, 122, 123, 204
Nouripour, Omid, 99, 135
Nowak, Wolfgang, 135
Obama, Barack, 12, 28, 105, 127, 218, 219, 221, 233, 241
Obermann, Rene, 163
Odendahl, Peter, 186
Oetker, Arend, 101, 116, 117, 135
Oettinger, Günther, 96
Olt, Reinhard, 63

Oppenheim, Christopher von, 136
Orwell, George, 164
Otto, Michael, 102, 117
Özdemir, Cem, 109
Pahlavi, Reza Cyrus, 39
Paul, Jens Peter, 196, 198, 199, 240, 241
Pearl, Daniel, 73
Peters, Stephan, 96
Petkovic, Andrea, 194
Pflüger, Friedbert, 136
Pischetsrieder, Bernd, 102
Plättner, Anke, 115
Podak, Klaus, 40
Polenz, Ruprecht, 136
Powell, Colin, 113
Primor, Avi, 136
Princip, Gavrilo, 143
Putin, Wladimir, 13, 28, 128, 219, 221, 233, 241
Qabus, ibn Said, 42, 45, 46, 131
Quandt, Johanna, 35, 122, 133, 140
Ramsauer, Peter, 95
Rau, Johannes, 38
Reißmüller, Johann Georg, 62, 63
Rice, Condoleezza, 118
Richter, Maike, 90
Riesbeck, Peter, 137, 138
Rieu, Andre, 201
Robbe, Reinhard, 136
Rohde, Armin, 87
Rohloff, Joachim, 140
Roller, Lars-Hendrik, 92
Ronny S., 59
Rosen, Lawrence A., 99
Rösler, Philipp, 94
Roth, Claudia, 109
Roth, Thomas, 55, 110
Rothe, Rudolf, 108
Rothkopf, David, 148
Rothschild, 99
Rüb, Matthias, 32
Rüttgers, Jürgen, 89

Salbuchi, Adrian, 129
Sandschneider, Eberhard, 136
Sarkozy, Nicolas, 91
Sarrazin, Thilo, 77, 225
Savimbi, Jonas, 73
Scalbert, Augustin, 90
Schachtschneider, Karl Albrecht, 181, 194, 197
Scharping, Rudolf, 55, 56, 91, 117
Schäuble, Wolfgang, 112, 188
Scheidt, Herbert J., 122
Schenk, Heinz, 188
Schicha, Christian, 162
Schily, Otto, 106
Schirrmacher, Frank, 93, 122, 138-142, 234
Schlauch, Rezzo, 95
Schmidbauer, Bernd, 75
Schmidt, Harald, 196
Schmidt, Helmut, 48, 101, 122, 130, 186, 187, 189, 240
Schmidt-Eenboom, Erich, 108
Schneider, Manfred, 102
Schneider, Romy, 25
Scholl-Latour, Peter, 25, 87, 88, 175
Schönburg-Glauchau, Alexander von, 142, 143
Schrempp, Jürgen E., 102
Schröder, Gerhard, 70, 87, 89, 170, 171, 173
Schulte-Noelle, Henning, 96, 102
Schuster, Rudolf, 177
Schwartau, Silke, 52
Schwarzer, Alice, 88
Schweiger, Til, 87
Schwencke, Olaf, 180, 239
Schwenker, Burkhard, 99
Seibert, Steffen, 92, 184
Sethe, Paul, 175

Siegwart, Horst Günther, 215
Sinclair, Upton, 24, 234
Skulimma, Peter, 172
Snowden, Edward, 37, 104, 128, 166, 214
Söder, Markus, 95
Sommer, Theo, 15, 55, 56, 58, 147, 181
Sommer, Ulrich, 158
Soros, George, 128, 133, 137, 138, 213
Spreng, Michael H., 48, 62, 89, 93, 94
Springer, Axel, 60, 88, 89, 90, 94-96, 99, 111, 112, 133, 146, 147, 149, 150, 154, 232
Stadler, Thomas, 15
Stahl, Kate, 141
Starbatty, Joachim, 181
Stawski, Dominik, 153, 236
Steingart, Gabor, 111, 214, 242
Steltzner, Holger, 35
Stelzenmüller, Constanze, 111
Stephan, Torben, 173
Stoiber, Edmund, 89, 95
Stone, Shepard, 34, 211, 220
Storz, Wolfgang, 172
Strache, Heinz-Christian, 95
Strauss-Kahn, Dominique, 71
Stuff, Eckart, 115
Stumberger, Rudolf, 132, 148
Sturbeck, Werner, 41
Stürmer, Michael, 110, 120, 122, 123, 204
Tappert, Horst, 167
Teltschik, Horst M., 136
Thern, Jürgen, 175
Thurn und Taxis, Gloria von, 142

Tichy, Roland, 34
Tilgner, Ulrich, 209
Trichet, Jean-Claude, 131
Uhl, Hans-Peter, 95
Uhlmann, Karsten, 99
Ulbrich, Sabine, 115
Vassiliadis, Michael Zissis, 99, 136
Verheugen, Günter, 177, 178
Vetter, Heinz-Oskar, 87
Vogel, Andreas, 18
Vogel, Bernhard, 95
Vogel, Hans Jochen, 151
Vogts, Berti, 185
Voigt, Karsten D., 136
Voregger, Michael, 119
Walters, David, 39
Walters, Vernon A., 97, 101, 102, 117, 229
Warburg, Max M., 99, 116, 118, 136
Warneck, Frank, 71
Weichert, Stephan, 142, 218, 220, 235
Weidenfeld, Werner, 104
Weimer, Wolfram, 151, 152, 236
Weizsäcker, Richard von, 88, 99, 136, 186, 189
Wenning, Werner, 136
Wernicke, Christian, 98, 112, 115
Wettig-Danielmeier, Inge, 171, 172
Wickert, Ulrich, 185-, 194, 240
Wiegand, Markus, 22, 24, 152
Witt, Katharina, 87
Witzer, Brigitte, 87
Woolsey, James, 37, 105
Woolsey, Suzanne, 105
Wowereit, Klaus, 136, 201
Zabel, Christian, 142, 218, 235
Zetsche, Dieter, 102

Author Biography

If you look up the German or English Wikipedia page to learn something about Udo Ulfkotte, the author, you'll get the impression that this man was just another crazy, right-wing conspiracy theorist. The fact that he spent most of his career writing for prestigious mainstream media outlets, working in close contact with top politicians and Western intelligence agencies, and making countless television appearances as a war correspondent and foreign policy expert, doesn't seem to count. At the bottom of his Wiki page, you'll also notice the long list of books he wrote, many of them run-away bestsellers in the German-speaking world – despite a virtual blackout on advertising. So, who was Udo Ulfkotte? Was he a highly-respected, mainstream journalist or just some crazy, right-wing conspiracy theorist?

To find the answer, you already have the best means at your disposal. The book you have in your hands is the closest the world will ever get to an Udo Ulfkotte autobiography. In referencing his own personal experiences throughout his career in the media, he details how easily young journalists are lifted up and swept along by the mainstream – how he and so many others were and still are unable to resist the reward system that still shapes the Western media. From his first nudge toward working with the German Federal Intelligence Service as a university student, to finally gaining official recognition for the mustard gas poisoning he suffered as a war correspondent (25 years after his exposure), Ulfkotte gives us a behind-the-scenes look at what we're being sold in major newspapers and on the evening news. In sharing so many personal experiences, *Presstitutes* is both an apology for his own personal conduct and a warning to a new generation of journalists.

Udo Ulfkotte admits that he was naive. His father died when he was 5 and he grew up as a latch-key kid, as his mother worked to make ends meet. Still, he managed to make it to university, working side jobs while he studied law and political science in Freiburg and London, also delving into criminology and Islamic studies. When a professor invited him to seminars in Bonn, to make a little money on summer holidays, he never suspected they were organized by the BND, the German CIA. Nor did he plan on writing for a living, yet somehow, fresh out of college and without any journalism experience, Ulfkotte landed a job as an assistant foreign policy editor – and not just anywhere, but at one of Germany's most prestigious international newspapers, the *Frankfurter Allgemeine Zeitung* (FAZ). He had been vetted by the CIA, the invisible hand at play in so many journalistic careers. Ensconced at the FAZ, he was helped along, initially copying articles or fleshing out pre-formulated reports before they were published in his name. As he explains, this practice continued throughout the 17 years he worked at the FAZ, a career in which he says he travelled to 60 countries and spent more time in the Middle East than in Germany.

Some will try to convince you that Udo Ulfkotte was a bitter man and only wrote *Presstitutes* to settle a grudge he had with his former employer. Others might think that in an us-versus-them world, he defected from them and joined us. However, there's no simple answer. Looking at his long list of published works, you can see that Dr. Ulfkotte was always concerned with crime, its causes and its effects on society. He also suffered from several serious health issues, and had many opportunities to reflect on the meaning and purpose of his life. After being exposed to chemical weapons near the Iran-Iraq border in 1988, he was also diagnosed with cancer. Recovering against all odds, he still stuck with the FAZ for another 15 years. Admittedly, he enjoyed the thrill of being an international correspondent with connections to the highest political and intelligence circles in Germany. Somewhere along the line though, things started hitting too close to home.

By the late 90s, Ulfkotte was starting to openly express his growing cynicism. His first critical title, *Classified Information: Federal Intelligence Service (BND)*, was published in 1997 and was promoted by the FAZ. In 1999 he released *Marketplace of Thieves: How industrial espionage is plundering and ruining German companies*. At the same time, he also began lecturing on "security management" in the University of Lüneburg's school of business administration. 2001 was a good year for conspiracy theorists and some may wonder why Ulfkotte's first critique of Islamism, *Prophets of Terror: The Islamists' secret network*, just happened to appear on bookshelves three weeks after 9/11. Later that December, Ulfkotte also released his first fiction title, a thriller titled *Gencode J*. It eerily mentions Osama bin Laden by name and features an airplane being flown into the Dome of the Rock. However, the revenge-driven plot revolves around a rogue Israeli Mossad agent who is trying to get his hands on a genetic weapon to specifically target Palestinian DNA. Although Ulfkotte's fiction didn't meet with much critical success, he did manage to make the point that terrorism isn't the sole property of one state or one religion. What did he know? Was there German involvement? Were journalists involved in distracting the masses and covering up crimes?

After that, it wasn't long before Ulfkotte did have a falling out with the Frankfurter Allgemeine Zeitung. After turning his eye to his own profession and publishing *How Journalists Lie: The fight for ratings and circulation*, in 2002, he suffered another serious physical injury in 2003. While recovering in the hospital, he once again saw his job advertised in his own newspaper. The first time had been in 1988. He was disgusted with himself for being in a position where politicians simply assumed he would spy on other politicians for a fee. He felt like a prostitute. Everybody has to so some dirty work from time to time, but when you find out the company you're working for is poisoning the whole town, you have to make a decision. Some people will keep quiet and keep working, hoping they make enough money to retire early and move somewhere far away before the storm hits. Others can't live with themselves and quit in the knowledge that what they're doing is wrong. It's a rare individual who goes as far as blowing the whistle, risking their own skin to wake everybody up.

After a short stint at a glossy high-society magazine and his first heart attack, Udo Ulfkotte knew that he had to do something meaningful with his life – not just for himself, but for his family and the country where he was born and raised. Knowing his days were numbered and being in the unique position of having so many top-ranking contacts, he decided to expose as much political corruption as he could before he died. He knew that Germany, a supposed democracy, was being sold out against the will of its people. First it was the euro. Then the War on Terror. In the mid-2000s, the European Union was quickly admitting every bankrupt country in Eastern Europe, and he didn't like where things were going. Udo Ulfkotte wanted to wake people up. That's when the house searches began. When asked why he was searched, he said, "Because I reported things in public that are not politically correct, especially things the public shouldn't know, things they would like to keep secret." … "It's always the case that the bearer of bad news is the first one to be hanged, beheaded or otherwise quartered."

He had crossed the line and was now an official persona non grata. Police and public prosecutors searched his and his wife's home and offices six times over the next 10 years. The searches were always reported in the media, and he also lost his teaching position at the University of Lüneburg, but curiously enough, nobody ever reported that the investigations were always dropped. No charges were ever filed. No one ever apologized for dragging his name through the mud. Summarily cut off, Dr. Udo Ulfkotte was finally free. He still had an extensive network of contacts from politics, intelligence, law enforcement and the media, many of whom who were just as fed up as he was, but not quite so willing to stick their own necks out. From that point on, Ulfkotte published about a book a year, each one more scathing than the last.

Presstitutes, Ulfkotte's most successful bestseller, stands out among all the books he published over the last decade of his life. If there was one issue that was dearest to Udo Ulfkotte it was the loss of European cultural identity, particularly in his home country of Germany. He was skeptical of the "increasingly powerful, commercial World Culture – also referred to as 'McWorld,'" that was being aggressively promoted through massive corruption in the government and media. In the last decade of his life, Ulfkotte withdrew to the countryside and wrote tirelessly, desperately trying to warn his fellow countrymen of what was in the works. He warned of the euro before the 2007-08 financial crisis. He warned of the dangers of uncontrolled, mass migration of culturally incompatible people before the assault, rape and murder rates shot off the charts. Afterwards, he always followed up by documenting the political deception at play and the media's collusion.

So, was Udo Ulfkotte a conspiracy theorist or a fortune teller? If he was just imagining connections where there weren't any, how could he consistently predict the future so well? Considering all the names he named in all his books and the dearth of lawsuits filed against him or his publisher, it doesn't seem like anyone has any factual objections with what he had to say. On the contrary, three German universities are now continuing the investigations of Uwe Krüger, whose work on media power Ulfkotte cites in this volume — thanks in part to the attention generated by this book.

It seems that the answer to the question of Udo Ulfkotte lies in knowing where to look. All the information is out there. However, it's readily apparent that the lazy man's information sources, the mainstream media and Wikipedia, want us to equate Ulfkotte with conspiracy theorist. They seem to have a vested interest in keeping this pyramid scheme going until the whole thing finally collapses. Maybe this is why an average of 175,000 well-educated Germans are emigrating every year.

Less than a year before he died in 2017, Udo Ulfkotte released internal documents that show where the German government is expecting the most violent unrest in the near future. These are towns and whole city districts where kids can't walk to school and women can't go jogging anymore, where insurance companies no longer pay out if your car gets set on fire in the night. Far away from all this, in the high Westerwald woodlands, Udo Ulfkotte spent the last years of his life with his family, living on the land. They operated a small, private animal sanctuary, taking in retired farm animals that had "outlived their economic usefulness." When asked why he liked animals so much in one of his last interviews, Dr. Ulfkotte replied, "Animals are more grateful than humans. Animals are not resentful. Animals are not deceitful or worse. However, I have experienced this in many people and especially with journalists, especially with alpha journalists and elite journalists. I experienced this corruption, that I already knew from politics, that I knew from the financial sector, up close and personal with journalists in the media industry. Although I was also one of them myself, so I also went through it myself too and lived like that in the past. I'm ashamed of that today."

Dr. Udo Ulfkotte survived a poison gas attack in Iraq, a bout with cancer, and head injuries from being pushed down the stairs of his home by a spy for the ISI, the Pakistani CIA. He died of his fourth heart attack on January 13th 2017, one week before his 57th birthday.

Glossary

Select German Media Acronyms and Terminology

10vor10 (10to10) – An in-depth news program broadcast by Swiss Radio and Television (SRF), equivalent in format to ARD's *Tagesthemen*

ACG – American Council on Germany – An NGO affiliated with the CFR, which works together closely with the Atlantik-Brücke, e.g. Young Leaders Program

ADAC – Allgemeiner Deutscher Automobil-Club e.V. (General German Automobile Club) – The largest automobile club in Europe, since 1903, over 20 million members

AG – Aktiengesellschaft (joint-stock company/corporation)

AI – Amnesty International – London-based NGO focusing on human rights

ALDE – Alliance of the Liberals and Democrats for Europe

Alliance 90/The Greens – The result of the merger of the East and West German Green Parties, commonly referred to as The Greens or Green Party

Allianz – A German multinational based in Munich, Bavaria, the world's largest insurance company, with over €1.9 trillion in assets under management

Anstalt (die) – Institute/Mental hospital – Name of a political satire program on ZDF

ARD – The first publicly funded, state operated television channel in Germany (1950). Arbeitsgemeinschaft der öffentlich-rechtlichen Rundfunkanstalten der Bundesrepublik Deutschland (Working Group of Public Broadcasters of the FRG)

Arte – French/German cooperative free-to-air public broadcasting channel with a cultural focus

Atlantik-Brücke (Atlantic Bridge) – Controversial, invitation-only transatlantic lobbying organization

auslandsjournal (Foreign Journal) – Weekly review of international politics and current events on ZDF

Axel Springer SE – Largest publisher in Europe, owns the *Bild* and *Die Welt*

BA – Bundesagentur für Arbeit (Federal Employment Agency) – Manages job centers

BamS – Bild am Sontag (Bild on Sunday) – The largest-selling German Sunday newspaper

Berliner Runde (Berlin Round Table) – Political debate program on ARD/ZDF TV

Berliner Zeitung (Berlin Newspaper) – Berlin's largest daily, center-left paper since 1945, redesigned in 1997 to become "Germany's Washington Post"

Bertelsmann AG – German multinational based in Gütersloh, NRW, world's largest book publisher and done of the largest mass media conglomerates including RTL Group, Penguin Random House, Gruner + Jahr, BMG and others

BG – Berufsgenossenschaft (Employers' Liability Insurance Association) – The statutory workers compensation provider for the German private sector. BGHW is the provider for Trade and Logistics companies

Bild (Picture) – German mainstream tabloid newspaper with the largest circulation in Europe. *Bild der Frau* (for women) – *Bild*'s weekly women's magazine with the greatest circulation in Europe

BK – Berufskrankheit (Occupational illness) – Classification prefix

BND – Bundesnachrichtendienst (Federal Intelligence Service) – Germany's foreign intelligence agency, reporting directly to the Chancellor's Office

Börse am Sonntag (Stock Market on Sunday) – German online financial magazine reporting on all German regional markets, in cooperation with *Die Welt* since 2012

BPA – Bundespresseamt – Press and Information office of German Federal Government, disseminates official publications

BR – Bayerische Rundfunk (Bavarian Broadcasting) – Regional public radio and television broadcaster based in Munich

brand eins (Brand One) – Monthly business magazine covering socio-political topics

BRD – Bundesrepublik Deutschland (Federal Republic of Germany) – Used for the former West Germany and the present German state

Bundestag – German Federal Parliament/House of Representatives

Bundeswehr (Federal Defense) – Armed Forces

Capital – German monthly business magazine published by Grüner + Jahr

CDU – Christian Democratic Union – Leading political party headed by Angela Merkel and characterized as "liberal-conservative" and "center-right"

CFR – Council on Foreign Relations – A US think tank (lobby) focusing on US foreign policy and international affairs, known for its neoconservative and neoliberal positions

Chancellor (Bundeskanzler) –Title of Germany's official head of state or prime minister

Cicero – Monthly German magazine focusing on politics and culture

CSIS – Center for Strategic and International Studies – Washington D.C. based think tank

CSU – Christian Social Union in Bavaria – The "somewhat more conservative" arm of the CDU, operating exclusively in Bavaria

DDVG – Deutsche Druck- und Verlagsgesellschaft (German Print and Publishing Company) – A media holding company of the SPD

ddp – Deutscher Depeschendienst (German Dispatch Service) – Former competitor of the dpa, it was a news agency based in Berlin from 1972-2010

DDR – Deutsche Demokratische Republik (GDR) – The former East Germany

DGAP – Deutsche Gesellschaft für Auswärtige Politik e. V. (German Council on Foreign Relations) – German version of the CFR, a network and foreign policy lobby

Die Linke (The Left) – Germany's largest left-oriented political party

DJV – Deutscher Journalisten-Verband (German Journalists Association) – One of Europe's largest journalists' organizations with around 38,000 members

DLG – Deutsche Landwirtschafts-Gesellschaft (German Agricultural Society) – A non-profit (lobbying) organization for the German agricultural industry

DM, D-Mark, Deutschmark, Deutsche Mark, Mark – Various names for West Germany (1948-1990) and united Germany's (1990-2002) official currency

dpa – Deutsche Presse-Agentur GmbH (German Press Agency) – The largest press agency in Germany with worldwide operations, providing news in four languages

DRPR – Deutscher Rat für Public Relations (German Council on Public Relations) – An organization for the "voluntary self-control" of PR professionals active in Germany

EADS (now Airbus SE) – European Aeronautic Defence and Space – Europe's largest air & space and second largest armaments company

ECFR – European Council on Foreign Relations – A pan-European think tank founded with funding from George Soros' Open Society Foundations

e. V. – eingetragener Verein (registered association) – Legally incorporated association

FAZ – Frankfurter Allgemeine Zeitung (Frankfurt Public Newspaper) – A very prestigious "leading media" broadsheet (top 4) in Germany, published in Frankfurt

FDP – Freie Demokratische Partei (Free Democratic Party) – Liberal-classic liberal political party considered to be center-right on the political spectrum

Focus – Illustrated weekly news magazine, among the top 3 in overall circulation

FR – Frankfurter Rundschau (Frankfurt Review) – Traditional (1945) daily newspaper published in Frankfurt

Freitag (Friday) – German national weekly newspaper founded in 1990 and aimed at an East-West readership; considered to be left-liberal

FRG – Federal Republic of Germany

FTD – *Financial Times Deutschland* – economic daily from Grüner + Jahr (2000-2012)

GDR – German Democratic Republic (former East Germany)

GEZ – Gebühreneinzugszentral (Fee Collection Center) – Now officially known as the ARD ZDF Deutschlandradio Beitragsservice (Contribution Service), it collects the mandatory television and radio license fees in Germany; in 2015 alone, it sent out 20 million dunning notices and forced 890,000 individuals to pay by liens or property seizures; often regarded as unconstitutional, there is a big resistance movement against it

Gladio (Operation) – Codename for a secret, stay-behind paramilitary special forces (specifically in Italy, other codenames were used elsewhere) run by NATO, ostensibly for the event of a Soviet invasion of Western Europe; but effectively anti-democratic, involved in terrorism and assassinations (Red Brigades, Baader Meinhof). See Richard Cottrell, *Gladio: NATO's Dagger at the Heart of Europe*, Progressive Press, 2015.

GmbH – Gesellschaft mit beschränkte Haftung – Corporation (Inc., Ltd., LLC, PLC, etc.)

GMF – German Marshall Fund – A "nonpartisan" American public policy think tank and grantmaking institution dedicated to "transatlantic cooperation"

GMH Gruppe – Georgsmarienhütte Holding GmbH – A consortium of 26 corporations involved in scrap metal recycling and steel production

Grüner + Jahr (G+J) – One of the largest publishing houses in Europe, a subsidiary of Bertelsmann based in Hamburg

Handelsblatt (Commerce Paper) – A leading business daily, under the same owndrship as *Wirtschaftswoche (Economic Weekly)*

Hartz IV – the fourth stage of the Hartz reforms, combining unemployment and welfare benefits (pre-retirement); beneficiaries receive housing, health care and €400/month

heute-journal (Today Journal) – A daily television news magazine broadcast by ZDF

heute (Nachrichten) (Today News) – A daily television news program broadcast by ZDF

IM – Informeller Mitarbeiter (Unofficial/Informal Collaborator) until 1968 Geheimer Mitarbeiter (GI) (Secret Collaborator) – Designation for informants who reported to the communist East German Ministry for State Security (Stasi)

junge Welt (Young World) – Founded in East Berlin in 1947, until 1990 is was the central mouthpiece for the FDJ (Free German Youth), a communist youth organization; now anti-imperialist and anti-capitalist

KfW – Kreditanstalt für Wiederaufbau (Credit Institute for Reconstruction) – A German state-owned development bank formed as a part of the Marshall Plan

(Kölner) *Express,* Cologne – A regional tabloid newspaper

Kölner Stadt-Anzeiger (Cologne City Gazette) – The largest daily regional paper in the Cologne/Bonn metropolitan area

Maischberger, Sandra – Host of *Maischberger* (formerly *Menschen bei Maischberger* (People with Maischberger), a politically-leaning talk show on ARD since 2003

MB – Member of the Bundestag (German Parliament)

Meedia – German online journal for all things media related

Medium Magazin – A trade magazine for journalists known for its independent reporting

MEP – Member of the European Parliament

Merkur (Mercury) – Monthly magazine "for European thinking," since 1947, Germany's oldest cultural magazine

Münchner Merkur (Munich Mercury) – Conservative regional daily paper in Munich

Mutti – *Mommy* – A common German nickname for Angela Merkel

N24 – A free-to-air television news channel owned by WeltN24, *Die Welt's* (The World's) parent company. Part of Axel Springer group.

NDR – Norddeutscher Rundfunk (Northern German Broadcasting) – Regional public radio and television broadcaster based in Hamburg, covering 5 of Germany's 16 states

Neue Züricher Zeitung (New Zurich Newspaper) – Swiss international newspaper known for its "free-thinking democratic orientation"

NRW – Nordrhein-Westfalen (North Rhine-Westphalia) West German state bordering the Netherlands and France

NRZ – *Neue Ruhr Zeitung* (New Ruhr Newspaper) – Ruhr regional newspaper also owned by the Funke Mediengruppe, formerly the WAZ Mediengruppe (SPD affiliation)

Phoenix – a free-to-air television channel operated jointly by ARD and ZDF specializing in documentaries, special events, news and discussions

Presseclub (Press Club) – Weekly political discussion program on ARD

Quick – Weekly illustrated news magazine published from 1948-1992

RTL – Radio Television Luxembourg – German commercial television conglomerate based in Cologne, NRW

saldo – A Swiss consumer reporting magazine

Sat.1 – Private German television station with a wide spectrum of programming

SE (Societas Europaea) – European Public Company

SPD – Social Democratic Party – The left-leaning party is the oldest in Germany (1863), but membership has declined steadily since the early '90s

Spiegel (der) (The Mirror) – Weekly news magazine, the largest in Europe

SRF – Schweizer Radio und Fernsehen (Swiss Radio and Television) – A Swiss broadcasting company serving Switzerland's German-speaking population

Stern (Star) – Hamburg weekly news magazine from Gruner + Jahr / Bertelsmann

Stern TV – *Star TV* – Television news magazine broadcast by RTL

SWP – Stiftung Wissenschaft und Politik ("Foundation for Science and Politics" – Institute for International and Security Affairs)

SZ – Süddeutsche Zeitung (South German Newspaper) – A prestigious, national "leading media" broadsheet (No. 2) in Germany, published in Munich

Tagesschau (Daily View) – Daily news broadcast of the ARD and oldest, continuously broadcasting program in Germany (1955), seen by up to 10 million viewers a day; Swiss Radio and Television (SRF) has a similar Tagesschau

Tagesspiegel (Daily Mirror) – Berlin regional daily with the highest circulation

Tagesthemen (Daily Issues) – Short background stories on the daily news, on ARD

taz – *Die Tageszeitung (The Daily Newspaper) – Daily newspaper co-op, focusing on current events,society, ecology,and linked to the Green Party*

Thyssen-Krupp – German multinational in industrial engineering and steel

TPN – Transatlantic Policy Network – Umbrella lobbying organization for large European and American corporations and networks with close ties to business

Union (CDU/CSU) – The political alliance of the two parties

UPI – United Press International – A news agency owned by Sun Myung Moon's Unification movement

VCI – Verband der Chemischen Industrie e.V. (Association of Chemical Industries)

Volkszeitung – *People's newspaper*

VS – Verschlusssache (Classified material)

WAZ – *Westdeutsche Allgemeine Zeitung* (West German Public Newspaper) – Germany's largest regional daily paper, covering the Ruhr area, owned by Funke Mediengruppe, linked to SDP.

WamS – Welt am Sontag (World on Sunday) – Sunday edition of *Die Welt*

WDR – Westdeutscher Rundfunk Köln (West German Broadcasting Cologne) – Regional public radio and TV broadcaster covering NRW from Cologne

Welt (die) (The World) – Prestigious, conservative German national daily broadsheet (top 5), published by the Axel Springer SE

Wirtschaftsjournalist (Economic Journalist) – Trade magazine for finance and business journalists

Wirtschaftswoche (Business Week) – Best-selling German weekly business news magazine

Zapp – NDR TV news magazine focusing on the media, known for investigative reporting

ZDF – Zweites Deutsches Fernsehen (Second German Television) – Publicly funded, state operated television channel (1963)

Zeit (die) (Time) – National weekly broadsheet considered to be a "newspaper of record"

Zeitung – *Newspaper*

Other Favorite Titles
from ProgressivePress.com

Before Our Very Eyes: Fake Wars & Big Lies: From 9/11 to Donald Trump. VoltaireNet's Thierry Meyssan tells the Inside Story of plots against Libya and Syria. 286 pp, $25.

ISIS IS US: The Shocking Truth. How and why the US and its allies created ISIS, by JP Leonard, Wayne Madsen et. al. 268 pp. $19.95.

JFK-911: 50 Years of Deep State. Evidence of an Israeli strategy behind the JFK and 9/11 murders. By Laurent Guyénot. 238 pp, $15.95.

Two by F. Wm. Engdahl

A Century of War: Anglo-American Oil Politics and the New World Order. Classic exposé: Control the oil to control the world. 352 pp, $25.

Gods of Money: Wall Street and the Death of the American Century. The banksters stop at nothing: setting world wars, nuking cities, keeping our world in chaos and corruption. 390 pp. $24.95.

Two by Dr. Webster Griffin Tarpley

9/11 Synthetic Terror: Made in USA — by a network of moles, patsies, killers, corrupt politicians and media. The 9/11 bible. "Strongest of the 770+ books I have reviewed" – R. Steele. 5th ed., 569 pp., $19.95.

George Bush: The Unauthorized Biography Vivid X-ray of the oligarchy dominating U.S. politics, with a full narrative of GWHB's links to Iran-Contra, Watergate, and a long list of war crimes. 700 pp, $19.95.

Conspiracies, Conspiracy Theories and the Secrets of 9/11, German bestseller. Conspiracy in evolution and history. 274 pp, $14.95.

Dope Inc.: Britain's Opium War against the United States. "The Book that Drove Kissinger Crazy." Underground Classic. 320 pp, $14.95

Gladio, NATO's Dagger at the Heart of Europe. The blood-red thread of NATO terror and assassinations, from 1945 to now. 487 pp, $24.95.

The Money Power: Empire of the City and Pawns in the Game. two classics in one volume. The illuminist Three World Wars conspiracy. 320 pp. $16.95.

The Nazi Hydra in America: Suppressed History of a Century. US plutocrats launched Hitler. "Shocking... deserves to be widely read." – Howard Zinn. 700 pp, $19.95.

Terrorism and the Illuminati: A 3000-Year History. Who controls "Islamic" terrorists? 332 pp, $16.95.

The Rape of the Mind. Tools for self-defense against social pressure in open and closed societies. Classic by Dr. Joost Meerloo. 320 pp, $16.95.

Terror on the Tube: Behind the Veil of 7/7, an Investigation. Exonerates the patsies, proves the false flag. 322 pp, $17.77.

Made in the USA
Las Vegas, NV
09 August 2022

53009372R00148